Including Students
with Severe and Multiple Disabilities
in Typical Classrooms

Including Students with Severe and Multiple Disabilities in Typical Classrooms

Practical Strategies for Teachers

Second Edition

by June E. Downing, Ph.D.
California State University, Northridge

with invited contributors

·P·A·U·L·H·
BROOKES
PUBLISHING Cº

Baltimore • London • Toronto • Sydney

Paul H. Brookes Publishing Co.
Post Office Box 10624
Baltimore, Maryland 21285-0624

www.brookespublishing.com

Typeset by Barton Matheson Willse & Worthington,
Baltimore, Maryland.
Manufactured in the United States of America by
Sheridan Books, Fredericksburg, Virginia.

The cases described in this book are composites based on the authors' actual experiences. Individuals' names have been changed, and identifying details have been altered to protect confidentiality.

The photographs in this book are printed with permission of the individuals pictured. The photographs on pages 148, 177, and 191 are by Margo Yunker. The photographs on pages 59, 60, and 178 are by Lavada Minor. The photograph on the back cover is by Gloria Rodriguez-Gil.

Figure 5.4 includes images from ClickArt Incredible Image Pak 65,000, which are protected by the copyright laws of the United States, Canada, and elsewhere. Used under license.

Library of Congress Cataloging-in-Publication Data

Downing, June, 1950–
   Including students with severe and multiple disabilities in typical classrooms: practical strategies for teachers/by June E. Downing with invited contributors, Joanne Eichinger, MaryAnn Demchak.—2nd ed.
      p.   cm.
   Includes bibliographical references and index.
   ISBN 1-55766-519-2
      1. Handicapped children—Education—United States.   2. Mainstreaming in education—United States.   I. Eichinger, Joanne.   II. Demchak, MaryAnn, 1957–.   III. Title.

LC4031.D69 2002
371.9'046'0973—dc21

2001035260

British Library Cataloguing in Publication data are available from the British Library.

Contents

About the Author

June E. Downing, Ph.D., Professor, Department of Special Education, California State University–Northridge, 18111 Nordhoff Street, Northridge, CA 91330

Dr. Downing prepares teachers to meet the needs of students with moderate to severe and multiple disabilities. In this capacity, she teaches courses, advises students, and supervises teachers in their practicum experiences. Dr. Downing has provided in-service training to teachers, administrators, parents, and support staff around the country. She has been interested in the education of students with severe and multiple disabilities (especially those with sensory impairments) since 1974 and has served as a paraprofessional, teacher, work experience coordinator, consultant, researcher, and teacher trainer. Areas of research include investigating related topics such as educating all students together, enhancing the social-communicative skills of students with severe disabilities, adapting for the unique needs of individual students, developing paraprofessional skills, and preparing teachers for inclusive education.

Also Contributing to This Volume

Joanne Eichinger, Ph.D., Professor, School of Education, University of Rhode Island, Kingston, RI 02881

Dr. Eichinger teaches graduate and undergraduate courses to students in elementary education and graduate courses to students in school psychology. Prior to obtaining her doctorate at Syracuse University in 1988, she taught learners with disabilities for 8 years. She also worked as the project coordinator and then director of the Northeast Region of The Association for Persons with Severe Handicaps technical assistance project, serving students with dual sensory impairments. Her research interests include promoting positive attitudes toward people with disabilities, examining job stress and satisfaction among special educators, and investigating the efficacy of promising educational practices in inclusive classes.

MaryAnn Demchak, Ph.D., Professor, Department of Curriculum and Instruction, University of Nevada–Reno, Reno, NV 89557

Dr. Demchak teaches graduate courses in severe disabilities. In addition, as the project director of the Nevada Dual Sensory Impairment Project, Dr. Demchak provides technical assistance to families and service providers of children who are deafblind. Her research interests include inclusion of students with severe disabilities in typical classrooms, meeting the unique educational needs of students with severe disabilities, and positive support for behavior problems.

Foreword
Values, Logical Practices, and Research:
The Three Musketeers of Effective Education

Michael F. Giangreco, Ph.D.

The motto of the Three Musketeers is legendary: "All for one and one for all!" The result of their unity was triumph! To triumph in the realm of meaningful and effective education, we, too, need to rely on an inseparable triumvirate: values, logical practices, and research. The order in which this trio is presented is purposeful. Effective education begins with values and proceeds to logical practices. Research informs the selection of our logical practices and helps us determine their effectiveness and impact.

SOCIETAL VALUES

Educating our children begins with what we value. Without an affirmative value orientation upon which to base our practices and research, they are at best haphazard, and at worst, dangerous. At the broadest level, I am referring to values deeply embedded in our national ethos. These values are the kind most people would agree with regardless of their political persuasion or educational philosophy, such as those articulated by our nation's founders as "life, liberty, and the pursuit of happiness."

Although no one is guaranteed his or her version of the "American Dream," as a society we purport to provide equal access to it. We espouse that everyone should have the opportunity to pursue his or her dreams and be included in community life, free of undue restrictions on personal liberties. These are values we aspire to but which still elude too many Americans—especially those with disabilities.

Historically, people with disabilities have been on the receiving end of many practices based on restrictive and exclusionary values, often under the guise of "helping." We now recognize these practices as interfering with the pursuit of living a "regular life" in the community. People with disabilities have been, and continue to be, institutionalized, sterilized, segregated, subjected to aversive procedures, denied access to medical treatment, devalued, and discriminated against in virtually every aspect of community life. These practices are now widely recognized as inconsistent with what our society claims to value. It has taken us a long time to own up to this realization—we still have quite a way to go to set things right.

Despite the slow pace of change, we are headed on a path in pursuit of values that affirm the inclusion, participation, self-determination, and support of people with disabilities in education, employment, community living, and recreation. These are values that, when put into practice, are good for people with disabilities, good for their families, and good for our communities and society as a whole. Like a canary in a mineshaft, how a society treats its citizens with disabilities can be an indicator of its overall health.

Our national values, at least in part, are reflected in our federal laws. Within the realm of education, the Individuals with Disabilities Education Act (IDEA) Amendments of 1997, PL 105-17, support access to a meaningful life in the community by ensuring that *all* children with disabilities receive a free, appropriate public education. IDEA emphasizes access to general education settings and curriculum, as well as opportunities for students with disabilities to be educated with peers who do not have disabilities. IDEA affirms the belief that all children can learn when provided with appropriately individualized curriculum, instruction, and supports. Further, it includes safeguards to avoid unduly restrictive placements and practices. Of course, IDEA reflects an ideal that is not always played out in reality.

VALUED LIFE OUTCOMES

For most people with disabilities and their families and friends, the lofty rhetoric of society's values is distant and somewhat removed from the joys and struggles of daily life. On an individual level, these broader societal values are played out in more practical terms. The following valued life outcomes are neither surprising nor are they unique to people with disabilities. Self-advocates and their families tell us that they value people, practices, and supports that allow them to

- Be safe and healthy
- Develop meaningful relationships with other people
- Have choice and control within their lives
- Engage in meaningful activities (e.g., employment, recreation, education)
- Participate in the full range of places available to other citizens
- Have a home in which to live, now and in the future

These valued life outcomes, as well as others, can be pursued through a combination of skill development on the part of the person with a disability and supports provided to that person. Most of us have come to expect that we will have opportunities to pursue our interests and aspirations in ways that we find personally satisfying and that hold potential to be of value to the broader community. Too many people with disabilities and their families wage a battle to attain the same opportunities many of us take for granted.

LOGICAL PRACTICES

Bridging the gap between values and reality requires the development and utilization of practices that logically lead to the realization of those values. In this context, logical practices refer to actions taken to educate our students that *make sense*. For example, if we want a student with a disability to learn how to interact with peers who do not have disabilities, it is logical to provide ongoing opportunities for these students to be together and participate in shared activities. If we want a student to learn an important skill, it is logical to explicitly teach that skill, provide repeated opportunities to practice and apply that skill, and provide ways for the student to get feedback on his learning. If we want a student to learn to make reasonable choices, it is logical to provide a range of reasonable options, teach the student communication skills that allow her to indicate her choices, and then honor the choices she makes.

ILLOGICAL PRACTICES

In too many places in our country we find ourselves in a sort of educational "twilight zone." While more people are espousing inclusive values about educating students with disabilities, our practices reflect an odd mixture of the old and the new. Much of our "politically correct" rhetoric is without substance. Our hybrid practices are not as successful as they could be because too many of them are consistent with values from a past era. As a result, we see *illogical practices.*

If we want a student with challenging behaviors to have positive models of appropriate behaviors, it is illogical to place him in a classroom where he will only interact with other students who exhibit a range of challenging behaviors. If we want students to learn how to treat others fairly and with kindness, it is illogical to use classroom management methods that are based on humiliation, threats, or punishment. If we want a middle school student to have opportunities to make friends with classmates, it is illogical to teach her recreational activities meant for much younger children. If we want students to lead regular lives, it is illogical to make everything we do with and for them "specialized" and "disability different." We desperately need to rely on logical practices that are congruent with the valued life outcomes sought by people with disabilities and their families.

PURSUING LOGICAL PRACTICES REQUIRES CREATIVITY

In pursuing actions that make sense, there is a danger that the pursuit of "logical practices" might be interpreted too narrowly. Some people might limit what makes sense only to what is rather than what could be. For example, some people might think it does not make sense to include a student with severe disabilities in an academic class where the vast majority of other students are working on objectives that are different or more advanced. It is not uncommon to hear a teacher say, "I don't get it! How does it make sense to include a student with severe disabilities in my class?"

Limiting ourselves to what is restricts the boundaries of our thinking. These artificial limitations have led us to wrongly assume that

- All students in the same class must have the same learning outcomes
- The format of a class (e.g., lecture) must stay the same
- All students must be evaluated in the same ways

Reexamining practices that might appear illogical when viewed from a "what is" perspective can actually provide fertile ground for creative problem-solving when we approach them as "what if" situations. In fact, when we challenge our existing practices in an effort to include students with disabilities, invariably we identify changes that improve educational practices for many other students who do not have disabilities, often by making instruction more individualized, participatory, and cooperative.

RESEARCH

Where does educational research fit into an approach that begins with values and proceeds to logical practices? Within this framework, educational research serves at least two important purposes. First, descriptive research can help us deepen our understanding, reframe our questions, challenge our thinking, and extend our insights. Second, educational research is well-suited to helping us evaluate our practices to determine the extent of their effectiveness and impact on desired outcomes. Both of these purposes can inform our selection, development, and utilization of logical practices that match valued life outcomes sought by students with disabilities and their families.

It is important to recognize and distinguish between helpful and unhelpful research. Helpful research aids us in better understanding or pursuing valued life outcomes for students who have disabilities. Unhelpful research offers trivial findings, interferes with innovation, or hinders efforts to advance valued life outcomes for students with disabilities. Sometimes unhelpful research unnecessarily or artificially pits two or more valued outcomes against each other by suggesting that one can be pursued but only at the expense of another. Helpful research has resulted in more students with severe disabilities acquiring and applying skills resulting in improvements in valued life outcomes that would not have been considered priorities or possibilities 10 or 20 years ago.

Few issues in special education are more contentiously debated than the inclusion of students with the full range of disabilities in general education classes. Some people ask, "Where is the research supporting the inclusion of students with disabilities within general education?" Whether the inclusion of students with disabilities within general education should be supported at the level of social policy and school-based practice is not a question for research to answer—it is a question of values.

It would be more helpful to pose research questions that help us to clarify and to advance valued outcomes.

- How do students with disabilities and their families experience and think about inclusion and exclusion?
- How can we successfully include a wider range of students with disabilities in general education classes?
- What curricular and instructional approaches are effective for teaching heterogeneous groups of students who may be pursuing different learning outcomes?
- How can schools and classrooms be organized to account for greater student diversity?
- What are barriers to effective inclusion, and how can they be overcome?
- How can school personnel be supported to successfully teach students with and without disabilities?

LOCAL RESEARCH

When people talk about research, they usually mean the kind they read in journals. Typically, this is research carried out somewhere else, by someone else, with someone else's students. Although such research can be very useful, how we think about research need not be limited to articles in journals.

There is an old saying, "All politics are local." In much the same way, I would like to suggest that "All research is local." Although it is helpful to know that a practice has been successful elsewhere, ultimately, when relying on research to make decisions about whether a particular practice makes sense, the decision is a local one.

Just because something is published in a journal does not mean it makes sense in your situation. Conversely, just because research is lacking does not mean a practice that makes sense to an educational team should not be attempted. Do not be held back by the age-old conundrum, "We can't implement an innovative practice because we don't have enough research supporting it. Yet, we don't have enough research because not enough people are implementing it." What matters is whether the practices under consideration make sense for the specific students for whom their use is proposed. Once team members have decided that a proposed practice is logical and is consistent with the valued life outcomes being sought, they have enough reason to move forward with initial implementation.

At this point, educational team members become researchers to study the effectiveness and impact of the practices locally to see if they are helping to effectively achieve desired outcomes for their students. This means establishing important questions and developing valid systems to answer them.

In other words, to be accountable for our decisions about practices that we utilize, we have to collect and analyze data to determine if students are achieving reasonably established objectives. Second, we must extend our evaluation of impact in an attempt to ascertain whether achievement has resulted in strides toward valued life outcomes. For example, having a student learn social skills is commendable, but ultimately, these skills are only useful if they result in the development or enhancement of personally meaningful relationships with other people.

SEQUENCE AND SYNERGY

Espousing inclusion's values without implementing logical practices and learning from research is of little consequence and is unlikely to yield positive results. Implementation of practices without values leads to misuse and abuse. Segregation and use of aversive procedures are two prime examples. Values and logical practices without research leave us with too many unanswered questions about effectiveness and impact. But used together, values, logical practices, and research can have a positive and synergistic effect on education and the lives of students with disabilities.

In this book, June E. Downing and her colleagues present a wide array of logical practices that are firmly based on inclusionary values and research. Our challenge as a field is to create the conditions (e.g., class size, caseload size, proportion of students with special needs, personnel preparation and support) that allow teams to implement these and other innovative practices. Downing's practical and value-based insights into including students with severe and multiple disabilities present "what is" for a small portion of students with severe disabilities and the promise of "what could be" for many others. She accomplishes this important task by relying on the synergy of values, logical practices, and research— the Three Musketeers of meaningful and effective education.

Michael F. Giangreco, Ph.D.
University of Vermont
Center on Disability and Community Inclusion

Preface

Upon tackling the task of reworking the first edition of *Including Students with Severe and Multiple Disabilities in Typical Classrooms: Practical Strategies for Teachers*, I was initially relieved that in updating the text it did not appear that extensive revisions would be needed. At the same time, I was somewhat dismayed that extensive revisions would not be needed. I guess I felt that as a field we should have made sufficient progress since the early 1990s (when I began work on the first edition) to require some fairly substantial changes. Yet, that did not appear to be the case. In fact, several friends and colleagues who have used the first edition of this text for courses they taught told me to leave it alone—it was fine. They probably thought I'd make a mess of things for the second edition. I hope I haven't done that. In fact, I have really tried to adhere to advice given by a handyman friend of mine from Tucson, Arizona. His advice was, "Don't fix things if they're not broken." (Actually, his business card read, "I *only* fix things that aren't broken," which may have accounted for his relative success.)

I hope I have been successful at preparing an improved text over the first edition. Those who liked that edition can rest assured that I left the essence of it intact, including all the examples provided throughout. Because the feedback I received indicated that real examples helped to "make the book," I added even more.

In addition to updating information as needed (certainly the reauthorization of the Individuals with Disabilities Education Act in 1997 warranted some changes), the major changes include separating the material on middle and high school students into two chapters. This allowed me to provide a lot more examples of students at these ages. I also wanted to add a bit of information about block scheduling, service learning, and what to try during challenging times for the students when the teacher was lecturing or there were large group discussions.

I also felt the need to address the topic of assessment. I'm not sure why. Certainly my students (those I am trying to help become certified teachers) held no great love for assignments I gave in this area. Collecting data on student progress seemed at the bottom of their "to do" list. I think I was fascinated by the somewhat vague, but always creative reporting of progress made on individualized education program (IEP) goals and objectives at the many IEP meetings I attended while supporting families. I'm sure this served as some kind of catalyst to write Chapter 10 on assessing progress. I guess I believe that it is important to document student progress in inclusive situations. I am hoping that at least some of the readers believe this as well.

Specific information on using daily schedules with students was added to Chapter 3, which I hope will prove helpful. I inadvertently left this information out when writing the first edition and am glad I have this opportunity to correct that oversight. I also added information on scheduling (in Chapter 9) for the benefit of teaching staff. Orchestrating where team members will be during the course of a day or week can be very challenging. Perhaps this information with examples provided for the elementary and high school years will make this aspect of inclusion clearer.

When I asked friends and past students what was missing from the first edition, one individual made the following comment. "Remind everyone that this is *hard* work. It will never be perfect no matter how hard you try, and there will always be something that needs to be done" (M. Taylor, personal communication, August 27, 1999). I'm not sure if that was the exact quote because her call came fairly late at night and was somewhat "out of the blue," and I was exhausted. Still, I remember the call, and I think I captured the gist of her message. I never intended to imply that teaching was easy (regardless of placement or type of student). It *is* hard work and there will always be elements of frustration (on everyone's part). Despite this fact, we can at least try. My hope is that with this second edition, the thoughts and ideas of those who are trying very hard to educate all children together will help others try as well. Good luck to all of you.

Acknowledgments

The completion of this second edition was made possible with the assistance of a number of people. My co-authors, Joanne Eichinger and MaryAnn Demchak, agreed to revise the chapters they had written with me for the first edition of this book. Their ongoing support was both needed and greatly appreciated. I am so grateful I can count on their expertise and their friendship. Yet another friend, Mike Giangreco, agreed to write the foreword despite a very busy schedule. This foreword is a unique contribution to the book. Mike wanted to do more than write a traditional foreword, and this book was the lucky recipient. His words in these beginning pages provide wonderful insight into why we all strive so hard to look beyond superficial differences and include everyone. I only hope this book measures up to such an impressive treatise. Thank you, Mike.

I am very grateful to the families who let me use photographs of their children in this book. Their fight to keep their children as full-time members of their appropriate general education classes is truly inspiring. They should not have to struggle so long and so hard to do so. My hope is that one day the fear that exists regarding those who appear different will cease and differences will be celebrated. The students pictured in this book have given so much to those fortunate enough to know them. I hope that one day everyone will benefit from interactions with students like these. Their photographs add significantly to what I have tried to say.

Of course, these photographs never would have been a part of this book unless certain friends had been willing to take them for me. I am indebted to Margo Yunker for once more capturing images of students she has supported in general education classrooms. Thank you, Margo. In addition, Lavada Minor photographed the images of two close friends at play. Their picture in Chapter 8 represents the friendships that are possible despite extremely diverse abilities.

Carolyn Gross, an English major working on her master's degree and serving as a part-time clerical assistant, was an unbelievable source of support. She made edits, formatted material, created tables, and checked web sites. She was indispensable. Carolyn and her then fiancé, Tom Darin, also used their digital camera to take pictures of the schedules in Chapter 3. I really appreciate their generous offer to help, which went way beyond any expectation I had.

Several friends and colleagues offered both their suggestions and encouragement. I relied on their much-needed support. Thank you all so much. And last, but not least, I would like to thank those at Paul H. Brookes Publishing Co. who were so helpful with the development and final completion of this book. Janet Betten kept everything moving to fruition. Her skillful edits aided clarity and conciseness. Finally, I'd like to thank Lisa Benson for her positive support and enthusiasm for this book. Without her interest, there would be no second edition.

To the students I have known who desire to learn,
their families whose strength and courage continue to amaze me,
and those in the schools who tirelessly provide quality support
to ensure that all students are valued and belong

Chapter 1

Educating Students with Diverse Strengths and Needs Together

Rationale for Inclusion

June E. Downing and Joanne Eichinger

The children and young adults with severe and multiple disabilities who are the focus of this book have varying strengths and needs. They have been assigned many labels by the educational system: *severely disabled, multihandicapped blind, multihandicapped deaf, deafblind,* and *severe-profound/multihandicapped.* Yet, such terms do not convey who these children are as people, how they learn, what they want to learn, what they need to learn, and what they prefer not to learn. It is therefore best to avoid using labels if possible and to address each child as a unique learner, with specific strengths as well as limitations (as is true of anyone). However, to provide some direction for readers in applying the information contained in this and the following chapters, some general characteristics of these students are described here.

Children and young adults with severe and multiple disabilities are extremely diverse in their ages, abilities, interests, and experiences. They all, however, have difficulty learning through the visual or auditory mode or both. These students also may find it difficult to remain seated while performing deskwork. They tend to learn better when they are actively involved in the learning process and provided with tactile cues, pictures, objects, parts of objects, and clear models of behavior in addition to verbal information. They need to be allowed time to examine objects of interest and given many opportunities to perform meaningful tasks. Routines and repetition help to support understanding (Maxson, Tedder, Marmion, & Lamb, 1993).

When visual and auditory information is unclear or not readily accessible, the impact on learning can be dramatic (Prickett & Welch, 1998). Most teachers teach using these two sensory modes, so the student who does not have clear access to this information or does not understand this type of information will not experience the same rich learning environment as other children. The problem is compounded when the student has limited movement, as well, or has limited experiences or opportunities to practice skills.

Many students with severe and multiple disabilities have trouble making and maintaining friendships. Communication impairments can cause even basic social interactions to be quite limited (Downing, 1999; Mar & Sall, 1999; Romer & Haring, 1994). These individuals may have little idea of how friendships are made, what social skills are needed, or how to act in public. Some of these young people may have retreated inside themselves, engaging in unique behaviors because of their inability to obtain necessary levels of stimulation, which further ostracizes them from their peers.

HISTORICAL OVERVIEW

Historically, students with severe and multiple impairments were often denied access to public educational services because it was assumed they were unable to learn (Donder & York, 1984). The passage of the Education for All Handicapped Children Act of 1975 (PL 94-142) allowed for these students to be educated in segregated environments, including state developmental centers and segregated schools (Biklen, 1985; Donder & York, 1984). During the 1980s, there was a movement toward closing state institutions entirely or dramatically reducing their populations (Bruininks & Lakin, 1985). As a result of various court cases, there was a parallel shift in the delivery of services in schools. Many of the segregated schools were closed or reduced in size, and their students were gradually transferred to self-contained classes on general school campuses (Meyer & Kishi, 1985). With this move came an emphasis on social inclusion programs such as Special Friends (Voeltz, 1980, 1982), whereby students from general education classes spend time interacting socially with students with severe and multiple disabilities in special education classrooms.

Less than 20 years after the federal mandate, national organizations (The Association for Persons with Severe Handicaps, cited in Hardman, 1994; The Association for Retarded Citizens, 1992; National Association of State Boards of Education, 1992), parents (Obierti, 1993; Vargo & Vargo, 1993), and some educators (Stainback & Stainback, 1990, 1992) began advocating for inclusion. Inclusion, the philosophy that students with disabilities be educated in general education classes regardless of whether they can meet grade-level curricular standards, emerged in the early 1990s (Janney, Snell, Beers, & Raynes, 1995). Coupled with these advocacy efforts, the Individuals with Disabilities Education Act (IDEA) of 1990 (PL 101-476) and its 1997 amendments (PL 105-17) funded projects that emphasize education in inclusive environments (Friend & Bursuck, 1999). Thus, since the 1970s dramatic changes have occurred and continue to be proposed in the delivery of services to students with severe and multiple disabilities.

IMPORTANCE OF SYSTEMIC CHANGE

The 1990 reauthorization of PL 94-142 as PL 101-476, IDEA, emphasizes the placement of students with disabilities in general education classes. Educational data revealed that indeed IDEA has had an impact on educational placements for students with severe and multiple disabilities. U.S. Department of Education data note that during the 1990–1991 school year, for students ages 6–21, only 6.7% of students labeled as having multiple disabilities and 10.9% of students labeled as deafblind were placed in a general education class (Snyder & Hoffman, 1994). Furthermore, for the 1990–1991 school year, more than half of students labeled as multiply disabled were served in very restrictive environments including public or private separate schools, separate classes, public or private residential programs, and homebound or hospital institutional settings. In the *Annual Report to Congress on the Implementation of the IDEA Act*, U.S. Department of Education data revealed that during the 1997–1998 school year, for students ages 6–21, 10% of students labeled as having multiple disabilities and 13.6% of students labeled as deafblind received instruction in the general education class as their primary learning environment (Snyder, 2000).

Although these data are somewhat encouraging, it is important that all schools begin to address inclusion in a systematic fashion as the number of students who are included continues to increase. Inclusion of learners with severe and multiple disabilities is more likely to be successful and sustained if approached from a systemic perspective (Villa & Thousand, 2000; Villa, Thousand, Stainback, & Stainback, 1992). This involves a shared-values philosophy that is articulated in the school's mission statement (Kennedy, 2001; Schattman & Benay, 1992) and operationalized in the policies and behaviors of the professionals involved. One example of a district that embraced the inclusion of its students with severe disabilities is Johnson City Central School District in New York State. Salisbury, Palombaro, and Hollowood (1993) documented the systems change process that occurred in an inclusive elementary school in that district over a 30-month period. Their study revealed that the change to an inclusive school occurred slowly, systematically, and within a collaborative process of decision making involving administration and staff. Staub, Spaulding, Peck, Gallucci, and Schwartz (1996) described a similar inclusion process for a junior high school in another region of the country.

Ideally, for successful inclusion to occur, a school district, family members, university training program, and state education department all share the same philosophy and work collaboratively toward that goal. When this collaboration occurs, large-scale inclusion can take place. For example, in the San Francisco Bay Area, where researchers in higher education (i.e., San Francisco State University) have been implementing federal grant initiatives for several years, 47 of the 85 students with severe disabilities in one urban district were full-time students in general education in either their neighborhood schools or schools of choice (Hunt, Alwell, Farron-Davis, & Goetz, 1996).

Because this level of university involvement may be the exception rather than the rule, the next best scenario is for a particular school to develop a cohesive mission statement, along with an action plan for how inclusion will be implemented and what supports will be provided to teachers and students. This ongoing planning effort should involve all of the key players in this service delivery shift (e.g., teachers, parents, paraeducators, administrators). One key support that has been identified as critical to inclusion is a block of time for collaborative planning (Jorgensen, 1994; Jorgensen, Fisher, Sax, & Skoglund, 1998; Logan et al., 1994–1995). This aspect, in particular, would be very difficult to achieve without planning and support from the administrative level.

Several authors address the systems change process in professional literature (Calculator & Jorgensen, 1994; Salisbury et al., 1993; Villa & Thousand, 2000). The emphasis of this book, however, is not on strategies for systemic change. An underlying premise of this book is that schools and school districts are committed to educating all students together and have made an effort to support this philosophy using a variety of general inclusive strategies (e.g., development of an inclusive mission statement, schoolwide staff training). Accepting this premise allows us to focus on specific teaching strategies and unique curricular adaptations across the age range (preschool through high school) that support effective educational programming for students with severe and multiple disabilities. The emphasis is on ensuring appropriate supports. Although no standard definition of inclusion exists, for the purpose of this text, inclusion is defined as full-time placement of a student in a chronologically age-appropriate general education classroom(s) with the necessary and appropriate supports and services to facilitate learning.

WHY EDUCATE THESE STUDENTS IN TYPICAL CLASSROOMS?

Students labeled as having severe and multiple disabilities may appear to have such challenging impairments that their educational limitations are perceived as far exceeding their abilities. Their needs may appear to be so basic (e.g., simple communication skills; appropriate manipulation of objects; learning to sit, stand, or walk) that teaching these students in highly academic, typical classrooms seems improbable or, at the least, impractical. Yet, these students can benefit considerably from the learning opportunities that typically occur in general education classrooms. With limited information available to these students from the two major sensory modes—vision and hearing—these students need the almost constant stimulation, the numerous opportunities to interact, and the readily available instructional models from peers that occur in typical classrooms.

Special educators, no matter how highly motivated or skilled, cannot provide the necessary ongoing stimulation in self-contained classrooms. The battle against the relatively long periods of time during which students must wait for adult attention in such classrooms has been well documented (Houghton, Bronicki, & Guess, 1987; Richards & Sternberg, 1992). In addition, interaction among students who possess the same multiple and challenging disabilities is minimal, if it occurs at all (Logan et al., 1998; Romer & Haring, 1994). These individuals require very responsive communicative partners to reinforce their attempts to interact. Educating students together who have the same difficulty in communication provides neither the necessary responsive partners nor the typical communicative role models that are essential for enhancing social interactions.

For instance, when the special educator is assisting one student, the other students in the room are unable to help each other or even socialize with one another in any sort of fulfilling way. In a typical classroom, when adults cannot attend to a given student, the time can be filled with peer interactions for general social reasons or for more specific learning purposes. General education classrooms offer stimulation, challenge, and learning opportunities that are extremely difficult to replicate in a self-contained classroom. Yet, mere physical presence in typical classrooms is not sufficient to ensure the development of communicative, social, or friendship skills (Schnorr, 1997; Schwartz, 2000). These students need to be an integral part of the classroom and accepted as full-time members who contribute in a positive way to the overall dynamics of the learning environment. Ford and Fredericks (1994), for example, documented the success of the inclusion process for a fourth grader with deafblindness. Their book contains numerous other examples of the benefits for all students of including students with multiple impairments in the general educational environment.

Many general education teachers and parents have reported that their students who do not have disabilities lose valuable learning opportunities if they do not experience inclusive education (Cushing & Kennedy, 1997; S. Hughes, personal communication, February 18, 2000). Learning with and from students with severe disabilities provides students without disabilities unique opportunities for personal growth and understanding of differences. Therefore, no excuses are needed for the presence of a student with severe and multiple disabilities in a typical general education class. One parent once asked the principal of her children's new elementary school where the students were who had severe disabilities. Her children, who did not have disabilities, had classmates with severe disabilities at their former school, and the parent perceived their presence as an essential element in her children's education. A parent of a child with severe multiple disabilities, including deafblindness and physical disabilities, also reported similar requests for other students to be placed with her son (Boisot, 2000). All children have gifts to share with others. What educators need to do is make sure that everyone can recognize them.

DESIRED OUTCOMES FOR STUDENTS

Regardless of whether a student has severe and multiple disabilities, graduation goals for all students are similar. In general, students should become productive, contributing members of society who follow rules of social conduct and get along with others. We also hope that students will lead happy, rewarding lives. In interviews with parents about their dreams and hopes for their children with multiple disabilities and deafblindness, Giangreco, Cloninger, Mueller, Yuan, and Ashworth (1991) found that parents' valued outcomes included a safe, stable home, access to a variety of places to engage in worthwhile activities, meaningful relationships, personal choice and control, safety, and health. Such valued outcomes are certainly not limited to children with severe disabilities. Recognizing the shared common goals for all students clarifies the rationale for educating students together and greatly diminishes the need for separate education.

OUTCOMES OF INCLUSIVE EDUCATIONAL PRACTICES

Numerous researchers have examined the outcomes of inclusive educational practices from various perspectives (parents, general education teachers, special education teachers, and students). This research has generated information relative to the benefits not only to students with severe disabilities but to their peers without disabilities, as well.

Benefits to Students with Severe Disabilities

Numerous benefits for students with severe disabilities exist to support their inclusion in typical classrooms. These benefits include those perceived by others (parents, teachers, and students) as well as behaviors of the students that have been observed.

Teacher Perspectives   Much of the literature documenting positive outcomes for students with severe disabilities in inclusive classrooms comes from research involving teachers. Giangreco, Dennis, Cloninger, Edelman, and Schattman (1993) interviewed 19 general education teachers who had at least one student with a severe disability in their class. They reported that students with severe disabilities were more aware and responsive and had increased skill acquisition when educated in general classrooms than in self-contained environments.

York, Vandercook, Macdonald, Heise-Neff, and Caughey (1992) used questionnaires to survey general and special education teachers. Four of the seven general education teachers surveyed said that students with disabilities were part of the class and were accepted. The special educators surveyed noted that students with severe disabilities who were educated in general classrooms were included more in the school community and experienced growth in terms of skill acquisition.

Downing, Eichinger, and Williams (1997) interviewed nine general education teachers and nine special education teachers relative to perceived benefits of inclusion for students with severe disabilities. Results indicated that teachers regarded the rich learning environment of the typical classroom as beneficial to the student with severe disabilities in developing appropriate social and behavior skills as well as friendships.

Finally, Janzen, Wilgosh, and McDonald (1995) interviewed five general educators and one resource room teacher. All reported that students with moderate and severe disabilities developed a sense of belonging to the group and were aware of their classmates as demonstrated by smiles, high fives, eye contact, and reaching toward them. These teachers also felt that the students with disabilities had progressed in physical skill development, had increased appropriate behaviors, and had decreased inappropriate behaviors.

Student Perspectives   York et al. (1992) surveyed middle school students about their perceptions of the inclusion of students with severe disabilities. Overall, the students noted positive changes in the students with severe disabilities since the inception of inclusion. The perceptions of the students were that students with disabilities had changed socially (e.g., were more talkative, fun, cooperative, happy), had more friends, and had reduced levels of inappropriate behaviors (e.g., inappropriate hugging).

Fisher, Pumpian, and Sax (1998) interviewed 1,413 typical students from two high schools (one inclusive and one in which students with disabilities were in self-contained classes). Findings revealed that students without disabilities from the inclusive high school were more positive in general with regard to their attitudes and perceptions of students having severe disabilities. The students without disabilities also felt that students with severe disabilities could increase social skills, be better prepared for the future, and be challenged to learn if included in typical classrooms.

Multiple Perspectives   For 2 years, Peck et al. (1994) followed 35 preschool-to middle school–age students with mild to severe disabilities who were in inclusive environments. They used multiple measures to collect data, including parent and teacher interviews, surveys, videotape recordings, and narrative records of the teachers and students in classroom and other school environments. They reported three major outcomes for the students with disabilities. First, the students achieved membership and a sense of belonging. Second, there were numerous opportunities to develop meaningful social relationships. Third, the authors noted developmental changes, including increased social and communication skills, improved academic skills for the older students, and improved preacademic skills for the preschoolers.

Based on observational and interview data from a year-long program in which students without disabilities or students with mild disabilities served as aides who worked with students with severe disabilities, Staub et al. (1996) reported increased levels of independence, social growth and more opportunities for social networking, and academic and behavioral growth for the four learners.

Parent Perspectives Parent perspectives also have been examined. Davern (1999) conducted semistructured in-depth interviews with 21 parents representing 15 families who had children with disabilities ranging from mild to severe. All the children were being educated in inclusive environments. She reported that although parents remarked about the challenges involved with inclusive education, parents were extremely enthusiastic about the impact of inclusive education on their children's development. In another study, interviews with 13 parents of children with severe disabilities educated in general education classrooms indicated that the children had acquired academic, communication, social, and behavior skills, as well as developed friendships and a sense of belonging (Ryndak, Downing, Jacqueline, & Morrison, 1995).

A large-scale study regarding inclusive education for learners with severe disabilities surveyed parents of children with severe disabilities. The children, ages 3–22, were being educated in self-contained classrooms, and 476 parents responded to the survey. Results indicated that the parents perceived inclusion to be beneficial in terms of social interactions, acceptance, and treatment of their children, but the parents expressed concern about the quality of education their children would receive in an inclusive program (Palmer, Borthwick-Duffy, & Widaman, 1998). However, given the fact that these parents had children who had not experienced inclusion, their views may not be representative of parents in general.

Student Outcomes Hunt, Farron-Davis, Beckstead, Curtis, and Goetz (1994) compared outcomes for students with severe disabilities in general education classes with outcomes for students with disabilities in special education classes. The areas examined were quality of the individualized education program (IEP), curricular content of the IEP, engaged time, inclusive activities, affective demeanor, and social interactions. The authors found that the IEP objectives for students in inclusive environments included more instruction of basic skills and more participation with peers who do not have disabilities than for students in self-contained classes. The overall quality of the IEP objectives was considered higher for the students in general education environments. Students in the inclusive environments had more academic activities and fewer recreation and leisure activities than did students in the self-contained classrooms. When the authors observed the actual behaviors of students, the students in the general education classes were alone less and were more often actively engaged in the activities of the day than were students in self-contained classes. They were also more involved in academic skill activities and less involved in critical skill activities than students in special education classes. Regarding social interactions, students in general education classes initiated more interactions, and these interactions were more social and less task-related. Similar findings were noted by Hunt and Farron-Davis (1992), who followed students with severe disabilities from their self-contained classes to inclusive general education. When these students were in general education classrooms, the overall quality of their IEPs was higher, and their IEPs included more inclusive activities than when they were in self-contained classrooms.

Other researchers have documented actual change in the behaviors of students with severe disabilities in inclusive environments. Hunt, Staub, Alwell, and Goetz (1994) described the results of a study involving three students with severe and multiple disabilities who were included in three second-grade classes. They demonstrated communication and motor skill acquisition for all three students during a mathematics unit, in which each lesson was structured using cooperative learning groups. Specifically, by the end of the second intervention phase, the students were consistently and independently passing out materials, acknowledging other group members (via eye contact and smiling), and asking for a turn (via hitting a switch to activate a prerecorded message). The researchers also documented that the students continued to demonstrate those skills in follow-up sessions with different students in newly configured cooperative groups.

Logan et al. (1998) investigated the impact of interaction among students with profound and multiple disabilities and their peers without disabilities. The five targeted students showed a higher percentage of behavior that was described as happiness when typical peers were present versus classmates with similar disabilities. These researchers felt that peers without disabilities produced much higher social and physical interactions (more stimulation) and that interactions were of a higher quality.

In the realm of social development, Kennedy, Shukla, and Fryxell (1997) compared social interactions, social support behaviors, and friendship networks of students with severe disabilities educated full time in general education classes in neighborhood schools with students with severe disabilities educated in self-contained classes in typical public schools. They found that students in general education classes experienced more frequent interactions with their peers without disabilities, a larger proportion of social support during social interactions, and bigger and more durable friendship networks than students in self-contained classes. Interestingly, they also noted that students with severe disabilities in inclusive environments gave more social support during interactions with peers without disabilities than did the students in self-contained classes.

Extending beyond social interactions, Staub, Schwartz, Gallucci, and Peck (1994) examined four friendships among elementary students with severe disabilities and their classmates without disabilities. All of these relationships developed from nontutorial activities and contexts.

Benefits to Students without Disabilities

Students with severe disabilities are not the only ones to benefit from an inclusive education. Several studies have reported the benefits available to their classmates who have no disabilities. This recommended practice of inclusive education for students with severe disabilities does not interfere with but in fact enhances educational opportunities for all students.

Teacher and Parent Perspectives   As was the case when describing benefits to students with severe disabilities, much of what we know about benefits to students without disabilities in inclusive environments has been reported by teachers and parents. Peck, Carlson, and Helmstetter (1992) examined the perceptions of 125 parents of typical children and 95 teachers involved with children with mild to severe disabilities included in general education classrooms at the preschool or kindergarten level. They reported that overall parent perceptions were very favorable, with five positive outcomes emerging. These were that the children without disabilities 1) became more accepting of individual differences, 2) were more aware of other children's needs, 3) were more comfortable with people with disabilities, 4) were more helpful in general to other children, and 5) were less prejudiced about people who are different. Similarly, teacher responses were positive overall, with the same first three positive outcomes as noted by parents, as well.

In interviews involving teachers who had at least one student with a severe disability in their class, acceptance, improved social and emotional development, and flexibility emerged as benefits for the students without disabilities (Giangreco, Dennis, et al., 1993). Similarly, the majority of the general education teachers interviewed by York et al. (1992) stated that students without disabilities benefited by becoming more accepting, more understanding, and more aware of the similarities they shared with students with disabilities. Downing et al. (1997) found that teachers (both special and general education) felt that students without disabilities acquired appreciation for and demonstrated acceptance of students with severe and multiple disabilities. Teachers also reported that students without disabilities acquired leadership skills and enhanced their self-esteem.

Student Perspectives   Helmstetter, Peck, and Giangreco (1994) surveyed 166 high school students to determine outcomes of interactions with students with severe disabilities. The respondents interacted with the students with moderate or severe disabilities through attendance in general education classes, Special Friends programs (Voeltz, 1980, 1982), or tutorial programs. The authors reported seven positive outcomes: increased responsiveness to others' needs, valuing relationships with people with disabilities, personal development, more tolerance for others, increased appreciation for human diversity, development of personal values, and positive changes in peer status. The study of high school students by Fisher et al. (1998) supported these findings with students from the inclusive high school reporting an increase of understanding and acceptance of their classmates with severe disabilities as a result of inclusive practices.

One benefit of inclusion to students without disabilities is opportunities for friendship. Using a case study approach, Staub et al. (1994) discussed the nature of friendships among four elementary students without disabilities and four classmates with severe disabilities. The authors described these relationships as rich and varied. Turnbull, Pereira, and Blue-Banning (2000) also reported that true friendships can and do occur among students with and without disabilities. For example, one student without disabilities in their study stressed the feeling of total acceptance that he felt in his relationship with a friend with severe disabilities. Similarly, in a survey of 1,137 middle and high school students, between 55% and 65% of typical students indicated that they would benefit from a friendship with a student with disabilities (Hendrickson, Shokoohi-Yekta, Hamre-Nietupski, & Gable, 1996).

Multiple Perspectives   Observational data and interview data from students, parents, teachers, and paraeducators identified five outcomes for the 31 student aides without disabilities involved in a year-long project to support inclusion: increased social networks; acknowledgement and appreciation for helping; more awareness, appreciation, and understanding of people with disabilities; more patience for people who learn differently; and a greater sense of responsibility (Staub et al., 1996).

Impact on Learning   Although concerns have been expressed regarding the impact of inclusion on learners without disabilities—specifically, that inclusion will negatively affect their learning (Shanker, 1994–1995)—the literature does not seem to bear this out. When asked to respond to the statement that having children with disabilities in the class resulted in children without disabilities receiving less teacher attention, both teachers and parents disagreed with the statement (Peck et al., 1992). In fact, Fisher, Sax, and Grove (2000) found that inclusive education for students with mild, moderate, and severe disabilities actually increased the impact of academic achievement of students without disabilities in elementary school. In another study examining the effects of cooperatively structured groups, students without disabilities provided cues, prompts, and reinforcement to a student with severe disabilities in their cooperative group. The researchers examined the achievement levels of the students without disabilities who provided the assistance to students with severe disabilities. They found that the students providing assistance made gains in achievement of mathematics skills comparable to those made by students without disabilities who were part of control groups in which there were no students with severe disabilities (both groups of students without disabilities were at similar math levels to begin with) (Hunt et al., 1994).

POTENTIAL BARRIERS TO SUCCESSFUL INCLUSION

Perhaps the greatest barrier to the successful inclusion of children with severe and multiple impairments in typical learning environments is the fear of what might happen or what might have to happen. Because relatively few students with these disabilities are included in general education classes, information pertaining to their successful learning and to the necessary supports to promote this success are not readily available or known to most teaching teams. These children tend to be judged on how they perform in self-contained classrooms and on developmental scales (Linehan, Brady, & Hwang, 1991). This instructional context obscures the ability to perceive them as capable learners in need of typical interactions and educational situations. Not knowing what is possible and how supports can be used to promote all students' learning can create an unwillingness to change. A change in attitude is the basic step that must occur before educating all students together can be successful. With a change of attitude from "You can't do it, so you can't be a part of it" to "You can't do it now, so I must find a way to help you be a part of it," the movement toward inclusive education can be realized. The focus must shift from a deficit orientation to an ability orientation, with the realization that additional support may be necessary and is acceptable. Inclusive education builds on the principle of interdependence among learners and the realization that students will excel in some skill areas but not others. The heterogeneity of learners in typical classrooms allows the give and take necessary for students to learn from each other.

Due to the relatively recent trend of including children with severe disabilities in general education environments, there may be a shortage of trained personnel to promote this type of learning situation (Eichinger, Downing, Evans, Feck, & Ike, 2000; Luiselli, Luiselli, DeCaluwe, & Jacobs, 1995). Until personnel preparation programs can shift their training strategies to an inclusive approach, schools and school districts must engage in intensive in-service training of their staffs. Although certain staff members may have considerable experience working with the target population, the skills required for inclusive programming are substantially different and will require additional training for most people. Skills needed to use traditional assessments, implement developmental curricula, and remediate skills deficits will be considerably less important than collaborative teaming skills, peer in-services, facilitating peer interactions, and adapting the typical curricular materials for diverse learners (Edelson-Smith, Prater, & Sileo, 1993).

OVERVIEW OF SUCCESSFUL
STRATEGIES FOR INCLUSIVE EDUCATION

Perhaps the most critical strategy for creating successful learning experiences for all children in general education environments, regardless of disability, is teamwork. Much has been written about the need for effective team collaboration in the educational planning of students with severe and multiple disabilities (Giangreco, Cloninger, & Iverson, 1998; Meyer & Eichinger, 1994; Rainforth & York-Barr, 1997; Romer & Byrne, 1995; Utley, 1993). The need for creative problem solving and innovative delivery of services requires cooperative and ongoing interactions among trained professionals, paraeducators, and family members. Setting realistic goals for the whole student demands a commitment from all team members to contribute their expertise in such a way that the student does not become fragmented into various specialty areas. Respect for others' ideas, experiences, and skills, regardless of degree or certification, is essential if the student's best interests are to guide the process.

The recognition that all students learn differently and at different rates and are motivated to learn different things assists the process of inclusive education. Not all students in a classroom obtain the same level of knowledge or understanding in the course of a school year. What is critical, however, is that all students have access to the information, regardless of whether similar goals are reached. When confronted with a new learning task, not all individuals will master the material; some will attain only a partial level of understanding. Nevertheless, individuals should not be denied access to information for which mastery is doubtful. Motivation to learn, the individual's perception of the need to learn the material, plus natural ability to learn will combine to play major roles in the level of skill mastery.

The concept of partial participation (Ferguson & Baumgart, 1991) supports the idea that participation in various learning activities will be realized differently by different students. Whereas active participation in the learning process is a goal for all students, the level of participation will vary depending on such factors as abilities, interest, and past experiences. Realizing that all individuals will acquire different levels of skill and understanding of material/activities may help teachers to welcome diverse learners in the classroom. For instance, while Joe, a typical fifth grader, masters the multiplication tables from 0 to 10, Jeff, a fifth grader with severe intellectual, visual, and behavior impairments, learns to match numbers to a large calculator in preparation for shopping excursions. The skills of both students were learned during the same mathematics class in fifth grade. The mastery level is significantly different, but both boys attain the skills needed for their present and future lives. In addition, they each learn how to work together in a cooperative manner that fosters respect for differences.

Cooperative learning has been one positive strategy in support of the inclusion of students with different learning abilities (Putnam, 1998). Cooperative learning typically allows for greater interactions among students, movement from one learning group to another, and greater acceptance of individual learning styles (Johnson & Johnson, 1999; Stevens, Slavin, & Madden, 1991). For the student with multiple impairments including a sensory loss, the action focus of this type of learning can provide the stimulation needed to maintain interest in and attention to the task. In addition, the enhanced focus on hands-on, active involvement of students in learning is particularly beneficial to students who require more information than a strict lecture format can provide. Students with severe and multiple disabilities will learn more effectively if given the opportunity to explore, touch, interact, and perform. Of course, this type of instruction also has obvious benefits for students without disabilities. Outcomes such as higher achievement, increased use of higher-level reasoning strategies, more positive relationships with students with disabilities, and higher levels of self-esteem have been documented in the literature (Johnson, Johnson, & Maruyama, 1983; Johnson, Maruyama, Johnson, Nelson, & Skon, 1981).

Finally, the creativity of teaching staff (teachers, paraeducators, support staff) and other students will make it possible to see beyond imposed barriers and develop ways of including all students. The emphasis on critical thinking skills and creative problem solving for today's students applies equally well to today's teachers. The presence of a student with severe and multiple disabilities in the typical classroom provides a challenging opportunity to apply such skills. Personnel preparation programs will do well to develop creative thinking skills, problem-solving skills, and team collaboration on the part of future teachers.

PURPOSE OF THIS BOOK

This book's primary purpose is to provide educators, support staff, parents, and other family members with strategies they can use successfully to include students with severe and multiple impairments in the typical learning environment of public schools on a full-time basis. Practical suggestions are given for children of different ages and abilities, to serve as catalysts for effecting the changes needed for individual children. Specific examples—many from the authors' actual experiences—are included to aid in implementing the suggested ideas. To assist teachers who are specifically teaching students with sensory impairment in addition to other challenges, all examples target these students; however, the authors strongly believe that the information and examples provided in this book hold considerable value and are applicable to a wide range of students with moderate to profound disabilities without a sensory impairment. Students without sensory impairments will likely need fewer or less extensive curricular modifications.

Although each student must be treated as a unique individual and every situation is different, the intent of this book is to stimulate the critical thinking and problem solving that are crucial to any team effort to include those children who may learn differently than the typical child. The underlying assumption is that all children can learn once we identify their special strengths and support them in their effort to achieve desired outcomes.

REFERENCES

The Association for Retarded Citizens of the United States. (1992, October). *Report card to the nation on inclusion in education of students with mental retardation.* Arlington, TX: Author.

Biklen, D. (1985). *Achieving the complete school: Strategies for effective mainstreaming.* New York: Teachers College Press.

Boisot, T. (2000). Ben. *Mental Retardation, 38,* 375–377.

Bruininks, R.H., & Lakin, K.C. (Eds.). (1985). *Living and learning in the least restrictive environment.* Baltimore: Paul H. Brookes Publishing Co.

Calculator, S.N., & Jorgensen, C.M. (1994). *Including students with severe disabilities in schools: Fostering communication, interaction, and participation.* San Diego: Singular Publishing Group.

Cushing, L., & Kennedy, C. (1997). Academic effects of providing peer support in general education classrooms on students without disabilities. *Journal of Applied Behavior Analysis, 30,* 139–151.

Davern, L. (1999). Parents' perspectives on personnel attitudes and characteristics in inclusive school settings: Implications for teacher preparation programs. *Teacher Education and Special Education, 22,* 165–182.

Donder, D.J., & York, R. (1984). Integration of students with severe handicaps. In N. Certo, N. Haring, & R. York (Eds.), *Public school integration of severely handicapped students: Rational issues and progressive alternatives* (pp. 1–14). Baltimore: Paul H. Brookes Publishing Co.

Downing, J.E. (1999). *Teaching communication skills to students with severe disabilities.* Baltimore: Paul H. Brookes Publishing Co.

Downing, J., Eichinger, J., & Williams, L. (1997). Inclusive education for students with severe disabilities: Comparative views of principals and educators at different levels of implementation. *Remedial and Special Education, 18,* 133–142.

Edelson-Smith, P., Prater, M.A., & Sileo, T. (1993). The impact of current issues in teacher education on the preparation of special educators. *Issues in Special Education and Rehabilitation, 8*(1), 7–16.

Education for All Handicapped Children Act of 1975, PL 94-142, 20 U.S.C. §§ 1400 *et seq.*

Eichinger, J., Downing, J.E., Evans, K., Feck, A., & Ike, R. (2000). Special education faculty positions advertised from 1991–1997: Reflective of current practice? *Journal of The Association for Persons with Severe Handicaps, 25,* 104–108.

Ferguson, D.L., & Baumgart, D. (1991). Partial participation revisited. *Journal of The Association for Persons with Severe Handicaps, 16,* 218–227.

Fisher, D., Pumpian, I., & Sax, C. (1998). High school students' attitudes about recommendations for their peers with significant disabilities. *Journal of The Association for Persons with Severe Handicaps, 23,* 272–282.

Fisher, D., Sax, C., & Grove, K.A. (2000). The resilience of changes promoting inclusiveness in an urban elementary school. *The Elementary School Journal, 100,* 213–227.

Ford, J., & Fredericks, B. (1994). Inclusion for children who are deaf-blind. *Network, 4*(1), 25–29.

Friend, M., & Bursuck, W.D. (1999). *Including students with special needs: A practical guide for classroom teachers* (2nd ed.). Needham Heights, MA: Allyn & Bacon.

Giangreco, M.F., Cloninger, C.J., & Iverson, V.S. (1998). *Choosing outcomes and accommodations for children (COACH): A guide to educational planning for students with disabilities* (2nd ed.). Baltimore: Paul H. Brookes Publishing Co.

Giangreco, M.F., Cloninger, C.J., Mueller, P.H., Yuan, S., & Ashworth, S. (1991). Perspectives of parents whose children have dual sensory impairments. *Journal of The Association for Persons with Severe Handicaps, 16,* 14–24.

Giangreco, M.F., Dennis, R., Cloninger, C., Edelman, S., & Schattman, R. (1993). I've counted Jon: Transformational experiences of teachers educating students with disabilities. *Exceptional Children, 59,* 359–372.

Hardman, M.L. (1994). *Inclusion: Issues of educating students with disabilities in regular education settings.* Needham Heights, MA: Allyn & Bacon.

Helmstetter, E., Peck, C.A., & Giangreco, M. (1994). Outcomes of interactions with peers with moderate or severe disabilities: A statewide survey of high school students. *Journal of The Association for Persons with Severe Handicaps, 19,* 263–276.

Hendrickson, J.M., Shokoohi-Yekta, M., Hamre-Nietupski, S., & Gable, R.A. (1996). Middle and high school students' perceptions on being friends with peers with severe disabilities. *Exceptional Children, 63,* 19–28.

Houghton, J., Bronicki, G.J., & Guess, D. (1987). Opportunities to express preferences and make choices among students with severe disabilities in classroom settings. *Journal of The Association for Persons with Severe Handicaps, 12,* 18–27.

Hunt, P., Alwell, M., Farron-Davis, F., & Goetz, L. (1996). Creating socially supportive environments for fully included students who experience multiple disabilities. *Journal of The Association for Persons with Severe Handicaps, 21,* 53–71.

Hunt, P., & Farron-Davis, F. (1992). A preliminary investigation of IEP quality and content associated with placement in general education versus special education classes. *Journal of The Association for Persons with Severe Handicaps, 17,* 247–253.

Hunt, P., Farron-Davis, F., Beckstead, S., Curtis, D., & Goetz, L. (1994). Evaluating the effects of placement of students with severe disabilities in general education versus special education classes. *Journal of The Association for Persons with Severe Handicaps, 19,* 200–214.

Hunt, P., Staub, D., Alwell, M., & Goetz, L. (1994). Achievement by all students within the context of cooperative learning groups. *Journal of The Association for Persons with Severe Handicaps, 19,* 290–301.

Individuals with Disabilities Education Act (IDEA) of 1990, PL 101-476, 20 U.S.C. §§ 1400 *et seq.*

Individuals with Disabilities Education Act Amendments of 1997, PL 105-17, 20 U.S.C. §§ 1400 *et seq.*

Janney, R.W., Snell, M.E., Beers, M.K., & Raynes, M. (1995). Integrating students with moderate and severe disabilities into general education classes. *Exceptional Children, 61,* 425–439.

Janzen, L., Wilgosh, L., & McDonald, L. (1995). Experiences of classroom teachers integrating students with moderate and severe disabilities. *Developmental Disabilities Bulletin, 23*(1), 40–57.

Johnson, D.W., & Johnson, R.T. (1999). *Learning together and alone: Cooperative, competitive, and individualistic learning* (5th ed.). Needham Heights, MA: Allyn & Bacon.

Johnson, D.W., Johnson, R., & Maruyama, G. (1983). Interdependence and interpersonal attraction among heterogeneous and homogeneous individuals: A theoretical formulation of a meta-analysis of the research. *Review of Educational Research, 53,* 51–54.

Johnson, D.W., Maruyama, G., Johnson, R., Nelson, D., & Skon, L. (1981). The effects of cooperative, competitive, and individualistic goal structures on achievement: A meta-analysis. *Psychological Bulletin, 89,* 47–62.

Jorgensen, C.M. (1994). Essential questions—inclusive answers. *Educational Leadership, 52*(4), 52–55.

Jorgensen, C.M., Fisher, D., Sax, C., & Skoglund, K.L. (1998). Innovative scheduling, new roles for teachers and heterogeneous grouping: The organizational factors related to student success in inclusive, restructuring schools. In C.M. Jorgensen (Ed.), *Restructuring high schools for all students: Taking inclusion to the next level* (pp. 49–70). Baltimore: Paul H. Brookes Publishing Co.

Kennedy, C.H. (2001). Administrative leadership. In C.H. Kennedy & D. Fisher, *Inclusive middle schools* (pp. 17–26). Baltimore: Paul H. Brookes Publishing Co.

Kennedy, C.H., Shukla, S., & Fryxell, D. (1997). Comparing the effects of educational placement on the social relationships of intermediate school students with severe disabilities. *Exceptional Children, 64,* 31–47.

Linehan, S., Brady, M., & Hwang, C. (1991). Ecological vs. developmental assessment: Influences on instructional expectations. *Journal of The Association for Persons with Severe Handicaps, 16,* 146–153.

Logan, K.R., Diaz, E., Piperno, M., Rankin, D., MacFarland, A.D., & Bargamian, K. (1994–1995). How inclusion built a community of learners. *Educational Leadership, 52*(4), 42–44.

Logan, K., Jacobs, H.A., Gast, D.A., Murray, A.S., Daino, K., & Skala, C. (1998). The impact of typical peers on the perceived happiness of students with profound multiple disabilities. *Journal of The Association for Persons with Severe Handicaps, 23,* 309–318.

Luiselli, T.E., Luiselli, J.K., DeCaluwe, S.M., & Jacobs, L.A. (1995). Inclusive education of young children with deaf-blindness: A technical assistance model. *Journal of Visual Impairment and Blindness, 89,* 249–256.

Mar, H.H., & Sall, N. (1999). Profiles of the expressive communication skills of children and adolescents with severe cognitive disabilities. *Education and Training in Mental Retardation and Developmental Disabilities, 34,* 77–89.

Maxson, B.J., Tedder, N.E., Marmion, S., & Lamb, A.M. (1993). The education of youth who are deaf-blind: Learning tasks and teaching methods. *Journal of Visual Impairments and Blindness, 87,* 259–262.

Meyer, L., & Eichinger, J. (1994). *Program quality indicators (PQI): A checklist of most promising practices in educational programs for students with disabilities.* (Available from TASH, 29 W. Susquehanna Avenue, Suite 210, Towson, MD 21204)

Meyer, L.H., & Kishi, G.S. (1985). School integration strategies. In K.C. Lakin & R.H. Bruininks (Eds.), *Strategies for achieving community integration of developmentally disabled citizens* (pp. 231–252). Baltimore: Paul H. Brookes Publishing Co.

National Association of State Boards of Education. (1992, October). *Winners all: A call for inclusive schools.* Alexandria, VA: Author.

Obierti, C. (1993). A parent's perspective. *Exceptional Parent, 23*(7), 18–21.

Palmer, D.S., Borthwick-Duffy, S.A., & Widaman, K. (1998). Parent perceptions of inclusive practices for their children with significant cognitive disabilities. *Exceptional Children, 64,* 271–282.

Peck, C.A., Billingsley, F., Staub, D., Gallucci, C., Schwartz, I.S., & White, O. (1994, December). *Analysis of outcomes and contexts in inclusive school environments.* Paper presented at the meeting of The Association for Persons with Severe Handicaps, Atlanta, GA.

Peck, C.A., Carlson, P., & Helmstetter, E. (1992). Parent and teacher perceptions of outcomes for typically developing children enrolled in integrated early childhood programs: A statewide survey. *Journal of Early Intervention, 16*(1), 53–63.

Prickett, J.G., & Welch, T.R. (1998). Educating students who are deaf-blind. In S.Z. Sacks & R.K. Silberman (Eds.), *Educating students who have severe visual impairments with other disabilities* (pp. 139–159). Baltimore: Paul H. Brookes Publishing Co.

Putnam, J.W. (Ed.). (1998). *Cooperative learning and strategies for inclusion: Celebrating diversity in the classroom* (2nd ed.). Baltimore: Paul H. Brookes Publishing Co.

Rainforth, B., & York-Barr, J. (1997). *Collaborative teams for students with severe disabilities: Integrating therapy and educational services* (2nd ed.). Baltimore: Paul H. Brookes Publishing Co.

Richards, S.B., & Sternberg, L. (1992). A preliminary analysis of environmental variables affecting the observed biobehavioral states of individuals with profound handicaps. *Journal of Intellectual Disability Research, 36*(4), 403–414.

Romer, L.T., & Byrne, A.R. (1995). Collaborative teaming to support participation in inclusive education settings. In N.G. Haring & L.T. Romer (Eds.), *Welcoming students who are deaf-blind into typical classrooms: Facilitating school participation, learning, and friendships* (pp. 143–169). Baltimore: Paul H. Brookes Publishing Co.

Romer, L.T., & Haring, N.G. (1994). The social participation of students with deaf-blindness in educational settings. *Education and Training in Mental Retardation and Developmental Disabilities, 29,* 134–144.

Ryndak, D.L., Downing, J.E., Jacqueline, L.R., & Morrison, A.P. (1995). Parents' perceptions after inclusion of their child with moderate or severe disabilities in general education settings. *Journal of The Association for Persons with Severe Handicaps, 20,* 147–157.

Salisbury, C., Palombaro, M., & Hollowood, T. (1993). On the nature and change of an inclusive elementary school. *Journal of The Association for Persons with Severe Handicaps, 18,* 75–84.

Schattman, R., & Benay, J. (1992). Inclusive practices transform special education in the 1990s. *School Administrator, 49*(2), 8–12.

Schnorr, R.F. (1997). From enrollment to membership: "Belonging" in middle and high school classes. *Journal of The Association for Persons with Severe Handicaps, 22,* 1–15.

Schwartz, I.S. (2000). Standing on the shoulders of giants: Looking ahead to facilitating membership and relationships for children with disabilities. *Topics in Early Childhood Special Education, 20,* 123–128.

Shanker, A. (1994–1995). Full inclusion is neither free nor appropriate. *Educational Leadership, 52*(4), 18–21.

Snyder, T. (2000). *Digest of education statistics* (Publication No. NCES 2000-034). Washington, DC: U.S. Department of Education, Office of Educational Research Improvement.

Snyder, T.D., & Hoffman, C.M. (1994). *Digest of education statistics* (Pub. No. NCES 94-115). Washington, DC: U.S. Department of Education, Office of Educational Research and Improvement.

Stainback, S., & Stainback, W. (1992). *Curriculum considerations in inclusive classrooms: Facilitating learning for all students.* Baltimore: Paul H. Brookes Publishing Co.

Stainback, W., & Stainback, S. (Eds.). (1990). *Support networks for inclusive schools: Interdependent integrated education.* Baltimore: Paul H. Brookes Publishing Co.

Staub, D., Schwartz, I.S., Gallucci, C., & Peck, C. (1994). Four portraits of friendship at an inclusive school. *Journal of The Association for Persons with Severe Handicaps, 19,* 314–325.

Staub, D., Spaulding, M., Peck, C.A., Gallucci, C., & Schwartz, I.S. (1996). Using nondisabled peers to support the inclusion of students with disabilities at the junior high school level. *Journal of The Association for Persons with Severe Handicaps, 21,* 194–205.

Stevens, R., Slavin, R., & Madden, N. (1991). Cooperative integrated reading and composition (CIRC): Effective cooperative learning in reading and language arts. *Cooperative Learning, 11*(4), 6–18.

Turnbull, A.P., Pereira, L., & Blue-Banning, M. (2000). Teachers as friendship facilitators: Respeco and personalismo. *Teaching Exceptional Children, 32*(5), 66–71.

Utley, B. (1993). Facilitating and measuring the team process within inclusive educational settings. *Clinics in Communication Disorders, 3*(2), 71–85.

Vargo, J., & Vargo, R. (1993). Inclusive education: Right for us. *Inclusion Times for Children and Youth with Disabilities, 1*(2), 3.

Villa, R., & Thousand, J. (2000). *Restructuring for caring and effective education: Piecing the puzzle together* (2nd ed.). Baltimore: Paul H. Brookes Publishing Co.

Villa, R.A., Thousand, J.S., Stainback, W., & Stainback, S. (Eds.). (1992). *Restructuring for caring and effective education: An administrative guide to creating heterogeneous schools.* Baltimore: Paul H. Brookes Publishing Co.

Voeltz, L. (1980). Children's attitudes toward handicapped peers. *American Journal on Mental Deficiency, 84,* 455–464.

Voeltz, L. (1982). Effects of structured interactions with severely handicapped peers on children's attitudes. *American Journal on Mental Deficiency, 86,* 180–190.

York, J., Vandercook, T., Macdonald, C., Heise-Neff, C., & Caughey, E. (1992). Feedback about integrating middle-school students with severe disabilities in general education classes. *Exceptional Children, 58,* 244–258.

Chapter 2

Instruction in the
General Education Environment

Joanne Eichinger and June E. Downing

Since 1980, numerous changes have occurred in education, fueled by the publication of *A Nation at Risk* (United States Department of Education, 1983). As part of an emphasis on increased accountability in education, school districts are focusing on content standards (typically developed by national organizations in various fields, e.g., National Council of Teachers of Mathematics), performance standards (National Center on Education and the Economy and the University of Pittsburgh, 1997), and teaching standards (e.g., National Board of Professional Teaching Standards).

This chapter highlights the changes that have occurred in approaches in general and special education since 1980 and considers parallels in these changes. This analysis is followed by a discussion of "promising practices" in general education for the inclusion of learners with severe and multiple disabilities. Each of these discussions has four components: first, a description of the practice; second, the empirical or theoretical base related to that practice, including data for learners with disabilities, if these data exist; third, the rationale for utilizing the practice with students with severe and multiple disabilities; and, fourth, strategies for using the practice with students with severe and multiple disabilities.

EDUCATIONAL REFORM EFFORTS

In terms of curricular approaches, there has been an increasing emphasis on a more holistic approach to education. This is a result of the constructivist movement that emphasizes that learning is individualized, social, and occurs in context. Students construct and build on their own knowledge via interactions with their environments (Reid, Kurkijian, & Carruthers, 1994). Thus, the teacher serves as a facilitator or mediator of learning, as opposed to a disseminator of knowledge. The work of Vygotsky (1978) has been influential in this shift in thinking and practice. The constructivist approach runs counter to a strict behaviorist/reductionist approach to teaching and learning that tends to stress the remediation of deficit skills. Poplin and Stone (1992) provided an excellent description of the differences between these two learning theories, and Brooks and

Brooks (1993) compared characteristics in traditional classrooms with those in constructivist classrooms. The constructivist approach lends itself to inclusion because it emphasizes that learning is a social process, thus stressing peer-to-peer learning and support. It is also compatible with individual student goals and outcomes because acquisition of knowledge is based on students' abilities and interests. Jackson, Reid, and Bunsen asserted that constructivism

> Provides a framework for accepting all students as equal members of a community of learners rather than as differentially positioned achievers on a hierarchical skill sequence. This acceptance contrasts markedly with one of the legacies of past interpretations of the reductionist perspective: requiring individuals to "earn" membership in the school community through the acquisition of externally defined "functional" or "appropriate" skills. (1993, pp. 292–293)

Instructional strategies to teach literacy, for example, that are active; meaningful; and include reading, writing, listening, and speaking follow such a constructivist approach (Atwell, 1998). This type of comprehensive approach uses the child's own experiential base for learning oral and written communication and, as such, is very child-centered. Literacy skills are integrated within meaningful contexts (e.g., listening to classmates share something brought from home, writing daily journals), as opposed to instruction on specific skills such as decoding, grammar, and letter–sound association that are only taught in an isolated manner. Teachers balance different types of literacy instruction (e.g., explicit skill instruction with opportunities to read and write authentic texts) so that students can benefit from a more holistic approach (Pressley, Rankin, & Yokoi, 1996). Children acquire literacy skills as they engage in various activities throughout the day.

Cooperative learning (Johnson & Johnson, 1987; Johnson, Johnson, & Holubec, 1993) has also gained widespread acceptance as a promising practice in general education since the 1970s. Used at all grade levels, although more frequently in elementary classes, cooperative learning operates under the principle that learning is social. A departure from traditional lecture and workbook approaches, in which students work independently, within the cooperative learning model students actively assist each other in the learning process.

Thematic teaching units, another approach that harmonizes with the holistic trend, has gained prominence in general education classrooms (see Forte & Schurr, 1994; Kovalik & Olsen, 1992; Udall, 1997). Thematic teaching units ensure that content is integrated across several curricular areas, highlighting the natural linkages for students. There is more repetition of content and therefore more opportunity for learning because related concepts may be developed in more than one curricular area.

Another concept that is consistent with the holistic model and that has influenced educational practices in some schools is the theory of multiple intelligences (Gardner, 1983; Teele, 1999). According to this theory, individuals possess and demonstrate intelligence in various ways (e.g., spatially, interpersonally). When this theory is applied in practice, the curricular content moves beyond linguistic and logical mathematical areas to incorporate other facets such as the visual arts and interpersonal relationships. By using this approach, students from diverse backgrounds can draw on their strengths for further educational development.

Increased emphasis has been placed on assessments of students at various grade levels (typically fourth, eighth, and tenth), via standardized assessments and performance assessments, as part of the move toward increased accountability in education. To ensure educational accountability, Congress enacted Title II of the Goals 2000: Educate America Act of 1994 (PL 103-227), National Educational Reform Leadership, Standards, and Assessment. This called for the development of statewide assessments for all students as a major element of Goals 2000 (Kleinert, Kearns, & Kennedy, 1997). Although these efforts toward increased accountability are laudable, Vanderwood, McGrew, and Ysseldyke (1998) reported that students with disabilities were often excluded from statewide and local testing and hence were not represented in national or state databases. Gronna, Jenkins, and Chin-Chance (1998) reported that approximately 35% of Hawaii's students with disabilities were excluded from large-scale norm-referenced assessments in 1995. Most of these assessments excluded students who were considered to have severe disabilities. In a study examining changes in assessment data collected for students with disabilities in 1991 and 1995, Elliot, Erickson, Thurlow, and Shriner (2000) reported increases in the number of states using achievement, school participation, and exit data in their state or local accountability measures.

To address the lack of focus on educational outcomes for students with disabilities, the IDEA Amendments of 1997 (PL 105-17) mandate that students with disabilities be included in district and statewide assessments. Also, IDEA mandates that IEPs describe accommodations needed for students to participate fully in assessment. Furthermore, IDEA stipulates that alternative assessments should have been in place by July 1, 2000, for those who are unable to participate in state and districtwide assessments. Typically, students with severe and multiple disabilities would be included in this latter group.

RECENT CHANGES IN EDUCATIONAL APPROACHES FOR STUDENTS WITH SEVERE DISABILITIES

There have been dramatic shifts in the recommended approaches for educating learners with severe disabilities. Until the late 1970s, a developmental curricular approach dominated instruction for these students. This approach was characterized by a belief that in each curricular area (e.g., cognitive, motor), a hierarchical sequence of skills existed, and that students needed to acquire prerequisite skills before moving on to higher-level skills. Assessments based on developmental checklists yielded developmental ages that were used to determine instructional activities, materials, and performance criteria.

In the late 1970s, a functional curricular model was proposed (Brown et al., 1979). This model stated that students with severe disabilities should be taught the skills they need to be as independent as possible in school, home, community, and work environments. Instead of teaching individual motor skills, socialization skills, communication skills, and so forth, at a designated time (often out of context) and according to a prescribed hierarchy, these skills would be embedded in skill routines that would be taught at naturally occurring times (e.g., communication skills could be addressed at recess, lunch, and in small-group instruction). This shift toward contextually based instruction appears to parallel the shift toward more holistic concepts that came to dominate general education practices.

In addition, the shift from a multidisciplinary service delivery model to a transdisciplinary model or an integrated therapy model (a variation of the transdisciplinary model) for students with severe disabilities parallels the shift in service delivery in general education. Within a transdisciplinary model, the child is viewed holistically by all team members, and family members play a key role on the team (Giangreco, 1996; Orelove & Sobsey, 1996). Each of the related services providers (e.g., occupational therapist, orientation and mobility specialist, physical therapist) assesses the student and makes recommendations that can be implemented by a number of people, one of whom choreographs the instructional program (typically the teacher). These recommendations involve skills to be taught in natural contexts, rather than in isolation. For example, a physical therapist might recommend that a kindergarten student learn to transfer from his wheelchair to a standing position, then use a wheeled walker to go 10 feet from the play center to the snack table with minimal assistance. The therapist would show the teaching staff how to have the student do this. Once they were trained, the therapist would provide ongoing consultation to monitor the student's progress, ensure that the training was being implemented correctly and targeted at other appropriate times (e.g., on the way to physical education [PE] or lunch), and answer any questions the staff might have. Assessment of performance would occur on an ongoing basis using the natural routines and contexts for instruction. In a study by Anderson, Hawkins, Hamilton, and Hampton (1999), three students with severe and multiple disabilities increased and maintained their target motor behavior as a result of transdisciplinary teaming and integrative therapy.

The shift from the specialist-reliant approach to an integrative-related services delivery as an exemplary model supports the practice of educating students with severe and multiple disabilities in general education classes (Giangreco, Edelman, MacFarland, & Luiselli, 1997). The specialist-reliant approach asserts that related services providers have specialized skills, knowledge, and training that others (e.g., parents, teachers) do not and therefore only these skilled professionals can provide the necessary service; integrating related services providers' expertise into students' overall progress so that all service providers could adequately support the student when needed does not require the student to be removed from typical classes and routines to receive therapeutic support from specialists. In particular, two approaches have been developed to enable students with severe and multiple disabilities to utilize typical home, school, and community environments: natural supports and only-as-special-as-necessary (Giangreco et al., 1997). Both of these approaches recognize the importance of enabling the student with severe and multiple disabilities to gain access to the general education environment in a way that is less stigmatizing and more reflective of "belonging" and "interdependence."

A major change in the education of students with severe disabilities resulted from the 1997 IDEA amendments. This legislation stresses the rights of students with disabilities to participate fully in the general curriculum. Furthermore, a general education teacher is to be a member of each student's IEP team. Given the national significance of the educational movement discussed previously and the IDEA amendment mandates, it is imperative that all students with disabilities be included in standards-based education reform (Boundy, 2000; Lipsky & Gartner, 1997).

Alternative assessments for students with severe disabilities, as part of accountability measures from IDEA '97 is a relatively new phenomenon in the education of students with severe disabilities. Kentucky has been a leader in terms of accountability for all students. Kleinert et al. (1997) described Kentucky's alternate portfolio assessment for students with moderate and severe cognitive disabilities. In their article, they provide portfolio content and standards for evaluating portfolios, along with reliability data. To examine whether their alternate portfolio system correlated with other best practice measures, on-site observations and interviews were conducted. A high correlation of .703 (p <.0001) existed between alternative portfolio scores and observation of best practices program characteristics. Subsequently, Turner, Baldwin, Kleinert, and Kearns (2000) examined the extent to which Kentucky's alternative assessment scores correlate with program quality and overall school effectiveness. They found a significant relationship between alternative portfolio scores and overall program quality, as measured by the Program Quality Indicator Checklist (Meyer, Eichinger, & Downing, 1992). An even more impressive finding was that the alternative portfolio scores were significantly related to the school's educational accountability index for all students.

ANALYSIS OF CURRICULAR CHANGES
FOR STUDENTS WITH AND WITHOUT DISABILITIES

Several parallels exist between the evolution of curricular program implementation for learners with severe disabilities and for students without disabilities. Both fields have embraced a more holistic approach to education that is child-centered, with teaching taking place in natural and social contexts. As a result, activities planned for students tend to be more meaningful. Other approaches to assessment, such as portfolio assessment, that stress more authentic evaluation, are being used in conjunction with standardized assessment.

Several of the instructional approaches that have formed the cornerstone of education for learners with severe disabilities rely on a behavior model (e.g., shaping using reinforcement of successive approximations). As stated previously, strict adherence to behaviorism can run counter to a holistic constructivist approach because behavioral interventions support the identification of and instruction in discrete learning steps. Many behavioral approaches also rely on the use of highly individual and direct instruction. Moreover, past educational practices for students with severe disabilities were developed for use in self-contained classes or segregated schools because these were the predominant environments for learners with severe disabilities in the 1970s and 1980s. With the move toward inclusive practices, people involved in special education are rethinking practices that would be suitable in general education environments.

Given that instruction in a general education environment should be a collaborative effort among general education and special education teachers, it is important to examine the beliefs, attitudes, and curricular frameworks adhered to by general education teachers because they are key decision makers in these settings. In a qualitative study involving five general education teachers, each of whom taught a student with severe multiple, physical, and intellectual disabilities, Udvari-Solner (1996) conducted participant observations and interviews to determine 1) the elements of classroom culture and teacher behavior that promote inclusion and 2) what influences a teacher's ability to teach a diverse group of students. She noted that three of the teachers identified constructivist, Vygotskian theory, and/or multiple intelligences theory as central to their teaching philosophy and practices:

The teachers who clearly espoused one or more of the learning theories expressed perceptions of their students as whole, intact and contributing class members. The disabilities appeared secondary to their view of the child as a learner. A student's inability to participate as a typical learner was not considered an inherent problem to the individual. Instead, teachers presumed the right tools or channel to advance the child's knowledge had not been uncovered and the appropriate methodology to do so must be pursued. The presence of this student appeared to promote the belief that all children can learn and the task to facilitate that process is a worthy one. (p. 110)

Giangreco, Dennis, Cloninger, Edelman, and Schattman reported that "teachers frequently favored the use of typical activities, materials, and approaches over special ones" (1993, p. 367). Downing, Eichinger, and Williams (1997) found that of 18 general and special educators interviewed, 11 (61%) felt that some form of adaptations were important to use with students having severe disabilities in inclusive environments. Half of the respondents mentioned the need for multimodal instruction, and seven felt that one-to-one instruction was important. Five of the teachers stated that the same teaching strategies work for all students.

Due to the relative novelty of inclusion for students with severe and multiple disabilities, a database of empirically validated "best practices" for these learners in general education classes is still emerging. A holistic constructivist-oriented approach may be optimal overall, but with some students or some learning outcomes (e.g., those involving more motor components, such as eating routines), a blend with a behavioral approach may be more appropriate.

PROMISING PRACTICES FOR STUDENTS WITH SEVERE DISABILITIES IN GENERAL EDUCATION ENVIRONMENTS

This section addresses educational approaches used in typical learning environments that, because they accommodate diversity among learners, appear to be promising for learners with severe and multiple disabilities. Because of the still-infrequent cases of inclusion for learners with severe and multiple disabilities in general education classes, few efficacy studies have been conducted to determine teaching strategies that are successful with these learners. Thus, the strategies cited here are offered as "promising practices" for two reasons. First, for some of these techniques (e.g., cooperative learning), data indicate that the technique was successful for learners with severe and multiple disabilities in general education classes and other contexts. Second, for other strategies (e.g., thematic teaching units), learning characteristics of students with severe and multiple disabilities suggest the need for such an approach.

Cooperative Learning

Johnson et al. (1993) described four components of cooperative learning: positive interdependence; individual accountability, interpersonal and small-group skill development and group processing, and face-to-face interactions. Given these characteristics, cooperative learning has value in enhancing both educational and social skills (Johnson et al., 1993; Slavin, 1996).

Positive interdependence refers to the cooperative goal structure built into each lesson. Students work together to attain a common goal (e.g., a group product). Often students share materials (e.g., jigsaw approach) to promote positive interdependence (Johnson et al., 1993).

Individual accountability means that every student must contribute to the final product or outcome, so students are typically assigned various roles within cooperative groups (e.g., praiser, checker, encourager, materials manager). Regarding interpersonal and small-group skill development, a social skill objective is taught and evaluated within each lesson. The same social skill objective may be pursued over a long time period. For example, in a kindergarten class, sharing might be the targeted social skill. Processing is done at the end of the lesson by asking the students how they performed relative to the social skill objective and then by offering constructive feedback to the students.

In addition to monitoring social skill acquisition, academic skill acquisition is monitored. The teacher's role is to observe and provide feedback to the students. Observation sheets can be used to aggregate feedback relative to academic or social skill performance.

Students in cooperative groups have numerous opportunities for face-to-face interactions. These communicative exchanges occur within the interdependent structure that is created. Teachers should ensure that cooperative groups are formed heterogeneously, with students mixed by culture, ethnicity, gender, and ability. Typically, groups stay intact for approximately 4–6 weeks so that the desired interaction skills can be acquired.

Empirical Database   Much of the literature on the use of cooperative learning with students with disabilities involves students with mild disabilities who were mainstreamed into general education classrooms after the passage of the Education for All Handicapped Children Act of 1975 (PL 94-142). Several studies found that cooperative learning promoted more helping among students with and without disabilities than did individualistic or competitive learning (Armstrong, Johnson, & Balow, 1981; Cooper, Johnson, Johnson, & Wilderson, 1980; Johnson & Johnson, 1982).

Other researchers examined the effects of goal structure on the social interactions among students without disabilities and students labeled as having moderate mental retardation and found that a cooperative approach was associated with more positive social interactions than an individualistic one (Johnson, Rynders, Johnson, Schmidt, & Haider, 1979; Rynders, Johnson, Johnson, & Schmidt, 1980).

Putnam, Rynders, Johnson, and Johnson (1989) studied the effects of cooperative skill instruction on the social interactions among students without disabilities and students with moderate and severe disabilities in a science class. They found that students with disabilities who had been explicitly instructed in cooperative behaviors had higher levels of eye contact and vocalizations with students without disabilities. In two other studies involving students with severe and multiple disabilities, the cooperative method was found to be more effective, at least initially, than a nonstructured (laissez-faire) condition (Cole, 1986; Cole, Meyer, Vandercook, & McQuarter, 1986). Eichinger (1990) compared social interactions among students with severe and multiple disabilities and fourth and fifth graders without disabilities as a function of goal-structured activities. Again, a cooperative as opposed to an individualistic approach was more beneficial in promoting social interactions among students with and without disabilities.

As described in Chapter 1, Hunt, Staub, Alwell, and Goetz (1994) documented the success of cooperative learning in terms of communication and motor skill acquisition for three students with severe and multiple disabilities who were being educated in three second-grade classes. Jones and Carlier (1995) noted that increased social initiations and responses occurred and decreased behavioral needs occurred among students with moderate cognitive abilities (IQ score = low 50s) in a team-taught classroom, when cooperative learning strategies were employed to teach academic content.

All of the teachers interviewed as part of a qualitative study on inclusive education indicated that they used cooperative learning as one strategy to promote social relationships among students with and without disabilities in elementary school classes (Salisbury, Gallucci, Palombaro, & Peck, 1995). Thus, although none of these studies compared the use of cooperative learning with other types of goal structures in general education classrooms, four studies (Hunt et al., 1994; Jones & Carlier, 1995; Putnam et al., 1989; Salisbury et al., 1995) demonstrated the efficacy of this practice for students with severe disabilities in general education classes. Along with the evidence supporting cooperative learning with students with severe disabilities in other instructional contexts, this suggests that cooperative learning would be an effective instructional practice.

Why Cooperative Learning Is Appropriate   Cooperative learning allows students to be actively involved in their own learning. For children with severe and multiple impairments including a sensory loss, this approach can provide the stimulation needed to maintain interest and attention to the task. In addition, the hands-on involvement of students in the learning process is particularly beneficial to students who require more information than that embodied in a traditional lecture format. Students with impaired sensory input learn more effectively if given the opportunity to explore, touch, interact, and perform. The assignment of a specific role within the cooperative group ensures that each student is an active participant, although perhaps assistance is required.

The interpersonal objectives built into every cooperatively structured lesson are highly recommended for students with severe and multiple disabilities, who often need to develop more adaptive social skills. Students are thus provided numerous opportunities to work on basic social skills (e.g., taking turns, sharing materials) as well as more sophisticated social skills (e.g., initiating conversations).

How Cooperative Learning Can Be Used   Putnam (1998) provided a detailed exploration of cooperative learning practices in inclusive environments. As a general suggestion, when planning cooperative learning lessons, teachers should attend to cultural and language issues. For example, if a child has limited English proficiency, that child should be in a group with a student who speaks the child's native language as well as English and can act as a mediator for the child. Harry et al. (1995) provided an excellent discussion of cultural and language issues pertaining to the inclusion of learners with severe disabilities in general education classes. Individual case examples of cooperative learning are included next.

Michaela, age 6, loves to be with people, is interested in books, and has good auditory discrimination skills. She also has severe spastic quadriplegia, a moderate vision impairment, and a mild hearing loss and is nonverbal. She is a member of a half-day kindergarten class. After reading various books on different animals and visiting the local petting zoo, her class breaks into groups of five. Each group is instructed to work together to create a wall mural for the hall outside the classroom. One large sheet of paper and one set of markers are given to the group. Because all of the kindergarten students are working on the floor, Michaela is positioned prone (on her stomach) over a small wedge at the edge of the paper. Physical assistance is provided to her as needed to help her draw or to pass supplies to a peer. The social skill of sharing is targeted for instruction. Michaela performs the role of praiser by hitting a switch to activate a tape recorder with prerecorded messages on it (e.g., "That looks really pretty. You are all working really hard. Good for us!"). Michaela's objectives enable her to be working on Standard 5 of the Rhode Island Language Arts framework: All students will be effective communicators in varied settings and for varied purposes. Her communication mode is the use of an augmentative system.

Antwan, age 8, is in third grade, eager to learn, and quite strong willed. He is blind and just learning to use some speech. His science class is working on a unit on the solar system. As part of this unit, students work in groups for different activities. Each group is assigned a planet and is instructed to write a one- to two-page report on the planet as well as to make a papier-mâché replica of the planet. Antwan performs the role of materials manager. He makes sure that all of the resource texts and other materials are taken out at the beginning of the work session and are put away afterward. After listening to a videotape on the solar system, Antwan contributes information for the written report by responding to yes/no questions asked to him by his peers. He also works with his group members on the papier-mâche planet.

Juan, age 10, is a member of a fifth-grade class that uses whole language instruction as the basis for reading instruction. Juan has strong preferences, likes to tease, and is curious. He has a hearing impairment, developmental delays, and a physical impairment. It is decided that Juan's class will write a short play for the rest of the school and their parents. The teacher assigns students to work in cooperative learning groups. Each group is responsible for one aspect of the production, including making invitations; making scenery; making costumes; planning a menu and making food for parents the day of the play; and taking roles as actors and actresses in the play. Juan works with three peers to make the invitations. He works with Kyle on typing on the computer, printing out, and then delivering invitations to 10 classes in the building, using a bag attached to his wheeled walker. The group works on the social skill of listening to other people's ideas and providing feedback to come to consensus on the design of the invitations. Juan gives feedback by shaking his head yes or no when asked if he likes specific aspects of the design.

Paula, age 14, is in eighth grade. She is very sociable, loves to laugh, and has several friends. Paula has a severe hearing impairment, substantial cognitive delay, and some emotional challenges. She is taking a class in home economics that meets twice a week. During cooking activities, her teacher assigns students to groups of five. Each group is responsible for making enough food for the group, including preparation and clean-up. A pictorial recipe is used. Paula is assigned the role of checking to see that everyone completes their job; in addition, she will set the table.

Carmen, age 17, attends PE class with her high school classmates. Carmen has strong opinions on most topics, wants to be included in everything, and is sensitive to others' feelings. She also has a mild hearing impairment, is very myopic (nearsighted), has severe physical impairments, and uses facial expressions, objects, and some pictures for her expressive communication. Instead of a competitive game, the PE teacher organizes groups of six students. One activity involves rotating the basketball among the six students to see how many baskets they can make from a designated spot within 5 minutes. Then, they play again to try to beat their combined scores. They are working on providing encouragement and support. All students are encouraged to provide praise (e.g., group cheers). Carmen uses her prone stander and throws the ball to a teammate of her choice, who then takes a shot at the basket. Using a switch to activate a voice output communication aid (VOCA), she also cheers on her team.

Thematic Teaching Units

Thematic teaching units expand on a previously used teaching strategy called unit teaching, in which a series of lessons is centered around a particular theme in one content area (e.g., science). Thematic teaching also centers around a specified theme (e.g., "the world of work"), but lessons are taught in a number of different content areas that relate to the theme. Language and reading activities related to the theme transcend the various content area lessons.

Empirical or Theoretical Base   Thematic teaching relates to a body of knowledge called brain-based learning that contends that the disciplines relate to each other and share common information that can be recognized and organized by the brain (Caine & Caine, 1991).

On the basis of brain research conducted by numerous individuals, Kovalik and Olsen (1992) enumerated eight components that they believe are directly connected to improved performance for children and adults: absence of threat (trust), meaningful content, choices, adequate time, enriched environment, collaboration, immediate feedback, and mastery. The "integrated thematic instruction model" was developed to represent what is known about brain research, curriculum development, and teaching strategies in which curriculum and instruction correspond to the way children naturally learn.

Other writers have examined how thematic instruction can be used. Jacobs, Hannah, Manfredonia, Percivalle, and Gilbert (1989) and Jacobs (1991) have provided excellent discussions of interdisciplinary curricula and include examples of interdisciplinary units for a kindergarten through sixth-grade class and for a high school class. Additional information on thematic units is available (Forte & Schurr, 1994; Foster, Konar, Williamson, & Brumbaugh, 1991; Perkins, 1989).

Why Thematic Teaching Units Are Appropriate   Thematic teaching units allow greater continuity in programming around a particular topic. Thus, natural connections can intentionally be ensured for all students. This is extremely important for students with severe disabilities because they have difficulty generalizing to other environments or people (Coon, Vogelsberg, & Williams, 1981; Horner, Bellamy, & Colvin, 1984).

Also, lessons taught within thematic teaching units tend to be very project based (Wolk, 1994). As a result, students are actively engaged in the learning process. Art activities (e.g., dioramas), reading/language arts activities (e.g., writing and acting out a play), and social studies activities (e.g., simulating a city government within a classroom) all promote student participation.

How Thematic Teaching Can Be Used   A high school thematic teaching unit could focus on the theme of "social responsibility." The teaching team decides that the students will be given a framework in which to work, but that students will decide the particular social issue they wish to pursue in various classes. The germination of the unit begins in government class, in which students generate a list of social problems that exist in our world. Using a brainstorming approach, they generate possible solutions to four current problems in society (crime, drugs, social injustice, homelessness). As a class, they decide they would like to focus on homelessness.

At this point, the team meets to plan how this topic can be developed across the curriculum. In English class, students read and discuss the excerpt in the *Utne Reader,* "A Day in the Homeless Life," by Collette Russell (1990). Students then decide which of two activities they wish to pursue. The first option is to research the extent of the problem in their own and surrounding communities and provide a brief written and oral report on the topic. This would be followed by writing letters to local and state officials highlighting the problem and the need to remedy it. The second option is to research the organization Habitat for Humanity and prepare a written and oral report on the work of this organization worldwide. Students are encouraged to work in small groups (two to four students) on the selected activity. This aspect of the unit addresses Standard 8 within the Rhode Island Language Arts framework: All students will develop and apply their language skills using the community as a learning laboratory.

In PE, students have designed a fundraising program called "Hoops for Homes." Students ask for pledges for the number of hoops they make over a 1-month period. One week of class time is devoted to this mini basketball unit. Students also are given the opportunity to make hoops after school when the gym is not in use. All of the money is donated to Habitat for Humanity.

In art class, students are asked to choose a medium to create an artistic representation of homelessness. Some students use pencil line drawings, although others use chalk, paint, or three-dimensional paper representations. One student, with his parents' assistance, obtains participants' permission and does a photographic essay on homelessness.

In government class, students conduct a 2-week food and clothing drive. This involves generating notices of the drive on the computer and distributing them to other classes. The collected food and clothing are then sorted and taken to a local shelter.

Jose is a friendly teenager who enjoys sports and most recreational activities. Jose, who has Down syndrome, a mild to moderate hearing loss, and a moderate vision loss, participates in the homeless project in English class by listening to the story read to him by a partner. He works in a group of three to research homelessness in his community and compose two letters to various officials. He offers one idea for how the problem can be addressed. After the letter has been handwritten by other students, he types it using a computer. Once the letter is completed and addressed, he puts it into the envelope, seals it, puts a stamp in the proper corner, and gets it to the outgoing mailbox in the school's main office. While Jose will be working on his IEP objectives that align with Language Arts Standard 8, the expectations and performance standards may be different from those of his peers due to his disabilities.

In PE class, Jose participates in the Hoops for Homes program and collects his pledges. He assists with collecting and counting the pledge money each day (first sorting it into easily recognizable denominations). In art, he cuts pictures out of magazines to depict what homelessness means to him. In government class, he works with five other students to sort the food and clothing and deliver it to a homeless shelter.

A Balanced Approach to Literacy

Literacy instruction has traditionally been perceived as a hierarchy of reading skills that include presumed prerequisite skills of auditory and visual discrimination as well as several others. Using direct instruction, these skills were to be taught in a prescribed order and in a repetitive, isolated manner (Teale & Sulzby, 1986). Successful accomplishments of each successive skill in the sequence lead to increased literacy achievement.

Given a broader and more comprehensive perspective, literacy can be considered the use of reading, writing, listening and speaking in an individual's life. Furthermore, components of literacy can be taught interactively by making use of meaningful opportunities for each individual (Koppenhaver, Pierce, Steelman & Yoder, 1995; McLane & McNamee, 1990). In this view, literacy is not limited to one area of instruction but is a pervasive factor in all areas of the curriculum. The teacher acts as a facilitator of learning in this student-centered approach, drawing on the student's experiential background and understanding, and thus building on the student's strengths as opposed to impairments.

Oral language is used as the basis for acquiring written expression. Teachers create a print-rich environment (e.g., label things in the classroom, have numerous books and magazines available for students to read by themselves or with a partner, and have various written material on walls and blackboards). They provide stimulating language experiences, encourage students to pursue their unique literacy interests, and offer specific instruction on elements designed to improve literacy development. Reading to students is recommended at all age levels, and books on tape are readily available in the classroom and library. For young children, predictable books are used to stimulate a child's receptive and expressive language capabilities.

Instruction of specific literacy skills such as decoding strategies takes place both within isolated and meaningful contexts. For example, young children might write letters to classmates or pen pals using invented spelling, and later receive instruction in conventional spelling. Older students might carry on a dialog with teachers or peers via written communication in journals, receiving feedback from the teacher to make their written expression more effective. There is a strong emphasis on developing comprehension of meaningful text in conjunction with decoding skills.

Empirical or Theoretical Base In order to develop literacy skills, children need to be read to on a frequent and regular basis, see others reading, have access to reading and writing materials, and be encouraged to respond to specific questions regarding literacy activities (Anderson & Stokes, 1984; Cochran-Smith, 1984; Snow, 1983; Teale & Sulzby, 1986; Van Kleeck, 1990). While being immersed in a rich literate environment, children creatively engage in their own unique or authentic reading and writing activities (Atwell, 1998; Calkins, 1994). A balanced approach to literacy instruction encompasses the diverse aspects of literacy (e.g., listening, speaking, reading, and writing.) By defining literacy more broadly to include communication skills, literacy applies to all children, not just those who can decode the printed word (Rossi, 2000).

Why a Comprehensive Literacy Approach Is Appropriate All students have the right to attain as high a literacy level as possible, and literacy for all students is targeted as a goal in Goals 2000: Educate America Act of 1994 (PL 103-

227). Literacy skills enhance one's ability to communicate effectively, gain information, and be entertained. As such, teaching literacy skills to students with severe disabilities is very relevant, and a comprehensive approach to teaching literacy skills makes considerable sense given the unique needs and different learning styles of these students. Furthermore, even when students with moderate or severe disabilities receive literacy instruction well after the elementary school years, meaningful literacy instruction can be very beneficial (Ryndak, Morrison, & Sommerstein, 1999).

Children with disabilities, especially those with severe and multiple disabilities have been shown to have fewer opportunities to engage in literacy activities (Marvin, 1994; Marvin & Mirenda, 1993). Children with visual impairments in addition to other disabilities may not be able to access a print environment or even respond to pictorial information. Students with limited communication skills that make it difficult to ask questions or respond to questions regarding literacy activities may not be very reinforcing for parents or other adults who read to them (Marvin, 1994). Parents may spend an inordinate amount of time in caregiving activities, thus limiting the time available for reading and writing activities (Katims, 2000; Marvin, 1994). In addition, parents of children with severe and multiple disabilities appear to have lower expectations for their children regarding literacy skill attainment (Marvin, 1994). As a result, students with severe and multiple disabilities may be further hindered in their ability to acquire basic literacy skills.

Students with severe and multiple disabilities can be included in literacy activities when the emphasis is placed on the broader view of literacy and not limited strictly to readiness skills. In fact, Koppenhaver, Coleman, Kalman, and Yoder (1991) felt that teachers have a moral obligation to enhance the literacy of all people. Because this more balanced or comprehensive approach is based on a constructivist view that learning is somewhat unique for each learner, it affords the student with severe and multiple disabilities numerous opportunities to develop a wide range of literacy skills (e.g., listening to a peer read a story, writing by sequencing pictures, reading picture books).

How Literacy Instruction Can Be Applied A comprehensive approach to literacy instruction allows for the individualization of instruction that is the foundation of special education. The student with severe and multiple disabilities may require considerable individualization in their instruction to gain from literacy experiences. It is up to the teacher to provide the necessary support to connect the student to literacy activities (Kliewer & Landis, 1999). For example, in a fifth- and sixth-grade combination class, students read the story, *Sarah, Plain and Tall* (MacLachlan, 1985). After the students read the story, the teacher encourages them to generate information about the story, which she places on a web or map on the board. The information is used by students to report on the story. In addition, students make dioramas depicting various aspects of Sarah's life and the period during which she lived.

One student in this class, Kathy, age 11, is curious and good with her hands. She is totally blind, has moderate hearing loss, and uses a hearing aid. She listens to the story *Sarah, Plain and Tall* read by a partner. She is learning to raise her hand and provide information about the setting when the class is constructing the web. With the assistance of a paraeducator, she dictates a few sentences about the story. She works with two other students to construct a diorama of Sarah's home.

During recess, she plays with one girlfriend, using a slightly adapted version of hopscotch, a game that was also popular during Sarah's life.

During more direct reading instruction, some time is spent working alone or in small groups, with the teacher circulating around the classroom to offer assistance as needed. During this time frame, students with severe and multiple disabilities might be working with a peer tutor or paraeducator on related reading activities. For example, Jenna, age 9, might be sequencing and then reviewing her line-drawn picture schedule for the day with her friend, Tatiana. Simple books with appropriate tactual information (e.g., actual materials) can be made by students, purchased at local book stores, or obtained from the American Printing House for the Blind for students with no vision.

Meaningful writing activities could be taught during this time using a variety of different modes (see Chapter 5). Using pictures, students could "write" lists of gifts desired for a birthday, Hanukkah, or Christmas or lists of friends and their birthdays. For older students, writing activities could range from developing a pictorial grocery list, to making a telephone tree of friends, to filling out a job application. Modifications to the classroom environment also can be made to accommodate learners with sensory impairments. For example, when labeling things in the classroom, the teacher can label them with a word in braille or print, a sign representation, and a line-drawing representation.

Multiple Intelligences

The theory of multiple intelligences purports that intelligence is not a single construct that can be quantified as an isolated unit of measure. Gardner's 1983 analysis questioned the validity of attempting to measure intelligence by removing a person from his or her environment to test performance on isolated tasks that have no relevance to everyday life. He contended that intelligence goes beyond what is typically measured by such tests (linguistic and logical problem-solving skills). Gardner reconceptualized intelligence as the ability to solve a problem or to create a product that would be considered useful in at least one cultural setting (Goldman & Gardner, 1989).

Gardner describes eight categories of intelligences: logical-mathematical, linguistic, musical, bodily kinesthetic, spatial, interpersonal, intrapersonal, and naturalist (Armstrong, 2000). Logical-mathematical intelligence is the ability to use numbers or logical reasoning well. Linguistic intelligence refers to the ability to use words effectively, either verbally or in writing. Musical intelligence is manifested in the ability to hear themes, to think in musical terms, to understand how themes are transformed, and to be able to follow the themes in a musical piece (Goldman & Gardner, 1989). Bodily kinesthetic intelligence refers to the ability to successfully manipulate one's body to express feelings or ideas or to use one's hands to create or transform something. Spatial intelligence is characterized by the capacity to view the world in a spatial framework and to transform elements spatially. Interpersonal intelligence refers to the capacity to understand others, including perceiving the moods and cues of others. Intrapersonal intelligence is the ability to self-reflect and understand oneself and to use this knowledge to guide one's behavior. Naturalist intelligence refers to the ability to recognize and classify species (flora and fauna) present in a person's environment.

Empirical or Theoretical Base   In recent years, some schools have implemented practices that support the multiple intelligences theory of learning. Project Spectrum, for example, is designed to assess students' capabilities in all of the intelligences (Krechevsky, 1991). Others have described programmatic efforts to use the multiple intelligences throughout the curriculum (Hoerr, 1992; Olson, 1988). Ellison (1992) described how students and parents are involved in setting goals for the coming school year. This individualized approach has helped parents appreciate the gifts their children bring to a learning situation.

An additional informative resource is Armstrong's (2000) book on the theory and practical application of the multiple intelligences theory, including a chapter on the application of this theory to students with special needs. Hanson (1997) also discusses how multiple intelligences theory builds children's strengths instead of focusing on deficit areas.

Why Multiple Intelligences Is Appropriate   By its nature, the theory of multiple intelligences is vital to the field of special education. It encourages educators to move away from a deficit-oriented, remediation model of service delivery to a student-centered, resource-oriented, and compensatory model of service delivery. The gifts and strengths of students who have been labeled as having severe and multiple disabilities often have been overlooked in favor of an overall IQ or mental age score. The assessment process used to obtain this score removes the student from any familiar or practical environment and depends on strong communication skills. Such an evaluation process places this student at a distinct disadvantage and fails to identify strengths the student possesses (e.g., the ability to hide hearing aids within seconds despite constant observation).

Armstrong (2000) enumerated differences between a deficit paradigm and a growth paradigm. A focus on deficits only serves to exclude individuals from many valued activities, further limiting their life experiences and opportunities for growth. A focus on abilities and ways to compensate for limitations (e.g., synthesized or digital speech to allow access to computer programs) highlights the unique gifts and talents that all students possess and allows individuals to learn together.

How Multiple Intelligences Can Be Used   Students with severe and multiple disabilities, and especially those with sensory impairments, need teachers who can recognize their strengths in different areas and use these to enhance learning. The multiple intelligences theory can be used when developing an IEP for a student with severe disabilities, including sensory losses, by drawing on the strengths of the child. For example, Mary, age 15, has profound hearing loss and moderate vision loss. Her teacher develops activities in which Mary is encouraged to use her residual vision to obtain information (e.g., pictorial schedule, photographs of activities). She is sociable, and the teacher encourages her to further develop those skills via extracurricular activities. Last year, she served as a student council representative.

In terms of classroom practices, the theory of multiple intelligences places much less emphasis on passive learning (e.g., lecture) and more emphasis on alternative ways of learning, including movement, manipulation of objects, music, and social interactions. Students are encouraged to develop their strengths and interests, with the teacher following their lead and taking advantage of incidental learning opportunities as they emerge. Teachers are less "directors of learning" or givers of knowledge and more facilitators of learning. For example, Brise is 12 years old and deafblind (although she does have functional vision and hearing). She has a strong interest in life and death issues (e.g., she is fascinated by dead leaves, trees, plants, and animals). When allowed to pursue this interest, she goes to the library and looks through books and magazines for relevant pictures. She expresses her interest to both peers and adults using a few signs (DEAD, NOT GROW, BLACK) and she uses gestures to gain another's attention to share her interest. When "forced" to spend significant time investigating other topics, Brise can become aggressive toward others and destructive of property. Knowing Brise's strengths and interests helps her teachers plan accordingly so that different skills such as comprehending information, expressing oneself, and comparing similarities and differences can be taught using the subject matter of Brise's choice. Topics that Brise has limited interest in are introduced to her, but the time spent on these topics fluctuates according to her needs. She is always provided with choices of topics so that she can maintain the highest possible interest in the learning process.

SUMMARY

This chapter has highlighted the changes that have occurred in general and special education since the mid-1980s. A brief analysis of the parallels that exist between these changes was provided so that the similarities of these two systems can be seen. Based on these changes, promising educational practices for students with severe and multiple disabilities in general education environments were described. Although this chapter contains a few specific examples of the techniques and strategies presented here, numerous other examples are found in the succeeding chapters.

As special and general education become less disparate systems and, instead, collaborate to address the needs of all school-age children, the perceived need to isolate individual students based on limitations will become less common. Creating one unified educational system can foster the professional development of teachers and administrators alike through access to combined skills and knowledge. An enriched learning environment is then available for all students.

REFERENCES

Anderson, A., & Stokes, S. (1984). Social and institutional influences on the development and practice of literacy. In H. Goelman, A. Oberg, & F. Smith (Eds.), *Awakening to literacy* (pp. 24–37). Westport, CT: Heinemann.

Anderson, N.B., Hawkins, J., Hamilton, R., & Hampton, J.D. (1999). Effects of transdisciplinary teaming for students with motor disabilities. *Education and Training in Mental Retardation and Developmental Disabilities, 34,* 330–341.

Armstrong, B., Johnson, D.W., & Balow, B. (1981). Effects of cooperative versus individualistic learning experiences on interpersonal attraction between learning disabled and normal progress elementary school students. *Contemporary Educational Psychology, 6,* 102–109.

Armstrong, T. (2000). *Multiple intelligences in the classroom* (2nd ed.). Alexandria, VA: Association for Supervision and Curriculum Development.

Atwell, N. (1998). *In the middle: New understanding about writing, reading, and learning* (2nd ed.). Westport, CT: Heinemann.

Boundy, K. (2000). Including students with disabilities in standards-bound education reform. *TASH Newsletter, 20*(4), 4–5, 21.

Brooks, J.G., & Brooks, M.G. (1993). *In search of understanding: The case for constructivist classrooms*. Alexandria, VA: Association for Supervision and Curriculum Development.

Brown, L., Branston, M., Hamre-Nietupski, S., Pumpian, I., Certo, N., & Gruenewald, L. (1979). A strategy for developing chronological age appropriate and functional curricular content for severely handicapped adolescents and young adults. *Journal of Special Education, 13*(1), 81–90.

Caine, R.N., & Caine, G. (1991). *Making connections: Teaching and the human brain*. Alexandria, VA: Association for Supervision and Curriculum Development.

Calkins, L. (1994). *The art of teaching writing*. Westport, CT: Heinemann.

Cochran-Smith, M. (1984). *The making of a reader*. Stamford, CT: Ablex.

Cole, D.A. (1986). Facilitating play in children's peer relationships: Are we having fun yet? *American Educational Research Journal, 23*, 201–215.

Cole, D.A., Meyer, L.H., Vandercook, T., & McQuarter, R.J. (1986). Interactions between peers with and without severe handicaps: The dynamics of teacher intervention. *American Journal of Mental Deficiency, 91*, 160–169.

Coon, M.E., Vogelsberg, R.T., & Williams, W. (1981). Effects of classroom public transportation instruction on generalization to the natural environment. *Journal of The Association for Persons with Severe Handicaps, 6*, 46–53.

Cooper, L., Johnson, D.W., Johnson, R., & Wilderson, F. (1980). Effects of cooperative, competitive, and individualistic experiences on interpersonal attraction among heterogeneous peers. *Journal of Social Psychology, 111*, 243–252.

Downing, J., Eichinger, J., & Williams, L. (1997). Inclusive education for students with severe disabilities: Comparative views of principals and educators at different levels of implementation. *Remedial and Special Education, 18*, 133–142, 165.

Education for All Handicapped Children Act of 1975, PL 94-142, 20 U.S.C. §§ 1400 *et seq.*

Eichinger, J. (1990). Goal structure effects on social interaction: Nondisabled and disabled elementary students. *Exceptional Children, 56*, 408–416.

Elliot, J.L., Erickson, R.N., Thurlow, M.L., & Shriner, J.G. (2000). State-level accountability for the performance of students with disabilities: Five years of change? *Journal of Special Education, 34*, 39–47.

Ellison, L. (1992). Using multiple intelligences to set goals. *Educational Leadership, 50*(2), 69–72.

Forte, I., & Schurr, S. (1994). *Interdisciplinary units and projects for thematic instruction for middle grade success*. Nashville, TN: Incentive Publications.

Foster, A., Konar, S., Williamson, S., & Brumbaugh, A. (1991). Connect your curriculum. *Instructor, 101*(2), 24–32.

Gardner, H. (1983). *Frames of mind: The theory of multiple intelligences*. New York: Basic Books.

Giangreco, M.F. (1996). *Vermont interdependent services team approach (VISTA): A guide to coordinating educational support services*. Baltimore: Paul H. Brookes Publishing Co.

Giangreco, M., Dennis, R., Cloninger, C., Edelman, S., & Schattman, R. (1993). I've counted Jon: Transformational experiences of teachers educating students with disabilities. *Exceptional Children, 59*, 359–372.

Giangreco, M.F., Edelman, S.W., MacFarland, S.Z., & Luiselli, T.E. (1997). Attitudes about educational and related service provision for students with deaf-blindness and multiple disabilities. *Exceptional Children, 63*, 329–342.

Goals 2000: Educate America Act of 1994, PL 103-227, 20 U.S.C. §§ 5801 *et seq.*

Goldman, J., & Gardner, H. (1989). Multiple paths to educational effectiveness. In D.K. Lipsky & A. Gartner (Eds.), *Beyond separate education: Quality education for all* (pp. 121–139). Baltimore: Paul H. Brookes Publishing Co.

Gronna, S.S., Jenkins, A.A., & Chin-Chance, S.A. (1998). Who are we assessing? Determining state-wide participation rates for students with disabilities. *Exceptional Children, 64*, 407–418.

Hanson, R. (Executive Producer). (1997). *Multiple intelligences: Discovering the giftedness in all* [Videotape]. (Available from National Professional Resources, 25 South Regent Street, Port Chester, NY, 10573; 800-453-7461)

Harry, B., Grenot-Scheyer, M., Smith-Lewis, M., Park, H., Xin, F., & Schwartz, I. (1995). Developing culturally inclusive services for individuals with severe disabilities. *Journal of The Association for Persons with Severe Handicaps, 20*(2), 99–109.

Hoerr, T.R. (1992). How our school applied multiple intelligences theory. *Educational Leadership, 50,* 67–68.

Horner, R.H., Bellamy, G.T., & Colvin, G.T. (1984). Responding in the presence of non-trained stimuli: Implications of generalization error patterns. *Journal of The Association for Persons with Severe Handicaps, 9,* 287–295.

Hunt, P., Staub, D., Alwell, M., & Goetz, L. (1994). Achievement by all students within the context of cooperative learning groups. *Journal of The Association for Persons with Severe Handicaps, 19,* 290–301.

Individuals with Disabilities Education Act Amendments of 1997, PL 105-17, 20 U.S.C. §§ 1400 *et seq.*

Jackson, L., Reid, D.K., & Bunsen, T. (1993). Reader response, alternative dreams: A response to Felix Billingsley. *Journal of The Association for Persons with Severe Handicaps, 18*(4), 292–295.

Jacobs, H.H. (1991). The integrated curriculum. *Instructor, 101*(2), 22–23.

Jacobs, H.H., Hannah, J., Manfredonia, W., Percivalle, J., & Gilbert, J.C. (1989). Descriptions of two existing interdisciplinary programs. In H. Jacobs (Ed.), *Interdisciplinary curriculum: Design and implementation* (pp. 39–51). Alexandria, VA: Association for Curriculum and Development.

Johnson, D.W., & Johnson, R. (1982). Effects of cooperative and individualistic instruction of handicapped and nonhandicapped students. *Journal of Social Psychology, 118,* 257–268.

Johnson, D., & Johnson, R. (1987). *Learning together and alone: Cooperation, competition, and individualization.* Upper Saddle River, NJ: Prentice-Hall.

Johnson, D.W., Johnson, R.T., & Holubec, E.J. (1993). *Circles of learning: Cooperation in the classroom* (4th ed.). Edina, MI: Interactive Book Company.

Johnson, R., Rynders, J., Johnson, D.W., Schmidt, B., & Haider, S. (1979). Producing positive interactions between handicapped and nonhandicapped teenagers through cooperative goal structuring: Implications for mainstreaming. *American Educational Research Journal, 16,* 161–167.

Jones, M.M., & Carlier, L.L. (1995). Creating inclusionary opportunities for learners with multiple disabilities: A team-teaching approach. *Teaching Exceptional Children, 27,* 23–27.

Katims, D.S. (2000). *The quest for literacy: Curriculum and instructional procedures for teaching reading and writing to students with mental retardation and developmental disabilities.* Reston, VA: Council for Exceptional Children, Division on Mental Retardation and Developmental Disabilities.

Kleinert, H.L., Kearns, J.F., & Kennedy, S. (1997). Accountability for all students: Kentucky's alternate portfolio assessment for students with moderate and severe cognitive disabilities. *Journal of The Association for Persons with Severe Handicaps, 22,* 88–101.

Kliewer, C., & Landis, D. (1999). Individualizing literacy instruction for young children with moderate to severe disabilities. *Exceptional Children, 66,* 85–100.

Koppenhaver, D.A., Coleman, P.P., Kalman, S.L., & Yoder, D.E. (1991). The implications of emergent literacy research for children with developmental disabilities. *American Journal of Speech/Language Pathology, 1,* 38–44.

Koppenhaver, D.A., Pierce, P.L., Steelman, J.D., & Yoder, D.E. (1995). Contexts of early literacy intervention for children with developmental disabilities. In S.F. Warren & J. Reichle (Series Eds.) & M. Fey, J. Windsor, & S. Warren (Vol. Eds.), *Communication and Language Intervention Series: Vol. 5. Language intervention: Preschool through the elementary years* (pp. 241–274). Baltimore: Paul H. Brookes Publishing Co.

Kovalik, S., & Olsen, K.D. (1992). *Integrated thematic instruction: The model.* Village of Oak Creek, AZ: Susan Kovalik and Associates.

Krechevsky, M. (1991). Project Spectrum: An innovative assessment alternative. *Educational Leadership, 48,* 43–48.

Lipsky, D.K., & Gartner, A. (1997). *Inclusion and school reform: Transforming America's classrooms.* Baltimore: Paul H. Brookes Publishing Co.

MacLachlan, P. (1985). *Sarah, plain and tall.* New York: Harper & Row.

Marvin, C. (1994). Home literacy experiences of children with single and multiple disabilities. *Topics in Early Childhood Special Education, 14,* 436–454.

Marvin, C., & Mirenda, P. (1993). Home literacy experiences of preschoolers enrolled in Head Start and special education programs. *Journal of Early Intervention, 17,* 351–367.

McLane, J.B., & McNamee, G.D. (1990). *Early literacy.* Cambridge, MA: Harvard University Press.

Meyer, L., Eichinger, J., & Downing, J. (1992). *The program quality indicators (PQI) checklist: A checklist of most promising practices in educational programs for students with severe disabilities.* Syracuse, NY: Division of Special Education and Rehabilitation.

National Center on Education and the Economy and the University of Pittsburgh. (1997). *Performance Standards: Vol. 2. Middle school.* Author.

Olson, L. (1988). Children flourish here: Eight teachers and a theory changed a school world. *Education Week, 7*(1), 18–19.

Orelove, F.P., & Sobsey, D. (1996). *Educating children with multiple disabilities: A transdisciplinary approach* (3rd ed.). Baltimore: Paul H. Brookes Publishing Co.

Perkins, D.N. (1989). Selecting fertile themes for integrated learning. In H.H. Jacobs (Ed.), *Interdisciplinary curriculum: Design and implementation* (pp. 67–76). Alexandria, VA: Association for Supervision and Curriculum Development.

Poplin, M., & Stone, S. (1992). Paradigm shifts in instructional strategies: From reductionism to holistic/constructivism. In W. Stainback & S. Stainback (Eds.), *Controversial issues confronting special education: Divergent perspectives* (2nd ed., pp. 153–179). Needham Heights, MA: Allyn & Bacon.

Pressley, M., Rankin, J., & Yokoi, L. (1996). A survey of instructional practices of outstanding primary-level literacy teachers. *Elementary School Journal, 96,* 363–384.

Putnam, J. (Ed.). (1998). *Cooperative learning and strategies for inclusion: Celebrating diversity in the classroom* (2nd ed.). Baltimore: Paul H. Brookes Publishing Co.

Putnam, J.W., Rynders, J.E., Johnson, R.T., & Johnson, D.W. (1989). Collaborative skill instruction for promoting positive interactions between mentally handicapped and nonhandicapped children. *Exceptional Children, 55,* 550–557.

Reid, K., Kurkijian, C., & Carruthers, S. (1994). Special education teachers interpret constructivist teaching. *Remedial and Special Education, 15,* 267–280.

Rossi, P.J. (2000). Many ways in the way: Supporting the languages and literacies of culturally, linguistically, and developmentally diverse children. In T. Fletcher & C. Bos (Eds.), *Helping individuals with disabilities and their families: Mexican and U.S. perspectives* (pp. 171–187). Tempe: AZ: Bilingual Review Press.

Russell, C.H. (1990, September/October). A day in the homeless life. *Utne Reader, 41,* 52–53.

Ryndak, D.L., Morrison, A.P., & Sommerstein, L. (1999). Literacy before and after inclusion in general education settings: A case study. *Journal of The Association for Persons with Severe Handicaps, 24,* 5–22.

Rynders, J.E., Johnson, R., Johnson, D.W., & Schmidt, B. (1980). Producing positive interaction among Down syndrome and nonhandicapped teenagers through cooperative goal structuring. *American Journal of Mental Deficiency, 85,* 268–283.

Salisbury, C.L., Gallucci, C., Palombaro, M.M., & Peck, C.A. (1995). Strategies that promote social relations among elementary students with and without severe disabilities in inclusive schools. *Exceptional Children, 62*(2), 125–137.

Slavin, R. (1996). *Education for all: Contexts of learning.* Lesse, France: Swets & Keitlinger Publishers.

Snow, C. (1983). Literacy and language: Relationships during the preschool years. *Harvard Educational Review, 53,* 165–189.

Teale, W.H., & Sulzby, E. (1986). Emergent literacy as a perspective for examining how young children become writers and readers. In W.H. Teale & E. Sulzby (Eds.), *Emergent literacy: Writing and reading* (pp. vii–xxv). Stamford, CT: Ablex.

Teele, S. (1999). *Rainbows of intelligence: Explaining how students learn.* Redlands, CA: Sue Teele Associates.

Turner, M.D., Baldwin, L., Kleinert, H., & Kearns, J.F. (2000). The relation of a statewide alternate assessment for students with severe disabilities to other measures of instructional effectiveness. *Journal of Special Education, 34,* 69–76.

Udall, A. (Narrator). (1997). *Big questions, big ideas: Themes that matter. Workshops with master teachers* [Videotape]. (Available from Zephyr Press, Post Office Box 66006, Tucson, AZ 85728-6006)

Udvari-Solner, A. (1996). Theoretical influences on the establishment of inclusive practice. *Cambridge Journal of Education, 26,* 101–119.

United States Department of Education, by the National Commission on Excellence in Education. (1983). *A nation at risk: The imperative for education reform: A report to the nation and the Secretary of Education.* Washington, DC: Government Printing Office.

Van Kleeck, A. (1990). Emergent literacy: Learning about print before learning to read. *Topics in Language Disorders, 10*(2), 25–45.

Vanderwood, M., McGrew, K.S., & Ysseldyke, J.E. (1998). Why we can't say much about students with disabilities during education reform. *Exceptional Children, 64,* 359–370.

Vygotsky, L.S. (1978). *Mind in society.* Cambridge, MA: Harvard University Press.

Wolk, S. (1994). Project-based learning: Pursuits with a purpose. *Educational Leadership, 52*(3), 42–45.

Chapter 3

First Steps

Determining Individual Abilities
and How Best to Support Students

June E. Downing and MaryAnn Demchak

This chapter examines key educational concerns of inclusive environments from preschool through high school. For inclusion to be a successful experience for the student with severe and multiple impairments, careful attention must be paid to determining individual student strengths and needs, the type of support concerned, the most appropriate people to provide the support, and the most appropriate manner to provide it. These topics are addressed as the first steps in an ongoing process for including students with severe and multiple impairments in typical educational classrooms.

DETERMINING STUDENTS' STRENGTHS AND NEEDS

Too often, assessment procedures in the educational system target student deficits, especially when the student has severe and multiple impairments. The focus tends to accentuate what the student cannot do, rather than what he or she can do. The emphasis is thus on remediating skill deficits without much regard for whether the skills are valued by the individual, family, friends, or community. In addition, many assessment procedures require the student to demonstrate skills out of the typical context in which they are used and at the whim of the assessor. If the student fails an item (i.e., the skill is not demonstrated), little if any consideration is given to the reason for the failure. It is not clear whether the student is actually unable to perform the desired skill, lacks sufficient motivation at the time, or has no reason to perform the skill when requested. As a result, assessments that use developmental scales and anticipated behavior normed on typical child development tend to provide a very negative picture of a student who has severe and multiple impairments. What is more, the typical approach to assessment does not include any reference to the actual demands of the natural environment or to the preferences of the individual. Therefore, the assessment results provide very limited information regarding what the student actually needs to learn and wants to learn. Consequently, considerable time can be devoted to determining a student's developmental profile that may have little to do with helping him or her learn what needs to be learned (Fewell, 2000; McConnell, 2000).

An additional consequence of deficit-oriented assessment that portrays the individual in a negative light is the low expectations for success that others accept and may use as an excuse not to teach (Peter, 2000). In a study of an adult with intellectual impairments and blindness who was institutionalized for most of his life, Peter (2000) clearly articulated the danger of detrimental labels on this individual's life. The focus on this man's low IQ scores as determined by standardized IQ tests prevented service providers from seeing what he could learn, thus further handicapping his development. Students with severe and multiple disabilities, not to mention their teachers and parents, find this practice frustrating and unrewarding.

Functional-Ecological Approach

An alternative assessment process—functional-ecological assessment that is both observational and activity based—is recommended because it does not expect the student with multiple impairments to perform tasks out of context. Rather, such an assessment takes into account the student's motivation and need to perform a given task (Downing, 1996), thus enabling a more accurate picture of a student's interests and abilities, as well as areas requiring intervention (Campbell, Campbell, & Brady, 1998; Downing & Perino, 1992; McConnell, 2000). This type of assessment leads directly to intervention strategies that occur in natural contexts at natural times of the day and also helps the student acquire the skills needed to be as successful as possible within meaningful activities.

Who Is This Student?   The first step in this assessment process is to identify what the individual can do, enjoys doing, and needs to do as determined by individual and family preferences and environmental demands. This information can be obtained formally by using a number of individual and parent interview formats (see Giangreco, Cloninger, & Iverson, 1998). Alternatively, the information can be collected informally by talking with the student and/or those closest to him or her about present and future aspirations and by observing the student in typical environments. This person-centered approach has been referred to by a number of different terms including Group Action Planning (GAP), Essential Lifestyles Planning (ELP), Personal Futures Planning (PFP), and Making Action Plans (MAPS) (Menchetti & Sweeney, 1995). All of these approaches involve obtaining a positive description of the individual versus labels or IQ scores, a vision for the future, and an action plan so as to reach the desired vision.

The MAPS process, described by Falvey, Forest, Pearpoint, and Rosenberg (1997), is often used with school-age children. The purpose of MAPS is to assemble significant people in the student's life who can identify strengths and needs, which will be used to implement a program in a general education environment. Individuals who are typically involved include the student, the student's parents, sibling(s), other relatives, classmates, friends, teachers, support personnel, and anyone who knows the student and wants to contribute to this process. Two individuals facilitate the process, one serving as a host and the other serving as a recorder. Having same-age friends present is extremely important so that the plan is socially valid. This is particularly true for students unable to clearly express their opinions during this process. Falvey et al. and Vandercook,

York, and Forest (1989) discussed the seven questions that typically are asked of each participant. Modifying the questions asked is advised depending on who is present. For example, Question 3 originally asked about the nightmares others might have concerning the student's future. However, it might be more appropriate (especially for young children) to change the word *nightmares* to *concerns.* Questions 4 and 5 can be combined as a time-saving measure. The following questions are asked during the MAPS process. (For additional information see www.inclusion.com.)

1. What is the individual's history?
2. What is your dream for this individual?
3. What are your concerns for this individual?
4. Who is the individual?
5. What are the individual's strengths, gifts, and abilities?
6. What are the individual's needs?
7. What would the individual's ideal day at school look like, and what must be done to make it happen?

The MAPS process culminates in a graphically represented plan of action, which is then implemented collaboratively by the involved parties. Responses to these questions determine what environments and activities need to be assessed to determine how best to reach the goals or dreams identified in Question 2. In this way, information gathered on the student leads directly to an intervention that should lead to desired outcomes.

Regardless of how the information is gathered, it is important to remember that this type of assessment is dynamic and ongoing; the information will need to be checked, rechecked, and revised as individual abilities, needs, and desires change. Although this information can be reviewed any time the individual or other team member believes it would be helpful, it should be reviewed at least once a year.

The information obtained from this interaction with the student, family members, and significant others helps to determine activities that the student likes to do (e.g., play in water) as well as activities that need to be performed (e.g., get dressed in the morning). It also identifies the environments in which these activities will most likely be performed (e.g., operating a computer in the computer lab). The importance of empowering the family and student to play a major role in this assessment process is well supported by the special education field (Giangreco et al., 1998; Turnbull & Turnbull, 1997). The family as a primary source of information to determine a student's strengths, needs, and future aspirations is critical to meaningful assessment and intervention (Schwartz, 1995). Family input helps to determine skills and activities that are important to the student. These activities then become critical areas of immediate intervention if the requisite skills are lacking. Also, general skill areas will emerge as either strengths or needs (e.g., Jill enjoys being with people but needs a different way to express herself). These general skill areas (e.g., communication, social skills) are required in many activities across different environments. The functional-ecological assessment approach allows these types of skills to be assessed and subsequently targeted for intervention in the actual settings and activities where needed, rather than assessing the skills in isolation, as they frequently are in a developmental approach.

What Does the Student Need to Learn?   The second major step in this assessment process is to delineate the typical skills required by the activity. Delineating steps in the activity to be assessed puts a focus on what is typically expected of students without disabilities. If students with severe disabilities are to be
successful participants in typical activities with others who do not have disabilities, it is imperative for them to know the expectations within these activities.
Once these skills are documented (by watching a same-age individual perform
the activity), the individual student's performance is evaluated to determine skills
that are already in the student's repertoire and those that are lacking. Figure 3.1
provides an example of this procedure for Jason, an eighth grader who has myopia, a hearing impairment, moderate mental retardation, and a short attention
span. See Downing (1996) for a detailed description of the entire process and accompanying forms. By recording possible reasons why a skill is lacking during the
performance (e.g., student cannot hear the teacher direct the class to line up at
the door), considerable information can be obtained to aid in the development of
the IEP and the overall intervention process. The more activities that are assessed
across different settings and situations, the more accurate and thorough is the understanding of the student's abilities and needs.

Careful documentation of how the student responds under natural conditions in age-appropriate settings (e.g., general education classrooms) provides
valuable information on ways the student receives information and acts on it.
Part of the functional-ecological assessment process involves determining the natural cues that exist to prompt or guide behavior for all students. Some of these
cues are obvious and clearly related to the desired behavior (e.g., the teacher says
to put materials away and line up for recess). Other cues are harder to determine,
yet have a definite impact on resulting behavior (e.g., feeling the need to use the
restroom serves as a catalyst to raise one's hand and request permission to leave
the classroom). Identifying the typical or expected behaviors of various activities
and the natural cues that exist to prompt the behaviors helps to pinpoint where
a student with severe and multiple disabilities may have difficulty responding as
desired.

For example, a student who has very limited vision and a severe hearing impairment will not receive the verbal cues from the teacher to prepare for the next
activity. This student may also miss the visual cues of classmates putting away
their work and getting out needed material for the next activity. The student cannot be expected to follow cues not received. Because there may be no way to facilitate this student's reception of the natural cues in the classroom to perform,
adaptations that enhance the student's independence and facilitate ongoing
placement with his classmates need to be made. The adaptations do not need to
be complex and may be as simple as having a classmate tactually and visually cue
this student to check his tactile schedule of activities in order to understand the
need to make the transition. The steps involved in a functional-ecological assessment are outlined in Table 3.1.

It is important to obtain as much information as possible regarding how a
student performs during various activities and responds to the natural cues that
exist for all students in order to help clarify the most effective way that the student learns. Analyzing several activities and documenting the student's performance in these activities will help to determine areas in which adaptations in materials and instruction will be necessary. Information from this assessment can

Student:	_Jason_			
Activity:	_Science class—eighth grade_			

Peer inventory	Cues	Student performance	Discrepancy	Intervention strategies and/or adaptations
1. Enter science class	Time to go to science class; sees door	+		
2. Find seat and sit down	Knowledge of seating assignments; sees seat	−	Not motivated; can't hear well, doesn't understand	Peer cues him to sit down, uses body to guide
3. Listen to teacher for 15 minutes	Teacher giving instruction, information	−	Not motivated; can't hear well, doesn't understand	Jason does adapted work of organizing materials for the assignment; he receives praise for attending to task.
4. Get out materials	Teacher directions; not having what is needed	−	Has difficult time staying on task; doesn't understand	Paraeducator directs attention to peers; praises any effort; starts to take out materials to cue Jason.
5. Perform assignment within allotted time (come up with list of rules that differentiate one species from another)	Assignment/ knowledge of teacher expectations	−	Has difficult time staying on task; doesn't understand	Teacher uses colorful pictures of different species and pairs with a peer. Jason sorts pictures into _same_ and _different_ piles. Peer models task and provides corrective feedback. Paraeducator uses timer and praises for 5 minutes of on-task behavior. Jason takes a short break then returns to task. Peer writes rules for him.
6. Put away materials	Teacher directions/ time	−	Doesn't hear teacher or understand; dislikes change	Paraeducator directs attention to his peers; shows him pictorial schedule of next class; praises any effort; starts to put away items as a cue to him.
7. Get ready to go to next class	End of science class	−	Doesn't like next class	Teacher pairs him up with other students going to class. Paraeducator allows a water fountain break before class.

Figure 3.1.   Skill documentation sheet for Jason, a student with myopia, a hearing impairment, mental retardation, and a short attention span. (Key: + = independent; P = required prompts; − = did not perform skill.)

Table 3.1.   Completing a functional-ecological assessment

Step 1:	Gather information regarding activities the student can do, enjoys doing, and needs to do. Determine priority activities and environments for intervention.
Step 2:	Watch a same-age peer to identify the typical skills required for the activity and the cues that exist naturally to cue desired behavior.
Step 3:	Observe the student to determine the skills that he or she can already do and those that he or she cannot.
Step 4:	Record possible reasons the student cannot perform a particular skill (discrepancy analysis).
Step 5:	Develop the IEP using the above information.
Step 6:	Implement instruction using natural cues, appropriate adaptations, and effective teaching strategies.

contribute significantly to the development of the IEP and to the manner in which IEP goals and objectives or benchmarks are met. In addition, cumulative information from this assessment procedure becomes part of a portfolio on the student, providing future teachers and other team members with an important tool to support the student's continued progress.

DEVELOPING THE IEP

The IEP should be developed by a team composed of family members as well as the various professionals and paraprofessionals who work with the student. Professionals from numerous disciplines could potentially be on the team: teacher(s), vision specialist, hearing specialist, audiologist, occupational and physical therapists, orientation and mobility specialist, communication specialist, adapted physical educator, and others. Paraeducators involved in the classroom are also crucial team members who will frequently be involved in implementing instruction or overseeing various activities. Therefore, they should be active, contributing members.

As mentioned previously, it is imperative that family members be active participants on the educational team. It is inappropriate to simply present the family with a completed IEP for approval. Rather, family members can 1) provide information during the assessment process, 2) identify priorities, 3) help develop goals and objectives, 4) provide input regarding how and where instruction will occur, and 5) assist with carryover to the home. However, it is essential to remember that degree of family involvement will vary from family to family. Families should be provided with choices regarding the type and amount of involvement that they wish to have in the IEP process.

IEP goals and objectives/benchmarks are derived from the results of the assessment process (i.e., those skills needed to complete an activity that are apparently lacking for a specific student). IEP objectives will not target all missing skills but only those considered most critical for more independent performance in the most meaningful activities and that have a high probability of being attained. Billingsley, Gallucci, Peck, Schwartz, and Staub (1996) recommended using an outcome framework that targets participation in valued roles, settings, and activities. A few high-quality objectives that target a number of critical skills within valued and frequently engaged-in activities are recommended over numerous objectives that target skills in isolation from any recognizable purpose. For example, an objective such as "Sally will make better use of her vision" would be replaced by what Sally needs to do with her vision to perform more efficiently (e.g., "During computer lab, Sally will follow the cursor and make appropriate choices from the software program in 18 of 20 opportunities"). IEP objectives do not target isolated skills written by individual specialists on the team (e.g., vision specialists, speech-language pathologists [SLPs], occupational therapists). Instead, these team members, along with family members, pool their expertise to create one IEP that includes objectives that are activity-based and reflect the numerous skills required by the activity.

Team members also rely on their experience and knowledge of the student to determine the criterion that will be used to measure IEP goals and objectives or benchmarks. There are no right or wrong criteria; the purpose of having criteria is to ensure objectivity in measuring student progress. Therefore, criteria set by the team should be high enough to challenge the student and clearly indicate attainment of desired behavior, yet not so high that the student will not be able to demonstrate success. When benchmarks, instead of short-term objectives, are used, the skill(s) to be addressed will remain the same, while the criterion used will change to show progress toward goal attainment. For instance, for the goal of a student learning to recognize 10 new words, the following benchmarks might be used.

- In 3 months, Terza will recognize five words in her schedule for 5 of 10 trials per word.
- In 6 months, Terza will recognize eight words in her schedule for 7 of 10 trials per word.
- In 9 months, Terza will recognize 10 words in her schedule for 9 of 10 trials per word.

There are no strict guidelines for establishing criteria. The team must decide what will represent mastery for each student. Depending on student progress, criteria measures may need to be lessened or made more difficult.

Once IEP goals and objectives/benchmarks have been drafted from assessment information, they should be sent in draft format to parents or guardians to review. In this way, family members can examine their child's proposed educational plan in the comfort of their home without time constraints and the potential pressure of professionals in attendance. Of course, the drafted IEP should be in the parents' native language so they can review it easily, make changes as needed, and ask questions. The school team can then adjust the IEP accordingly and set an IEP meeting. This way the actual meeting does not bring any surprises. Table 3.2 provides samples of IEP goals and objectives for students with severe and multiple impairments. Several objectives could be written per goal.

DETERMINING THE MOST
APPROPRIATE GENERAL EDUCATION CLASSES

Once individual strengths and needs have been identified and documented in the IEP, the next step is to implement the program. Because IEP goals and objectives usually target typical skills required to perform similarly to others of the same age, much of the functional-ecological assessment process naturally takes place within typical classrooms and other settings frequented by same-age students. In-

Table 3.2.   Examples of IEP goals and objectives for individual students with severe and multiple disabilities

Goal	Objective
Jeff will develop at least one friend as determined by self-report.	When approached by a peer, Jeff will not react by hitting but will take the arm offered him for sighted guidance and walk cooperatively with classmate from the playground back to class once a day for 3 weeks.
Karen will independently go to all of her classes for at least a 1-week period.	Following each class period, when asked by a peer using sign WHERE NOW?, Karen will look at the picture schedule, point to the next activity, then proceed without stopping until she reaches the correct destination for each scheduled period for 5 consecutive days.
Robin will respond to peers in an appropriate manner at least 10 times a day for 2 weeks.	During third-grade music class, Robin will look at a peer when the peer says her name, extend her hand, and grasp the instrument or book given to her by her peer in 9 of 10 consecutive opportunities.
Casey will demonstrate decision-making skills 80% of all opportunities for a 2-week period.	During lunch, Casey will look at each food item before indicating her choice to a peer by reaching for one item in 9 of 10 opportunities.
Jenny will respond appropriately to peers 90% of the time for a 3-week period.	While shooting baskets with classmates (at recess or PE), Jenny will look toward a peer who calls her name, extend her arms to try to catch the ball, and throw the ball at the basket or to another classmate in 10 consecutive attempts.
Robert will respond appropriately to peers 90% of the time for a 3-week period.	At the beginning of each new class period, when a peer or teacher greets Robert by name, Robert will turn toward the person in 9 of 10 opportunities.
Frank will acquire mathematics skills needed to successfully make at least four purchases.	During seventh-grade pre-algebra class, Frank will successfully complete 8 of 10 word problems involving purchases (determining sufficient funds to purchase items) for 5 consecutive mathematics classes.
Susan will use signs to express herself at least 12 times a day for 2 weeks.	During creative writing period, Susan will spontaneously produce a two-word signed phrase describing a picture or photograph for 10 consecutive pictures that comprise her journal.

formation obtained from such assessment has a direct relationship to the classroom situation. There is no need to interpret developmental scores to determine what they mean in terms of the daily curriculum in the classroom. (Other portions of this assessment will occur at home and in the community, but for the purposes of this book, the focus remains on classroom and school settings.)

In the course of the assessment process, it may emerge that the structure and dynamics of the classroom and the needs of the student appear to be at odds with one another. For instance, a classroom may be very noisy and unstructured, which tends to create problems for the student who responds better to quiet and structure. Physical considerations also may arise. A small classroom with limited access may be difficult for a student who uses a wheelchair or has medical equipment needs. Students who have limited or no vision may perform more efficiently under conditions in which they can maneuver easily without fear of tripping or being hurt and in which they can count on materials being in a specific place. Identifying the advantages and disadvantages of various classroom environments represents a critical component of the ecological process. Factors to consider include teaching style, organization, room layout, accessibility, noise level, lighting, acoustics, and other similar variables.

In many schools, options for students allow a match between student strengths and needs and the characteristics of the classroom. There may be two or three classrooms and teachers at a specific grade level, one of which may represent a better match than the others. At the middle and high school levels, the variety of class options for students eases the difficulty of finding the best match between student needs and learning environments; however, even when no options exist (e.g., one fifth-grade class), certain modifications can be made to facilitate learning. For instance, the student may need to be seated close to the classroom teacher, have access to better lighting, and use an FM system to gain more auditory information. The team works together to creatively enhance the learning environment to meet the unique needs of a given student. Accommodations should not be overly extensive or interfere with the learning of the other students. In fact, accommodations often can enhance everyone's learning ability. For example, better lighting and contrast may make it easier for all students to view information on a chalkboard.

The important factor to remember when analyzing a typical classroom for a particular student is to avoid focusing mostly on deterrents (e.g., teacher doesn't like other adults in the room, is strict, likes quiet, has high expectations). Rather, the emphasis should be on what the teacher is doing that could be supportive (e.g., teacher encourages students to problem-solve, has computers in the room and uses them frequently, has interactive materials and activities, has high expectations). Concentrating on potentially negative aspects will only produce barriers and will thwart inclusive education. Focusing on strengths and skills allows for the development of building blocks for a firm inclusive foundation.

WORKING ON IEP OBJECTIVES IN TYPICAL CLASSROOMS

The IEP does not address all activities performed in a typical classroom on a daily basis; however, many skills targeted in IEP objectives are likely required throughout the day in a range of ongoing activities. The team needs to identify the various opportunities to practice targeted IEP skills across different functional activities. An activity/IEP objective analysis form developed by Fox and Williams (1991) is recommended for this purpose. An adaptation of this form for a student with severe and multiple disabilities is provided in Figure 3.2. Obviously, inclusion is not something that is done after IEP objectives have been worked on in another setting. Rather, full-time participation in typical activities and classrooms with classmates who do not have disabilities provides the necessary environment in which to meet these objectives. The importance of this full-time participation is particularly clear when the outcomes desired for students include belonging to a social group and working collaboratively with peers (Schnorr, 1990, 1997).

Activity/IEP Objective Matrix

Student: _Jennifer_

Grade: _Fifth_

School year: _2000–2001_

Teachers: _Mrs. Hill (fifth grade), Ms. Lott (support)_

Activities/subjects IEP objectives	Social studies	Math	Reading	Physical education	Lunch
To recognize pictures for expressive communication purposes	Use daily schedule to get out book Match pictures related to social studies	Determine story problem for peers by matching same pictures	Answer questions by pointing to pictures Sequence three pictures in order to retell story	Choose equipment using photographs Choose partner using school photographs	Use pictures to request type of milk from cafeteria person Point to pictures to converse with peers
To follow directions quickly	Watch peers get out materials and follow their lead Sequence pictorial cards in order Put away materials and get ready for next subject	Watch peers get out materials and follow their lead Work on math skills as instructed Change activity when directed	Watch peers get out materials and follow their lead Find appropriate page in book Answer questions by pointing Put away materials and get ready for next subject	Line up for PE Move to area on floor by PE teacher Follow teacher and group	Line up for lunch with class Go to lunch room Stay at table until dismissed
To interact with peers in a positive way	Sit with classmate Do not destroy peer's work Pass out materials	Sit with classmate Do not destroy peer's work Pass out materials Respond to three offers of help	Sit with classmate Choose book to read from peer Respond to peer's questions	Respond to peers when they initiate Share equipment Clap for peers when they do well	Respond to peers when they initiate Initiate topics using schedule and magazine Respond to peer's questions

To make decisions	Decide who will read to her Request help when needed Pick appropriate pictures from three pictures based on question	Decide which math activities to do Decide which manipulatives to use: first, second, third.	Choose book to read Choose peer to read with Choose place to read	Decide which two of three exercises to do and in what order	Choose milk Choose person to sit next to Choose where to go when finished eating and with whom
To increase physical strength and endurance	Sit at desk with good posture for 10 minutes Squeeze glue to get picture on paper	Sit at desk with good posture for 10 minutes	Sit at desk with good posture for 10 minutes Hold book upright for peer to read	Add one more exercise at warmup Exercise each week Hold door open for class	Open milk carton Carry own tray to table
To work independently	Stay on task without adult nearby for 10 minutes Raise hand to get help	Stay on task without adult nearby for 10 minutes Raise hand to get help	Stay on task without adult nearby for 10 minutes Raise hand to get help	Stay on task without adult nearby for 10 minutes Start each exercise/activity on own Raise hand to get help	Stay on task without adult nearby for 10 minutes Obtain milk with peer support Eat meal with no prompts

Figure 3.2. Activity/IEP objective matrix for Jennifer, a fifth-grade student.

   This analysis of opportunities for learning (i.e., examining typical classroom activities) according to targeted IEP objectives or benchmarks for a given student can occur across the age range from preschool through high school. Horn, Lieber, Li, Sandall, and Schwartz (2000) found that early childhood educators were successful at identifying and embedding learning opportunities into inclusive preschool classrooms for young children with disabilities. The teachers believed that the procedure fit into their natural routine and made it easier for them to focus on the individual student's needs. Once opportunities to target needed skills have been identified by the team, each activity will need to be carefully analyzed to determine the most effective way for learning to occur for a given student. The team will need to determine the most appropriate physical position for the student, the most effective way for the student to participate, and the most efficient means of providing needed support. Table 3.3 lists specific questions that need to be addressed by the team to ensure the successful inclusion of students with severe and multiple disabilities.

DETERMINING INDIVIDUAL LEARNING STYLES

Although the students targeted in this book have at least one sensory limitation in addition to other multiple disabilities, each has a distinct and unique way of learning. Some children, for instance, acquire considerable information via the auditory mode even though they have a moderate hearing loss, whereas others will not find auditory information helpful, and in fact, it may even prove confusing. Some students make considerable use of visual information, despite the fact that they have a severe visual impairment, whereas others will not be able to process any visual information because both eyes have been enucleated (surgically removed). For some students, encouraging tactile exploration of information will be very informative, whereas others, especially those with a physical impairment such as cerebral palsy that affects all limbs, may not find this information beneficial. Many students with multiple disabilities may need to actively engage in an activity in order to understand it. These students learn by doing, especially if the distance senses of vision and hearing do not provide the needed information. Still other students, owing to their severe physical impairments, may not be able to fully engage in an activity and will need other ways to learn.

   There is no formula to determine the modes that best help a given student to learn. Some students do better with a certain learning mode in one situation and need a different strategy for another situation. Often, the type of activity has a direct bearing on how best to teach a student. For example, learning to bring food to one's mouth to eat may be best taught by having the student do it; however, to learn how to get the teacher's attention, watching other students raise their hands may be the most powerful way to teach this behavior. Providing students with multiple ways of obtaining the necessary information (whether visual, auditory, kinesthetic, or tactile) and drawing their attention to the most important aspects of the lesson may be the most effective strategies. This approach not only has merit for students who are having difficulty obtaining information via one mode (usually the visual mode) but also could obviously benefit many students without disabilities. The focus of the intervention should be on ensuring that the student understands what is expected (through a variety of sources) and then as-

Table 3.3. Questions for the educational team to ask to accommodate inclusive learning

What is the best position for the student?
Where are the other students? On the floor? At desks? Standing at tables?
What allows the student the greatest movement needed for the activity? The best vision? The best hearing?
Is the student physically isolated or right with the others?

Is the student able to obtain information from the teacher?
What is the learning style of the student?
Does the student learn in an auditory, visual, tactile, and/or kinesthetic way? Is the necessary information available in the activity?
Can additional information be added to an activity to make it more understandable to a given student?

How can the student participate?
Can the student raise his or her hand to gain attention? Is another way possible (e.g., switch-activated voice output mode)?
Can the student respond verbally to questions? If not, can he or she be given choices of objects and/or pictures as responses?
Can the student engage in movement related to the activity (e.g., act out a skit, pass items, get out and put away materials)?
How does participation in each activity support the student's IEP objectives?

Who can assist in the learning process?
Can other students help? Teachers? Support staff? Volunteers? Older students?

sisting the student to use whatever information is available to learn the steps of the activity.

When students remove their hearing aids or take off their glasses, it may signal to teachers that the information obtained via these modes may not be helpful or that it may be overwhelming (e.g., the student who has just begun wearing glasses to correct a severe visual impairment and who must learn to use vision). Alternative approaches to teaching can then be considered. The question to ask is whether the child needs to see or hear to perform as expected or whether the child can bypass these sensory modes and still learn. In other instances, the child may gradually learn to use the information obtained through hearing or vision. The emphasis is on helping the child to be most successful, not on conforming to a specified style of learning.

DIRECT INSTRUCTION

It is essential that all students—with and without disabilities—receive some direct instruction and are taught in systematic ways. Instructors of typical students teach reading, writing, spelling, and mathematics systematically by breaking down targeted activities into steps and teaching in a sequential fashion. Similarly, a student with severe and multiple disabilities must be taught in an organized fashion. Some students with severe impairments may not be learning the academics targeted for their peers. Other students with severe and multiple impairments will be learning academics but may be taught in a different manner from that used with their typical peers owing to different learning styles. That is, more specialized instruction may be needed for particular skills or activities (Odom, 2000). General education teachers, however, can embed these specialized instructional procedures in classroom activities (Wolery, Anthony, Snyder, Werts, & Katzenmeyer, 1997). Regardless of the activities and targeted skills, all students need to be taught in a planned manner.

For example, students without disabilities are frequently taught using procedures that have the same theoretical basis as those used with students with disabilities. A student may be taught to spell the word *receive* through a process of gradually providing greater degrees of assistance. First, the student may simply be told to "remember the rule." If the student is still unable to spell the word, an additional prompt may be given to "remember *i* before *e*." If the student is still having difficulty, the final prompt may be given: "Remember the rule is *i* before *e* except after *c*." The student is systematically given greater assistance until the task is performed correctly. Similarly, students are provided with corrective feedback when errors are made, as well as with reinforcement for correct or improved responses.

Students with severe and multiple disabilities are also taught through prompts, corrective feedback, and reinforcement; however, their prompts may be a bit different from those used with students without disabilities. Teaching procedures may be used to teach the student with severe impairments alternative skills from those targeted for other students. For example, a student learning to use a switch as a means of participating in an activity will initially need to be taught to activate the switch. The student might first be prompted to activate the switch by having someone tap the switch to draw the student's attention to it. If the student does not respond, a teacher or peer might tap the student's hand. If another prompt is needed, someone might provide minimal physical assistance to aid the student in turning on the switch. The prompts provide increasing degrees of assistance until the student is able to complete the targeted skill (similar to providing increasing assistance to spell *receive*). Simply including a student with severe and multiple disabilities in a typical classroom does not mean that instruction of that student no longer needs to occur. If an activity is important enough to target in the IEP as an objective, it is important enough to teach systematically. Effective instruction of students with severe disabilities can and does occur in general education settings (McDonnell, 1998).

The effectiveness of systematically instructing students with severe and multiple impairments is well documented (Silberman, Sacks, & Wolfe, 1998; Snell, 1997). All students learn skills, and subsequently maintain those skills, through an instructional paradigm that includes 1) procedures (e.g., response prompts) designed to make it more likely that a targeted behavior will occur (i.e., the student initially learns a behavior or attempts to more fluently perform the behavior) and 2) procedures that follow correct and incorrect responses (e.g., reinforcement and corrective feedback, respectively). These procedures are briefly described here. Resources that examine the procedures in greater detail are listed in Appendix A, at the end of this book.

Prompting Behaviors to Occur

All students can learn many skills through shaping procedures that are frequently used in conjunction with teaching prompts. Shaping initially involves accepting approximations of the targeted behavior that ultimately lead to the desired behavior. For example, with a young child who is learning to sign, the teacher may accept approximations of initial signs to teach the child that signing is valuable and meaningful. Eventually, the child will be expected to produce the signs accurately. Shaping procedures occur across classrooms, grade levels, and curricular activities. Teachers teach all students to read, write, complete art products, use computers, and do numerous other activities by shaping behavior. For example, teachers will frequently accept "invented spellings" that approximate correct spellings from beginning writers prior to expecting those students to spell accurately. Sometimes this shaping procedure occurs quickly for students, and at other times the process is quite lengthy, with students requiring many opportunities to practice the skill. Frequently, shaping procedures are used in tandem with teaching prompts that are designed to increase the likelihood that the target behavior will occur.

All teachers typically use a variety of teaching prompts: verbal instructions, modeling or demonstrations, gestures, pictorial or other visual cues, and various degrees of physical assistance. Regardless of the prompt used, it is essential to remember that the prompt should be systematically faded, or removed, so that the student is cued by the natural cues in the setting (e.g., the student is cued by occurrences in the classroom to activate a switch, rather than by someone providing physical guidance). Demchak (1990) described several prompting techniques that have been successfully employed with students having a wide range of disabilities: increasing assistance, decreasing assistance, graduated guidance, as well as progressive and constant time delay. Wolery, Ault, and Doyle (1992) provided concrete guidelines for using these and other procedures to teach various skills and activities. Table 3.4 briefly explains each prompting procedure.

In addition to following the guidelines provided by Demchak (1990, 1997) and Wolery et al. (1992) regarding how prompts can be systematically removed, it is important that the student have sufficient time to respond after being given any prompt. Providing a delay before giving another prompt avoids overmanipulation and allows the student time to determine what behavior is expected or needed so that he or she can initiate a response. Sufficient response time (i.e., several seconds) should always be provided to increase the likelihood that the student will respond to natural cues rather than contrived prompts.

Variations of prompting procedures may be necessary for students who have difficulty receiving visual and/or auditory information or difficulty engaging in physical movements. Deciding which teaching prompts and cues to use with the student with severe and multiple disabilities will depend on how the student best learns and the particular aspects of a given task (e.g., what skills are required). For example, learning to run a software program usually relies on vision, with the learner watching the teacher activate the machine, insert the disk, and push different keys. If the student does not have sufficient vision to learn the skills involved, then the teacher will have to adapt to a tactile mode with auditory cues. The student will feel for the disk-insert slot and may use small tactile markers (e.g., hardened glue dots on a sticky backing) to identify the important keys to push. Auditory cues (e.g., "first . . . , then . . .") may help the student acquire the appropriate sequence of steps. Obviously, chronological age–appropriate software programs that provide auditory information/feedback will be critical for this student.

Modeling the desired response is one of the most commonly used ways to teach a new skill. Modeling can be done verbally, as when teaching a foreign language; visually, as when teaching a matching task or tumbling skill; and both visually and auditorily, as when teaching reading. The natural tendency to rely on vision is obvious, with teachers often giving cues such as "eyes on me," "watch

Table 3.4. Procedures for prompting students with severe disabilities

Increasing assistance Consists of a hierarchy of prompts arranged in order from presumed least informative to most informative assistance for a given activity; also known as system of least prompts or least-to-most prompts

Decreasing assistance Begins with the most informative prompt needed for the individual to respond in a given activity and moves through a specified hierarchy to less-informative levels of assistance; also known as most-to-least prompts

Graduated guidance Degrees of physical assistance provided from most intrusive to least intrusive, with amount of assistance varying within a teaching instance as the student responds (i.e., teacher makes moment-to-moment decisions regarding amount of assistance) and if appropriate

Constant time delay Initial teaching opportunities provided at a 0-second delay, with all subsequent teaching trials provided at a predetermined delay interval (e.g., 5 seconds)

Progressive time delay Initial teaching opportunities provided at a 0-second delay, with the amount of time between the natural cue and the prompt gradually increased (e.g., increments of 2 seconds) to allow the student to respond

me," or "do it like this." A severe visual impairment can put a student at a serious disadvantage in a classroom that relies heavily on students imitating modeled behavior. In addition, if the child also has a severe auditory impairment that prevents him or her from hearing the cue to watch the model, then the child may completely miss general interactions as well as specific instructional information.

Many children with severe and multiple disabilities can use their vision for learning; however, they may need the demonstration or relevant stimulus to be brought closer and made clearer or brighter. They may also need to have their attention specifically directed to the stimulus, and they will require sufficient time to assimilate the available information. This student can still benefit from this teaching technique; however, students who do not have sufficient vision to benefit from this approach will need to receive information in another way. A tactile model may need to be provided, so that the information can be received through touch. For instance, in PE class, a student who is blind (or deafblind) and is being taught softball will need to use a batting tee as well as have time to explore the tee tactually (feel the tee and the ball on it). This student should then be allowed to stand behind a batter who demonstrates the swing needed to hit the ball. The student needs to feel the bat and that the ball is no longer on the tee. The student's hands can be placed over the batter's hands to gain an understanding of the movement involved. To teach a new skill, considerable tactile modeling may be necessary (done on the sidelines with help from peers who are not batting). Once the student understands the expectation, just feeling the batting tee, being given the bat, and being appropriately placed to best make contact probably will suffice. A runner can then offer to be a sighted guide for this student around the bases.

Although students with severe and multiple disabilities are often physically manipulated through activities, greater control over the learning process and less resistance may develop if at an early age the child can be encouraged to put his or her hands on the instructor's and obtain information that way. This technique of modeling allows the student more control over the situation and may be particularly beneficial for students who display tactile defensiveness. It also encourages taking initiative in the learning process and actively making use of the sense of touch to compensate for the loss in visual and auditory input. Biederman,

Fairhall, Raven, and Davey (1998) found that passive observation by children with developmental disabilities and minimal language was more effective than hand-over-hand and verbal prompting involving tasks such as doing puzzles, washing hands, and zipping coats.

Other examples of tactile modeling involve giving the student a model to examine before expecting the behavior. For instance, if students are given an assignment to write a book, the student without visual or auditory access will need to feel a book with tactile illustrations in it. He or she will need to examine the number of pages, binding, and cover before being expected to relate the materials he or she has been given to the expected final product.

A multimodal approach to prompting is generally recommended for all students, so that individual learning styles can be addressed within the same lesson (Sobsey & Wolf-Schein, 1996). Recognizing the natural cues for any given activity can help teachers determine the most appropriate prompts to use (i.e., those that attract the student's attention to the natural cues, if at all possible). The previously discussed modifications to teaching prompts also provide considerable information as to the teacher's expectations for performance.

Students with access to limited sensory information as well as difficulty processing that information and/or acting on it typically require numerous opportunities to learn most skills. Breaking down steps into small skills as needed by the individual student, and consistently applying specific prompting strategies across the teaching staff are recommended practices (Alberto & Troutman, 1999; Orelove & Sobsey, 1996). Figure 3.3 provides an example of a step in an activity that has been broken down into smaller skills to better identify student strengths and needs and to document progress in learning the step (the analyzed step is taken from the eighth-grade science activity featured in Figure 3.1). In Figure 3.3, Step 5 (performing the assignment within the allotted time) is analyzed specifically for Jason, the eighth grader who has myopia (nearsightedness), a hearing impairment, moderate mental retardation, and a short attention span.

For each skill required to do this step, specific teaching prompts are provided and space is available to collect data on the student's performance. Clearly identifying the desired skills of this step in the activity as well as specific strategies to shape the behavior help all instructional staff be more consistent in their teaching approach. The overall goal in teaching new behavior is to have the student recognize when the behavior is needed or expected across natural environments, and to attempt the new behavior at that time. Once demonstrated (even if only partially), the behavior can be guided into a closer approximation and then reinforced so that it will be strengthened over time.

These prompting techniques are not only beneficial for students with disabilities but hold merit for students without disabilities, as well. Perhaps the most critical factor to remember about any instructional technique with any student is that it be provided in a manner that is positive, respectful to the learner, consistent across teachers and activities, and efficient.

Responding to Correct Behaviors: Reinforcement

The purpose of reinforcement is to strengthen desired or targeted behaviors by presenting a consequence contingent on the occurrence of the behavior. Ultimately, the only way that teachers know whether a particular reward is reinforc-

Student: _Jason_

Activity: _Science class—eighth grade_

Step 5 (of Figure 3.1): _Perform assignment within allotted time_

Wait time = _3 seconds between prompts_

Date: _9/10_

Task analysis for student	Trial 1	Trial 2	Trial 3	Trial 4	Trial 5	Strategy for teaching and/or adapting
Takes picture given to him	P	+				Wait; move picture across visual field to gain attention; hold in palm close to him; wait; praise any approximation.
Scans materials to find picture that is similar to the simple picture	–	–				Slowly model desired behavior at least three times; draw attention to pictures; wait; use flashlight to cue him to start scanning; wait; praise attention to pictures.
Correctly puts similar pictures of animals together	–	–				Reduce number of pictorial choices; keep choices different so right match is obvious; tap near correct match; guide hand; give immediate feedback.
Responds in an appropriate way to feedback (whether right or wrong); does not get angry and continues to work	P	P				Model correct match; physically guide him to make correct match; praise for staying on task, not just for doing it correctly; go to next item.
Works for at least 5 minutes without leaving task or becoming upset	P, 3 minutes	P, 3 minutes				Let him use timer—he sets; let him take break for 2 minutes if he requests one using the request card; praise for staying on task.

Figure 3.3.   Task analysis of an eighth-grade science activity for Jason, a student with myopia, a hearing impairment, mental retardation, and a short attention span. (Key: + = independent; P = required prompts; – = did not perform skill.)

ing is by its effect on behavior. If a consequence is a reinforcer, then the future probability of the targeted behavior increases (i.e., the behavior is strengthened). If the behavior does not increase, the consequence that the teacher chose to use was not actually a reinforcing one, even though the consequence may have been viewed as pleasant by the student.

Providing reinforcers to the student with severe and multiple disabilities can be difficult, depending on how the student receives information. Usually teachers let students know when their efforts have been successful by giving a smile, nod, or verbal praise. Some students with sufficient vision or hearing can receive and respond positively to such feedback. Other students may require a pat on the back, in addition, to understand that they have done as expected. If the student is self-motivated to engage in the activity, then the successful completion of the activity may provide sufficient feedback.

Considerable information exists on using reinforcement when teaching, especially when tasks are not inherently motivating (Haney & Falvey, 1989; Kennedy & Haring, 1993; Orelove & Sobsey, 1996). This information is not repeated here, with the exception of a few critical points.

Reinforcement Is Unique to the Individual   Reinforcers are idiosyncratic; what is effective for one person may be ineffective for another. Even primary reinforcers, such as food and drink, hold unequal value per individual. Discovering what reinforces a given student can require considerable investigative work involving the individual, family members, friends, and professionals on the team. This precise determination is especially necessary when the individual cannot communicate preferences or desires clearly and/or may have become comfortable interacting with a limited number of things to the exclusion of other possibilities. One student may be very motivated by looking at motorcycle pictures, whereas another child may do his or her assignments for a luggage tag. Assuming that all students are motivated by the same rewards would be a faulty premise. Furthermore, the rate that reinforcement is required will vary from individual to individual and from activity to activity. That is, one student may require more frequent reinforcement than another student. The art of teaching requires that the student not receive too much or too little of the needed reinforcement to maintain successful performance.

Reinforcement Is Dynamic   The perceived value of reinforcers can change from moment to moment for the person receiving the reinforcer. Thus, what is effective today may be ineffective tomorrow. In some instances, what is initially effective early in a school day may no longer be effective later in the day. This dynamic nature of reinforcement can frustrate both parent and teacher who may be struggling to motivate a given student; however, this aspect of reinforcement is true for all of us. Our interests change, and we can quickly become satiated with one consequence if it is readily available. In addition, other environmental factors (both internal and external) may play a major role in determining the strength of a given reinforcer. For example, the student may not feel well, causing any reinforcer to lose its effectiveness. In addition, other students in the classroom may have access to something new and interesting that distracts this particular student and reduces the power of the reinforcer.

Reinforcers Must Be Thinned   The overall goal of education is to teach individuals to learn how to learn and to be motivated to learn. Therefore, it is essential that the teacher move from providing external, contrived reinforcers to natural reinforcers or self-reinforcement. The goal of self-motivation across different activities is a valuable aspiration for everyone; however, self-motivation may not always be possible. Even though many adults may enjoy their careers, few would work for no pay. There may always be situations requiring that external reinforcement be present. The goal may be for the student to learn to work for deferred gratification rather than an immediate reward, so as not to interrupt efficiency of performance. Again, the teacher's skill is called on to provide sufficient reinforcement to acquire and maintain the skill, but not so much reinforcement as to create dependency on immediate rewards and thus reduce proficiency. Carefully monitoring students' progress under different reinforcement conditions (e.g., type of reinforcer, frequency of reinforcement) and thinning as quickly as possible to natural reinforcers (e.g., natural teacher praise, feeling good about engaging in or completing the task) will help to determine the most effective procedure for each student.

Responding to Incorrect Behaviors: Corrective Feedback

When the student provides an incorrect response, corrective feedback is needed so that the behavior can be changed as targeted. Providing such feedback should be immediate so that the student can distinguish between desired and ineffective behavior. In addition, if the student has not produced the desired response, continuing the task incorrectly can further confuse him or her and interfere with efficient learning.

Teachers inform students of errors by verbally stating that they made a mistake, asking them to try again, pointing out where the mistake occurred, or providing the correct response. For some students with severe and multiple impairments, corrective feedback can be very confusing. It may seem like another step in a sequence of steps that has already confused them. Care must be taken to quickly intercede to shape the desired response before inappropriate responses are learned. For example, Sharon is learning to affix her name on her tactile artwork using braille labels of her name. She gets the sheet of braille labels of her name and removes one from the sticky backing. She tries, however, to put her name on the tactile artwork where it will not stick well, rather than on the paper holding the artwork. Her teacher prevents her from making this mistake by blocking the action and guiding Sharon's hands to the edge of the paper instead.

ADAPTATIONS

In addition to a variety of teaching strategies, adaptations play a major role in helping students acquire valuable skills. This section gives general information about adaptations that can be helpful for the student with severe and multiple disabilities. The first section suggests adaptations that would be applicable for a wide range of students with disabilities (adapted activities, adapted materials, and daily schedules). Following this are four specific categories of adaptations for different types of disabilities: 1) adaptations for visual impairments, 2) adaptations for hearing impairments, 3) tactile adaptations, and 4) adaptations for physical disabilities. The chapters following provide multiple examples of adaptations used across the age span and in different situations.

Adapted Activities

If students with severe and multiple disabilities cannot perform all aspects of a given activity, then adaptations need to be made that allow participation based on the students' strengths. Adaptations can take many forms and can be simple or complex as suggested in the previous sections. The critical point is to recognize when adaptations are necessary and to be able to apply them as effectively as possible. Instead of excluding these students because they cannot do certain steps (even major steps) in an activity, teachers and other team members can identify the steps that provide the most appropriate learning opportunities. Sometimes steps can be skipped altogether and another student can complete them as a partner to the student with a disability.

For example, removing a sheet of cookies from an oven during home economics class may not be possible for a student who is deafblind and has severe physical limitations. A classmate does that step for him or her. Or, during a softball game in PE class, a student may be supported in a standing position while he or she hits the ball off a batting tee, but a team member may then run the bases. In other instances, students with severe and multiple disabilities can perform the activity, but in a different manner. For example, Sharon gives her report in English class using a switch, cassette recorder, and prerecorded report. Sometimes students participate in the activity but use different materials. James may do his mathematics problems using a talking calculator. Sometimes rules can be modified to allow for the participation of all students. For example, during sustained silent reading, one student is permitted to read quietly to a classmate who is unable to read. During basketball practice, a student with multiple disabilities is allowed to move as close to the basket as she desires instead of having to stay at the free throw line. Considerable information exists on ways to adapt activities to more effectively include all students in school activities (Bauer & Shea, 1999; Block, 2000; Brown & Lehr, 1993; Fisher, Sax, & Pumpian, 1999; Gee, 1995; Hamre-Nietupski, McDonald, & Nietupski, 1994; Janney & Snell, 2000). In determining adapted activities, the team is limited only by their creativity and commitment.

Adapted Materials

Although it is always preferable to obtain lesson plans and activities prior to the lesson, sometimes such preparation is not possible. For these times, it is helpful if teachers and paraeducators have immediate access to materials that can quickly modify the lesson to meet individual student needs. Items in Table 3.5 are inexpensive, easily portable, and offer multiple ways of adapting lessons to allow full participation and learning by different students. Parents, teachers, and students can be asked to contribute to these items so that a regular supply can be maintained. When pictorial information is needed and unavailable, classmates may be able to draw illustrations of subject matter that student's with severe disabilities can use.

Schedules for Student Use

One general adaptation that can prove beneficial to all students is the use of a daily schedule. Considered a best practice (Hodgdon, 1995; Massey & Wheeler,

Table 3.5. A "bag of tricks" for support teachers

The following items need to be kept with the teacher or paraeducator for times when on-the-spot adaptations are needed:

Colored pictures grouped by category (e.g., food, animals, scenery, people, toys, appliances, clothes) for writing and for understanding topic matter

Post-It notes (different colors and shapes) to provide a quick way for a student to choose the correct word or number and add to a worksheet

Blank white labels for a permanent way for a student to add words or his or her name to a report

Felt tip marker (black) to darken and make bold words that are hard to read

Two-sided tape/glue sticks to add pictures to reports, letters, worksheets

File folders to hold student's work and to use as paper for reports written with objects

HandiTak and/or Stickback Velcro to affix objects or parts of objects to file folder/cardboard

Duct tape for a variety of purposes

Colored markers/highlighters to add color to black and white graphics and to highlight certain words and/or numbers

Batteries for switch-activated devices and augmentative and alternative communication devices

2000; Schmit, Alper, Raschke, & Ryndak, 2000), schedules provide multiple opportunities for students to learn a variety of skills, such as communication, self-control, self-management, reading, writing, and math. Because schedules are used by students several times each day, numerous opportunities naturally exist for repetition and practice of targeted skills.

Although schedules have been used to help students anticipate events of their day and thus, reduce behavior disruptions (Hodgdon, 1995; MacDuff, Krantz, & McClannahan, 1993; Schmit et al., 2000), schedules have many more important uses to facilitate learning. For instance, a teacher can use a student's schedule to enhance receptive communication when giving directions or asking questions that involve transitions. Expressively, students can make use of their schedules to ask questions about upcoming events, request certain activities, or respond to a direct question from another person.

The design of the schedule can facilitate the teaching of certain academic skills such as reading, writing, and math (Downing & Peckham-Hardin, 2001). Because words or short sentences can be paired with pictures to provide a means of teaching sight-word recognition related to the student's school day, over time pictures can be faded and a greater emphasis placed on word recognition. Even for students who may not develop any reading skills, sentences related to each activity can be read by classmates and teachers to aid in interactions with the student.

As students become familiar with their schedules, they can organize them or "write" their schedules by sequencing pictures and words in the appropriate order. Some students may be able to match words and/or pictures, while others can copy words or use letter stamps to "write" the first letter of critical words. For example, in Figure 3.4, the student's task is to identify the correct label for this activity (PE) from two distracters and place the correct yellow sticky note on the number and label. Even though some students may know the sequence of their day, the regular use of a schedule can be an effective way to teach a variety of practical skills.

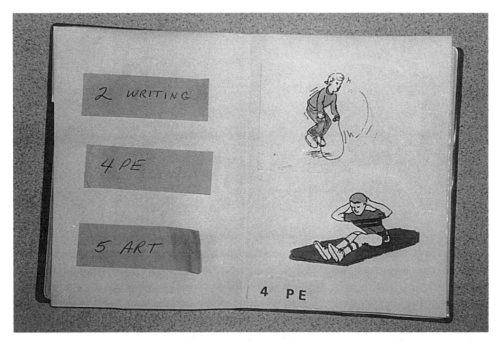

Figure 3.4.   One page in a pictorial/written schedule. For each new activity, the student reads the three Post-It notes (on the left), finds the correct number label, and places it over the number label on the right. (Photograph by Lavada Minor.)

Math skills can be targeted by using numbers to represent periods of the day, individual pages in the schedule, room numbers, or order of activities. Students can learn to recognize numbers, match them, sequence them, and understand the concepts of first, second, third, and so forth. Students can learn to write these numbers by connecting the dots that the teacher has used to make the numbers or by tracing them (if laminated). In addition, students can find the correct number stamp from a set of three or four different numbers or use numbers written on yellow sticky notes to place on the right page of the schedule (e.g., to "write" by matching numbers). For some students, adding important times of the day to their schedules can allow them to work on telling time, relating it to something relevant.

Schedules can be in a variety of formats according to the physical, cognitive, sensory, and preferential needs of the student. Table 3.6 provides ideas for a sample tactile schedule. Figure 3.5 depicts two periods using an object daily schedule for a student who needs this type of schedule. Individual schedules can be used at any age and can become increasingly sophisticated and challenging as the student develops greater skills. Their use before and after each change of activity or time period provides the teacher with several opportunities each day to practice valuable lifelong skills. To be most practical, student schedules must be portable so that the student has ready access to them throughout the day.

Adaptations for Visual Impairments

Specific adaptations for children with visual impairments are individualized according to the student's particular needs and visual condition. Adaptations can as-

Table 3.6.   Sample tactile schedule for fifth grader

Activity	Representation
1. Opening[a]	Cross piece of flag pole
2. Mathematics	Small calculator
3. Reading	Cassette tape
4. Physical Education	Wristband
5. Lunch	Plastic wrap
6. Science	Magnet[b]
7. Writing	Piece of plastic mesh the student "writes" on
8. Art	Clay[b]

[a] Numbers (1–8) are tactually represented as glue dots.

[b] Item changes with the topic.

Note: These items are placed in order on separate cardboard pages in a small (4-inch by 6-inch) three-ring binder. The schedule is read at the beginning and end of each activity.

sist students with visual impairments to use any residual vision that they have more effectively and efficiently. (For detailed information on teaching children with visual impairments to use their vision, the reader is referred to Downing & Bailey, 1990, 1993.) Adaptations also accommodate the needs of the student with no vision by recognizing the potential need to move safely in a given environment, organize materials for easy recovery, and have sufficient room for tactile materials.

In general, it is important to remember that children with severe and multiple impairments should be positioned appropriately before teachers make visual demands. If children are not positioned appropriately, their energy is more likely to go toward maintaining upright posture, balance, and so forth, than toward using their vision efficiently (Smith & Levack, 1996; Utley, Roman, & Nelson, 1998). As with motor skills, it is recommended that a team member, or consultant to the educational team, have expertise in the vision area in order to make perti-

Figure 3.5.   A sample object daily schedule for a student with severe and multiple disabilities. (Photograph by Lavada Minor.)

nent recommendations regarding specific adaptations for a particular child. Several resources exist for assisting teachers to make adaptations for students with visual impairments, as well as those with multiple disabilities, including Bailey and Downing (1994), Lueck, Dornbusch, and Hart (1999), Levack (1994), Smith and Levack (1996), and Utley et al. (1998). According to Levack, adaptations can be made in the following areas: in color and contrast, in illumination, in space and illumination, in size and distance, with vision devices, in visual cues, in materials, in the immediate work space, and in the larger environment.

Frequently, several modifications can be combined to meet the needs of a particular student. Again, the adaptations are specific to the student's concerns and to his or her particular impairment. In specifying adaptations it is important to be knowledgeable as to the type of visual impairment. For example, the following recommendations may be relevant for a preschooler with a cortical visual impairment. Cortical visual impairment refers to damage that has occurred to the visual cortex or visual pathways (i.e., there is difficulty processing visual information), rather than to the eye structure. Such impairment can result in fluctuating vision, inattentiveness to visual cues, preference of touch to vision in exploring objects, greater peripheral than central vision, and difficulty with visual clutter (e.g., with figure–ground discrimination or seeing objects placed close together) (Levack, 1994). Some adaptations that are specific to Seth, a child with such impairments, are as follows:

1. When Seth is in his wheelchair, he frequently uses a tray that attaches to the chair. It is possible to see through the tray, however, and it becomes difficult for Seth to discriminate visually what is on the tray versus what is underneath the tray. Therefore, the educational team covered the underside of the tray with black, nonglare paper to reduce visual clutter.

2. With cortical visual impairment, color vision is typically intact, and it was observed that Seth generally responds well to items that are in bright, fluorescent colors. Thus, toys (e.g., balls, balloons, puppets, blocks), playdough and clay, paints, construction paper, and other materials that are brightly colored were used. Bright yellow or red is often used to attract attention.

3. One of Seth's educational goals targets making a choice between two objects or items during free play, snack, or any other appropriate time. To enhance the likelihood that Seth can visually discriminate between the two choices, it was recommended that the items used for choice making be placed several inches apart from each other. Seth was then taught to look at first one choice and then the other (by moving first one then another to trigger the use of his peripheral vision) before selecting his preference.

4. Seth is also encouraged to touch each of the choices, as a supplement to using his vision to explore options.

5. At snack time, Seth sits in a bolster chair at a table with other children. A blue nonslip place mat is used to provide a contrasting background on the table to assist Seth in using his vision to locate snack items as well as to keep them from sliding on the table.

6. Seth has more difficulty using his vision if he is tired, if there are numerous extraneous distractions (e.g., noise) or if he is positioned inappropriately. The team tries to keep this in mind before placing demands on Seth to perform visually.

7. Finally, Seth appears to be unusually sensitive to bright sunlight during out-
    side play. Therefore, his family provided both sunglasses and a hat with a
    visor so that Seth could choose, on a daily basis, which he would wear for
    outside play.

Although adaptations of this nature may be made specifically to benefit a student who has visual difficulties, they also can benefit other students. Students
without disabilities may find that visual adaptations (e.g., greater contrast, brighter
colors, movement) are more interesting. Again, such adaptations can serve to
bring children together, which is another goal of inclusive education.

Adaptations for Hearing Impairments

For many students with severe and multiple disabilities, teachers will also need
to modify instructional strategies or environmental arrangements to facilitate
hearing and listening skills. For example, part of the curriculum may incorporate
teaching basic signs to everyone in the classroom. All of the students and adults
may have name signs as well as learn to use basic signing vocabulary. These name
signs, plus fingerspelling the alphabet and basic vocabulary, could be incorporated
into classroom routines and activities (e.g., spelling practice, attendance, requesting permission to go to the restroom).

In addition, adults and students in the setting will likely need to attend to the
manner in which they interact with the student who has a hearing impairment.
Students who have hearing impairments may need to be specifically prompted to
attend to peers and adults who are speaking to them. Everyone should be encouraged to speak to the student at a normal rate; it is not necessary to speak unusually slowly. Communication partners should speak at normal levels at close
range rather than attempting to talk to the student from across the room. Keeping mouths clear of obstructions (e.g., hands away) and facing directly toward the
student also improve reception. The student will be better able to use residual
hearing when the environment is quiet (i.e., background noise is minimized)
rather than noisy. Therefore, adaptations to reduce noise levels by carpeting
floors or using acoustic-enhancing ceiling tiles or wall panels are recommended
(Prickett & Welch, 1995). Preferential seating (e.g., sitting closer to the teacher)
also can help to increase volume and decrease background distractions. It may be
easier for students with severe and multiple disabilities to follow instructions
when they are given verbally as well as paired with visual or concrete cues and/or
natural gestures.

For students with the ability to understand some auditory information, assistive listening devices may be of value. The team audiologist can provide information concerning the types of assistive learning devices that may be helpful. If
any amplification is used (e.g., hearing aids or FM systems), then the adults in the
setting will need to be familiar with the devices. Someone on the educational team
should be trained in problem solving (e.g., checking batteries, determining appropriate volume settings). With the help of the audiologist, the team also will need
to understand the student's audiogram, which provides information regarding
what speech sounds the student can hear aided and unaided as well as those that
the student will have difficulty hearing. This information can assist the teacher and
inclusion facilitator to predict when auditory cues will need to be supplemented.

Even when the student cannot understand speech, an exaggerated tone of voice and pitch can help the student understand when a question is being asked or a direction is being given and some action is expected. Using sound to draw attention to important information may also help the student respond as expected. For example, tapping the item to be examined can draw the student's attention to the item even when speech cannot be understood sufficiently to add other information. Being directed to certain environmental sounds (e.g., doors slamming shut, children running, books being dropped) can alert the student to things happening around him or her. Using auditory information of this nature can help students understand events and act on them when necessary (e.g., move out of the way when someone is running toward you, or stop and pick up the book that has fallen).

Tactile Adaptations

For students who require tactile information either to supplement or substitute for visual and auditory information, adaptations may require even greater thought and preplanning. Touching and tactually examining objects being directly studied (e.g., sedimentary rock), as well as objects indirectly related to the topic (e.g., feathers, egg, and a nest in the study of birds), provide critical information and help to maintain interest. Obviously, allowing extra time for such examination is one needed adaptation. The goal, however, is not simply to provide tactile information but to provide information that facilitates learning. Factors to be considered when adapting to the tactile mode are presented in Table 3.7. Because tactile information can be valuable for all students, considering the best way to incorporate it for the whole class should be addressed by the team during joint planning sessions.

Tactile information should be selected that is most relevant to the subject of study (Downing & Eichinger, 1990). This type of information should also be concrete and easily understood by the student (Rowland & Schweigert, 1998). Tactile representation of all aspects of the lesson may not be possible, but certain directly or indirectly related aspects could be presented tactually to add information. For example, a study of the desert could involve a terrarium of sand, rocks, a desert tortoise, and certain cactus plants that would allow some careful tactile exploration. A unit on electricity could involve the use of a switch and a vibrating pillow or any appropriate device (e.g., fan, blender, radio). A history lesson on Christopher Columbus could involve a globe, a replica of a sailboat on water, or a tactile compass.

The use of miniatures to represent ideas, activities, and so forth, however, may not be the most meaningful approach for a given student. For instance, the study of animals (either at an elementary or secondary level in biology) is best done with real animals and not small, plastic miniatures. The small size of miniatures makes it difficult to tactually discriminate one from the other, and they lack other relevant information, such as texture, smell, and movement. Miniatures, in fact, are very visual in the information they provide—not tactile. To try to convince a student with significant visual, auditory, and intellectual challenges that a 1- to 2-inch plastic dog is a dog would be confusing and impractical.

When providing tactile information for any lesson, it is important to determine whether the information would clarify or confuse. Sometimes the object

Table 3.7. Factors to consider when adapting a tactile mode

Can some or all of the information for the lesson be presented tactually?

What aspects can be presented tactually?

How should some or all aspects be presented tactually in order to provide the clearest, most relevant information?

How will tactile information be used and when?
- Does it truly benefit the student?
- Does it benefit all students?

Obtain feedback from students for evaluation/modification.

adds information for others in the class and can be held by the student who enjoys feeling it, regardless of whether it helps the student gain a better understanding of the subject. Letting the student be in charge of tactile items to show others and to hold during group instruction time could help create opportunities to practice appropriate social interactions and provide a calming activity (similar to doodling) until a more active response is required.

Adaptations for Physical Disabilities

Restrictions on a student's ability to move and manipulate items require that teachers facilitate these abilities as much as possible while finding alternative means for these students to actively participate in activities. Fortunately, there are many accommodations that can be employed to assist a student who must deal with physical limitations. In general, these accommodations include physical positioning, assistive technology (both light and high technology), and an emphasis on expressive communicative abilities.

Physical Positioning   Rainforth and York-Barr (1996) emphasized the critical importance of effective physical positioning for students with physical disabilities. Teachers must ensure that students are comfortable and in a position that supports their ability to engage in meaningful activities. Students without disabilities change their body position almost constantly throughout each day; therefore, it is imperative that teachers remain sensitive to the need for students with physical disabilities to adjust their positions, as well.

Adaptive positioning equipment allows students to sit, stand, kneel, and lie on their side, front (prone), or back (supine). Direct services providers must assume responsibility for assisting students into different positions throughout each day depending on the student's abilities, needs, physical limitations, and the demand or expectations of each activity. In addition, the physical position of students without disabilities will affect the decision regarding the appropriate position for a student with physical disabilities. For example, when young preschool or elementary students sit on the floor to listen to a story being read, the student with severe physical disabilities also should be on the floor in a supported sitting position as opposed to being placed in a wheelchair or bolster chair that elevates this student above the other children. Or, if students gather on the floor to work on a project, it may be a good opportunity for a student to be positioned prone on a wedge while working with this group.

At the preschool and elementary level, it is relatively easy to match the student's positioning needs because children at this age often work in a variety of positions during the school day. Fewer options may exist for secondary students in middle and high school. At the secondary level, students may spend considerable time in wheelchairs as their classmates spend most of their time at their desks. During these school years, teachers and related services professionals will need to be particularly creative in ensuring that students experience different physical positions during each day. Arranging schedules so that students avoid taking numerous sequential classes that require the use of a wheelchair as the primary positioning equipment is one strategy. Such classes are best alternated with classes that permit a wider variety of positions.

For example, a PE class would allow students to exercise on a mat in a prone or supine position, watch team sports on a bolster chair or in a standing table or a prone or supine stander, and participate in various activities by sitting or standing. Choir, art, drama, home economics, and woodshop, to name a few, also offer options for students to participate in class activities in a standing position versus sitting in a wheelchair.

Because changing positions involves the use of various pieces of equipment, the educational team will need to come up with creative ways of getting the necessary equipment to the classes in which it will be needed. Employing the assistance of classmates to address this potential difficulty can be very helpful to teachers and paraeducators who have several students to support.

Assistive Technology   Technology is pervasive in today's society, enhancing almost everyone's life in some manner (Inge & Shepherd, 1995; Reed, 1998). The use of assistive technology for students with severe and multiple disabilities has contributed significantly to their ability to participate in typical environments. A wide range of assistive technology from simple or light technology to complex or high technology is available to support students having severe and multiple disabilities. As mandated by IDEA, educational team members need to be aware of available technology to ensure the greatest level of student participation. Educators also need to be aware of cultural differences with regard to the acceptance and use of assistive technology. Certain cultural beliefs concerning assistive technology (e.g., potential stigmatizing effects or failure to fit into family's lifestyle) can present a distinct barrier to using available technology despite the professional belief of its benefit (Kemp & Parette, 2000; Parette, 1998). Therefore, respecting familial and cultural values is essential before introducing any type of assistive technology.

Low or Light Technology   Assistive technology does not have to be expensive or complex to be highly useful. Almost any adaptation to material or an entire activity can fall under this category. Many adaptations or examples of light technology can be readily purchased from common retail stores (e.g., pencil grips, step stools, HandiTak to hold objects, nonslip place mats, signature stamps, headphones, calculators with extra-large numbers). Other relatively simple types of adaptive technology are commercially available via companies producing specialized equipment for individuals with disabilities (e.g., adapted spoons, pictorial communication systems, orthotic splints, bolsters, simple switches).

A wide variety of switches can be activated with various body parts and require varying amounts of pressure for activation. For example, plate switches in the form of lever, disc, or membrane switches can be positioned so that any part of the body can activate the switch (e.g., hand, elbow, back or side of the head, knee, foot). Some switches can use air pressure (e.g., the sip-and-puff switch) for activation. Mercury switches can be attached to the head (e.g., on an age-appropriate hat or hair ribbon) and activated with head movements. A final example involves a switch activated by the child's voice. The type of switch and the body part used to activate the switch will be determined by the child's educational team, with input from a person with expertise in motor skills.

Many adaptations that are not complex in nature can be made by family members, teachers, volunteers, and other students. Examples of handmade light technology could include pressure switches, jigs to perform different jobs, adaptive mitts, handles for a variety of objects, bags to attach to wheelchairs or walkers, pictorial conversation books, Velcro clipboards to hold objects, and page fluffers.

Light or low technology can help a student perform more efficiently in almost any daily activity and can be specifically designed to the individual's needs. This type of technology facilitates communicative interactions, task performance, and care of one's personal needs. The effective use of light technology demonstrates the creativity of the educational team in resolving potential barriers.

High Technology   This area of technology has grown substantially since the 1980s and continues to make progress in addressing human needs. High technology is considerably more complex than light technology and usually carries a higher price tag as well as a need for training in its use. Careful assessment of an individual student's needs and careful analysis of how that student's needs would be most effectively and efficiently addressed by a given piece of technology are needed to avoid purchasing the expensive, yet wrong, equipment.

The personal computer has revolutionized the way people interact with one another. It has opened countless doors for individuals with severe physical disabilities. Furthermore, individuals with disabilities have access to this type of technology with just a few adaptations (Langone, 2000). Software programs with voice output, adapted keyboards, and touch windows have enabled students to participate in a wide range of activities using computers. Students of any age can learn about the relationship between their movements and related consequences (cause and effect) using software programs that create colorful and changing designs or that allow creative musical expression. Aspects of such programs are fascinating to anyone of any age, and therefore the teacher does not have to worry about using software that is age-inappropriate for older students.

High technology has had a major impact on the development of augmentative and alternative communication (AAC) systems for individuals with severe physical disabilities. Numerous electronic communication systems are available and can be adapted to meet individual student needs (see Beukelman & Mirenda, 1998; Goetz & Hunt, 1994). For example, Zygo's Macaw and Prentke Romich's Introtalker (as well as Touch and Light Talkers) allow for a wide range of symbols (e.g., objects, pictures, photographs) to be used with these systems. In addition, digitized speech for these products creates a natural sounding voice to accompany a selection. These electronic systems continue to decrease in size, allowing them to be more easily portable. They also have become more user friendly; however, this aspect of technology is still inconvenient for students with the most challenging needs.

Communication as an Emphasis   Although a physical disability may limit a student's ability to move and handle objects, meaningful participation still can occur in school activities when the student's ability to convey information is emphasized. The student will be a part of whatever activity is occurring for the class but will capitalize on the ability to make choices, reject or request actions or items, and express opinions instead of participating in the actual manipulation of materials. Other students will make the actual products, whereas the student with severe and multiple disabilities including a severe physical disability will direct, decide, and comment.

The major accommodation that must occur is for those without disabilities (students and teachers) to provide the opportunities to allow the student unable to move well to be an active participant. Too often students with severe and multiple impairments will be physically close to the other students but merely passive observers. No expectation is present for these students to participate. This situation can be changed to include any student when those without disabilities take the time to offer choices (e.g., "Would you like Aaron or Jonah to mix the chemicals?"), ask for direction (e.g., "Where should I put this?" "What's next?"), request feedback (e.g., "Do you like it this way?" "Is it better with yellow or black?"), or allow a comment (e.g., a student vocalizes and looks interested in a mural being made, and his peer responds with, "Yeah, Tracy, I like that, too").

Many options exist for students with severe and multiple disabilities to communicate, including highly symbolic means via the use of high technology and nonsymbolic means via the use of facial expressions, vocalizations, or slight body movements (Beukelman & Mirenda, 1998; Downing, 1999). The important point to remember is that everyone has something to say, even though it may prove very difficult to say it. Expecting each student to express himself or herself through whatever means is available is the key. The next step is to provide each student with the most appropriate means to communicate and to give that student time and supportive instruction to be successful. The examples across age ranges provided in Chapters 4, 5, 6, and 7 highlight the importance of expecting students to communicate their thoughts, despite an inability to use speech or other symbolic means.

SUMMARY

This chapter has examined educational strategies for working with students of all ages who have severe and multiple disabilities. Emphasis has been placed on first determining who the student is (identifying strengths, hopes, interests) and then assessing the student within typical activities and environments that lead toward the goals that the student and/or parents have targeted as priorities. Helping the student acquire needed skills according to individual interests, strengths, and limitations, as well as the demands of the environment, is done in a positive and least intrusive way. Respect for the student is shown, first, by recognizing that individuals learn differently and require varying support across different activities; and, second, by providing as many options as practicable and giving each student as much decision-making power over educational goals and methods of attaining them as possible.

REFERENCES

Alberto, P.A., & Troutman, A.C. (1999). *Applied behavior analysis for teachers* (5th ed.). Upper Saddle River, NJ: Prentice-Hall.

Bailey, B.R., & Downing, J. (1994). Using visual accents to enhance attending to communication symbols for students with severe multiple disabilities. *RE:view, 26*(3), 101–118.

Bauer, A.M., & Shea, T.M. (1999). *Inclusion 101: How to teach all learners.* Baltimore: Paul H. Brookes Publishing Co.

Beukelman, D.R., & Mirenda, P. (1998). *Augmentative and alternative communication: Management of severe communication disorders in children and adults* (2nd ed.). Baltimore: Paul H. Brookes Publishing Co.

Biederman, G.B., Fairhall, J.L., Raven, K.A., & Davey, V.A. (1998). Verbal prompting, hand-over-hand instruction, and passive observation in teaching children with developmental disabilities. *Exceptional Children, 64,* 503–512.

Billingsley, F.F., Gallucci, C., Peck, C.A., Schwartz, I.S., & Staub, D. (1996). "But those kids can't even do math": An alternative conceptualization of outcomes for inclusive education. *Special Education Leadership Review, 3,* 43–55.

Block, M.E. (2000). *A teacher's guide to including students with disabilities in general physical education* (2nd ed.). Baltimore: Paul H. Brookes Publishing Co.

Brown, F., & Lehr, D. (1993). Making activities meaningful for students with severe multiple disabilities. *Teaching Exceptional Children, 25*(4), 12–17.

Campbell, P.C., Campbell, C.R., & Brady, M.P. (1998). Team environmental assessment mapping system: A method for selecting curriculum goals for students with disabilities. *Education and Training in Mental Retardation and Developmental Disabilities, 33,* 264–272.

Demchak, M. (1990). Response prompting and fading methods: A review. *American Journal on Mental Retardation, 94,* 603–615.

Demchak, M. (1997). *Teaching students with severe disabilities in inclusive settings.* Washington, DC: American Association on Mental Retardation.

Downing, J. (1996). *Assessment of the school age student with dual sensory and intellectual impairments.* Monmouth, OR: Traces Technical Assistance Project.

Downing, J.E. (1999). *Teaching communication skills to students with severe disabilities.* Baltimore: Paul H. Brookes Publishing Co.

Downing, J., & Bailey, B. (1990). Developing vision use within functional daily activities for students with visual and multiple disabilities. *RE:view, 21,* 209–220.

Downing, J., & Bailey, B.R. (1993). *Helping young children with visual impairments make use of their vision.* Terre Haute: Indiana State University, Blumberg Center for Interdisciplinary Studies in Special Education.

Downing, J., & Eichinger, J. (1990). Instructional strategies for learners with dual sensory impairments in integrated settings. *Journal of The Association for Persons with Severe Handicaps, 15,* 98–105.

Downing, J.E., & Peckham-Hardin, K. (2001). Daily schedules: A helpful learning tool. *Teaching Exceptional Children, 33*(3), 62–68.

Downing, J., & Perino, D. (1992). Functional versus standardized assessment procedures: Implications for educational programming. *Mental Retardation, 30,* 289–295.

Falvey, M., Forest, M., Pearpoint, J., & Rosenberg, R. (1997). *All my life's a circle. Using the tools: Circles, MAPS, and PATHS.* Toronto, Ontario: Inclusion Press.

Fewell, R.R. (2000). Assessment of young children with special needs: Foundations for tomorrow. *Topics in Early Childhood Special Education, 20*(1), 38–42.

Fisher, D., Sax, C., & Pumpian, I. (1999). *Inclusive high schools: Learning from contemporary classrooms.* Baltimore: Paul H. Brookes Publishing Co.

Fox, T., & Williams, W. (1991). *Implementing best practices for all students in their local schools: Inclusion of all students through family and community involvement, collaboration, and the use of school planning teams and individual student planning teams.* Burlington: University of Vermont, Center for Developmental Disabilities.

Gee, K. (1995). Facilitating active and informed learning and participation in inclusive school settings. In N.G. Haring & L.T. Romer (Eds.), *Welcoming students who are deaf-blind into typical classrooms: Facilitating school participation, learning, and friendships* (pp. 369–404). Baltimore: Paul H. Brookes Publishing Co.

Giangreco, M.F., Cloninger, C.J., & Iverson, V.S. (1998). *Choosing outcomes and accommodations for children (COACH): A guide to educational planning for students with disabilities* (2nd ed.). Baltimore: Paul H. Brookes Publishing Co.

Goetz, L., & Hunt, P. (1994). Augmentative and alternative communication. In E.C. Cipani & F. Spooner (Eds.), *Curricular and instructional approaches for persons with severe disabilities* (pp. 263–288). Needham Heights, MA: Allyn & Bacon.

Hamre-Nietupski, S., McDonald, J., & Nietupski, J. (1994). Enhancing participation of a student with multiple disabilities in regular education. *Teaching Exceptional Children, 26*(3), 60–63.

Haney, M., & Falvey, M.A. (1989). Instructional strategies. In M.A. Falvey (Ed.), *Community-based curriculum: Instructional strategies for students with severe disabilities* (2nd ed., pp. 63–90). Baltimore: Paul H. Brookes Publishing Co.

Hodgdon, L.A. (1995). *Visual strategies for improving communication: Practical supports for school and home.* Troy, MI: Quirk Roberts Publishing.

Horn, E., Lieber, J., Li, S., Sandall, S., & Schwartz, I. (2000). Supporting young children's IEP goals in inclusive settings through embedded learning opportunities. *Topics in Early Childhood Special Education, 20,* 208–223.

Inge, K.J., & Shepherd, J. (1995). Assistive technology applications and strategies for school system personnel. In K.F. Flippo, K.J. Inge, & M. Barcus (Eds.), *Assistive technology: A resource for school, work, and community* (pp. 133–166). Baltimore: Paul H. Brookes Publishing Co.

Janney, R., & Snell, M.E. (2000). *Teachers' guides to inclusive practices: Modifying schoolwork.* Baltimore: Paul H. Brookes Publishing Co.

Kemp, C.E., & Parette, H.P. (2000). Barriers to minority family involvement in assistive technology decision-making processes. *Education and Training in Mental Retardation and Developmental Disabilities, 35,* 384–392.

Kennedy, C.H., & Haring, T.G. (1993). Combining reward and escape DRO to reduce the problem behavior of students with severe disabilities. *Journal of The Association for Persons with Severe Handicaps, 18,* 85–92.

Langone, J. (2000). Technology for individuals with severe and physical disabilities. In J.D. Lindsey (Ed.), *Technology and exceptional individuals* (pp. 327–352). Austin, TX: PRO-ED.

Levack, N. (1994). *Low vision: A resource guide with adaptations for students with visual impairments* (2nd ed.). Austin: Texas School for the Blind and the Visually Impaired.

Lueck, A.H., Dornbusch, H., & Hart, J. (1999). The effects of training on a young child with cortical visual impairment: An exploratory study. *Journal of Visual Impairment and Blindness, 13,* 778–793.

MacDuff, G.S., Krantz, P.J., & McClannahan, L.E. (1993). Teaching children with autism to use photographic activity schedules: Maintenance and generalization of complex response chains. *Journal of Applied Behavior Analysis, 26,* 89–97.

Massey, N.G., & Wheeler, J.J. (2000). Acquisition and generalization of activity schedules and their effects on task engagement in a young child with autism in an inclusive preschool classroom. *Education and Training in Mental Retardation and Developmental Disabilities, 35,* 326–335.

McConnell, S.R. (2000). Assessment in early intervention and early childhood special education: Building on the past to project into our future. *Topics in Early Childhood Special Education, 20*(1), 43–48.

McDonnell, J. (1998). Instruction of students with severe disabilities in general education settings. *Education and Training in Mental Retardation and Developmental Disabilities, 33,* 199–215.

Menchetti, B.M., & Sweeney, M.A. (1995). *Person-centered planning: Technical assistance packet* (No. 5). Gainesville: University of Florida.

Odom, S.L. (2000). Preschool inclusion: What we know and where do we go from here. *Topics in Early Childhood Special Education, 20,* 20–27.

Orelove, F.P., & Sobsey, D. (1996). *Educating children with multiple disabilities: A transdisciplinary approach* (3rd ed.). Baltimore: Paul H. Brookes Publishing Co.

Parette, H.P. (1998). Cultural values and family-centered assistive technology decision-making. In S.L. Judge & H.P. Parette (Eds.), *Assistive technology for young children with disabilities: A guide to providing family-centered services* (pp. 184–210). Cambridge, MA: Brookline.

Peter, D. (2000). Dynamics of discourse: A case study illuminating power relations in mental retardation. *Mental Retardation, 38,* 354–362.

Prickett, J.G., & Welch, T.R. (1995). Adapting environments to support the inclusion of students who are deaf-blind. In N.G. Haring & L.T. Romer (Eds.), *Welcoming students who are deaf-blind into typical classrooms: Facilitating school participation, learning, and friendships* (pp. 171–194). Baltimore: Paul H. Brookes Publishing Co.

Rainforth, B., & York-Barr, J. (1996). Handling and positioning. In F.P. Orelove & D. Sobsey (Eds.), *Educating children with multiple disabilities: A transdisciplinary approach* (pp. 79–118). Baltimore: Paul H. Brookes Publishing Co.

Reed, P. (1998) Assistive technology: Putting the pieces together. *Disability Solutions, 3*(2), 1–11.

Rowland, C., & Schweigert, P. (1998). Enhancing the acquisition of functional language and communication. In S.Z. Sacks & R.K. Silberman (Eds.), *Educating students who have visual impairments with other disabilities* (pp. 413–438). Baltimore: Paul H. Brookes Publishing Co.

Schmit, J., Alper, S., Raschke, D., & Ryndak, D. (2000). Effects of using a photographic cueing package during routine school transitions with a child who has autism. *Mental Retardation, 38,* 131–137.

Schnorr, R.F. (1990). "Peter? He comes and goes . . .": First graders' perspectives on a part-time mainstream student. *Journal of The Association for Persons with Severe Handicaps, 15,* 231–240.

Schnorr, R.F. (1997). From enrollment to membership: "Belonging" in middle and high school classes. *Journal of The Association for Persons with Severe Handicaps, 22,* 1–15.

Schwartz, I.S. (1995). Using social-validity assessments to identify meaningful outcomes for students with deaf-blindness. In N.G. Haring & L.T. Romer (Eds.), *Welcoming students who are deaf-blind into typical classrooms: Facilitating school participation, learning, and friendships* (pp. 133–142). Baltimore: Paul H. Brookes Publishing Co.

Silberman, R.K., Sacks, S.Z., & Wolfe, J. (1998). Instructional strategies for educating students who have visual impairments with severe disabilities. In S.Z. Sacks & R.K. Silberman (Eds.), *Educating students who have visual impairments with other disabilities* (pp. 101–137). Baltimore: Paul H. Brookes Publishing Co.

Smith, M., & Levack, N. (1996). *Teaching students with visual and multiple impairments: A resource guide.* Austin: Texas School for the Blind and Visually Impaired.

Snell, M.E. (1997). Teaching children and young adults with mental retardation in school programs: Current research. *Behavior Change, 14,* 73–105.

Sobsey, D., & Wolf-Schein, E.G. (1996). Children with sensory impairments. In F.P. Orelove & D. Sobsey (Eds.), *Educating children with multiple disabilities: A transdisciplinary approach* (3rd ed., pp. 411–450). Baltimore: Paul H. Brookes Publishing Co.

Turnbull, A.P., & Turnbull, H.R. (1997). *Families, professionals, and exceptionality: A special partnership* (3rd ed.). Upper Saddle River, NJ: Merrill/Prentice-Hall.

Utley, B.L., Roman, C., & Nelson, G.L. (1998). Functional vision. In S.Z. Sacks & R.K. Silberman (Eds.), *Educating students who have visual impairments with other disabilities* (pp. 371–412). Baltimore: Paul H. Brookes Publishing Co.

Vandercook, T., York, J., & Forest, M. (1989). The McGill Action Planning System (MAPS): A strategy for building the vision. *Journal of The Association for Persons with Severe Handicaps, 14,* 205–215.

Wolery, M., Anthony, L., Snyder, E.D., Werts, M.G., & Katzenmeyer, J. (1997). Training elementary teachers to embed instruction during classroom activities. *Education and Treatment of Children, 20,* 40–58.

Wolery, M., Ault, M.J., & Doyle, P.M. (1992). *Teaching students with moderate to severe disabilities.* New York: Longman.

Chapter 4

The Preschool Student

MaryAnn Demchak and June E. Downing

For young children, the first educational experiences should be centered on play, which is young children's "work." When approached as play, learning has a greater impact on a young child's development and is more enjoyable for the child (Burton, 1991). Early childhood education should involve active learning that consists of choice making, abundant materials for children to manipulate in various ways, and an emphasis on language development (Tompkins, 1991). Active learning can occur in various types of play: 1) dramatic play or role play, in which children pretend; 2) constructive play, in which children use materials to make something; 3) exploratory/manipulative play, in which children physically manipulate materials by banging, pushing, pulling, and so forth; 4) social play routines that involve turn taking and reciprocal interactions; and 5) functional play, in which children use two or more play materials together in a conventional manner (e.g., a doll in a stroller) (Buchanan & Cooney, 2000). Through play, young children learn about objects and events and the language for talking about them. In addition they develop a variety of interaction skills (Lifter, Sulzer-Azaroff, Anderson, & Cowdery, 1993). Play also contributes to cognitive, social, and physical development on an incidental, or informal, basis in numerous areas, including object permanence; memory; attention; cause and effect; problem solving; color, shape, and size identification; grasping and manipulation; gross motor skills; turn taking; and expressive and receptive communication skills.

A typical schedule for a preschool program includes, first and foremost, a generous amount of play time (inside and outside) stressing free play as well as planned activities at centers and play in small and large groups. In addition, the schedule typically includes greeting time (i.e., morning circle), snack time, storytime, and closing circle at departure time. These various activities allow young children to learn the skills previously identified, as well as to learn about self and others, to participate in a group, to follow directions, to complete self-help skills, and to respect the property of others.

EDUCATING YOUNG CHILDREN TOGETHER

The current emphasis in early childhood education is on a play-based, family-centered, and teacher-facilitated program (Hanline & Fox, 1993; McLean & Odom, 1993; Weber, Behl, & Summers, 1994). These standards are also relevant to early childhood special education (Bailey, McWilliam, Buysse, & Wesley, 1998). In fact, compatibility between these fields is important because there is increased emphasis on educating young children with disabilities in inclusive environments. Bailey et al. reviewed the legal, moral, rational, and empirical foundations for educating young children with disabilities with their typical peers. All young children benefit from an inclusive preschool program. Preschoolers with disabilities have a more challenging educational environment, can observe and learn from typical peers, and are in a more socially stimulating environment, whereas preschoolers without disabilities learn about differences and develop acceptance of those with disabilities. Buysse (1993) also cited what is perhaps a more important result of inclusive education for young children, the reciprocal friendships that develop among young children with and without disabilities. The empirical basis for inclusive preschool education is substantial, whereas empirical support for segregated preschool programs is minimal (Bailey et al., 1998).

The activities that occur in typical preschools are perfectly suited to young children with severe and multiple impairments who usually are learning to communicate, to take care of bodily functions, to play appropriately with toys, to interact with others their age, and to follow the rules of social conduct. If young children with disabilities are placed in homogeneous groupings according to ability (or rather disability), lack of appropriate role models will hinder the development of targeted skills and place the burden of teaching on a few adults. Being surrounded by appropriate role models at a very young age and experiencing typical expectations for behavior can set a critical foundation for future learning. Some evidence exists that preschool children in inclusive environments score higher on standardized measures of development than children with comparable disabilities in special education environments (Hundert, Mahoney, Mundy, & Vernon, 1998). The value of educating preschoolers with and without disabilities together is clear.

BARRIERS TO INCLUSIVE PRESCHOOL EDUCATION

Perhaps the biggest barrier to inclusive education for preschool-age children with disabilities is the lack of public preschool programs for typical children (Lieber et al., 2000; Odom, McConnell, & Chandler, 1993). Children without disabilities receive early childhood education and child care in a range of programs that include 1) in-home care by others, 2) family child care, 3) preschools, 4) child care centers, and 5) federal Head Start programs. Unfortunately, many preschoolers with disabilities do not have access to peers without disabilities because they receive their early education in separate schools or separate classes in public schools. The youngest children in most public schools are in kindergarten. Fowler, Donegan, Lueke, Hadden, and Phillips (2000) found that the least restrictive environment requirement was one of the most difficult for school districts to meet for young children transitioning into preschool services.

Nonetheless, there are options for educating preschoolers with disabilities in the typical environments previously listed. For example, early childhood special education teachers may collaborate with local private preschools (e.g., Montessori preschools or others) or with public programs for at-risk preschoolers (e.g., Head Start). In some instances, a school district may choose to open its own preschool program for all children or may rent space to a private preschool on an elementary school campus. Inclusion of young children with disabilities has occurred successfully within existing child care and preschool options (Lieber et al., 2000; Odom et al., 1999). It is likely, however, that the early childhood special educator and the early childhood general educator will need to collaborate to ensure that necessary adaptations are implemented for young children with severe and multiple impairments. The adaptations to be implemented should be developed by the educational team that includes family members and should be linked to the goals and objectives specified in the IEP.

Despite the benefits documented for young children with severe and multiple disabilities in inclusive preschools, children with more severe disabilities tend to be educated in specialized environments to a greater degree than children with milder disabilities (Odom, 2000). Therefore, few early childhood teachers have had the opportunity to teach a child with a severe disability. Naturally, fear and apprehension sometimes exist on the part of these teachers, especially when children have complex health concerns in addition to sensory and other disabilities. These teachers will need to receive sufficient information and support to ease concerns and feel comfortable including a child with these kinds of disabilities.

Although young children tend to be quite accepting at this age, when a classmate does not respond or behave as expected, children may opt to avoid this child. In addition, children at this young age are just developing skills of sharing toys and engaging in cooperative and interactive play. Their typical level of development in play skills (especially for 3-year-olds) may make interactions with a child who has complex needs all that more challenging. When children are rejected or avoided by their peers, teachers will need to facilitate individualized activities and group friendship activities to build a foundation for positive social relationships (Frea, Craig-Unkefer, Odom, & Johnson, 1999; Wolfberg et al., 1999).

Although barriers to inclusive preschool education do exist, they can be overcome. Preschool children with severe disabilities should be educated with their peers without disabilities (Cavallaro & Haney, 1999; Downing, 1999a). The IEP is a key means for the educational team to address some of the barriers that may be present.

DEVELOPING THE PRESCHOOL CHILD'S IEP

The educational team comprising family members, relevant professionals, and paraprofessionals develops the IEP. (An individualized family service plan to focus on the family's concerns and priorities may also be developed at this time.) The educational team should collaborate in targeting IEP goals and objectives that are meaningful and appropriate for a preschooler. Any areas that were identified as priorities by the family should be targeted within the IEP. The various professionals involved with the child should write IEP objectives that address basic skills (e.g., motor, communication, vision, and hearing) in the context of meaningful activities. Each professional is not allotted a separate section within the IEP; rather, there is a common set of IEP goals and objectives.

Pretti-Frontczak and Bricker (2000) discussed five dimensions for writing quality IEP goals and objectives for young children: functionality, generality, instructional context, measurability, and hierarchical relationship. The targeted skills should be functional in that they should increase children's independence in their daily environments, as well as address behaviors that would otherwise need to be targeted by someone else. Goals and objectives address generality by focusing on general concepts or classes of behaviors that are generic rather than specific to particular materials or environments. The skills targeted in the IEP should be those that can be taught frequently and easily in a naturalistic manner in ongoing routines. As is true for any student, the targeted skills should be directly observable and measurable and should have specific criteria delineated. Finally, short-term objectives should be hierarchically related to the long-term goals—that is, achieving an objective should be directly related to attainment of the goal. Subsequent implementation of IEP objectives should occur within the context of ongoing class activities. Embedding opportunities to address children's IEP objectives in existing routines and activities leads to improved performance in the targeted objectives (Horn, Lieber, Li, Sandall, & Schwartz, 2000).

The following objective demonstrates the incorporation of these guidelines as well as collaborative efforts by the educational team: "When greeted by name, Seth will respond by looking at or turning toward that peer or teacher in 9 of 10 opportunities." Seth's teacher had identified greetings as an important aspect of the arrival routine, and the parents had indicated that greetings were a priority for them. The communication specialist collaborated regarding the meaningful use of greetings, whereas the hearing specialist provided guidelines to facilitate the likelihood that Seth would hear the greetings (in addition to subsequent communications). In addition, the physical therapist provided input regarding appropriate positioning to enable Seth to turn his head in response to greetings. Finally, the objective was targeted within the existing arrival routine. A similar process is followed in developing all goals and objectives for the preschooler with severe and multiple disabilities.

Table 4.1 lists skills that could be targeted to the IEP and the manner in which they can be incorporated into the ongoing preschool routines. The actual IEP objectives are written to reflect the class activities and routines in which the objectives can be meaningfully addressed. Writing IEP objectives in this manner leads to targeting of skills in a relevant fashion throughout the day, rather than in isolation.

POTENTIAL ADAPTATIONS

A variety of relatively simple adaptations can be incorporated into a typical preschool schedule to facilitate the purposeful participation of children with disabilities. (Although the examples discussed here focus on preschoolers, it should be noted that many of these adaptations cross ages and are relevant to older children, as well.) Due to limited sensory input and possible physical limitations, one critical and relatively simple adaptation may involve allowing children with multiple impairments more time to explore the learning environment. This may be particularly important when a child has both visual and physical impairments

Table 4.1.   Sample preschool schedule with skills to meet IEP objectives

Activity	Potential IEP objectives
Arrival and greeting	Greet peers Respond to peers' greetings Mobility (e.g., use walker) Assist with removing coat/jacket Anticipate next activity using object calendar (e.g., toy car and ramp)
Free play	Choose activities, partners Maintain head control Maintain balance Grasp and manipulate objects (e.g., toy cars) Anticipate next activity using object calendar (e.g., cassette)
Good morning circle and music	Maintain sitting posture Grasp and manipulate objects Activate a switch (e.g., to turn on a cassette recorder) Anticipate next activity using object calendar (e.g., clay, blocks)
Center time	Maintain head control, balance, sitting posture Choose activities, partners Grasp and manipulate objects (e.g., blocks) Interact with peers (e.g., pass items) Mobility (e.g., use walker to move between centers) Anticipate next activity using object calendar (e.g., beanbag)
Active play	Use walker Maintain head control and balance Grasp and manipulate objects (e.g., beanbags) Choose activities and partners Interact with peers (e.g., pass balls, beanbags) Assist with putting coat/jacket on for outdoor play Assist with removing coat/jacket after outdoor play Anticipate next activity using object calendar (e.g., cup)
Snack time	Maintain head control, balance, and sitting posture Choose food, drink, and who is to help Self-feeding and drinking Interact with peers (e.g., request snack food or pass objects) Personal hygiene (e.g., wipe face, bathroom break) Anticipate next activity using object calendar (e.g., book)
Storytime	Maintain head control, balance, and sitting posture Grasp and manipulate objects (i.e., those related to the story) Anticipate next activity using object calendar (e.g., backpack)
Closing circle and departure	Respond to peers' good-byes Communicate good-bye to peers Mobility (e.g., use walker) Assist with putting on coat/jacket Anticipate trip home using object calendar (e.g., part of a seat belt)

(Downing, 1999a). Adaptations may require collaboration among professionals from various disciplines to ensure that a specific child's concerns are met (Cavallaro & Haney, 1999). For example, early childhood educators and early childhood special educators may work with occupational and/or physical therapists to address motor impairments.

In some instances, adaptations are incorporated into numerous, if not all, activities throughout the day, rather than being limited to one particular activity at a specific time. For example, equipment allowing for proper positioning to enable a child to interact and stay involved in the learning activities to the greatest extent possible will be used throughout the day. This equipment could include corner chairs, bolster chairs, prone standers, wedges, bolsters, sidelyers, standing tables, or other equipment as recommended by physical and/or occupational therapists. The therapist(s) will assist in deciding what adaptive equipment will be necessary and in acquiring the equipment. In general, the equipment needed by an individual student is determined both by physical strengths and limitations as well as by functional concerns to interact with others most efficiently.

The goal of using adaptive positioning strategies should be to increase meaningful and active participation in ongoing activities and routines within the classroom (Breath, DeMauro, & Snyder, 1997). Equipment should not be used solely to achieve an alternate position for some specified time period. A child positioned on a piece of adaptive equipment without concern for meaningful interaction or participation in ongoing class activities can become bored and frustrated and miss valuable learning opportunities. A more appropriate use of adaptive equipment is provided in the following example. If children are playing on the floor, positioning equipment (e.g., a corner chair) may allow the child with severe and multiple disabilities to also play on the floor. The child's position is determined by physical concerns as well as the activities in the classroom and where those activities occur (i.e., on the floor, at a table, or standing). Table 4.2 shows examples of incorporating the use of adaptive equipment into ongoing class activities.

Adaptive devices also are available to help young children with fine motor tasks (e.g., grasping and maintaining that grasp) with which they might otherwise have difficulty. For example, a mitten with Velcro attached enabling the hand to be shaped into a fist can help a child to hold and examine a doll, pinwheel, kaleidoscope, or any other object that a strong extensor pattern and/or floppy tone might hinder grasping.

Switches and environmental control units can be used to allow the student with motor impairments access to and control of various items in the classroom that might otherwise not be possible. For example, the frequent repetition of familiar songs or the use of predictable books facilitates the use of AAC devices that allow a child to press a switch to participate vocally with peers (see Downing, 1999b; Glennen & DeCoste, 1997). Switches allow the child to learn the impact of his or her actions on the social environment as well as to participate more meaningfully in class activities. An additional benefit is that the use of switches can be fascinating for typical peers. This fascination results in young children's gathering around the child using the switch (he or she may be less able to move toward them). Moreover, when all students are allowed to share a switch to activate a toy or appliance, it helps to validate for the student with disabilities that such an adaptation is accepted and even valued by others. (Chapter 3 discusses a variety of switches that can be activated with various body parts.)

Not only is it important to adapt activities to accommodate motor impairments, but it is also essential to make the appropriate modifications to address visual and hearing impairments (Downing, 1999a). Chapter 3 discusses potential adaptations for accommodating impairments in vision and hearing. In general, activities involving the use of vision and hearing should be meaningful and functional as well as incorporated into regular preschool routines. For example, it is not meaningful to remove the child from classroom activities to locate fabricated sounds, such as a drum being hit behind him or her. The child must learn to hear the sound for a purpose that has relevance for the child in the classroom envi-

Table 4.2. Sample preschool schedule incorporating adaptive equipment

Activity	Potential adaptive equipment
Arrival and greeting	Adapted wheelchair Walker
Free play	Supported sitting device on floor Prone over wedge Sidelyer
Good morning circle and music	Supported sitting device on floor
Center activities	Adapted wheelchair Stander Corner chair Bolster chair
Active play	Adapted wheelchair Walker
Snack time	Adapted wheelchair Bolster chair
Storytime	Supported sitting device on floor
Closing circle and departure	Adapted wheelchair Walker

ronment. That is, a functional listening activity can involve asking the child to respond to sounds relating to the task at hand. Responding when the teacher calls
a child's name is one obvious example that can occur many times a day. Musical
chairs is another common example, because it requires all children to use their
hearing and to respond according to the presence or absence of sound. The teaching staff will direct the child's attention to other environmental sounds that occur
on an incidental basis (e.g., classroom telephone ringing, school bell) and will instruct the child to respond differently to each sound. Incorporating activities that
involve vision and listening into the ongoing preschool routines provides the
child with numerous worthwhile opportunities to practice the skills in a distrib-
uted fashion throughout the day.

MEETING INDIVIDUAL STUDENT
CONCERNS THROUGHOUT DAILY ROUTINES

The need for specified adaptations is contingent on individual student strengths
and needs. When a child's particular learning needs require adaptations, these
are brought to the child and incorporated into meaningful activities throughout
the day. This section reviews typical activities from an inclusive preschool schedule in order to provide examples of the manner in which adaptations can be
incorporated.

Arrival and Greeting

As children arrive at the classroom, it is important to facilitate the child's greeting
of peers on a one-to-one basis by encouraging individual children to come together long enough to exchange a look, a touch, and/or a verbalization. This informal interaction helps to ensure that the children are aware of one another. In
addition, the child with severe and multiple disabilities should be encouraged to
greet the teacher. If the child has extremely limited vision and hearing, it is im-

portant for each person to have a unique name sign or object cue so that the child will know with whom he or she is interacting. For example, if a particular staff person always wears a certain ring, that staff person may always initiate interactions with the child by having the child feel the ring as a way of identifying the staff person. Similarly, other staff and peers should have unique ways of identifying themselves. One little boy, for instance, frequently wore a baseball cap with an insignia patch on the front. This patch came to represent this boy to his classmate who could not see or speak. Another patch glued to a small piece of cardboard became this student's means of requesting interactions with his peer.

Free Play

Frequently, preschool activities begin with free time activities for children as they wait for the other children to arrive. To facilitate independence at this time, materials for all children should be easily accessible and visible (i.e., not hidden away in cabinets) and have a specific place where they can be found. Brightly colored toys with interesting sounds and textures may encourage children with severe and multiple disabilities, as well as other children, to explore the toys. A sufficient number and variety of toys should be provided. Toys that may be used alone (e.g., puzzles, clay) as well as those that encourage cooperative play (e.g., balls, wagons, puppets) should be available. All children should be allowed to pick their desired activity. Some children will choose without prompting, whereas others will need minimal prompts such as the models provided by other children choosing activities. Children may also need simple gestures that direct their attention to what other children are doing or verbal prompts such as "Susie is playing with the dolls. Would you like to join her?" Other children will need to have their choices provided in a more structured format.

A child may choose an activity after being provided with actual objects or parts of objects used in the activity or after being shown picture cues representing the available activities. For example, Seth, who has a mild hearing loss and a cortical visual impairment as well as mobility and cognitive impairments, uses actual objects to choose his free time activity. Seth is typically given two activities to choose from at a time—for example, headphones (to represent listening to preferred children's music) and brightly colored bristle blocks that self-stick. Seth's choices are presented to him separately, several inches apart from each other and tacked on a contrasting background, and he has a chance to explore each one tactually. Seth is then asked to look at first one object and then the other before expressing his preference. When Seth chooses to listen to songs, he also is taught to activate the tape player with a switch. The choices provided should allow for independent play as well as play with other children. The teaching staff may need to carefully balance the time the child plays with other children and the time spent playing alone, so that the child does not spend more time playing alone than other children do.

Good Morning Circle and Music

The songs, nursery rhymes, and rhythmic activities that are frequently part of circle time and other activities are excellent activities for teaching children with hearing impairments about the rhythm and structure of spoken language. Turn-taking activities and games also permit the child to learn about the "give and take" of communicative exchanges. In group activities, where various children are taking turns, the teacher can develop a procedure that allows the child to know who is taking a turn or contributing to an activity and when it is the child's turn (Luetke-Stahlman, 1994). For example, a peer may tell the child where to look and point in that direction.

To help maintain attention and interest, all children should be actively involved in the morning circle. Children frequently sing the same "good morning songs" in unison each morning. The child who is unable to sing vocally might be taught to use a switch to activate a prerecorded song to sing with the other children. If other children choose songs to sing, then the child with disabilities can also choose a song through representative picture or object cues. Providing all children with rhythm instruments to play involves everyone. The child with severe and multiple disabilities can choose his or her instrument by using picture or object cues and can then be encouraged to play the instrument. If necessary, the occupational therapist might provide suggestions regarding assisted grasping. During this circle routine, the class also frequently sings a special song of greeting to each other. To facilitate the participation of the child with sensory and motor disabilities, the teacher may choose two or three preferred friends of the child and provide tactile and/or visual cues to name cards. The child with disabilities can hold the name cards, explore the cards tactually, and respond to peers by passing the name cards as requested.

It is important that children with motor impairments be positioned on the floor close to the other children and the teacher. In some cases, it may be necessary to use specialized equipment such as a corner seat to allow the child to sit without adult assistance. Using equipment allows the child to be as independent as possible during the activity and frees the adult to assist with the activity in other ways. The physical therapist on the team can input his or her expertise in this area to help determine optimal seating for the child during different activities.

Center Activities

A variety of center activities are typically available in any preschool. These frequently include art, dramatic or dress-up play, books or reading, fine motor manipulatives (e.g., building blocks, puzzles, sticker play, magnet play), water play, sand play, and others. In some preschools the available centers may be related to a thematic unit that is incorporated throughout all preschool activities. For example, in the spring a unit may involve plants and flowers. Thus, the book center may include books about plants. The sand area may be replaced by one that allows the children to plant seeds. The art center may provide the children with materials to create artistic "plants." Regardless of the types of centers available and whether or not thematic units are used, children with severe disabilities can be involved meaningfully.

As with choosing free time activities, all children should be provided with choices regarding center activities. When the child with severe and multiple disabilities is instructed to choose a center activity, the early childhood educator may speak to the child as well as provide him or her with objects representing each center. Thus, the child is given auditory input and visual information as well as a concrete object that can be explored tactually. Prior to giving the auditory and visual cues, it is important to also use language that stresses hearing and listening (e.g., "Listen to Anna. She is calling your name and asking you to play with her," or "Listen, Jake is making car sounds"). Using such vocabulary combined with gestures (e.g., pointing to your ear) can help to prompt listening behaviors (Flexer, 1999). When asking the child for a response, it is essential that the child be given sufficient time to respond (Downing, 1999b). If teachers expect responses too quickly and step in to complete activities for children rather than allowing them to respond independently, children may believe their communicative efforts are not really valued.

Once the child has chosen a center, the child becomes actively involved in manipulating, exploring, and passing objects to peers. For example, art activities allow the child to make multiple choices regarding the medium to be used, where artwork is to be located on a piece of paper, or the implement to be used. Art activities allow the use of materials of varying textures (e.g., various fabrics, colored sand, rice, playdough) that some children will enjoy tactually exploring. If the child with disabilities is working on paper, the paper may be taped to the table-top or wheelchair tray to keep it from being pushed off by accidental, involuntary movements. Materials may be placed on nonslip place mats or on trays or pans with raised edges to confine the materials. For other activities, adapted scissors or easy-to-use glue bottles (e.g., those that simply require tapping on the paper rather than squeezing) may be provided. The final product does not need to look like that of other children. Of primary importance is that it is the child's work, not the teacher's or the teaching assistant's. All children can be recognized for their unique and creative work.

In a book center, all children will be given choices of books. The child with severe and multiple disabilities can be provided books with accompanying tapes. Page fluffers that elevate individual pages with varying thicknesses of foam may be used to assist the child in turning pages. Tactile books (with braille or raised drawings) can be used that allow the child to tactually explore the page. For the child for whom hearing is a strength, books that allow the child to press a button to hear the page read aloud or to hear particular sounds related to the story may encourage greater involvement. For the child with visual impairments, it may be beneficial to provide books with pictures that are clear and uncluttered and that have contrasting backgrounds. In some instances, books may be made that incorporate specific visual adaptations. A slant board with small ledges to hold objects in front of the child can assist in providing access to information (e.g., looking at a book). To enhance communication skills, the child can be asked very simple questions (e.g., "Can you show me where the red ball is?") and then shown how to point to the pictures in the book or representative objects to respond.

Various adaptive skills can be incorporated into center activities. For example, prior to completing an art activity, all children may be expected to put on a smock. For the child whose IEP targets self-care skills such as dressing, this activity provides a natural opportunity to work on putting on an oversized shirt or smock and later removing it. Similarly, the dramatic or dress-up center gives children a chance to practice putting on oversized clothing of various types (e.g., shirts, dresses, hats, gloves). In addition, many art exercises, sand play, water play, and other activities will require that the children wash and/or dry their hands following completion of the activity.

Addressing all of the potential activities that can occur in centers is not possible within the confines of this chapter. It is essential, however, to ensure that the child with severe and multiple impairments is actively involved in any center in which the child chooses to participate. Involvement is limited only by the creativity of the educational team.

Active Play

Most preschools include gross motor activities, or active play, both indoors and outdoors. Once again, the child with severe and multiple disabilities can be given choices of activities as previously discussed. Whenever possible, peers can be encouraged to provide the child with these choices. For the child with physical disabilities, it is essential to encourage interactions with peers during active play so that the child's active play does not consist of only being pushed in a wheelchair around the playground by an adult. In order for the child to participate on the playground, it may be necessary to make physical adaptations (e.g., adapted swings). In some activities, the child may participate in the same activity but in a different way (e.g., pushing a ball off a wheelchair tray rather than throwing it).

During active play, the physical therapist can incorporate hands-on activities for the child who has physical impairments. For example, the physical therapist can add therapy equipment (e.g., large bolsters, therapy balls) into the active play area of the classroom, and all children can be encouraged to use them. Thus, all children can have fun with the equipment, and the preschooler with motor impairments is not singled out in any way. In addition, the physical therapist should share with the staff information on ways to incorporate specific skills into the ongoing routines of the class (e.g., the manner in which the child sits on the floor, how the child moves from sitting to standing).

Outdoor active play provides an opportunity to work on self-dressing skills, depending on the weather and climate. For example, the child may need to put on a jacket or coat, hat, gloves, and boots. If the child cannot perform such tasks independently, then partial participation is encouraged (e.g., the student pushes an arm into a coat sleeve that is held for her). Students who have very limited physical movement can participate by deciding which coat belongs to them and requesting help to put it on. Obviously, on returning to the classroom, the child can then assist in removing these items of clothing and/or ask for help to do so.

Snack Time

The impact of motor difficulties may be evident at snack time, and some children may benefit from the use of adaptive equipment at this time. The specific equipment to be used is determined by student need with input from an occupational therapist. Equipment that may be used at snack time includes the following:

1. Nonslip place mat: Holds plate or bowl in place
2. Plate guard: Allows child to scoop food against it
3. Scooper bowl: Assists with scooping because one side is built up
4. Utensils with built-up handles: Allows a better gripping surface
5. Utensils with Velcro cuffs: Assists child in maintaining grasp
6. Nonmetal or coated utensils: Assists children with bite reflex and other feeding problems
7. Weighted utensils: Aids children with tremors or sensory integration problems

8. Cutout plastic cups: Allows children to drink without extending their necks, and allows staff to see how much they are drinking
9. Two-handled mugs: Allows for two-handed grasping

Regardless of the adaptive equipment employed, it is imperative that the child be positioned correctly so that he or she can appropriately manipulate the adaptive equipment and participate more meaningfully at snack time. A physical therapist should consult with the educational team to provide recommendations regarding positioning for snack time.

The child also works on communication skills by being allowed to make choices throughout the activity, as appropriate. For example, the child can be given the choice of where to sit, what to eat and drink, and who is to help. Because snack and mealtimes tend to be social occasions, communicative and social exchanges among peers can be targeted for instruction. All children should be encouraged to talk to one another, to request more of the snack or drink, and so forth. For example, Anna is a very social young girl who has limited verbal communication skills and some motor and visual impairments. At snack time, she uses a simple AAC device that allows her to choose one of four messages. Each quadrant of the device is a different color (permitting her to use her limited vision to aid in making her choice) and is paired with a line drawing representing the communicative message. The device requires minimal pressure, and Anna is able to use a device with voice output to ask for more snack or drink as well as to talk to her peers. Similarly, if necessary, some children might use any of the switches previously discussed that are connected to AAC devices to activate prerecorded messages. Other children may be encouraged to use pictures or manual sign to communicate at snack time. The SLP, along with teachers and paraeducators and other therapists (e.g., occupational, physical), should discuss options as a team to determine the communication demands of the situation, the current communicative skills of the child, and the need to find an augmentative or alternative mode of communication. What is effective in one situation may not be as effective in another, reflecting the dynamic nature of communication and interactions in general.

Snack time also provides an opportunity for all the preschool children to work on various adaptive skills. For the child with severe disabilities, some of these skills may be targeted within the child's IEP. For example, all children are typically asked to wash and dry their hands prior to snack. Following snack, the children are likely to be asked to once again clean up. Depending on the snack, they may be asked to wash and dry both their faces and hands when finished with snack. At this time, it may also be appropriate to target participation in brushing teeth as part of the ongoing snack routine. These adaptive skills involve all the children and do not single any one child out, but may involve different levels of participation depending on the child's abilities. A child with disabilities who cannot physically perform the task can either partially participate (e.g., grasp the toothbrush) or indicate choices involving the task (e.g., choosing a flavor of toothpaste).

Storytime

As the daily schedule is winding down, the class may move to a quiet activity such as storytime. As in the morning circle, the child with disabilities should be assisted to sit on the floor close to peers and the teacher, supported either by positioning equipment or by adult staff. For example, Tracy, who has limited vision, is given preferential seating so that she is able to see the pictures. Teachers can use "big books" that are commercially available and thus enhance the likelihood that Tracy (as well as the other children) will be able to see the pictures. If big books are not available, an effort should be made to show Tracy each picture. For example, a peer may have a duplicate copy of the book and can be encouraged to show her each picture. The teacher also may attempt to select books that have pictures with contrasting backgrounds and/or pictures that are relatively uncluttered visually.

Similarly, the teacher may provide the child having hearing impairments with preferential seating so that the child is more likely to use any residual hearing that is present. If the child uses assistive listening devices, these should be in place for storytime. In some instances, it may be appropriate for the child to listen to a prerecorded story on tape with headphones.

If children assist with turning pages of the story, the child with physical disabilities may use page fluffers. The child also can participate by asking what will happen next, using AAC devices (e.g., prerecorded loop tapes or prerecorded messages such as those described for snack). Similarly, if the teacher periodically asks the class questions regarding the story, the child may have a prerecorded answer on an AAC device so that he or she can participate in this part of the activity, as well.

As with other activities, active involvement should be encouraged whenever other children are also actively involved. For example, when particular stories are favorites and are read repeatedly, the class may begin to "read" along with the teacher. In this instance, the child with multiple disabilities may be asked to use a switch to activate a prerecorded tape of the story. Or the child may be asked to activate a tape that tells the rest of the class "Ready? Begin reading!" Thus, the child provides the cue to begin the activity. The child can be cued by peer or teacher, requiring the child to respond to a specific request. In some instances, children may be provided with objects or items related to the story. For example, when reading a story related to puppetry, the children may be provided with puppets that they are expected to hold up or manipulate at various points in the story. The child with severe and multiple disabilities can be provided with an item and given time to explore it. The child will then receive instruction on how to respond similarly to the other students.

Closing Circle and Departure

The child with severe and multiple disabilities needs to be encouraged to say good-bye to peers in a similar manner in which greetings were facilitated. Once again, the child can be positioned on the floor close to peers and the teacher, as opposed to in a wheelchair at the back of the group. Saying good-bye could mean waving, lifting an arm partway, looking at a peer, or raising one's head. The teacher, paraeducator, or classmate can cue these behaviors. If the class sings a farewell song, the child can use a switch to activate a prerecorded tape of the song. Involvement in any songs sung at this time can be similar to involvement discussed for the good morning circle.

Summary

Although the preschooler with severe and multiple impairments may have numerous needs as well as many professionals involved on the educational team, it is important to remember that the child must be treated in a holistic fashion. That is, the team members must work together collaboratively to meet the needs of the whole child. Team members share roles and move beyond traditional discipline boundaries to facilitate addressing the needs of the whole child. Such an approach also will have value for all children, who have different needs regardless of ability level.

GENERAL GUIDELINES TO ENHANCE INTERACTIONS

General modifications to the classroom environment can establish occasions for children with severe disabilities to interact with their peers without disabilities. For example, the early childhood educator can provide certain materials that encourage more than one child to play together simultaneously. Chandler (1998) recommended developing a specific center within the preschool classroom that emphasizes peer interactions. This center then becomes one of the options during center time. This peer interaction play center (the PALS center) is structured around the following variables: 1) children are paired so that those with social delays play with peers with more age-appropriate social skills; 2) adults prompt and reinforce positive social interactions; 3) materials that promote social play are used and materials are limited in number; and 4) adults provide the initial structure for activities by introducing them, describing or modeling how materials are used, and asking the children to play together. For many children, the skills developed in the PALS center will generalize to other activities and interactions (Chandler, 1998). For other children, adults in the class will need to prompt and reinforce positive peer interactions in play activities outside the PALS center to facilitate generalization of these skills.

Favazza, Phillipsen, and Kumar (2000) examined ways to promote acceptance of young children with disabilities by their classmates. They found that a structured program using stories about children with disabilities and supported play was much more effective at facilitating acceptance than no stories or supported play. Favazza et al. concluded that teachers play a critical role in establishing an accepting environment. Considerable data exist to support the notion that simply putting children physically together to learn will not necessarily lead to truly social and interactive play. Rather, children with and without disabilities (and children with severe disabilities in particular) need instructional support to learn how to interact (Favazza et al., 2000; Frea et al., 1999; Wolfberg et al., 1999). For example, in a qualitative study of 16 preschools in 5 states, Wolfberg et al. (1999) found that the children with significant disabilities expressed the desire to participate in the peer culture but lacked the social competence to be successful. Their study confirmed that both the children with significant disabilities and those without disabilities needed to be taught how to interact. The teachers needed to help the children find common goals. Adults can take a facilitative role by suggesting activities, directing children to play together, recommending sharing of toys, and providing feedback and redirection as needed.

PLANNING FOR DAILY TRANSITIONS

Following a clear routine that does not change considerably from day to day will help children of all ages anticipate events and order their world. Access to a pictorial or object schedule prior to and following each activity can help reduce anxiety regarding transition times and can facilitate communication (Hodgdon, 1996; Schmit, Alper, Raschke, & Ryndak, 2000). In Table 4.1, a sample preschool schedule, an object schedule is used throughout the day to facilitate smooth transitions between activities. Use of either an object schedule or a picture schedule typically involves providing the child with a concrete, visual representation of the next activity in which that child will be participating. If an object schedule is being used, the child might be asked to hold onto an object as he or she moves to the next activity, thus helping to clarify the representative role of the object. For example, if a small car is used to represent free play, Seth would then use that car at least part of the time during free play. Subsequently, the child would be asked to place the object in a "finished" or "done" location to indicate for the child that the activity has ended and that it is time to move to a new activity. This type of object representation works well so long as children remain in one classroom. When they move from class to class, as at the secondary level, a more portable object system must be developed (e.g., small parts of objects can be placed in a small book) as described in Chapter 3.

Object and picture schedules can serve a communicative purpose if there is an expectation for active involvement on the part of the child (Rowland & Schweigert, 1989). For example, the child may give the symbol for the activity to someone or place it in the finished bin to indicate an activity is completed. When the child is presented with the calendar or schedule, the child would be expected to point to, pick up, or touch the next symbol. Subsequently, the child might be expected to move in the direction of the activity indicated by the symbol, to look in that direction, to indicate preference for that activity (e.g., smiling, frowning), or to gather materials to participate in the activity. The use of such a system is essential in assisting children with severe disabilities to understand and anticipate what is happening to them and around them.

PROVIDING INSTRUCTIONAL SUPPORT

The interaction styles that the adults in the environment use with the child with severe and multiple impairments will likely influence the way in which peers interact with that child. For example, the adults should not baby or interact with the child with disabilities in an infantile manner. Sometimes adults interact in such a way unintentionally based on the child's disabilities or because the child is so much smaller in stature than the other children. The adults in the environment should interact with and talk to the child with disabilities in the same manner they would with others who are the same chronological age; however, adults in the preschool environment should remember that there is typically a 2- or 3-year age range within the environment. The manner in which they interact with 3-year-olds will be different from that used with 5-year-olds.

In addition, the manner in which instructional support is provided must be monitored and should facilitate the child's ability to interact with peers, engage in active play, and learn specific critical skills. At this age, the child is learning how to function as part of a larger social group. Overdependence on a special caregiver or instructor will teach the child to look to this individual for direction and assistance and not toward the true leader of the class. Systematic fading techniques must thus be applied appropriately so that the child can learn to respond as others in the class respond. Considerable finesse and skill are required to ensure that the necessary support is provided as concerns arise without dominating the child's attention with an adaptation or unwittingly dominating the class with the child's concerns.

There is a fine line between providing too much support and not enough. Too often a well-meaning special educator or paraeducator may separate a child from other children in the classroom. For example, a young child is sitting on the lap of a paraeducator behind the other children and farthest away from the teacher when a story is read to the class. This adult may be trying to provide the necessary adaptations and instruction, unaware of the separation being created. Using adaptive equipment that supports this child in a sitting position near the teacher and other children will reduce this separation.

Providing too much support to the child can also negatively influence peers' perceptions of that child. Too much assistance or hand-over-hand manipulation might lead to peers viewing that child as less competent or as the "baby of the class" (Drinkwater & Demchak, 1995). Children with severe and multiple disabilities should be encouraged to be as independent as possible. For example, if children are moving independently from center to center, the child with impairments should also be encouraged to move as independently as possible, using adaptive equipment if necessary (e.g., a walker). In general, when teaching the child new skills or expanding on previously taught skills, overmanipulation of the child should be avoided. The physical manipulation (hand-over-hand guidance) of children draws the child's attention to the stimulation of being manipulated rather than to the activity itself.

Where and how adults physically manipulate a child to perform an activity may actually create an adverse response (e.g., a startle response and extension reaction) to the targeted behavior. For instance, manipulating a child to grasp a toy or spoon by placing a hand over the child's hand may cause the child to extend his or her hand and not maintain the desired grasp. Instead, it may be more efficient and much less intrusive to have the adult use one finger to press the item more firmly against the child's palm to stimulate the desired response (Klein & Delaney, 1995). This strategy allows the child to experience what a grasp is and receive the necessary proprioceptive feedback. Physical and occupational therapists can assist all direct services providers in the most efficient ways to provide the needed physical support without overmanipulation.

Although a temptation may exist to manipulate a child through various activities, especially the child with vision loss, an effort should be made to manipulate the learning activity and items used in the activity, rather than manipulating the child. The goal is to shape the desired behavior in a more subtle and less intrusive way. For example, when children are playing with building blocks, instead of using hand-over-hand guidance to produce the desired behavior, children can be placed close together, materials can be placed close to all children, and peers can be encouraged to touch a block to the child's hand to cue the child to grasp it. Using brightly colored materials and materials that are interesting to touch will facilitate the child's interest in the play. Guiding the elbow forward can assist in a pass to another student or in releasing the item where needed. (Magnetic building materials can be very helpful for the child with little or no vision.) The adult can concentrate on providing only the needed verbal and physical cues to enhance active participation without disrupting a typical play scenario.

NATURALISTIC TEACHING PROCEDURES

Naturalistic teaching procedures can facilitate acquisition and maintenance of targeted behaviors for all preschool children without disrupting play. Naturalistic instruction occurs in the natural environment, is brief and interspersed throughout the day, typically follows the child's lead, uses natural consequences, and targets functional skills (Rule, Losardo, Dinnebeil, Kaiser, & Rowland, 1998). Naturalistic teaching procedures include incidental teaching and naturalistic time delay.

Incidental teaching procedures involve the specification of a target behavior (e.g., use of an AAC device) and an initiation by the child (e.g., child points to a snack and begins to cry). If the teacher decides to use this situation as a teaching opportunity, the teacher asks the child for an elaboration (e.g., "I'm not sure what you want; where's your card?") and allows time for the child to respond. When the child responds, the teacher provides a snack. If the child does not respond or responds incorrectly, the teacher provides a prompt that will elicit the desired behavior (e.g., a model).

An example of the naturalistic time delay is applied to teaching Jacob to use a line drawing to ask for help (i.e., the targeted skill). At predetermined times when Jacob is likely to need help (e.g., putting coat on, taking coat off, getting a drink, reaching for items out of reach), the teacher approaches Jacob, withholds assistance, and looks at him with a questioning or "expectant" look. The teacher waits for at least 5 seconds to give Jacob an opportunity to respond. If Jacob responds appropriately (i.e., points to the help picture on his communication card), the teacher provides natural consequences by providing the assistance needed. If no response or an incorrect response occurs, the teacher provides a prompt (e.g., a model) and again waits for at least 5 seconds. Assistance (i.e., the natural consequence) is provided when Jacob responds following the prompt.

Naturalistic teaching procedures have been used to teach a variety of functional communication behaviors to young children with disabilities (Wolery, Ault, & Doyle, 1992). In addition, Fox and Hanline (1993) used naturalistic teaching procedures to teach a preschooler with severe and multiple disabilities, within the context of play, to put objects in a container, give objects to peers, and manipulate objects with both hands. Filla, Wolery, and Anthony (1999) used environmental modifications (i.e., dramatic play theme boxes and restricted play space) in combination with adult prompting to increase the rate of conversations and the number of turns per conversation for preschoolers with disabilities. These procedures are developmentally appropriate in that they respond to the child's interests and intent, occur within the context of ongoing routines, and use natural consequences.

TRANSITION FROM PRESCHOOL TO KINDERGARTEN

Transitions from one learning environment to another are challenging for most students of any age. The unfamiliarity of the new physical and social environment creates an adjustment period that may result in undesirable behaviors. In a survey of 3,600 teachers, it was indicated that 48% of children have moderate or serious problems entering kindergarten (Cox, 1999; LaParo, Pianta, & Cox, 2000). The child who requires more time to learn about any environment due to severe sensory, intellectual, and physical limitations will need a carefully planned transition when the learning environment changes significantly (O'Shea, 1994). Unfortunately, the most common strategies used by teachers for children making the transition to kindergarten tend to be informal and occur after the new school year starts: 1) talk with parents, 2) letter to parents, 3) an open house, 4) mailing a flyer or brochure, or 5) reading records (Cox, 1999).

Several months before the child is to attend kindergarten, the receiving and sending teams need to confer on the most appropriate and effective transition plan. Obviously, the parents need to be actively involved in the transition process. Moving from preschool to kindergarten is a major life transition and can be as difficult for the parents as for the child. Keeping everyone informed of options and encouraging parents to spend time visiting different kindergarten classrooms will help. The child and the parents need to visit the new environment, meet the new teacher, and spend time in a positive and interactive activity in the new environment. Beginning these transition activities while the child is still spending the majority of time in the preschool environment will provide the time needed for a successful transition (Cox, 1999). During the summer months, family members may wish to allow the child time to play on the playground at the new school and help the child to become accustomed to the physical layout of the school. Learning the route (if physically possible) from the car or bus drop-off location to the kindergarten classroom is one transition skill that could be acquired prior to the beginning of the new school year.

Assessing the Next Environment

Knowing what skills will be expected in the next environment will facilitate the adjustment process when the student enters the new learning environment. These expected skills can also guide the learning activities in the present environment before the transition occurs. Children in kindergarten are expected to follow group directions, attend to their own concerns, and show greater independence (Rous & Hallam, 1998). For the first time, children are being asked to coordinate their various skills (cognitive, motor, social) in a more formal environment than preschool (Cox, 1999). Being aware of such differences in expectations can help to alter both the content and method of instruction during the last year of preschool to ease the transition to kindergarten. The transition to kindergarten and resulting changes in expectations can be particularly difficult for the young child with severe and multiple disabilities. This child needs considerable learning opportunities to understand these new expectations and to participate to the maximum extent possible in kindergarten activities.

Assessing the skills needed in kindergarten should not be viewed as a requirement for placement in a kindergarten class (Rous & Hallam, 1998). Rather, the purpose is to increase the likelihood of success for the transition by planning appropriately and by specifying adaptations that may be needed. The kindergarten assessment entails examining the supports and teaching strategies that will be needed for activities in the new environment (Rous & Hallam, 1998). Planning and support are essential for any transition to be successful.

Developing a Portfolio to Assist in Transition

A portfolio is a systematic approach for keeping important current and historical information regarding a student in a concise, user-friendly format. Any transition can be exciting as well as stressful; a portfolio can assist in making the transition less stressful. The portfolio is developed by the preschooler's educational team, which should include family members, the sending and receiving general education teachers, and special education personnel (e.g., teachers, therapists). The information included in the portfolio should address some of the following areas (Demchak & Greenfield, 2000):

1. Personal information: Child's likes and dislikes, summary of information gained from completing a MAPS process
2. Communication: Touch and object cues used, nonconventional forms of communication (e.g., challenging behaviors) and their meaning, specifics regarding the child's AAC system
3. Medical concerns: Emergency contacts, allergies, medications administered and potential side effects, seizure history, situations that constitute an emergency
4. Strategies and adaptations needed for accomplishing IEP objectives in the context of the general education classroom: Positioning, curriculum/instructional adaptations and supports, vision and hearing adaptations
5. Behavioral support and reinforcement strategies: Form of the problem behavior, purpose of the behavior, intervention strategies, previously successful reinforcers

Other areas can be included in the portfolio as specified by the educational team. Every portfolio is student-specific.

As part of the team developing the portfolio, the kindergarten teacher will have the opportunity to learn important information about the child prior to the start of the next school year. The portfolio provides the teacher with a permanent record of the information exchanged at the transition meeting. This record will likely prove invaluable at the beginning of the school year. The kindergarten teacher may also request to observe the child in the preschool environment or to view a brief videotape of the child in the preschool class. All of these strategies increase the likelihood that the transition from preschool to kindergarten will be conducted efficiently and effectively.

REFERENCES

Bailey, D.B., Jr., McWilliam, R.A., Buysse, V., & Wesley, P.W. (1998). Inclusion in the context of competing values in early childhood education. *Early Childhood Research Quarterly, 13*, 27–47.

Breath, D., DeMauro, G.J., & Snyder, P. (1997). Adaptive sitting for young children with mild to moderate motor challenges: Basic guidelines. *Young Exceptional Children, 1*(1), 10–16.

Buchanan, M., & Cooney, M. (2000). Play at home, play in the classroom: Parent–professional partnerships in supporting child play. *Young Exceptional Children, 3*(4), 9–15.

Burton, L.H. (1991). *Joy in learning: Making it happen in early childhood classes.* Washington, DC: NEA Professional Library.

Buysse, V. (1993). Friendships of preschoolers with disabilities in community-based child care settings. *Journal of Early Intervention, 17*, 380–395.

Cavallaro, C.C., & Haney, M. (1999). *Preschool inclusion.* Baltimore: Paul H. Brookes Publishing Co.

Chandler, L. (1998). Promoting positive interaction between preschool-age children during free play: The PALS center. *Young Exceptional Children, 1*(3), 14–19.

Cox, M. (1999). Making the transition. *Early Development, 3*(1), 4–6.

Demchak, M., & Greenfield, R. (2000). A transition portfolio for Jeff, a student with multiple disabilities. *Teaching Exceptional Children, 32*(6), 44–49.

Downing, J.E. (1999a). Critical transitions: Educating young children in a typical preschool. In D. Chen (Ed.), *Essential elements in early intervention: Visual impairments and multiple disabilities* (pp. 378–420). New York: American Foundation for the Blind Press.

Downing, J.E. (1999b). *Teaching communication skills to students with severe disabilities.* Baltimore: Paul H. Brookes Publishing Co.

Drinkwater, S., & Demchak, M. (1995). The preschool checklist: Integration of children with severe disabilities. *Teaching Exceptional Children, 28*(1), 4–8.

Favazza, P.C., Phillipsen, L., & Kumar, P. (2000). Measuring and promoting acceptance of young children with disabilities. *Exceptional Children, 66*, 491–508.

Filla, A., Wolery, M., & Anthony, L. (1999). Promoting children's conversations during play with adult prompts. *Journal of Early Intervention, 22*, 93–108.

Flexer, C. (1999). *Facilitating hearing and listening in young children* (2nd ed.). San Diego: Singular Publishing Group.

Fowler, S.A., Donegan, M., Lueke, B., Hadden, D.S., & Phillips, B. (2000). Evaluating community collaboration in writing interagency agreements on the age 3 transition. *Exceptional Children, 67*, 35–50.

Fox, L., & Hanline, M.F. (1993). A preliminary investigation within developmentally appropriate early childhood settings. *Topics in Early Childhood Special Education, 13*, 308–327.

Frea, W., Craig-Unkefer, L., Odom, S.L., & Johnson, D. (1999). Differential effects of structured social integration and group friendship activities for promoting social interaction with peers. *Journal of Early Intervention, 22*, 230–242.

Glennen, S.L., & DeCoste, D.C. (1997). *Handbook of augmentative and alternative communication.* San Diego: Singular Publishing Group.

Hanline, M.F., & Fox, L. (1993). Learning within the context of play: Providing typical early childhood experiences for children with severe disabilities. *Journal of The Association for Persons with Severe Handicaps, 18*, 121–129.

Hodgdon, L.A. (1996). *Visual strategies for improving communication.* Troy, MI: Quirk Roberts Publishing.

Horn, E., Lieber, J., Li, S., Sandall, S., & Schwartz, I. (2000). Supporting young children's IEP goals in inclusive settings through embedded learning opportunities. *Topics in Early Childhood Special Education, 20*, 208–223.

Hundert, J., Mahoney, B., Mundy, F., & Vernon, M.L. (1998). A descriptive analysis of developmental and social gains of children with severe disabilities in segregated and inclusive preschools in southern Ontario. *Early Childhood Research Quarterly, 13*, 49–65.

Klein, M.D., & Delaney, T.A. (1995). *Feeding and nutrition for the child with special needs: Handouts for parents.* Tucson, AZ: Therapy Skill Builders.

LaParo, K.M., Pianta, R.C., & Cox, M.J. (2000). Teachers' reported transition practices for children transitioning into kindergarten and first grade. *Exceptional Children, 67*, 7–20.

Lieber, J., Hanson, M.J., Beckman, P.J., Odom, S.L., Sandall, S.R., Schwartz, I.S., Horn, E., & Wolery, R. (2000). Key influences on the initiation and implementation of inclusive preschool programs. *Exceptional Children, 67*, 83–98.

Lifter, K., Sulzer-Azaroff, B., Anderson, S.R., & Cowdery, G.E. (1993). Teaching play activities to preschool children with disabilities: The importance of developmental considerations. *Journal of Early Intervention, 17*, 139–159.

Luetke-Stahlman, B. (1994). Procedures for socially integrating preschoolers who are hearing, deaf, and hard-of-hearing. *Topics in Early Childhood Special Education, 14*, 472–487.

McLean, M., & Odom, S. (1993). Practices for young children with and without disabilities: A comparison of DEC and NAEYC identified practices. *Topics in Early Childhood Special Education, 13*, 274–292.

Odom, S.L. (2000). Preschool inclusion: What we know and where we go from here. *Topics in Early Childhood Special Education, 20*, 20–27.

Odom, S.L., Horn, E.M., Marquart, J.M., Hanson, M.J., Wolfberg, P., Beckman, P., Lieber, J., Li, S., Schwartz, I., Janko, S., & Sandall, S. (1999). On the forms of inclusion: Organizational context and individualized service models. *Journal of Early Intervention, 22,* 185–199.

Odom, S.L., McConnell, S.R., & Chandler, L.R. (1993). Acceptability and feasibility of classroom-based social interaction interventions for young children with disabilities. *Exceptional Children, 60,* 226–236.

O'Shea, D.J. (1994). Modifying daily practices to bridge transitions. *Teaching Exceptional Children, 26*(4), 29–35.

Pretti-Frontczak, K., & Bricker, D. (2000). Enhancing the quality of individualized education plan (IEP) goals and objectives. *Journal of Early Intervention, 23,* 92–105.

Rous, B., & Hallam, R. A. (1998). Easing the transition to kindergarten: Assessment of social, behavioral, and functional skills in young children with disabilities. *Young Exceptional Children, 1*(4), 17–26.

Rowland, C., & Schweigert, P. (1989). Tangible symbols: Symbolic communication for individuals with multisensory impairments. *Augmentative and Alternative Communication, 5,* 226–234.

Rule, S., Losardo, A., Dinnebeil, L., Kaiser, A., & Rowland, C. (1998). Translating research on naturalistic instruction into practice. *Journal of Early Intervention, 21,* 283–293.

Schmit, J., Alper, S., Raschke, D., & Ryndak, D. (2000). Effects of using a photographic cueing package during routine school transitions with a child who has autism. *Mental Retardation, 38,* 131–137.

Tompkins, M. (1991). Active learning: Making it happen in your program. In N.A. Brickman & L.S. Taylor (Eds.), *Supporting young learners: Ideas for preschool and day care providers* (pp. 5–13). Ypsilanti, MI: High/Scope Press.

Weber, C., Behl, D., & Summers, M. (1994). Watch them play, watch them learn. *Teaching Exceptional Children, 27*(1), 30–35.

Wolery, M., Ault, M.J., & Doyle, P.M. (1992). *Teaching students with moderate to severe disabilities: Use of response prompting procedures.* New York: Longman.

Wolfberg, P.J., Zercher, C., Lieber, J., Capell, K., Matias, S., Hanson, M., & Odom, S.L. (1999). "Can I play with you?" Peer culture in inclusive preschool programs. *Journal of The Association for Persons with Severe Handicaps, 24,* 69–84.

Chapter 5

The Elementary School Student

June E. Downing

This chapter addresses issues of inclusion facing the student from kindergarten through the fifth or sixth grade. Public school children from 5 years of age to 11 or 12 years of age typically remain in one classroom for the majority of the day and follow the directions of one classroom teacher. There is a strong sense of belonging among one group of children and one teacher for the entire year. Although the class may benefit from a music teacher, PE teacher, and art teacher, the primary instructor for the group is the classroom teacher. The child with severe disabilities will be placed with same-age peers in the appropriate classroom of his or her neighborhood school or preferred magnet school and provided with whatever additional supports may be necessary to ensure learning. In other words, the student is not placed in an existing special program; rather, an appropriate program is built around the student's needs. The student is not just physically integrated into the classroom but is an integral member receiving necessary support in terms of personal assistance, adapted materials, equipment, and instruction so that learning as part of a larger group can and does occur.

TRADITIONAL FORMAT OF ELEMENTARY CLASSROOMS

Children from kindergarten through sixth grade are typically not ready to spend long time periods at their desks doing seat work. They need to be more actively engaged in their learning (Katz, 1988; Kovalik, 1993; Teele, 1999). Classroom teachers who recognize this need alternate between independent sedentary seat work and active small-group instruction with plenty of movement and hands-on learning. With the acceptance of cooperative learning (Johnson & Johnson, 1989; Johnson, Johnson, & Holubec, 1993; Spenciner & Putnam, 1998) as a viable mode to promote learning, the traditional emphasis on quiet, independent paper-and-pencil work has evolved into a more active and child-centered approach. Teachers initially may present information (in longer periods as children reach the higher grades), demonstrate the desired behavior to follow the presentation, and then encourage students to work singly, in pairs, or in groups to accomplish their tasks. During the elementary school years, children learn the critical skills of reading, writing, and mathematical calculations. With these basic learning tools, they can explore various topics of interest. The typical curricula for these grades not only cover reading, writing, and mathematics but also science, computer technology, social studies, health, art, music, and PE. The skilled classroom teacher employs a variety of teaching techniques to meet all the individual learner's needs in the classroom.

ADAPTATIONS FOR STUDENTS WITH SEVERE AND MULTIPLE IMPAIRMENTS

To include the child with severe and multiple impairments in this type of learning environment, the educational team for each child must approach typical classroom activities with a slightly different perspective. Guiding each child's educational program is the clear identification of skills that the child already possesses and the skills that will be needed in present and future environments. Although many standardized and formal assessment instruments exist to determine skills and deficits of various children with disabilities, an alternative approach may be to look at quality-of-life indicators for all children and use those as guideposts for intervention planning.

As described in Chapter 3, the goals and aspirations of the individual and family members take precedence over the results of items on standardized assessment tools (Giangreco, Cloninger, & Iverson, 1998; McConnell, 2000; Myers, McBride, & Peterson, 1996). Quality-of-life indicators such as friendship development and the social and communicative skills that such development requires, health, safety, ability to earn money to obtain desired goods, and social acceptance in one's community may help keep the focus away from isolated skills measured by assessment tools that may have limited bearing on one's life. Most children can benefit from learning how to interact with peers and adults, follow directions, and creatively explore and manipulate objects for information and/or enjoyment. The child who has severe intellectual and other impairments may have considerable difficulty learning some of these skills and will need assistance to recognize what is expected and possible in various situations. Individually designed support provided for these children addresses these issues.

Because children with severe and multiple disabilities usually do not have strengths in typical academic areas such as reading, writing, and arithmetic, the traditional focus of most classrooms at this age appears at first to create a barrier to inclusion. This perception must be replaced with the goal of identifying what skills the child has and needs to learn and how these can be met within this typical context. One way to create the necessary curriculum adaptations is to view the academic skills of reading, writing, and arithmetic from a functional perspective. That is, the educational team must determine what level of academic skills will best meet the present and future needs of the student. For instance, one student may benefit from learning one-to-one correspondence and counting in order to be able to set the table and play board games with his family and friends. While other students learn adding, subtracting, multiplying, and dividing, the student with severe multiple disabilities can learn one-to-one correspondence and counting.

Different aspects of the same activity can be used to address all learning needs. There is no need to separate students because learning objectives are dif-

Table 5.1.   Basic skills learned across subjects

Attending to teacher

Following directions

Getting out materials and putting them away

Using materials appropriately

Requesting attention

Responding to direct questions/comments

Interacting socially with classmates

Attending to a task

Making decisions

Problem solving

Reading

Writing

Doing mathematics or using numbers

Asking for help

ferent. For example, four fifth graders are playing a game designed by their teacher to determine the probability of a certain number on a dice being rolled. One of the students needs to learn the four basic mathematics skills just mentioned as well as some basic interaction skills. He will learn these skills by counting the number of times that the dice is rolled, presenting the dice in front of each student for his or her turn, and taking his turn, as well. Students participate at different levels to master the skills they individually need to meet life goals. Table 5.1 features a list of some of these lifelong skills that occur across subject areas.

The following sections address, from a functional perspective, the academic areas that typically occur in elementary schools. Specific suggestions are made in each area for students with severe and multiple impairments. These suggestions are meant to serve as catalysts for educational teams who are presented with the opportunity to educate diverse learners together. Academic, instead of nonacademic, subjects have been targeted, owing to the tendency to exclude students from academic areas if they are not performing at grade level. Adaptations and a focus on various skills needed by students (e.g., communication, social interaction, dexterity) should be considered in nonacademic areas, as well.

Reading

Reading is one academic skill that may require a somewhat broader definition to allow for all students to participate and learn. Traditionally, reading has been considered the ability to recognize, decode, and comprehend the written word (Adams, 1990); however, for some students who have no or limited vision, reading occurs by tactile recognition, decoding, and comprehension of the braille code. For students with a severe visual and/or hearing disability as well as a severe intellectual impairment, neither the written word nor the tactile code of braille will facilitate the skill of reading. This does not mean that reading is not important, but that it must be targeted in another way.

The inclusion of listening, speaking, and thinking about literacy as part of a comprehensive literacy approach (Pressley, Rankin, & Yokoi, 1996; Rossi, 2000) applies equally well to all students despite considerably diverse learning levels. Reading can include recognizing and comprehending the meaning of photographs, pictures, or parts of objects. In fact, those who can read the printed word also obtain considerable information and enjoyment by simultaneously experiencing other visual as well as tactile information. For instance, many people browse through clothing or furniture catalogs; magazines on sports, famous people, and gardening; or comic books, to name just a few. These same individuals also may enjoy touching sculptures, various textures, seashells, and an array of interesting objects to add to their visual understanding of the written word.

Teaching students with severe intellectual impairments to obtain information and entertain themselves by "reading" alternative formats is valuable instruction that can occur at times when other students are concentrating more on the recognition and decoding of print. Of course, those students with severe and multiple disabilities who can acquire reading skills in a more traditional manner should be challenged to do so and be provided with the necessary supports (Kliewer, 1997). Students who can receive auditory input can benefit from learning how to hold a book appropriately, listening to a classmate read to them, responding to their cue to turn the page, and following along by looking at relevant pictures in the book or from other sources. This same form of auditory reading can be accomplished via tape-recorded information and headphones. Listening is one distinct aspect of a comprehensive approach to literacy (Berghoff, 1998; McLane & McNamee, 1990); therefore, reading should be relatively easy to adjust to accommodate the needs of the student with severe and multiple disabilities who have functional hearing. If allowed, students can choose to listen to a taped story, a recorded message from a parent or other family member, or a taped letter from a friend. These choices are provided by color coding or tactually coding the different tapes.

Regardless of how students engage in a reading task, it is critical to check for some level of comprehension. Although the social aspects of being read to by a peer are present, learning how to attend to, enjoy, and obtain information via the auditory mode also is important. Therefore, being a passive recipient of the reading process is insufficient. A common strategy to check for comprehension of material is to ask questions regarding content, tone, relationship to other information, and so forth. Although the student with severe and multiple impairments may have difficulty expressing thoughts concerning auditory information, an effort should be made to encourage some kind of response. For a student with visual abilities, pictures from the book or another source can be used to check for comprehension. Depending on subject matter, use of objects or parts of objects also can aid the student in responding to simple questions about the reading material. Clear choices are provided for the student to use in responding (i.e., two or three pictures presented with only one picture having any relevance at all to what was read). Even without pictures or objects, students can be asked if they like the story, if they think it's boring or exciting or important, or whether they agree with the information. Students need to learn that they will be expected to respond in some manner to questions, that their opinion is important and will be sought, and that listening to material requires active involvement on their part. Such interaction among teacher and students is typical, happens frequently during each school day, and provides an opportunity to support the development of conversational skills.

Table 5.2. Ideas for including students in reading activities

Students read their pictorial/written or tactile/written schedules before and after every activity.

Students read pictorial/written menus before lunch (if they buy lunch).

Students listen to a chosen library book read by a volunteer or older student.

Students listen to information on tapes.

Students read pictorial/written or tactile/written directions prior to performing steps in a familiar activity (e.g., recycling, getting ready to go home).

Students reread stories/reports they have created with pictures/words and/or tactile items/words.

Students read sequenced photograph albums of family or school outings.

Students read pictures in the newspaper, comic books, or magazines.

Students read significantly abbreviated stories made with pictures and a few simple sentences.

Some students have sufficient vision to see print. These students may acquire some sight word vocabulary and/or individual letter recognition that is paired with the information they more readily perceive (e.g., pictorial and tactile). Literacy instruction that is an active, integrative approach to reading holds considerable promise for students with various severe disabilities in general education classes (Ryndak, Morrison, & Sommerstein, 1999). Making sure the student has access to the printed word in the natural environment and encouraging the student to associate these words with pictures or items of interest expose the student to a whole-language approach to reading. Tefft-Cousin, Weekly, and Gerard (1993) documented the use of this approach for some students.

The technique of pairing the written word with pictorial and/or tactile information can be used effectively across activities and settings. For example, as mentioned in Chapter 3, students can read their schedules of pictorial/written combinations to organize their day. Alberto and Fredrick (2000) stated the many benefits of picture reading and outlined a systematic procedure for instruction. Pictures have been used successfully to teach students with multiple disabilities to perform different tasks, as well (Roberson, Gravel, Valcante, & Maurer, 1992). The aim is to be creative and flexible so that desired outcomes can be reached (e.g., following pictorial/written instructions for greater independence or learning ways to entertain oneself) without excluding students from the frequently occurring activity of reading. The student is not denied access to reading instruction, but is expected to partially participate in the activity to reach individually determined goals that may or may not resemble reading mastery. Table 5.2 presents examples of alternative ways to "read."

Writing

It may not be possible for many students with severe and multiple disabilities to write using a pen/pencil or traditional keyboard; however, writing is a form of self-expression that can take multiple forms. When students in various grades are engaged in writing activities, the student with severe and multiple disabilities can be provided alternative writing media from which to choose, including pictures, photographs, small objects, parts of objects, textures, stamp pad designs, stickers, paint, wide felt-tip pens, and so forth. For students without vision, a brailler can be used to create a tactile design, or a mesh screen can be used with thin paper and a blunt pointed instrument (pen, knitting needle) to make tactile creations.

Regardless of the medium used, students should be encouraged to express themselves. The printed word or words are added to this form of expression, either by a classmate or an adult. Later, this written work can be "read" by the student with the help of a peer. Even if students cannot physically manipulate the different media to express themselves, they can still choose from various symbols offered to them while a classmate or adult affixes those chosen symbols to the paper.

General education classes offer many opportunities to help students develop their creative writing or creative expression skills. Due to physical limitations, however, students may need to use adaptive writing tools (Wisniewski & Anderson, 1995). Simple adaptations such as adding foam, clay, or a rubber ball to a writing tool can allow a student easier means of grasping it. An empty roll-on deodorant bottle filled with paint can become an easy-to-roll applicator. Also, a T-shaped pencil or pen holder can be obtained commercially or made by melting the writing or painting instrument into and perpendicular to a wide glue stick (i.e., for a hot glue gun). The student grasps the glue stick and pushes the pen or pencil forward. For students unable to use their hands, a head or mouth stick might be more appropriate. The paper for these students will need to be elevated on a slant board for easier access. Students can also wear 1- or 2-ounce weighted cuffs to help stabilize arms and arm movements. In addition, paper may need to be firmly anchored to a table or wheelchair tray by being taped down, placed on Dycem (or rubberized place mat), or held by a clipboard.

A computer may be the most effective means by which some students express themselves during writing activities. Switch devices and adaptive keyboards may be needed. Obviously, software programs that have clear and colorful graphic symbols to choose from for students who have some vision will be preferred. Interesting auditory feedback for students without vision is another option.

Other light- or low-technology can be used to include a student with severe and multiple disabilities in writing activities as described in the following example. First graders are learning to make rhyming words by changing the first letter of the word and using the rhyming words in paired sentences. Although Raul doesn't spell or read, he is an active participant in this activity. Depending on the word to be rhymed, the paraeducator puts certain letters on Raul's Ablenet spinner that is turned by a squeeze switch. When Raul's partner requests a letter from him, he squeezes the switch and activates the spinner. When it stops on a letter, he is told what letter it is by his partner, who also tells him what rhyming word it makes.

For example, the students need a word to rhyme with *bat,* so the paraeducator only affixes letters to the spinner that would make a rhyming word, such as *c, f, h, m, p, r,* and *s.* In this way, no matter where the spinner points, Raul's answer will be correct. As the students progress with this letter, the paraeducator or teacher may decide to add letters that do not work, and then Raul's partner will need to decide if he can use the letter that Raul chose or if he needs to request another letter. If a student has more physical abilities than Raul, the same activity can be done with a student who might roll a specially made die to pick a letter, or the student may be given a letter to match from four different letters and when successful, that becomes the letter the pair uses. For Raul, once the poem of rhyming couplets is finished, his partner records it using a audiocassette recorder, and then Raul plays it for the teacher when she asks to hear what they have done. Raul is prompted by his partner to use a switch to activate the recorder.

Students using alternative means of writing can serve as illustrators of their own work or of a peer's written work. They can also be paired with a peer and assume the responsibility for choosing the topic to be written about (for an entire story, paragraph, or even sentence by sentence). For example, two boys in a third-grade class are given the assignment to write a story. One boy, Mike, has severe and multiple disabilities, although he does have vision and is learning to use it. Mike is offered three pictures to select the topic for the story. He chooses a picture of several different animals; his partner then gives him three different animal pictures to select which animal they are to write about. Mike picks a dog picture. His partner offers him different dog pictures to choose from for different pages of the story. Mike responds to each question from his partner and chooses what pictures to use, what color paper for each picture, where on the page to put the picture, and the order of the pictures. His partner writes a sentence or two per picture to create a story as determined by the order of the pictures. Mike adds page numbers using number stamps or numbered labels, which addresses his IEP objective to identify numbers.

This situation forces Mike to make multiple decisions and respond appropriately and consistently to his partner. It also forces Mike's partner to creatively produce a story that will fit with the pictures. This interplay can be challenging and can also be very helpful to a student who cannot decide what to write. An added benefit is the camaraderie that can occur between the two students as they respond to each other's comments and decisions. Creative works should be maintained so that the students can be paired up again to add to or reread the work.

Sending work home also provides family members with a practical means of discussing activities that happened during the school day. Of course, work always has the student's name on it. Signing one's name (or part of one's name) can be done with any writing instrument, a signature stamp (with an adapted handle if necessary), individual rubber stamp letters, braille labels, or self-adhesive labels with the name printed on it. Students should pick from two, three, or more options (stamps or labels of different names) so that it is a reading skill, as well. There are many opportunities during each school day for students to practice "writing" their names.

Spelling

Learning to spell is a typical activity in most elementary classrooms. Sometimes this lesson is integrated into other curricular areas such as reading, writing, science, and social studies. Other teachers treat spelling as a more separate skill area. In either case, adaptations are needed to include students with severe and multiple disabilities in spelling activities.

For students with severe disabilities who are learning to recognize some letters or words, participation in spelling activities can be similar to that of students without disabilities. Students can be helped to pick a few words most relevant to their learning needs and interests from the list of spelling words for the class, using a picture or object that matches the word. Students can learn to match the picture or object to the word, match the same words, or match the first letter of the word to the whole word. Color cues can be added for ease of teaching (to clarify the matching task) and then can be faded as the child begins to cue into the printed word (Jan & Groenveld, 1993; Kelley, Davidson, & Sanspree, 1993). The student can study with a peer who works on the entire spelling list but who also asks the student to do one or more of the matching tasks just described for the few words that are the student's.

During the spelling test, the student with severe disabilities may be asked to identify the correctly written word that is on a separate card and to glue that word to the paper to be handed in with the other tests (a matching test). The person supporting this student can decide if the choice is from a field of two words, three words, or any number of words depending on the student's ability. Another option is for the student to identify the first letter of the word to be spelled from a variety of letters offered and glue that letter (or use Post-Its) onto the correct space on the test paper (see Figure 5.1 for an example). The student "signs" his or her name using a signature stamp or self-adhesive label and hands in the test with the others. The goal for this student is to match the picture to the word or vice versa, the object to the word, or to identify initial letters of words in preparation for more advanced reading skills.

For the student with no ability to use print, other adaptations will be necessary. Students who can hear may work on listening for the spelling word (again, words most relevant to the student's daily needs/interests) and identify the correct picture (with the word attached). Objects can also be used in the same manner. Three or four options can be provided per word, depending on the student's ability to discriminate across different options and make decisions. Classmates studying their spelling words with this student can ask the student to find the correct picture or object and then spell the word describing that object, write the word, and use it in a sentence. Students can pair up to create picture/object dictionaries that can be referred to when necessary.

Still other students may be asked to select a spelling word for their classmates to spell by feeling different objects, making a selection based on preference, and handing it to a peer. The peer will spell the word represented by the object (or that could describe the object), use it in a sentence, and spend a few minutes interacting with the student and the item as a form of social interaction. The goal for this student is to attend to a classmate, follow tactual, visual, and auditory cues, tactually discriminate among objects, handle objects appropriately, and socially interact.

The student who is unable to handle objects due to a physical limitation may want to select the word(s) to be spelled by a peer by looking at the picture or actual object from a variety of possible choices. Pictures representing words to be spelled could be placed on a switch-activated Ablenet spinner for random selection of words for the class to spell. Spelling words written on strips of paper with an attached paperclip could be randomly selected by the student using an easy-to-grip magnetic wand and handed to the adult who is teaching, who then reads the word chosen to the classmate who spells it. As another option, this student could use a switch that would activate a tape recorder with the prerecorded spelling words on it. The goal for this student is to have an impact on the social environment through his or her actions. The student learns to respond to the

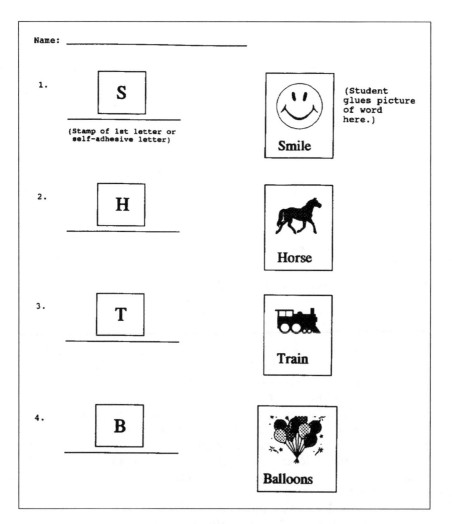

Figure 5.1. Example of an adapted spelling test. The student had previously chosen these words to learn.

prompts from classmates while selecting the next word. Greater fine and gross motor control can be developed depending on what the student needs to do.

Mathematics

Mathematics provides a highly rich and diverse arena in which to accommodate individual students. Determining the individual student's needs is perhaps the most difficult part of any adaptation process. The educational team must continually strive to keep a clear perspective of the student's current strengths and what mathematics skills he or she needs to be as independent as possible in daily activities. Skills such as counting and one-to-one correspondence have ready application to a number of daily activities such as setting the table, buying a sufficient number of items, passing out school materials, handling money, playing a board or card game, and performing a variety of packaging tasks (as an adult). Number

Name: _____

    1. $7 \div 2 =$ _____

    2. $9 \div 3 =$ _____

    3. $4 \times 5 =$ _____

    4. $2 \times 8 =$ _____

Figure 5.2. Sample mathematics worksheet.

recognition and matching also are valuable lifelong skills that enhance the individual's ability to determine, for example, if enough money is available to make a purchase. They will also be able to play card and board games and work in a library, retail store, or any place where numbers are used to organize items.

Basic mathematics skills such as these can be taught during any mathematics lesson, with some minor adaptations. To increase student motivation to learn, a calculator with large print numbers and possible voice output can be used to teach number recognition and matching, along with the appropriate fine motor skills. Students with sufficient vision can use the calculator to check peers' work. This partnership not only epitomizes what is meant by inclusive education but is highly practical, as well. Students can use the same textbooks and worksheets to work on their number recognition, counting, and number-matching skills. This eliminates the need to separate the student from the typical activity performed by the other students.

Figure 5.2 provides one example of an adapted worksheet for mathematics; its directions are as follows. First, the student chooses from three name stamps (the correct one is highlighted in bright yellow) or from three names on self-adhesive labels (the correct name is in bright red) and "signs" his or her name where indicated. The skills involved would be name-recognition, fine motor dexterity, recognizing the word *name*, and eye–hand coordination to place or stamp the name on the line. Then, the student finds the appropriate number to match the number of the problem by using number stamps or numbers on self-adhesive labels with the same cues used for choosing his or her name. The student places or stamps the number in the corresponding place on the worksheet. The skills used are number recognition, fine motor dexterity, number matching, eye–hand coordination, and number sequencing. Next, the student is given the first number (7) in Problem 1 on a blank card and asked to find it on a large, clear, easy-to-read number line and to place the card on top of the number. The student repeats this process with the second number (2) that has been written on a yellow card. The involved skills are number identification and matching. After that, the student is told and shown that the bigger number is to the right of the smaller number, and the student is asked to find the bigger number (7). Initially, some students may need the additional color cue of the card to help with the skill. The related skills are number identification and the concept of more. The student then picks up the bigger number (7) and finds the same number in the original problem (7 divided by 2) and marks that number with a blue marker. The student is applying the skills of number identification, concept of more, and writing by marking. A classmate who finishes the problem before others can volunteer to help the student fill in the answers or the student can use a calculator to do this. The student with severe disabilities gets credit for identifying the larger of the two numbers, while classmates get credit for doing the math problems as assigned.

Numbers used in problems like these should be related to other lessons (e.g., "You have 7 cans for recycling, and your friend Lindsey has 2. You have more.") or related to money and purchases (e.g., "You have $7.00. 7 is more than 2. You can buy more with $7.00.") Students unable to handle items could use a switch and rotary scanner to match the numbers in the problems and determine which one is bigger. Students who need to work on rote counting can use manipulatives to depict the problem (e.g., dollar bills, toothpicks in a holder or styrofoam square, or magnets.)

Manipulatives can and should be used to clarify the skills being taught. Students can use dollar bills, playing cards, dominoes, Unifix Cubes, Popsicle sticks, magnets, poker chips, marbles, building blocks, dice, stickers, toy soldiers, and so on (depending on what is appropriate for their age) any time they are working with numbers. Certain manipulatives—such as board games, cards, dominoes, and money—teach not only basic mathematics skills, such as number recognition, matching, and sequencing but also typical leisure activities and appropriate social skills. This use of manipulatives benefits the entire class, making the mathematical concepts easier to understand and more motivating. The use of manipulatives that relate to other topics being studied in language arts, science, and social studies helps to integrate lessons and helps students to see their interrelatedness.

When students do not have enough vision to engage in the basic arithmetic skills of number recognition and matching, the activity must be adapted somewhat to target counting real objects. For example, students in a sixth-grade class are learning beginning algebra. They are learning to manipulate equations to determine missing numerical values. The teacher is interested in the thought process of how this occurs and is not particularly concerned with what numbers are used. The students are working in groups of three to figure out individual problems. Cyndi, for example, is assigned to one group. Cyndi has very limited vision, moderate hearing loss, and mild quadriplegic cerebral palsy. She also puts most objects in her mouth, has a problem with excessive drool, and is not very responsive to her peers. In this mathematics lesson Cyndi uses a magnetic wand to pick up magnetic bingo pieces (or paper clips). She pulls the objects off the wand and is learning to hand them to a peer in response to their tactile and auditory request. The number of objects she hands them becomes one number in their equation. She does this twice per equation, while her peers figure out the third missing number.

Cyndi is learning to handle objects appropriately and respond to her peers. She also enjoys the feel of the magnet's strength, and pulling the objects off the magnetic wand improves her fine motor control. The special education support teacher or paraeducator prevents her from putting objects in her mouth by simply blocking those movements and redirecting her to manipulate the objects with her hands instead. All students' needs are being met within this one activity. (Obviously, the same process could be used for basic addition, subtraction, multiplication, and division practice, as well.)

To instruct her class on fractions, a fifth-grade teacher demonstrates what she would like the class to do on the board. Then, she provides each pair of students with a cardboard pizza. Students are to develop a number of word problems using the pizzas and targeting fractions. For every problem they develop, they must create the cardboard pizza that goes with the problem.

Ari does not have the math skills to do this exactly like the other students, but he is learning to count and that skill can be embedded within this lesson. Ari has no vision and does not use speech. He needs to learn to work with a peer and to ask for a break by handing someone a tactile card requesting this or by using a BIGmack (a voice output communication aid) instead of screaming. During the instructions and demonstration on the board at the beginning of this lesson, Ari works with a paraeducator (or vision teacher) to group the class in pairs using Popsicle sticks with names of class members on them. He uses a board with Handi-Tak drops placed in pairs on it. Ari must pick up a Popsicle stick and place it on the HandiTak until all the names have been used. While he is doing this, he gets repeated opportunities to learn counting to two, and he gets to recognize his name in braille on one of the Popsicle sticks. Then, when the teacher has finished with her demonstration and wants to pair students to work on their fraction problems, she asks Ari for the pairings. Ari must hand her the board on request and then will listen for his name to be called with his partner. His partner assumes responsibility for finding Ari and making sure that they have the materials they need.

To assist in the development of the word problems that address fractions, Ari rolls one specially designed die for the numerator (e.g., only numbers 1–4) and another die for the denominator (e.g., only numbers 5–9). The dice have glue drops on them for tactual information for Ari to learn counting. His partner must use the numbers that Ari rolls for the creation of word problems. When the pizza pieces are cut according to the problem, Ari is asked to get a certain number of pieces (count) and to put them together into a whole. In this way, both students are challenged by the task and learn to work together.

Another example targets a fifth-grade classroom where students study the concepts of volume and weight through the use of popped popcorn. One fifth grader, Paco, has no vision or hearing and uses a wheelchair for mobility. The classroom teacher thought that using popcorn would make good use of Paco's olfactory abilities and would be fun for everyone. Students were assigned to groups of six and given popcorn, a popcorn popper, oil, measuring tools, a scale, and so forth. Paco delivers these items to each group using his tray and the help of a classmate. Classmates thank Paco by rubbing his arm, which Paco likes. With his group, Paco explores the items tactually before helping to pour the popcorn into a measuring cup and then into the popcorn popper. (The popper is washed after Paco explores it.) He is learning to grasp and release items and to control his movements so as to better handle various items. Paco does this while members of his group decide how to determine the weight and volume of the corn once it is popped. Paco helps add oil and then uses a switch device to activate the popcorn popper. His classmates tactually cue him to start, maintain pressure, and stop when the popcorn is ready.

Members of Paco's group calculate the volume of popcorn and help Paco pour it into a bowl to weigh it. They fill out the worksheet accompanying the lesson while eating the popcorn. Paco is in charge of the salt shaker, and members of his group must tactually request it and then return it to him. Paco is learning to respond quickly and appropriately to all such requests. All groups report their findings while Paco and a few classmates clean up the materials. (A higher-grade level of students working on percentages and probability can engage in a similar activity by popping only a certain number of popcorn kernels at one time and trying to predict the probability of all kernels being popped and the percentage popped each time. This lesson provides opportunities for a student with severe and multiple disabilities to handle small items and count raw and popped kernels.)

Regardless of the materials used or how mathematics is targeted in a variety of activities, the emphasis should be on functionality for the learner as well as fun. Rote drill and practice, aside from being boring, may leave the student wondering how the information relates to anything meaningful. Teachers must be prepared to change activities frequently (still addressing the same or similar mathematics concepts, but in different ways). Whenever possible, students should be offered choices of materials, activities, partners, software programs, and so on, and the student should easily detect the element of fun. Because numerical concepts are prevalent in many games and enjoyable activities, keeping the learning of mathematics active and entertaining should not be too difficult.

Science

As in the area of mathematics, science offers countless ways to actively include a wide range of learners. Science activities typically involve hands-on manipulation of materials to determine the underlying principles being studied (Abruscato, 2001; Gurganus, Janas, & Schmitt, 1995; Mastropieri & Scruggs, 1995). Materials need to be gathered, arranged, and manipulated in such a way that an end result is attained. Some activities require that careful attention be paid to the precise manner in which materials are manipulated, whereas other activities allow more creative and independent actions. Either way, science activities offer numerous opportunities for students to learn how to properly handle an array of items, follow directions, and work cooperatively within a social group.

As with the other academic areas, certain adaptations will be needed to allow for full participation and active learning on the part of the student with severe and multiple disabilities. These adaptations will depend on the science activity, expectations for the entire class, the skills of the student in question, and the student's learning needs. Obviously, some activities will require more adaptation than others. For example, a fourth-grade class was studying dinosaurs, a theme that integrates reading, writing, spelling, mathematics, art, and science. The class researched dinosaurs and created a 4-foot-by-6-foot replica of a likely scene from the Jurassic period.

One student had 12-inch battery-operated plastic dinosaurs that had been adapted to be switch operated and were the focal point for the replication. Students in the class used mud, clay, dirt, rocks, and a variety of art materials to create a living area for these two dinosaurs. The owner of the dinosaurs (a student who had severe and multiple disabilities) assisted in the dinosaur research by choosing which book of two or three he wanted to have read to him (a communication objective) and by assisting in the creation of the replication (involving objectives for fine motor control and relaxation of overly tense muscles). He also chose different colors of paint for a peer to paint different parts of the replica (another communication objective). Finally, when the scenario had been replicated to size (involving considerable mathematics skills), this student received encouragement from his peers to activate the switches that moved the plastic dinosaurs within their "dinorama." Although this student may not have learned the same facts about dinosaurs as his classmates, or acquired the same mathematics skills that they practiced, he did have opportunities to practice his IEP objectives, to remain a part of his learning group, and to enjoy the experience.

As another example, a first-grade class is studying aerodynamics—a topic that addresses reading, writing, mathematics, art, and science. As one part of this lesson, students are paired with a classmate and given a paper airplane that they will decorate. Each airplane has been designed differently for varying aerodynamic purposes. The intent behind the buddy system and the decorating of the planes is not only to have fun but to get students to share the decision-making process of how the plane should look. One student chooses how to decorate the shared plane by looking and reaching for a crayon that her peer uses to color parts of the plane and by selecting a variety of stickers that her peer puts on the plane for her. Once the planes are decorated, the paired classmates go outside to see how their model flies.

One of the students just mentioned cannot throw a paper plane, and so a launcher has been designed for her that sits on the tray of her wheelchair. The launcher is essentially a piece of wood with a groove in it to hold the paper plane in the right position. A clothespin trigger with a rubber band is hit, which in turn launches the airplane. The student who is unable to throw the plane must follow her peer's advice to visually find the trigger (clothespin) and apply sufficient strength to it to launch the plane. She then proceeds to launch all of the planes, as one by one each pair places their plane on her launcher. This technique allows for a controlled way in which to see which aerodynamic design carries the plane the farthest, highest, or makes the most interesting maneuvers. In addition, it creates many opportunities for this young first grader to respond to her classmates via touch, gestures, and verbal encouragement. Following this activity, when her partner fills out the accompanying worksheet, this young girl chooses colors for the airplane illustration, assists in running a rubber stamp roller of an airplane design around the worksheet border, and writes her name in the appropriate place using a signature stamp with an adapted handle. She must choose her name stamp from one other to help her learn to recognize her name.

In Mr. Spink's fourth- and fifth-grade classes, students are studying various insects in an effort to learn what it means to be a scientist. They have visited the lab of an entomologist at a nearby university and are in various stages of collecting bugs, labeling them, and studying how they live. They are also engaged in creative writing activities, such as creating stories about bugs, "interviewing" bugs, and making insect diaries from the perspective of a given bug.

Adam, a fourth grader in this class, has a strong interest in computers and machines. Although myopic, he has some usable vision. He is also very good with his hands when he can concentrate on a task. Adam works with a group of three other boys who share his love of the computer. They have discovered some excellent web sites on insects that have very clear and colorful graphics. Adam's classmates ask him to select graphics that they can print out for their report. A large, bold cursor helps Adam track its movement, although his classmates move the cursor to the graphics he points to, and he then presses the mouse to select. They use the Writing with Symbols 2000 program that adds small graphics to the typed words while they compose their report.

Adam is in charge of deleting words to correct mistakes and identifying the word *insect(s)* by pointing to it. Adam types his name and chooses the colored paper to use when printing the report. Because Adam is nonverbal, when the group makes their presentation to the class, he walks around the room showing the small poster they have made of pictures and information downloaded from the Internet. During language arts, when the class is working on reading, Adam and a support teacher or paraeducator will help Adam point to the correct graphics as they read the report to him.

This activity allows Adam to work on the skills involved with operating a computer, finding information on the Internet, making decisions, interacting with classmates in an appropriate manner, typing his name, and recognizing words with the aid of graphic information. He also works on identifying and matching colors (using the bugs the class has collected) and on the concepts of big and little (also using the insects). Tests he takes for this unit of study will address these concepts using pictorial information (e.g., picture of a big bug and a small one).

Other science topics that can easily accommodate the needs of a student who has difficulty seeing, hearing, moving, and understanding abstract concepts include magnetic fields, health, plants, animals, recycling, gravity, and materials that change form (e.g., ice to water). Science activities include weighing items, identifying objects that float versus sink, and categorizing items by unique characteristics. It would be difficult to identify a science topic that would not provide a valuable learning experience for most students. Again, the objectives for the student with severe and multiple disabilities may differ substantially from those for other students. All students, however, can participate in learning, regardless of whether they attain the same end result.

Social Studies

The verbal nature of this topic poses more of a difficulty when attempting to include students whose verbal skills may be severely limited. Adaptations, however, can be made to successfully include students in these lessons and still meet individual needs. The team must be creative in working together to identify which parts of the lesson are most applicable, as well as the best way for the student to participate and learn.

Although reading about the topics typically addressed as part of a social studies curriculum is a common way to teach the information, creative teachers recognize the importance of hands-on, active learning experiences to teach their lessons. Teachers employ the use of films, field trips, guest speakers, and projects to maintain interest and heighten learning. These kinds of learning experiences are important to the student with severe and multiple disabilities. Working collaboratively, the classroom teacher and inclusion support teacher can determine the most appropriate way to make the lessons worthwhile to the student with special needs, while at the same time maximizing instruction for all students in the class.

Depending on the grade level, social studies covers a wide range of topics, such as environmental issues, careers, citizenship, current events, historical time periods, and cultures of different countries. All of these topics can be taught using a multimedia approach as well as by engaging students in a variety of different activities. It is not possible within the confines of this chapter to describe ways to adapt every topic in social studies for the student with severe and multiple disabilities; however, it is hoped that the following examples—on maps, environmental issues, historical periods, careers, and the history and culture of a country—will provide ideas for additional adaptations as needed across other topics.

Maps   In one second-grade class, students are learning to recognize the purpose of maps and to be able to read them. Because map reading tends to be a very visual skill, it needs to be adapted to accommodate the learning needs of students who do not have useful vision. Although Mara is very popular with her classmates and has many useful skills, she is a tactual and auditory learner. Mara says "hi," giggles and laughs a lot, and has good use of her arms and hands. She uses a walker for short and familiar distances and a wheelchair for all other routes. Mara is learning to use an object/piece of object daily schedule to organize her day.

Students have been shown different maps (e.g., street maps, shopping mall directories) and have learned of their importance in literature they have read. The teacher has also given them the assignment of making a map either of their neighborhood or of their school. For those who finish this assignment, they can create a treasure map. Students must decide what symbols to use for their maps and develop a key for the map. Mara is working on the association between various object symbols and locations in the classroom. In other words, she is learning to map the classroom using objects or parts of representative objects. This activity relates well to her IEP objective of using a tactual schedule and of maneuvering around the room. The other students are working independently on their projects, although the teacher does encourage classmates to help each other. Mara works with the special educator, vision specialist, or paraeducator (depending on their schedules) to recognize various objects and to find the location in the room that they represent. For instance, Mara is shown a pencil holder that represents the teacher's desk and is asked to find where that location is. She uses her walker with a bag attached to it to take the item to the correct location. In this way, she also works on an IEP objective of using her walker to maneuver around her classroom.

Environmental Issues   Environmental issues can be taught across grade levels and can involve a number of hands-on activities and informative field trips. For example, the class can request parents and neighbors to bring to school recyclable materials. Students sort and bag these materials and study future uses for them. Ryan, an active and creative fourth grader who cannot see or hear and has other learning difficulties, brings in recyclable items and helps classmates sort the items into appropriate bins. While classmates are discussing future uses for recyclable materials, Ryan continues to sort, crush aluminum cans, and organize materials for dropping off at the recycling center. In art, as part of this unit, students make sculptures out of wire, pop-tops from aluminum cans, and small cans. Ryan tactually examines several sculptures and then makes his own with assistance as needed from a paraeducator or parent volunteer.

The class also picks up litter around the school, sorts out the recyclable waste, and throws the rest away. A classmate serves as his sighted guide, and Ryan holds one of the garbage bags. He also participates in picking up the litter when there are several pieces of it in one spot and his sighted guide cues him to bend over and carefully feel for it. The class takes field trips to both a recycling center and a dump for waste. Ryan helps classmates unload the material they brought to these places and tactually explores containers and machinery that are safe to examine. Back in class, the students write reports sequencing the steps involved in either recycling or waste management. Ryan creates the design for the cover of a class-mate's report using small pieces of recyclable materials (e.g., shredded paper, pop-tops, cardboard, and Styrofoam). Both boys put their names on the report, Ryan using a prebrailled sticky label that he tactually differentiates from nonbrailled la-bels. Although Ryan does not read braille, he does this as standard practice on all individual and shared work, so he can recognize his work and eventually learn to recognize his name.

Historical Period As another example of a social studies adaptation, as part of a sixth-grade unit on the Old West, the class is engaged in playing the software program, *The Oregon Trail*. They work in cooperative groups making the numer-ous decisions as teams. Shawna has a cortical visual impairment, seeing better on some days than others. She uses a wheelchair for support and mobility and has a difficult time holding objects or manipulating them for any length of time. Shawna responds best to movement and bright colors and appears to like to watch the computer screen as the images change. She also smiles when she hears various sounds that are part of the software program. Shawna uses an adaptive switch and keyboard to play with her teammates. They cue her to activate the switch when decisions are made, and they visually cue her to look at the screen as needed.

As part of this unit, the class reads stories on the Old West and compares liv-ing conditions of the 1800s with the present. Students or volunteers read and tape short stories or parts of stories/reports so that Shawna can use her switch to activate the tapes at other times or play a section to the class when called on by the teacher. When writing descriptions comparing the 1800s to the present, Shawna uses color-coded cards containing specific information that she matches using a rotary scanner and switch (see Figure 5.3). Information from her correct matches (using the color highlights) is added to the report. Reports are presented orally to the class by each team. Shawna's part is prerecorded by a teammate, and she activates the tape when cued, using her switch. To culminate the unit, the class reenacts a day in the Old West by dressing up in appropriate clothing, preparing food that might have been eaten then, learning songs to sing, and stag-ing other appropriate activities. Parent volunteers help with the cooking, and the first-grade classes are also invited. Shawna participates in all these activities: preparation, dress-up, role playing, cooking, and tasting of food. She indicates her choices by looking and touching pictures and objects that represent different activities/items of interest. Her learning goals target communication, social inter-action, picture recognition, decision making, increased time on task, and appro-priate object manipulation.

Careers Awareness of different careers can and should begin early in the elementary years. A first-grade class learning about the different roles people play in their neighborhood and community engages in valuable hands-on activities as part of a social studies unit. Field trips are taken to local businesses and public ser-vice agencies. Photographs are taken of all of these places by the students, with help from the teacher and parent volunteers. Pamphlets, logos, and other infor-

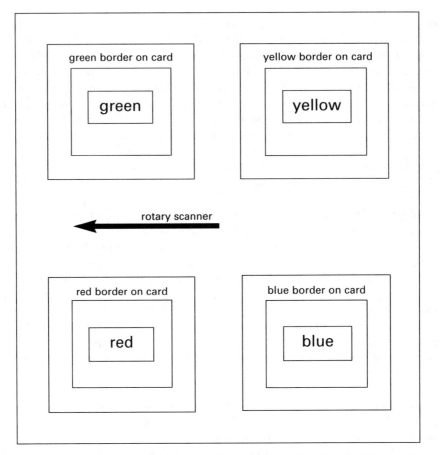

Figure 5.3.   Adaptation to teach matching skills to a student with severe and multiple disabilities in a sixth-grade social studies unit on the Old West. (*Use of scanner:* The student is shown a separate card with one of the four colored borders on it. On the card is one theme discussed during the Old West unit (e.g., transportation, clothing, trade). The student uses a touch-sensitive switch to activate the scanner until it stops at the matching colored square. A classmate then selects a card from the card holder attached with Velcro in this square and must answer a question pertaining to that theme. Numbers instead of colors can be used if the student is working on number recognition.)

mation also are gathered and taken back to school. Exhibits and maps of parts of the community are recreated using the photographs and other graphic information to designate places, businesses, and community members. Software programs such as KidArt and KidPix (by Brøderbund) allow children to create many computer-generated images of community helpers to supplement the other information on the community map. Stephen, a class member with moderate hearing loss and a visual impairment, is involved in all these activities. One of Stephen's strengths is his ability to move quickly and efficiently and manipulate items easily. He also has a short attention span and exhibits disruptive behaviors (destroying materials, throwing items, and screaming). He wears hearing aids and glasses, but he takes these off and throws them when frustrated or angry.

Stephen attends all field trips and is provided additional support by the inclusion support teacher, who clues him in to critical information, directs and redirects his attention, and simplifies the information using visual cues and fewer words. She also anticipates and blocks attempts on Stephen's part to destroy items

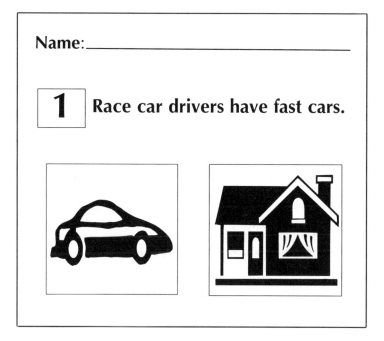

Figure 5.4.   Sample social studies worksheet. The student selects the appropriate illustration for each sentence.

or to run off. He collects pictures like the other children and puts them in a zippered fanny pack to avoid tearing them or throwing them away. In school, Stephen uses a keyguard on the computer to help him avoid hitting several keys at once and to encourage him to look at specific keys before touching them. Only keys needed to run the software program are left uncovered.

As a part of this unit, parents and other family members come to school to tell the class what careers they have chosen and what they involve. When Stephen's parents come in, Stephen introduces them to his classmates using signs for MOTHER and FATHER. On another day, the teacher reads stories to the class about different occupations, which the librarian reinforces when the class goes to the library. Stephen sits close to the person telling the story and occasionally is requested to hold the book toward the class so everyone can see the pictures. Sometimes Stephen needs to sit close to an adult (who rubs his shoulders) or in a beanbag chair for additional sensory input and physical support, while he looks through his own copy of the book being read. If particularly energetic, he may be given a small rubbery ball to hold and squeeze to calm him and help him attend to the story. When the teacher asks questions about the stories, Stephen holds up one of two pictures as his response. The questions are simplified to assist in his understanding of the expected response. For example, instead of asking the question, "Who puts out fires?" the paraeducator or teacher might offer Stephen two pictures and ask, using the sign for firefighter, "Which one is the firefighter?"

This study topic also involves written assignments. Worksheets can be adapted to allow Stephen to demonstrate skills and to hand in his work like the other students. These worksheets involve the use of pictures to write with as well as adapted means of writing numbers and one's name. Figure 5.4 provides an example of one such worksheet. To use this worksheet, the student chooses from three name stamps (the correct one is highlighted in bright yellow) or from three different self-adhesive labels (the correct name is in bright red) and "signs" his or her name where indicated. Then, a peer adds his or her name, as well, if both are turning in the paper together. The skills involved are name recognition, fine motor dexterity, recognizing the word *name*, and eye–hand coordination to place or stamp on the line.

Then, the peer writes a sentence related to the unit of study. The student finds the appropriate number to match the number of the sentence and uses rubber stamps or numbers on self-adhesive labels to place or stamp the number in the corresponding place on the worksheet. The student uses number recognition, fine motor dexterity, number matching, eye–hand coordination, and number sequencing.

The student then chooses from among two or three pictures the most appropriate one to describe the sentence that the peer writes and reads to him or her. For initial teaching, the peer cues by bringing the correct picture closer, tapping it, and/or preventing the student from picking up the incorrect picture by keeping the peer's hands on it. The applied skills are auditory comprehension, visual discrimination, recognition of pictures, matching auditory information to pictorial information, and responding to a peer or teacher.

Finally, the student uses a glue stick to adhere the correct picture to the spot below the sentence and places the picture with the correct visual orientation on the page. The student uses fine motor dexterity, visual recognition of picture and picture orientation, and eye–hand coordination. If the student is learning to recognize individual words, a choice of two or three words on small Post-Its could be used to allow the student to add (write) the correct label to the picture in addition to the sentence written by the peer.

In Stephen's class, the children choose their favorite occupation and dress up accordingly for an "our town" simulation. Stephen is given specific things to do in his role of mailman (a role he chose) to help him avoid becoming overstimulated. Because the activity can be somewhat noisy and confusing, at times, Stephen goes out in the hall to calm down for a few minutes before returning to the activity. The classroom teacher and special education support person determine when this becomes necessary. Either person may help Stephen to calm down, while the other adult remains in the classroom.

Studying a Country   This final example of a social studies unit describes a third-grade class study of the history, culture, language, and geography of Mexico. Students are grouped in fours to research various aspects of the country, each group deciding what they wish to research. They go to the library, listen to stories on Mexico, and obtain their own books. The teacher brings in different guest speakers (some of whom are parents of the children) to learn about the dress, music, customs, food, crafts, and folklore of Mexico. As part of the unit, students reproduce some of the folk art in art class, learn some Mexican folk songs in music, and play games in PE that are common to Mexico. As a bilingual class, they are already familiar with Spanish, which is woven throughout all lessons. Mathematics, reading, spelling, and writing also are integrated throughout activities involving this unit on Mexico. At the end of the unit, each team of four makes an oral report to the class on the information they have obtained. They use visual media, as well, to illustrate their points.

Certain accommodations need to be made for Carlos, who is a member of this class and has significant challenges that interfere with his learning. Carlos is beginning to say a few words in English and Spanish (e.g., "hi," "bye," "no," and "sí") when appropriate. He is also beginning to ambulate with a walker, although he uses a wheelchair for most mobility purposes. Carlos is totally blind and likes to find out about things by putting them in his mouth. He screams when frustrated, bored, or desiring attention.

Carlos is engaged in all learning activities. He chooses which peer reads to him, often preferring someone who can read to him in Spanish, the primary language spoken at home. He may not understand everything being read, but when the reader pauses, he does indicate by vocalizing and hitting the book that he wants the reader to continue. He also listens for longer periods of time when allowed to hold objects related to the unit (e.g., a gourd or onyx piece of artwork). He is prevented from putting objects in his mouth by the paraeducator, who uses her arm to block this movement. She immediately redirects him to explore the items with his hands only, but does not draw any negative attention to this behavior. He chooses topics for peers to help him investigate by indicating "no" or "okay" when asked.

Carlos practices walking with a walker from one work area to another in the classroom, and stands for added weight-bearing practice during some activities (e.g., cooking and art activities). For several activities, he is given different materials that are needed and is taught to respond to his classmates' requests for the materials. In this way, he is learning the names of some objects, how to handle objects appropriately, how to respond to specific requests, and how to tactually differentiate one item from another.

TARGETING INDIVIDUAL STUDENT NEEDS ACROSS EACH DAY

The preceding examples demonstrate ways in which all children can and do learn together across different subject areas. The educational team takes advantage of typical daily classroom activities, focusing on student strengths and adapting as appropriate to meet individual needs. As described in Chapter 3, an activity analysis is done for each student with disabilities to identify when specific IEP objectives will be targeted across different activities (an activity analysis for a first grader with severe and multiple impairments is presented in Table 5.3). Such analyses clarify for all team members how skills will be addressed during the day. They also help to clarify that content mastery may not be the primary objective but that participation in the same activities as the other students does provide sufficient opportunities to practice crucial skills. Once this analysis has been done by all team members, the daily schedule can be devised with the special and general educators, clarifying how desired outcomes will be addressed on a daily basis.

Analyzing the entire school day's activities needs to occur so that everyone involved in a student's education can see how, when, and where critical skills from IEP objectives will be taught and who can provide the necessary instruction and support. Not all of a student's IEP objectives can be met in one activity; however, seeing how the entire day unfolds aids the team in collaborating to ensure a comprehensive and coordinated program. Tables 5.4 and 5.5 provide examples of two students' daily schedules, specifying adaptations to enable each student to participate according to his or her strengths and identifying those available to

Table 5.3. Activity analysis for a first grader

Student: Joshua is 6 years old, eager to learn, and likes being with other children. He is totally blind and has developmental delays and cerebral palsy. He uses a wheelchair but has good use of his arms and hands.

Goals	A.M. Storytime	Spelling	Math	Science	Reading	Writing	Physical education
Increase comprehension skills	Ask who, what, when, where, and how—give choices for answers.	Define spelling words (says yes/no to meanings provided.) Peer puts word in sentence, and Joshua says yes/no if it makes sense, identifies first letter of word.	In 1:1 correspondence, simple story problem, Joshua makes up problem using different items for peers to add together (e.g., coins, Popsicle sticks).	What happened first, second, third . . . last? What materials were used? Who did what? (Give choices; Joshua confirms or denies.)	Ask one of the five W's. Give choices, choose book or program, tell story (sequence), and ask Joshua to confirm or deny order.	Peers write sentences, and Joshua confirms or denies whether they make sense or are funny, scary, and so forth.	What's going on in PE? Who's on what team? Who's the captain? What are the rules? What equipment is needed? Give limited choices for his answers.
Addition/ subtraction by 1	Ask number of people/animals/ items in stories. Add/subtract these people by having them come together or leave (use manipulatives).	Count number of words. Count children in group, then add self. Count letters in words.	Use manipulatives (cubes, beads, raised number lines), work on the same math problems in book using talking calculator.	Count objects used in the experiment, take 1 away and add 1. Count students in group.	Computer math program using manipulatives, number the questions of story: #1 Who—1+1=2; #2 What—2+1=3 #3 Where—...etc.	Label number of sentences written by peer using braille sticky labels.	Keep score, count students on each team, count warm-up exercises.

Goal							
Increase expressive communication; increase social skills with peers	Respond to questions about story (one word or yes/no).	Joshua asks peer to explain words used in spelling ("What?").	Tell answer to teacher by raising card with answer on it after confirming/denying it is correct.	Work with peer, ask question of peer, make comments (one word).	Work with peer who is finished working; ask for clarification from peer ("What?").	Pass brailled notes back and forth (underlined for classmates and spoken to Joshua).	Pair with peer who pushes wheelchair, thank peer, comment on game, cheer classmates.
Braille readiness	Follow along on brailled story, turn page at end, find top of page.	Braille initial letters, line up paper in a brailler, braille name to paper.	Count small manipulatives, count number of braille words per line, count braille designs per line.	Read 1 raised dot (first), 2 raised dots (second), etc. for assignments in science. Add brailled name to assignment.	Follow along in braille book, brailled keyboard for computer, feels brailled question.	Braille name, braille first letter of words written by peers.	Find braille label on door.
Increase orientation and mobility	Have Joshua trail walls to go places in the room, explain where he is, tell him who's to his left and right, where teacher is, give directions to get himself there.						

Table 5.4. Sample daily schedule for a first grader

Student: Celia, a first grader, is a young girl with strong preferences, good use of her hands, and a wonderful giggle. She appears to have much to say but has a difficult time doing so and may scratch or bite her arm when frustrated. Celia has no vision and uses a wheelchair. She uses an object schedule before and after each activity.

Time	Typical activities	Adaptations made for Celia	Goals
8:00 A.M.	Enter class, greet teacher/peers, put things away in cubby, go to desk, stand for Pledge of Allegiance, listen to morning teacher announcements.	Sixth-grader (neighbor) pushes Celia in a wheelchair into her room and helps her put things away after she identifies her own cubby tactually. Teacher and peers prompt Celia to greet them (a vocalization or head up). She listens to Pledge of Allegiance and announcements but is allowed to fiddle with onyx pieces that she collects. Paraeducator goes over daily schedule with her.	Greater independence in daily routines, social interactions with peers, receptive and expressive communication, recognizing her name, and reading her schedule.
8:20	Reading groups—students move from independent reading centers to a reading group with the teacher.	Teacher assigns Celia to a group that assumes responsibility for getting her from one center to the next. The group reads to her, asking her to indicate (by touching) which child she wants to read out loud. Teacher reads for Celia in her group. Celia indicates who goes next. She chooses between two objects to respond to simple questions on the story. She checks her schedule.	Decision making, attending to task, listening comprehension, and reading her schedule.
8:40	Creative writing—students work in small writing groups to create an ending to a story.	Supported by a paraeducator, Celia chooses between different objects she wants to incorporate into her story (to be read by a peer when finished). She hole-punches each page to number them (e.g., 1 hole = p. 1, 2 holes = p. 2)	Decision making, receptive and expressive communication, counting, and reading her schedule.
9:00	Transition time—clean up work, put away.	A paraeducator helps her to go to the bathroom. Celia partially participates in this activity. She throws away trash and puts materials away. She checks her schedule.	Increased independence in daily activities, receptive communication, and reading her schedule
9:05	Music	Celia goes to music room with peers, vocalizes, holds instruments, chooses where to sit and who pushes her wheelchair. She starts and stops vocalizing (singing) as directed. She checks her schedule.	Decision making, following directions, appropriate use of items, and reading her schedule.
9:45	Mathematics—students receive large-group instruction, then work in small groups. Cooperative learning groups work on addition/subtraction word problems related to story being read.	Paraeducator and teacher work with entire class: fifth grader having trouble in math assists Celia and others. Celia plays board games that incorporate counting, making money for items). She chooses her marker for the games. She checks her schedule.	Counting, following directions, receptive and expressive communication, and reading her schedule.

116

Time	Activity	Goals
10:30	Recess	Celia is helped outside by peers and plays with two best friends. She decides where to play and with what. She checks her schedule.	Friendship development, decision making, receptive and expressive communication, and reading her schedule.

Time	Activity	Activity (cont.)	Goals
10:30	Recess	Celia is helped outside by peers and plays with two best friends. She decides where to play and with what. She checks her schedule.	Friendship development, decision making, receptive and expressive communication, and reading her schedule.
10:50	Science—large-group instruction; cooperative learning groups of four do experiment, write results, report to class.	Depending on the unit studied, Celia follows directions from peers, holds objects (animals, plants, magnets, etc.), recognizes similarities, differences, and characteristics of items. She counts the number of items sorted by a similar characteristic. She checks her schedule.	Following directions, decision making, receptive and expressive communication, social interactions, appropriate use of items, counting, and reading her schedule.
11:30	Lunch	Paraeducator assists and physically supports Celia while eating with peers in lunchroom. Celia chooses food/drink items. She pays for her lunch with a lunch ticket, and she responds to comments and questions from friends. She checks her schedule.	Decision making, social interactions with peers, independence in daily activities, self-feeding skills, and reading her schedule.
12:00 noon	Recess	As before, a paraeducator assists Celia in bathroom before going to recess.	Increased independence in daily activities and receptive and expressive communication.
12:15 P.M.	Library—listen to story from librarian, check out book, read.	Teacher assists Celia while listening to the story. Celia holds objects related to story and later listens to her own chosen book on tape (activated by a switch). She responds to simple comprehension questions using objects. She checks her schedule.	Attending to task, appropriate use of items, switch use, comprehension skills, and reading her schedule.
1:00	Computer lab—students work independently on different programs.	Volunteer assists Celia to access computer with speech output—musical program, which she chooses. She checks her schedule.	Decision making, attending to task, appropriate use of computer, switch activation, and reading her schedule.
1:50	Prepare to leave school with class. Get belongings from cubbies. Say good-bye to teacher/peers.	Peers help Celia get her things and say good-bye; the neighbor helps her home.	Social interaction, decision making, appropriate handling of items, and name recognition.

Notes on related service support:
- On Mondays at 10:50 A.M. during science, the teacher certified in visual impairments works with Celia in the classroom, teaching her to make good use of her tactile discrimination skills and monitoring this part of the program. This teacher also works with Celia on Wednesdays at 8:20 A.M. during reading and assists the classroom teacher in promoting Celia's comprehension of aural material.
- On Tuesdays and Fridays, the physical therapist works with Celia at 9:05 A.M. during physical education (this class alternates with music and art). The therapist has Celia do exercises (stretches and range of motion) on a class mat, usually with two or three other students, and then adapts and supports her participation in the class activities. On Wednesdays, the speech-language pathologist works with Celia on clarifying her communicative intent during mathematics (9:45 A.M.) and on Mondays during creative writing (8:40 A.M.).
- On days when related service professionals work with students, the paraeducator or special education support teacher works with other students in other classrooms, helps the classroom teacher with other students in that room, or consults with the specialists.

117

Table 5.5. Sample daily schedule for a fifth grader

Student: Shaun, a fifth grader, has many skills, such as verbal comprehension, some verbal expression, and adequate fine motor skills. He also has no vision, some echolalia, and mental retardation. Shaun uses a tactual schedule of objects/parts of objects with raised dots to indicate page numbers that he reads before and after each activity.

Time	Sample daily activities	Goals
8:00 A.M.	Morning announcements over public address system. Daily oral language—a peer reads a sentence to be grammatically corrected to Shaun. Shaun tells the classmate what the sentence means to him, with help from the paraeducator. The peer corrects the sentence. Shaun checks his schedule.	Auditory comprehension, verbal expression, reading objects, and number recognition.
8:15	Reading—Shaun reads a library book on insects with a peer who reads it out loud. Shaun tapes his book report while others write theirs. The paraeducator facilitates Shaun's verbal expression and checks for comprehension. Shaun checks his schedule.	Auditory comprehension, verbal expression, reading objects, and number recognition.
9:00	Science—continuing unit on insects. Shaun helps to get the materials needed and the work area set up for a group of four. Peers perform dissection, telling Shaun what they're doing and helping him tactually explore. The peers and paraeducator help him with recording findings on a tape recorder. He checks his schedule.	Social interaction with peers, tactile discrimination, organizational skills, verbal expression, reading objects, and number recognition.
9:45	Physical education (PE)—Shaun uses a cane to walk to PE and then warms up with his class, following directions from the teacher. He runs laps using a peer as a sighted guide. Adaptations are used when and where needed to allow full participation (e.g., Shaun uses a batting tee and runs with a runner during softball). Shaun keeps score using an adapted abacus. He checks his schedule.	Physical development, following directions, social interaction, counting, learning rules of common sports, reading objects, and number recognition.
10:30	Mathematics—unit on fractions. Individual numbers from the mathematics text have been brailled for some problems. Shaun is learning to identify numbers and find them on his talking calculator. Peers help with function keys ($\times$, $+$, $-$) and ask him to check their work. Shaun also responds to peers' requests to roll a die, count dots when rolled, and report that number to peers for numerator/denominator in problems they are creating. The special education support teacher instructs Shaun and the other students.	Tactile discrimination of raised dots, counting, use of a calculator, responding appropriately to peer requests, and reading objects.
11:15	Free time to read or finish work from morning. Special education support teacher helps Shaun finish math or earlier work. Shaun checks his schedule.	Tactile discrimination of raised dots, counting, use of a calculator, responding appropriately to peer requests, and reading objects.

Time	Activity	Skills
11:30	Lunch—Shaun uses a cane to walk with peers to the lunch room, where he makes a choice of chocolate or white milk when asked by the lunch assistant. He pays with his lunch ticket. A peer or parent volunteer helps Shaun carry the tray to the table. He eats and socializes with his classmates. He checks his schedule.	Purchasing skills, orientation and mobility, decision making, social interaction, reading objects, and number recognition.
12:00 noon	Recess—Shaun plays tetherball with peers or walks around the playground with a group of kids from class. He checks his schedule.	Orientation and mobility, social interaction, reading objects, and number recognition.
12:30 P.M.	Social studies—unit on maps. The paraeducator helps Shaun create a tactile map of the school and his neighborhood using cardboard and string or pipe cleaners to delineate markers and boundaries. Shaun brailles some words to label the map. He checks his schedule.	Tactile discrimination, spatial awareness and organization, general knowledge of maps and map making, braille writing, reading objects, and number recognition.
1:15	Creative writing—students read part of a story and then write the ending working in pairs. A peer reads to Shaun. Shaun either records his story on a tape recorder or relays his thoughts and ideas to a peer with help from a paraeducator. They cowrite the ending. Shaun brailles his name and adds it to the paper. Students share their stories with the rest of the class. Shaun checks his schedule.	Listening skills, creativity, problem solving, cooperation with peer, verbal expression, reading objects, and number recognition.
2:00	Art—Shaun participates in all art media. He listens to directions and background information. Then, he creates artwork using materials other students are using, unless the materials are visual only. As necessary, adaptations are made (e.g., when students draw, Shaun uses paper on a mesh plastic screen and a dull pointed tool to create tactile designs). He cleans up after art projects and brailles his name to sign his work. He checks his schedule.	Following directions, creativity, appropriate use of tools, braille writing, reading objects, and number recognition.
2:45	Students finish up work, gather materials, and get homework. Shaun uses a cane to get to the school bus. He socializes with peers on the way home.	Following directions, orientation and mobility, and friendship development

Notes on related services support:
- On Tuesdays, the teacher certified in visual impairments works with Shaun on recognizing braille numbers during mathematics (10:30 A.M.). This teacher also works with Shaun on his listening skills and verbal expression on Thursdays during creative writing (1:15 P.M.) and on Fridays during reading (8:15 A.M.).
- On Mondays and Wednesdays, the speech-language pathologist works with Shaun on his comprehension and verbal expression skills during reading (8:15 A.M.).
- The orientation and mobility teacher works with Shaun on Mondays going to PE and on Thursdays going to lunch. This teacher assesses Shaun's skills, develops programs to teach him his daily routes, and monitors his progress throughout the year.

provide support. Both students are full-time class members who receive all of their support services within their typical classrooms.

TRANSITION TO MIDDLE OR JUNIOR HIGH SCHOOL

Expectations for middle or junior high school students can differ substantially from those for elementary school students (McKenzie & Houk, 1993). Students typically do not remain with the same teacher and peer group for the majority of the day, but instead take several classes from different teachers and interact with different classmates. Although cooperative planning by the educational team needs to occur as the child moves from grade to grade in elementary school, the learning arrangement in middle school places new demands on students and may be particularly challenging for some students, especially those with severe and multiple disabilities. Thus, the need to actively plan the transition from elementary to middle school is extremely important.

Due to a limited ability to receive visual or auditory input or both and to process that information easily, students with severe and multiple disabilities will need an opportunity to become familiar with their new school prior to attending it. They need the chance to physically explore the next environment in order to gain some comfort level with the actual physical transition. Supported by family members, this familiarization can take place at the new school in the months before summer break or during the summer months. As with all decisions, the way in which the transition occurs represents a team decision that best meets the student's and family's needs. A student's classmates can be a major asset to a successful transition (see Bishop & Jubala, 1994).

The receiving team also needs time to prepare for a smooth transition. They need information about the student (e.g., likes, dislikes, strengths, limitations), what the student needs to learn, and how the student learns. They also need specific information on what materials or assistive technology may be needed as well as which support services have been provided and how (Repetto & Correa, 1996). Written and videotaped information as part of a portfolio assessment must be shared with the receiving educational team (e.g., general educator, special education support teacher, administrator, counselor) well before the student plans to attend the new school. The sending team can answer questions regarding expectations for behavior, while the receiving team may have questions regarding the most effective ways to interact, expectations for the student's performance, and potential problem areas or issues for the student. Sharing this type of information with even some of the future team members can help to alleviate fears and ensure the most effective transition. Transition planning should begin no later than March for the following school year. Although not legally mandated, to avoid potential problems, collaborative planning for transition will remain important as the student progresses through each secondary grade level.

REFERENCES

Abruscato, J. (2001). *Teaching children science: Discovery methods for the elementary and middle grades.* Needham Heights, MA: Allyn & Bacon.

Adams, M.J. (1990). *Beginning to read: Thinking and learning about print.* Urbana-Champaign: University of Illinois.

Alberto, P.A., & Fredrick, L.D. (2000). Teaching picture reading as an enabling skill. *Teaching Exceptional Children, 33*(1), 60–64.

Berghoff, B. (1998). Multiple sign systems and reading. *The Reading Teacher, 51,* 520–523.

Bishop, K., & Jubala, K. (1994). By June, given shared experiences, integrated classes, and equal opportunities, Jaime will have a friend. *Teaching Exceptional Children, 21*(1), 36–40.

Giangreco, M.F., Cloninger, C.J., & Iverson, V.S. (1998). *Choosing outcomes and accommodations for children (COACH): A guide to educational planning for students with severe disabilities* (2nd ed.). Baltimore: Paul H. Brookes Publishing Co.

Gurganus, S., Janas, M., & Schmitt, L. (1995). Science instruction: What special education teachers need to know and what roles they need to play. *Teaching Exceptional Children, 27*(4), 7–9.

Jan, J.E., & Groenveld, M. (1993). Visual behaviors and adaptations associated with cortical and ocular impairment in children. *Journal of Vision Impairments and Blindness, 87,* 101–105.

Johnson, D.W., & Johnson, R.T. (1989). *Cooperation and competition: Theory research.* Edina, MN: Interaction Books.

Johnson, D.W., Johnson, R.T., & Holubec, E. (1993). *Circles of learning: Cooperation in the classroom* (4th ed.). Edina, MN: Interaction Books.

Katz, L. (1988). Engaging children's minds: The implications of research for early childhood education. In C. Warger (Ed.), *A resource guide to public school early childhood programs* (pp. 32–52). Alexandria, VA: Association for Supervision and Curriculum Development.

Kelley, P., Davidson, R., & Sanspree, M.J. (1993). Vision and orientation and mobility consultations for children with severe multiple disabilities. *Journal of Visual Impairments and Blindness, 87,* 397–401.

Kliewer, C. (1997). Citizenship in the literate community: An ethnography of children with Down syndrome and the written word. *Exceptional Children, 64,* 167–180.

Kovalik, S. (1993). *Integrated thematic instruction: The model* (2nd ed.). Oak Creek, AZ: Susan Kovalik & Associates.

Mastropieri, M.A., & Scruggs, T.E. (1995). Teaching science to students with disabilities in general education settings: Practical and proven strategies. *Teaching Exceptional Children, 27*(4), 10–13.

McConnell, S.R. (2000). Assessment in early intervention and early childhood special education: Building on the past to project into our future. *Topics in Early Childhood Special Education, 20*(1), 43–48.

McKenzie, R.G., & Houk, C.S. (1993). Across the great divide: Transition from elementary to secondary settings for students with mild disabilities. *Teaching Exceptional Children, 25*(2), 16–20.

McLane, J.B., & McNamee, G.D. (1990). *Early literacy.* Cambridge, MA: Harvard University Press.

Myers, C.L., McBride, S.L., & Peterson, C.A. (1996). Transdisciplinary play-based assessment in early childhood special education: An examination of social validity. *Topics in Early Childhood Special Education, 16,* 102–126.

Pressley, M., Rankin, J. & Yokoi, L. (1996). A survey of instructional practices of outstanding primary level literacy teachers. *Elementary School Journal, 96,* 363–384.

Repetto, J.B., & Correa, V.I. (1996). Expanding views on transition. *Exceptional Children, 62,* 551–563.

Roberson, W.H., Gravel, J.S., Valcante, G.C., & Maurer, R.G. (1992). Using a picture task analysis to teach students with multiple disabilities. *Teaching Exceptional Children, 24*(4), 12–16.

Rossi, P.J. (2000). Many ways is the way: Supporting the languages and literacies of culturally, linguistically, and developmentally diverse children. In T. Fletcher & C. Bos (Eds.), *Helping individuals with disabilities and their families: Mexican and U.S. perspectives* (pp. 171–187). Tempe, AZ: Bilingual Review Press.

Ryndak, D.L., Morrison, A.P., & Sommerstein, L. (1999). Literacy before and after inclusion in general education settings: A case study. *Journal of The Association for Persons with Severe Handicaps, 24,* 5–22.

Spenciner, L.J., & Putnam, J.W. (1998). Supporting young children's development through cooperative activities. In J.W. Putnam (Ed.), *Cooperative learning and strategies for inclusion:*

Celebrating diversity in the classroom (2nd ed., pp. 87–103). Baltimore: Paul H. Brookes Publishing Co.

Teele, S. (1999). *Rainbows of intelligence: Exploring how students learn.* Redlands, CA: Sue Teele & Associates.

Tefft-Cousin, P., Weekly, T., & Gerard, J. (1993). The functional use of language and literacy by students with severe language and learning problems. *Language Arts, 70,* 548–556.

Wisniewski, L., & Anderson, R. (1995). Managing the needs of students with physical and health challenges in inclusive settings. In D.L. Ryndak & S. Alper (Eds.), *Curriculum content for students with moderate and severe disabilities in inclusive settings* (pp. 243–268). Needham Heights, MA: Allyn & Bacon.

Chapter 6

The Middle School or
Junior High Student

June E. Downing

Compared with the elementary school years, the secondary school years feature considerably more complex academic work and subject-based learning. At the secondary levels, students are expected to obtain information more through a lecture and note-taking format, supplemented by textbooks, than through active, hands-on approaches. The emphasis on paper-and-pencil tasks at this level can pose a considerable barrier to the inclusion of students with severe and multiple disabilities.

In a study by York, Vandercook, MacDonald, Heise-Neff, and Caughey (1992), teachers at two middle schools in Minnesota reported that although they could see benefits of inclusion for students with severe disabilities, it was very difficult deciding how to involve the students. It seems reasonable to assume that teachers want students to learn in their classes and that students with severe and multiple disabilities present a unique challenge to teachers who may not be trained to make the necessary accommodations. Furthermore, teachers are pressured to bring their students to a level of mastery on national standardized tests that can interfere with the need to individualize instruction and accommodate differences in learning styles (Campbell & Olsen, 1994; Fisher & Kennedy, 2001). As a result, the educational team must take even greater care to ensure that the match between typical classes and the individual student's needs is a good one.

Both middle and junior high school students take a variety of courses requiring movement from one room to another and from one teacher to another. Not all students take the same courses; rather they follow a more individualized schedule. Students may follow a block schedule and be grouped for certain academic courses (language arts, science, mathematics, and social studies) so that they can relate to a smaller group of students and experience a more integrated curriculum. They also take an elective course (sometimes more than one) that offers greater individualization regarding interests and strengths.

Some courses offered during the middle school or junior high years involve sedentary instruction, whereas others are more active and encourage movement and more hands-on learning by all students. Teacher style and philosophy of learning determine to a great extent how a given topic is addressed and what student expectations will be. Considerable diversity among teachers exists in middle schools (as in elementary schools), and this factor must be considered when including students who have severe and multiple impairments. The use of cooperative learning groups, peer buddies, and peer tutors can represent very positive forms of support for a student with significant needs (Ryan & Paterna, 1997; Staub, Spaulding, Peck, Gallucci, & Schwartz, 1996).

Again, placement in general education classrooms is determined not by developmental or performance level but by the careful and creative blending of individual needs with the learning opportunities in a given classroom. These learning opportunities could be academic, communicative, social, or physical. Just being physically placed in a typical classroom is not inclusion. There must be an expectation that the student will learn, and attention must be paid to how the student will be actively involved in the learning process. As McDonnell (1998) contended, teachers need to infuse opportunities for students with severe disabilities to learn within ongoing classroom activities. The daily schedule of one seventh-grade student with severe and multiple disabilities in Table 6.1 represents the type of individualized schedule with unique expectations for learning that typifies inclusive education for a middle school student.

ANALYZING THE LEARNING ENVIRONMENT

Just as for the elementary-age student, participation for middle school students focuses on instructional adaptations to meet individual needs within the context of typical classrooms. These adaptations may look much like those designed for the younger student, except that the materials and activities selected and the manner in which they are presented are appropriate to the secondary levels. Age-appropriate materials and activities reflect the chronological age of the student, do not draw negative attention to the student because they are too juvenile in nature, and are such that others of the same age feel comfortable sharing the materials and engaging in the activity. For example, using real dollar bills, computer disks, pens, or baseball trading cards for solving math problems that involve counting would be more appropriate than using different colored plastic counting bears typically found in primary grades. Adaptations will involve both instructional procedures and materials and can make use of a number of potential assistants in the learning process.

Because many classes at this age are academic in nature, the process of including students with disabilities requires thoughtful analysis of the goals of the general education curriculum and how they relate to the student with severe and multiple impairments. The following four steps are suggested to assist in the problem solving that must inevitably occur.

1. The team must decide the underlying importance of the lesson to the student's everyday life. In other words, what parts of the general topic of study relate to the individual student's present and potential future needs?
2. The team must analyze how the classroom teacher is instructing the students to arrive at the overall goal for the lesson. It is vital to know the teacher's mode(s) of instruction to determine if that format is beneficial for the target student. For example, a straight lecture format will present significant barriers for the student who has no hearing or vision.

Table 6.1. Sample daily schedule for a seventh grader

Student: Sandi has many strengths such as effective use of her eyes for communication, some hearing, and a very social nature. She also has a moderate hearing impairment with her hearing aid, significant cognitive delays, and severe spastic quadriplegic cerebral palsy.

Time	Subject	Sample daily activities	Goals
8:00 A.M.	Homeroom	Announcements over the public address system. Discussion of news (school, local, state, and national). Sandi goes over her daily pictorial/word/number schedule with the inclusion support teacher to better understand her day. She refers back to this schedule following every period as a reading and math skill. She brings in a local newspaper for discussion of news and indicates by looking at one of two pictures what topic she would like to address.	Develop pictorial/sight word-reading skills, number recognition, concepts of before and after, first, second, third, and so forth, decision making
8:30	Social studies (unit on civil rights in different countries)	Students read a section of the text on this topic and watch a short video on the subject. They make lists and compare what rights are important to each of them, how these rights can be lost, and how they compare with others. Sandi participates in all these activities but has a peer read to her and explain what is read in terms related to her life. The inclusion support teacher uses pictures and simple phrases to help her understand; the teacher asks her to choose which rights she wants for herself and which she does not want. She reads her schedule.	Develop pictorial/sight word-reading skills, receptive communication, peer interactions, decision making, self-advocacy
9:25	Mathematics (computing areas of different geometric shapes, making comparisons, and relating findings to day-to-day situations—e.g., computing amount of paint needed to paint a house or amount of carpet needed for various rooms)	Sandi is shown which numbers to input into her calculator (calculator is large, with speech output). She inputs one of three numbers (given physical support) while her peers input the others to speed up the process. Sandi is working with two other students (one of these students has a learning disability). The inclusion teacher or mathematics teacher (who alternate monitoring the class and providing more in-depth instruction) provides extra help to all three students. As homework, two friends who are class members go to Sandi's home to measure rooms in her house. In class, they determine how much carpet her family needs. Using carpet samples, Sandi chooses her favorites based on texture and color, and her friends calculate the price. Using an adapted number line, Sandi determines the most/least expensive carpet. (Sandi leaves early with the inclusion support teacher to use the restroom after reading her schedule.)	Decision making, concepts of more/less, number recognition, use of a calculator, pictorial/sight word reading skills

(continued)

125

Table 6.1. *(continued)*

Student: Sandi has many strengths such as effective use of her eyes for communication, some hearing, and a very social nature. She also has a moderate hearing impairment with her hearing aid, significant cognitive delays, and severe spastic quadriplegia cerebral palsy.

Time	Subject	Sample daily activities	Goals
10:20	Language Arts (unit on discrimination)	The class reads stories and watches a film on individuals facing discrimination. The class discusses relevant issues. The students try to determine how additional factors could have affected the various stories of discrimination. Using pictures and/or sketches, Sandi indicates the sequence of different stories (e.g., what came first, second, third, etc.). The inclusion teacher helps Sandi to choose color of paper to use for her report as well as who will help her prepare it. The chosen peer puts the report on the computer using Sandi's sequenced pictures as a guide. Sandi chooses graphics to add to the report. She checks her schedule.	Enhance receptive communication, decision making, communication with peers, pictorial/word reading skills
11:10	Science (unit on biological differences among species—relates to social studies and language arts units on civil rights and discrimination)	Students categorize different species by certain characteristics, using actual cutouts and writing down characteristics of each group. Sandi uses her prone stander and chooses between two different forms to let the rest of her cooperative learning group know which form belongs to which category. She reads her schedule.	Recognize concepts of same and different, communicate with peers, improve physical strength and endurance, reading skills
12:00 noon	Lunch	Classmates ask Sandi whom she would like to push her wheelchair to the cafeteria. Sandi chooses by looking, and they go together. Her friends put her food on her tray as they push her through the line. She chooses items by looking at one option more than another. An inclusion support teacher helps her eat once she is seated next to friends. Sandi tells this assistant what she wants to eat or drink by looking at one of three choices offered. Her friends engage her in conversation by referring to teen magazines. She responds by looking at different pictures and using her facial expressions to convey her reactions. She checks her schedule.	Choice making, responding to peers, reading skills
12:30 P.M.	Breaktime	Sandi goes to the restroom to clean up after lunch. Sometimes a friend or two goes with her to socialize and discuss makeup.	Communication and social skills

126

Time	Activity	Description	Targeted skills
12:50	Physical Education (PE) (Monday, Wednesday, Friday) or Music (Tuesday, Thursday).	Since PE usually involves many team sports, Sandi receives her physical therapy (range of motion, stretches, etc.) at this time. She sits on mats on the side and can watch the class play. She has access to a switch device that allows her to send vocal messages to classmates during their game (e.g., "Way to go!" "All right!"). Anyone not playing sits with her and draws her attention to the game or otherwise converses. A paraeducator or physical therapist does physical therapy. Sandi is much more involved in certain PE units like swimming. In music, Sandi uses her prone stander during class to listen to classmates sing. She uses a head switch to turn on the metronome for everyone to keep the beat. Sometimes the switch activates a cassette recorder, and she tapes the songs the class is learning. A peer hits the appropriate buttons (record, rewind, or play) and asks Sandi to turn on the recorder according to the teacher's direction. She checks her schedule.	Greater comfort and use of her body, social interaction skills, enhanced physical strength, following directions, reading skills
1:45	Drama	Students have a number of creative projects that they do in this class. Sandi engages in all activities involving acting. She uses a simple VOCA to say her lines. Students in her group tend to give her lines that are repetitive so that she will have multiple opportunities to say them. During class discussions regarding specifics on how to say lines to project the intended message, Sandi works with a paraeducator or support teacher to make props that will be used for the skits. This requires her to gather materials and make choices as to color and type of material to be used. The drama teacher, who keeps her work for future classes, appreciates her efforts. She reads her schedule for the last time to see that it is time to go home.	Using a VOCA when cued by peers, making choices, asking for assistance to obtain materials, reading skills

Notes on related services support:
- Twice a week, a speech-language pathologist works with Sandi during drama class. She targets Sandi's interaction with peers and her use of AAC devices.
- The occupational therapist provides her with support during mathematics (twice a week). She is targeting Sandi's use of the calculator as well as manipulation of other materials used during this period.

3. The team will determine how to adapt the materials and instruction to address the underlying theme and highlight its importance for the target student while meeting individually determined educational objectives.
4. The team must determine ways of allowing students at considerably different learning levels and learning objectives to acquire the necessary skills and knowledge during the same (or essentially the same) activity. An example may help to clarify these steps.

In a sixth-grade science class, students are reviewing the human skeleton and the function of various parts of the body. They listen to the teacher present the information and explain what they will be doing in their lab work. Then, they use a paper model of various parts of the human skeleton to piece together and label. They also write the words used to label the bones and joints on separate index cards with a brief definition for study later on.

Although Isaac will not be expected to learn the same information as his classmates, he will be expected to learn what makes sense based on his needs. Learning about the human body does have relevance to Isaac's life, although it may not be the most critical information for Isaac. Nevertheless, he can learn other critical skills during this class. For instance, while the teacher is talking, Isaac, who has visual impairments, mild cerebral palsy, severe intellectual challenges, and very challenging behaviors, works with the special educator or paraeducator to read his pictorial/written daily schedule, and then prepares the materials that each group will be using (worksheets with skeletal drawings, index cards, brads, dictionary). With this task he is learning to follow directions and count. During group work on the assignment, Isaac follows the model of his group members to put his skeleton together. He also learns to identify some parts of his own body from the paper model and to demonstrate what movement the joint allows (e.g., knee, elbow, hip). Isaac learns to interact with his peers as a part of his task. While classmates are writing their definitions for the ulna, fibula, humerus, clavicle, and so forth, Isaac sorts a variety of pictorial cards with different body parts into separate piles while he is also encouraged to identify the same part on his body (multiple opportunities to practice). This aspect of the activity gives Isaac the opportunity to work on *same* and *different*.

This example illustrates how an analysis of an activity can help to determine what is relevant for a student with severe and multiple disabilities, what is not, and what adaptations are needed to make it relevant. Identifying the many skills that are meaningful for this student (e.g., following directions, gathering and handling materials, counting and social interaction with peers) is an important part of any activity.

The process of analyzing activities that typically occur during the secondary school years remains essentially the same regardless of the activity. It may be helpful to look for the essential elements of a given topic to find relevance for a particular student. For example, if the lesson is on modes of transportation, the students with severe and multiple disabilities may be learning to identify a car and determine its use. This could be done with pictures, car keys, seat belts, and actual cars. The study of various international and national confrontations (e.g., Civil War, World Wars I and II) could center on conflict resolution, dealing with negative emotions, and not hurting others. The study of electricity provides an opportunity to teach cause and effect using various switches and appliances to operate. Astronomy lessons can address the difference between night and day (dark and light) and big and little (using planets). All of these lessons could easily involve hands-on and active learning opportunities.

In general, it should be fairly apparent how the topic of study for the day, week, or longer period relates to the learning needs of the student requiring extra support (see Figure 6.1, for example, for an analysis of the skills that could be learned during an eighth-grade life science class). However, when the analysis reveals that little of the topic pertains to the student's life or that a meaningful adaptation would be difficult to achieve, then the team must consider alternatives. An alternative could mean taking another class.

Because earning all the required credits for graduation may not be the goal for a given student, less attention needs to be paid to "required" courses, and more freedom and creativity can be demonstrated in the development of the student's schedule. In other words, a student may choose to take several electives because those classes offer the means of instruction and subject matter that most closely pertain to the individual's learning needs. The same student may not take health, social sciences, or PE, which would all usually be required, but which do not meet either the student's instructional needs (e.g., active, hands-on learning in cooperative groups of peers) or do not easily permit adaptations of topic matter to make it relevant to the student's life. The activity/IEP objective analysis (first described in Chapter 3 and again illustrated in Chapter 5) is applicable to the older student, as well. Table 6.2 contains an example of such an analysis.

Community-based instruction is another alternative. Depending on student and family goals, learning in the community could be very appropriate at this age level (Agran, Snow, & Swaner, 1999; Schukar, 1997). With the increased emphasis on service learning for all students, community-based learning does not need to be unique for the student with severe disabilities. This student can learn targeted skills in the community as part of a class project or research (Gent & Gurecka, 1998). Analyzing the environment of the community to determine learning opportunities and the skills the student may need to acquire may be just as critical as analyzing activities at school. Although community-based instruction could easily be part of a middle or junior high school student's education program, information on this topic is dealt with in Chapter 7. Depending on student needs, it may be even more prevalent at the high school age.

EXAMPLES OF INCLUSIVE EDUCATION FOR MIDDLE SCHOOL AND/OR JUNIOR HIGH STUDENTS

Many of the adaptations described in the previous chapters are appropriate for secondary school students, as well. Approaches for teaching basic reading, writing, and mathematics to an adolescent with severe and multiple disabilities can closely resemble those discussed in Chapter 5. One word of caution is in order, however. Materials used at the secondary levels must not reflect negatively (e.g., in a juvenile manner) on the student. For example, pictures used should come from magazines geared to the appropriate age group, and pens or felt-tip markers should be used in lieu of crayons. Software programs clearly designed for young children would not be appropriate. Rather, facilitating active involvement of all students in typical learning activities is the goal. Such involvement not only promotes learning but also supports real membership for students (Williams &

Outcomes and specific underlying skills	The body — Building parts—structure and function	Ecology — Taking care of aquariums and terrariums	Classification systems — Sorting by species (same/different)	Mammals — Dissection, categorization (color, size)	Birds — Categorization (color, size)	Insects — Categorization (size, number of legs)
1. To have friends/social relationships						
• Greet peers and respond to greetings	✓✓	✓✓	✓✓	✓✓	✓✓	✓✓
• Share materials during laboratory activities						
• Request help if needed	✓✓	✓✓	✓✓	✓✓	✓✓	✓✓
• Respond to directions from laboratory partners						
• Ask to see what others are doing	✓	✓	✓	✓	✓	✓
2. To have control over certain aspects of life—to make decisions						
• Decide to participate in class activities	✓✓	✓✓	✓✓	✓✓	✓✓	✓✓
• Decide what needs to happen first, second, third, and so on in each task						
• Decide what materials are needed	✓✓	✓	✓✓	✓✓	✓	✓✓
• Determine same/different						
3. To get a preferred job						
• Follow directions given by classroom teacher	✓	✓	✓	✓	✓	✓
• Attend to task for duration of activity	✓✓✓✓	✓✓✓✓	✓✓✓✓✓	✓✓✓✓✓	✓✓✓✓	✓✓✓✓
• Obtain necessary materials for task						
• Handle materials appropriately						
• Work cooperatively with others						
• Put materials away	✓	✓✓	✓✓		✓✓	✓✓✓

Figure 6.1. Identification of potential outcomes and skills within an eighth-grade life science class.

Table 6.2. Activity/IEP matrix

Student: Iris has strong interests in music, color, and flowers. She will remain on a task of interest for almost 30 minutes and then does not like to move on to new things. Iris has low vision and moderate-severe intellectual impairments and primarily uses facial expressions, vocalizations, and pictures to express herself.

IEP goals	Math	Language arts	Science	3-D Art	Lunch	Horticulture
Reads meaningful words for recreation and information	Reads picture/word schedule prior to class Reads words on advertisements	Reads picture/word schedule prior to class Reads her own photograph word stories Reads picture/word stories created using Writing with Symbols 2000 software	Reads picture/word schedule prior to class Reads words on list of procedure used in class (with pictures)	Reads picture/word schedule prior to class Reads words in magazines used in art projects Reads words (with pictures) on clean up list	Reads menu words (some with pictures) to choose from lunch options Reads picture/word schedule prior to class	Reads picture/word schedule prior to class Reads words (with pictures) in steps of what to do Reads words that label photographs of herself in this class
Prints her name	Signs all work being turned in	Signs all work being turned in	Signs all work being turned in	Signs all work being turned in Prints name on different colored papers that are glued together to form a 3-D shape	Prints name and writes phone number (with help) to share with friends	Signs all work being turned in Prints name on labels to put on her plants
Identifies numbers 1–9 consistently	Uses calculator to find numbers in problems Points to the correct number that corresponds with each period on her schedule Points to individual numbers on the ads	Points to specific page numbers in stories/books being read Points to the correct number that corresponds with each period on her schedule	Finds number requested on a list of steps to do in lab Points to the correct number that corresponds with each period on her schedule	Identifies numbers on clean up list (first, second, etc.) Points to the correct number that corresponds with each period on her schedule Points to the numbers on ruler when used for projects	Identifies numbers on price of items in vending machine Points to the correct number that corresponds with each period on her schedule	Points to the correct number that corresponds with each period on her schedule Identifies numbers in steps of what to do Points to number label added to items sorted (e.g., one cone seed, three pumpkin seeds, etc.)

(continued)

Table 6.2. *(continued)*

Student: Iris has strong interests in music, color, and flowers. She will remain on a task of interest for almost 30 minutes and then does not like to move on to new things. Iris has low vision and moderate-severe intellectual impairments and primarily uses facial expressions, vocalizations, and pictures to express herself.

IEP goals	Math	Language arts	Science	3-D Art	Lunch	Horticulture
Responds to questions using pictures	Points to pictures in advertisements regarding what she'd like to buy Points to pictures in her schedule regarding her day	Points to one of three pictures to respond to simple questions regarding literature read to her Points to pictures in her schedule regarding her day Selects topics to write about using pictures	Points to picture representing steps of procedure when asked what comes first, second, third, and so forth. Points to pictures in her schedule regarding her day Indicates what is being studied by pointing to the correct picture (of three)	Uses photographs and pictures to choose topics for projects Points to pictures in her schedule regarding her day Responds to classmate's questions about what finished projects she likes	Responds to peers using pictures in conversation book and teen magazines Points to pictures in her schedule regarding her day	Points to pictures in her schedule regarding her day Responds to questions regarding subject matter using pictures (choice of three) Responds to questions regarding what tasks she'd prefer to do—choice of three pictures
Stays with peer group for at least 15 minutes	Works with group of four on comparison shopping	Works with group of three to "write" acrostic poetry using pictures Works with small group to study for tests (she randomly chooses questions)	Stays with lab group of four during science lab Stays with group to clean up	Works with small group on some projects Works with small group to clean up	Eats with a group of friends from her art and/or horticulture class Hangs out with at least two other students after eating	Works with a group of at least two other students on projects at lab table Assists with garden upkeep with rest of class

Downing, 1998). The following sections describe several middle school or junior high school classes (both academic and nonacademic) and the way in which certain students' learning needs were addressed within those classes.

Aey's Schedule in Seventh Grade

Aey, a seventh grader with a ready smile and an eagerness to please, needs to plan for her approaching year in middle school. She will be attending the same school as her older sister and will be learning in all general education classes. Aey has some speech and will respond to direct questions. She is ambulatory and uses an adapted cane and sighted guide to move around campus because she is totally blind. Aey is a very social young lady, who loves music and is talented in this area; however, she struggles to make friends. Her parents are interested in having her keep herself in good physical shape, make friends, and learn some braille skills. These skills and desires served as a basis for developing her class schedule.

In her middle school, students were automatically enrolled in English, math, PE, science, and social studies and could pick from one of several electives. Seventh graders could choose electives from five one-semester courses (art, chorus, drama, nutrition and health, and 3-D design) and six full-year courses (beginning orchestra, beginning band, intermediate band, advanced orchestra, advanced band, and yearbook and newspaper). Because Aey was not following a traditional diploma track, she was given greater latitude in developing her schedule. Aey's team debated the pros and cons of various classes and decided on the following schedule: PE, English (to work on listening and braille skills), science, chorus, band, and 3-D design and drama (one semester each). Aey does not need additional support in chorus or band due to her skills in music and her motivation to be a part of these classes. She listens to tapes of songs to be learned at home and memorizes the words in that manner because she cannot read music. In band, she plays the drums and does well sitting and keeping time with the music. Classmates serve as sighted guides to ensure that she gets to her classes on time.

The other classes require more support because they are harder for Aey, and she tends to be quiet and passively involved unless directly instructed to participate. A peer tutor as well as some classmates provide support in PE under the direction of the coach and the adaptive physical educator. She does not participate in team sports but does warm-up exercises, runs/walks laps, and works out using weights and exercise equipment. In English, the special educator or paraeducator provides support to help her attend to and understand the topics discussed, work on the computer with adapted, auditory-feedback software, work on her braille, and express herself orally on audiocassettes as opposed to written expression. The science teacher and either special educator or paraeducator, along with classmates, provide support to help her follow directions, handle a variety of materials, sort materials based on similar characteristics (e.g., seeds, leaves, rocks), respond to direct questions, perform experiments, and relate the information to daily tasks. In 3-D design, she typically has classmate and peer tutor support to follow directions, obtain and put away materials, express herself creatively, interact with peers, and initiate asking for help. In drama, the goals are for greater oral and gestural expression, voice production, stage presence (which supports choral presentations), response to peers, and acceptance of feedback. She is supported in this class by her classmates, a peer tutor or by a special educator, and, of course, the drama teacher.

Seventh-Grade Math Class

Mr. Webber, a mathematics teacher, starts class by having his students exchange homework papers and correct them as he reads off the answers. Kim is paired with a classmate for this activity. Kim is agile, moves quickly, and loves to draw and manipulate small items. She has severe myopia (nearsightedness), a mild hearing loss for which she wears a hearing aid, and significant intellectual challenges; at times, she engages in behavioral outbursts and self-injurious behavior.

Kim sits at the front of the class to be close to the teacher. Although Kim cannot do the same homework assignment as the rest of the class, she is expected to listen to the teacher and identify each mathematics problem the teacher is correcting by pointing to that particular number. Kim has a large number line (like a ruler) on her desk, and as Mr. Webber states the number of the problem, he taps that number on the number line as he reads off the answer. This visual cue helps to draw Kim's attention to the task. Kim then finds the number on the homework sheet, and her classmate provides her with a positive acknowledgment when she is correct or positive corrective feedback when she makes a mistake. Kim is learning to follow directions, to match numbers, and to sequence numbers. With these skills, she may be better able to use a calculator while shopping. She also may obtain a job that involves stocking shelves by matching stock numbers or doing data entry. During the activity of correcting homework assignments, Kim receives support from both the classroom teacher and her classmates. This allows a special education support person to spend more time with another student who needs physical assistance when using the restroom.

After the homework has been corrected, the papers are passed to the front, and Kim is asked to collect them and place them on Mr. Webber's desk. This task gives Kim the chance to follow directions from the teacher and to interact briefly with a few students (e.g., attend to their verbal cues of "Here, Kim," reach out to take the papers). Then, Mr. Webber has the class (as a whole) work on the manipulation of numbers and functions. He draws a square on the blackboard and asks students to raise their hands and give him a number less than 10. Kim is supported by the special education support person (paraeducator or teacher) to choose a number card (index cards) from three presented and wave it in the air to be called on. Kim and five other students are called on, and the six numbers are placed in strategic places around the figure on the blackboard (top, bottom, left, right, middle, and on one line). The same figure and numbers are drawn in black felt-tip pen by the support person for Kim to have at her desk.

The teacher then calls on students to make up problems by using words, not numbers from the figure (e.g., "top minus bottom times line"). Kim cannot do the mathematics involved, but instead works on her objectives of following directions and number recognition. She follows the directions of classmates (and the teacher, who repeats the question) and points to the stated location. Using her number line or from a choice of three separate index cards with numbers, she matches the number on the figure to the appropriate number. She does the first part of the different problems that the students invent—the ones she hears or attends to. The teacher touches her on the arm to focus her attention before he repeats the question that a student has created. Kim's support person also assists other students around her who appear to be having difficulty following the class or performing the mathematics functions.

Eighth-Grade Math Class

An eighth-grade math teacher is having his class learn about Newton's three laws of motion. This lesson is also being taught in their English and science classes, so that students gain greater depth and understanding of the concepts. In the math class, the teacher reviews the three laws and provides a demonstration to illustrate each point. Then, he instructs his class to work on problems that he has developed for them within their lab groups. Students need to get the necessary materials (an incline, marbles, and a small plastic cup) and perform the experiment as indicated. They will record their observations as a group and turn them in to be graded.

Armando belongs to a group with three other boys, one of whom pushes Armando in his wheelchair to where the materials are kept. The boys show Armando what is needed (using the actual items and his pictorial/written directions) and then ask him a couple of yes/no questions regarding materials acquisition. They show him the pictorial directions and then the marbles and ask if the marbles are needed. After a few seconds pause, they affirm that they are needed, model nodding their heads, and physically prompt a yes response (head nod down) from Armando. Then, they show him an irrelevant item (e.g., a sponge) and the pictorial/written directions again, and ask him if that item is needed. If Armando does not respond, they prompt him to make a no response, which in Armando's case is to turn his head away from it. The boys then go to their work area and begin to work.

Armando is offered two different colored marbles to choose from, and he places his hand on the one he wants. He is physically unable to pick up the marble, so another member of his group does this for him. He is also given two different colored plastic cups to choose from, which he does in a similar fashion. When his classmates ask him to confirm or deny his choice, he does so by saying yes or no as described in the previous paragraph. He is physically guided to hold the marble on the top of the incline and wait there until asked by his peers to release the marble. He enjoys watching the marble roll down the incline and displace the small plastic cup at the bottom. Because maintaining eye contact and tracking moving objects is a skill his vision teacher wants him to work on to improve his ability to take in information, this particular activity is not only enjoyable for Armando but also allows him to address a valued skill. His peers measure the displacement of the cup and perform all the necessary recording of the information gathered during this experiment. Armando signs his name to the worksheet using a signature stamp with an adapted handle that is chosen from three different stamps. In this way, the act of signing his name (which he does several times a day), teaches him to recognize his name from two distracters, grasp the correct stamp, and control its placement on a paper. When there is time, he is also given a choice of different colored ink pads for his stamp, which serves as a mild reinforcer.

Another Eighth-Grade Math Class

In another eighth-grade math class, students are learning about estimation and comparison shopping. Students are requested to bring in newspaper ads to help them get a better idea of approximate costs of different items. To aid the understanding of comparison shopping, the teacher in this class always plans field trips to various stores so that students can obtain some hands-on experiences with this concept. First, small groups of students develop a list of items that they would like to investigate (e.g., food, clothing, appliances). Then, they determine what stores are likely to carry the desired items, and they visit as many stores as possible to record the various prices per item. They also call stores they are unable to visit and request the information over the telephone. Because most items can be purchased via the Internet, this source is also used. Finally, the groups of students share their findings with everyone in the class.

Kyesha has little understanding of money and monetary exchanges. She has very basic math concepts (e.g., counting to 10); however, she does need to purchase items, and she loves to go into the community to obtain them. She is learning to use a pictorial/written shopping list to obtain items and, in fact, is learning that pictures represent items in general. In her group, Kyesha helps decide what items to price by pointing to pictures of her choice. Once in the community, she works on requesting assistance to find particular items, by handing a prewritten message to a store clerk (identified by his name tag), and then finding the exact item (by matching picture to item) once the clerk has helped her to the right location in the store.

If any choices based on color or size are possible, Kyesha makes those choices by pointing to the one she prefers. She is then asked what the next step is and is provided with a prompt (e.g., a gesture toward her purse). If she doesn't point to the purse to indicate that it's time to pay, she is asked a yes/no question regarding this. Then, she is assisted to find the cashier where she is to hand the cashier her wallet from her purse, which contains a prewritten message to remove the correct amount of money for the item and place change and receipt in the wallet. This strategy is used because Kyesha lacks the sufficient fine motor skills to handle money on her own. For Kyesha, the goal is not necessarily one of comparison shopping, but of making a purchase.

Eighth-Grade Physical Science Class

Carina attends eighth grade at Colter Junior High. Carina has a great smile, likes to be around people, and responds quickly to familiar voices. Carina has limited vision in her left eye, although it is uncertain what she sees and understands. She may have a mild hearing loss, but responds to most frequencies. She has extremely minimal movement of her head and arms and has significant intellectual challenges. Carina indicates "no" by slightly turning her head away from an item (e.g., food) and tightening her arms next to her side. She smiles and vocalizes to indicate "yes," "I like this," and "more."

Carina enjoys physical science class because many of the activities involve small groups of students. Examples of study units include rotational motion, structural soundness of buildings, and efficiency of machinery. These units typically involve some reading, lectures, and hands-on experimentation. When there is a lecture or when group instructions are being given that may last for 10–15 minutes, Carina uses her Walkman, which she activates with a switch positioned near her right cheek, to listen to her choice of music or taped material.

During the active small-group time periods, Carina, who uses a wheelchair, is helped by her lab mates. For a 3-week unit on structural soundness of buildings, students work in groups of four or five, constructing miniature towers and bridges from a variety of different materials (e.g., drinking straws, paper clips, tape, string). The students are to collaborate in the building and testing of these structures and in preparing their findings in a final report. Carina's teammates show her materials (two choices at a time) and ask for her decision regarding which material to use at different times during the construction. Carina responds by looking at one of the offered choices held against a pale blue backing (to eliminate extraneous visual information). Sometimes her teammates tell her and show her that they are using a specific material such as plastic drinking straws. Then, they ask her to select that particular material, again from a choice of two.

Once the structure is complete, Carina participates in testing its strength by using her momentary switch to activate devices that put pressure on the structure. For example, Carina activates a switch-adapted fan to apply wind pressure. Her teammates cue her to apply this force with verbal and tactile cues and then record the results. The final report contains both sentences written by her lab partners as well as pictures and object cues (e.g., pieces of straw) that Carina decides on. Carina is working on understanding how she can affect her environment through the use of switches and decision making. She also is learning to respond to her peers, to use her vision to make choices, and to match spoken words to objects.

Eighth-Grade Horticulture Class

David's horticulture class spends time doing sedentary work (e.g., discussions, lectures, note-taking, writing) and active work (e.g., planting and maintaining a garden) to learn the fundamentals of horticulture. David has friends in this class who help support him as well as a paraeducator or special educator. David does not have formal language and uses vocalizations, body movements, gestures, objects, and occasionally pictures to communicate. David has blurred central acuity but makes good use of his peripheral vision. He can be disruptive with his vocalizations and by leaving his seat when he is bored and not engaged. He typically works with his hands to perform various tasks related to the subject of horticulture and is allowed to listen to his Walkman using headphones. This seems to calm him down so that he does not make a lot of noise.

For instance, while the teacher is lecturing on the topic of deciduous and nondeciduous trees, David sorts two very different kinds of seeds from such trees into two containers. A classmate sitting close to David checks his work and helps him correct errors that he may make. Like other students in this class, David has plants that he is growing from seeds. These need to be watered and checked for growth. This allows David to get up and move around the room, find his plants (which are in specifically colored styrofoam cups), feel the soil and determine if it is wet or not, and water the plant if needed. These steps require David to make decisions, move quietly in a certain part of the room, use materials appropriately, and follow directions. When this is done he goes back to his sedentary task of sorting seeds. He will also make his report on this unit using actual seeds that he glues or uses HandiTak to attach to a file folder-type paper. He signs his name using a signature stamp that he is learning to recognize from other such stamps.

David particularly enjoys going outside and performing tasks involved in caring for a garden. He pushes a wheelbarrow to bring dirt to a specific plot, holds a strainer to sift out dirt from rocks, and rakes in preparation for planting. The adult support person in this class (special educator or paraeducator) tries to fade back and allow classmates to offer support.

ADDRESSING STUDENT NEEDS DURING
LECTURES AND OTHER CHALLENGING TIME PERIODS

Sometimes it is challenging to keep students with severe and multiple disabilities in general education classes actively involved in their learning. Usually these times address fairly complex cognitive skills of the students without disabilities and take place in a manner that makes it very difficult for a student who does not speak, read, or write. Examples include teacher lecturing while students take notes, group discussions on subject matter, and exam-taking. Not only may the topic make it difficult to include a student with severe and multiple disabilities (e.g., a discussion of poetry and the writer's intent), but often there is a require- ment for relative quiet and a focus on one person talking at a time. Unless care- ful preplanning has been done, the student with severe and multiple disabilities may just perceive this type of instruction as a waiting period and become bored and restless. No student should just be expected to sit, wait, and be quiet for long periods of time.

When educational staff do not see the relevance of what is being taught to the student with severe and multiple disabilities, there is a tendency to occupy that student with something that the student can do quietly, even if it is totally unrelated to what is occurring in the classroom. Sometimes completely different activities are warranted. For instance, Patrick, who has significant disabilities, does not learn well during lectures. He cannot see the teacher well, does not use speech, and does not read or write in the traditional sense. He also has a high need to keep moving and finds it difficult to be still for very long. Although his eleventh-grade English class is very good for him for a number of reasons (e.g., good support from classmates, welcoming teacher, access to a computer, lots of group work), there are definitely times when he cannot attend or contribute to the class activity. Therefore, it was decided that during the lecture part of some of the classes, Patrick would take the attendance to the office. Patrick is learning this route, as well as how to find the secretary, hand her the attendance sheet, so- cialize with anyone he sees on the way, and find his way back to class. This ac- tivity takes a lot of time, so when he returns to class, the students have moved on to an activity that makes his inclusion much easier and more relevant. Taking the attendance to the office also allows him time to move and unwind a bit. Although student workers from the office typically pick up the attendance sheet from each class, they don't come to Patrick's English class unless instructed to do so.

Before assigning the student a completely different and unrelated activity to perform during a challenging time period, it may be helpful to investigate other activities that relate to the activity (or upcoming activity). For example, when the teacher is lecturing or a group discussion is occurring, could the student with se- vere and multiple disabilities gather materials that will be needed and pass them out to students? This could be done relatively quietly and would teach one-to- one correspondence (one paper to each student), as well. There would be some movement around the class, but other students and the teacher could quickly be- come accustomed to this procedure.

Table 6.3. Suggestions for meeting the needs of the student with severe and multiple disabilities during challenging time periods

Could the student gather materials needed and pass them out?

Could the student organize the class into groups by making decisions using individual photographs of the class?

Could the student be given a model and/or specific pictorial/written instructions of the upcoming activity to preview?

Could the student make a visual representation of the content under study (a collage depicting the topic) to share with the class?

Could the student be asked to help pick out key words from the discussion by matching words and making a collage or list?

Could the student listen to keywords and simple explanations of what they are, using a cassette recorder and headphones?

Could the student help acquire and organize materials needed for group work that will follow a lecture or discussion?

Could the student randomly select discussion questions for the teacher to ask the class?

Could the student help the teacher display samples for the class to see?

Could the student make something that will be used in an upcoming class activity (e.g., a prop for a drama skit or an organizer for a science unit)?

If the student does not need to be up and about, perhaps he could spend the time organizing the class into various small groups for an upcoming activity. This organization could occur using photographs of classmates and having the student with severe and multiple disabilities randomly pick four students for Group 1, four students for Group 2, and so forth. Several different math concepts could be taught during this activity. Concepts of girl and boy could also be targeted if that were a criterion for group makeup. Table 6.3 lists different ideas for teaching the student with severe and multiple disabilities when the content of the lesson proves challenging for total involvement. Of course, one activity that could and probably should occur to some extent is the reading of one's daily schedule to see what has already transpired, what is currently happening, and what will happen next. Although this is an alternative activity, it provides several learning opportunities as explained in Chapter 3.

Finally, when students are being tested, tests can and should be adapted to address what the student with severe and multiple disabilities has learned. For example, vocabulary related to the topic can be checked by asking the student to find a specific picture or object or to group similar things together based on the topic being studied. This same skill of same and different should be the skill tested, again using pictures and/or objects. The actual adapted test or data on the student's responses should be collected and submitted to the teacher with all the other tests. Students with disabilities, no matter how severe, should be expected to learn and to demonstrate that learning. Students with severe and multiple disabilities, like other students, deserve the right to be exposed to high expectations.

TRANSITION TO HIGH SCHOOL

The transition to high school marks a significant step in the student's educational career. Although the focus of transition planning traditionally has been on the movement from high school to the adult community, important transitions occur continually throughout the student's school life (Repetto & Correa, 1996). To avoid potential problems and ensure a smooth transition from middle school or junior high school to high school, the receiving team needs to be well prepared. This is particularly important when the student has multiple challenges (Demchak & Greenfield, 2000). The educational team must ensure that the student follows a similar enrollment schedule as other students so that the student can start his or her classes on the first day of school and does not have to wait to seek special admission to classes after the school year has started. General educators should not perceive having a student with severe disabilities as an added "burden" on an already full class. Admitting students with severe and multiple disabilities to classes that best meet their needs should be done in a timely fashion that does not draw undue attention to the student. This will require early registration, not a last-minute approach that suggests the placement is an afterthought.

When helping a student plan a high school schedule, all opportunities for student learning should be explored. Extracurricular activities can become even more important during the high school years (Fisher, 1999). Being part of clubs and various social groups is critical at this age and can present additional opportunities for a student with severe and multiple disabilities to be included. Also, greater attention may be paid to obtaining a job to earn some money. Teenagers often have part-time jobs, which allows them the opportunity to explore potential careers or just become accustomed to job expectations and requirements. Similar opportunities should be planned for students with severe and multiple disabilities, who may work in the community as part of their educational program.

High school represents an achievement, and for many, could be their final years in the educational system. Furthermore, high school signifies a time of greater independence and greater awareness of potential career goals. Students individualize their course of study over the years following their strengths and interests much more extensively than during middle or junior high school. Therefore, the potential to create a highly unique educational program is even more apparent than in middle or junior high school. The team will want to work closely with the student to choose classes that will optimize learning during these critical school years.

REFERENCES

Agran, M., Snow, K., & Swaner, J. (1999). A survey of secondary level teachers' opinions on community-based instruction and inclusive education. *Journal of The Association for Persons with Severe Handicaps, 24,* 58–62.

Campbell, P., & Olsen, G.R. (1994). Improving instruction in secondary schools. *Teaching Exceptional Children, 26*(3), 51–54.

Demchak, M.A., & Greenfield, R.G. (2000). A transition portfolio for Jeff, a student with multiple disabilities. *Teaching Exceptional Children, 32*(8), 44–49.

Fisher, D. (1999). According to their peers: Inclusion as high school students see it. *Mental Retardation, 37,* 458–467.

Fisher, D., & Kennedy, C.H. (2001). Access to the middle school core curriculum. In C.H. Kennedy & D. Fisher, *Inclusive middle schools* (pp. 43–59). Baltimore: Paul H. Brookes Publishing Co.

Gent, P., & Gurecka, L. (1998). Service learning: A creative strategy for inclusive classrooms. *Journal of The Association for Persons with Severe Handicaps, 23,* 261–271.

McDonnell, J. (1998). Instruction for students with severe disabilities in general education settings. *Education and Training in Mental Retardation and Developmental Disabilities, 33,* 199–215.

Repetto, J.B., & Correa, V.I. (1996). Expanding views on transition. *Exceptional Children, 62,* 551–563.

Ryan, S., & Paterna, L. (1997). Junior high can be inclusive: Using natural supports and cooperative learning. *Teaching Exceptional Children, 30*(2), 36–41.

Schukar, R. (1997). Enhancing the middle school curriculum through service learning. *Theory into Practice, 36,* 176–183.

Staub, D., Spaulding, M., Peck, C.A., Gallucci, C., & Schwartz, I.S. (1996). Using nondisabled peers to support the inclusion of students with disabilities at the junior high school level. *Journal of The Association for Persons with Severe Handicaps, 21,* 194–205.

Williams, L.J., & Downing, J.E. (1998). Membership and belonging in inclusive classrooms: What do middle school students have to say? *Journal of The Association for Persons with Severe Handicaps, 23,* 98–110.

York, J., Vandercook, T., MacDonald, C., Heise-Neff, C., & Caughey, E. (1992). Feedback about integrating middle-school students with severe disabilities in general education classes. *Exceptional Children, 58,* 244–258.

Chapter 7

The High School Student

June E. Downing

From junior high or middle school, the student graduates to high school. High school typically offers greater opportunities for learning for students with severe and multiple disabilities. Although the emphasis on academic learning is certainly apparent, the options to specialize in different topics are much more prevalent. Students have choices of different courses to take each year, and each student's educational program is unique, regardless of whether the student has disabilities. Although students must complete a certain number of required courses, a degree of flexibility is allowed to foster individual preference and need. For instance, not all students will take German, physics, choir, or photography. Magnet high schools tend to offer an array of courses in specialized areas such as fine arts, technology, or science. Students can also opt to attend magnet high schools that offer programs geared to specific strengths and interests.

The greater the variety of course offerings in high school, the easier it should be to plan an appropriate program for the student with severe and multiple disabilities. Without the need to obtain a specified number and type of credits to graduate with a diploma, students with severe and multiple disabilities and their families can choose courses that more directly meet their highly individualized needs. Courses can be selected by subject matter, instructional methods used, or by personality of instructor. If one class is particularly beneficial for the student, the student may be able to enroll in the course twice a day (e.g., takes two keyboarding classes per day). Students may also repeat certain courses in subsequent years (e.g., take Spanish I during the junior and senior years of high school) if they enjoy the courses and can meet learning objectives while taking them. Determining a student's course of study is a team process based on information obtained during a traditional MAPS session (see Chapter 3), person-centered planning (O'Brien & O'Brien, 1998), other forms of discussion, review of past records and student portfolio, and interviews of significant others in the student's life. Allowing the student as much choice as possible in the selection of courses is recommended. This supports the development of self-determination.

DECIDING WHAT TO TAKE IN HIGH SCHOOL

While there is no prescribed course of study for high school students, certain steps can be followed to assist in the decision-making process. The suggestions in the following pages may serve as a guide for the educational team.

Determine Goals

The student should have a clear picture of what is to be accomplished during the 4 years of high school. Educational goals from middle or junior high school may carry over to high school and be very appropriate if the student has yet to master them and if they are still considered to be important. Other goals may no longer be appropriate or as critical. Perhaps the first step when entering high school is to gather the team together and review the previous MAPS, or if no MAPS process has occurred, to hold one. Because these are the last years of a student's formal education, the plan for the student's time in high school should be clear to all team members. The IEP should reflect what the student wants and needs to achieve before making the transition to the postschool arena. Because several classes may be able to meet a student's needs, student interest and compatibility with a given teacher can be used to select the courses.

For students 14 years and older, an individualized transition plan (ITP) also will be needed. This plan will specifically address transition issues and will begin the process of adult agencies becoming part of the team. Certainly, the IEP/ITP needs to reflect the student's strengths and build on previously acquired skills, which can change between the first year of high school and the last. A transition portfolio may be particularly helpful for the receiving team members (Demchak & Greenfield, 2000). Obtaining some direction with practical information on student preferences, means of communication, learning styles, and so forth without being overly restrictive is the key. Table 7.1 presents an activity/IEP matrix for an eleventh grader showing how this student's needs will be met across his school day.

Examine the Options

Depending on the high school, options can be limited or plentiful. Different classes can serve as beneficial learning environments based on the types of classes, when they are offered, and their relevance to the student's needs and interests. How a class is typically taught also has an impact on the decision-making process. Classes that have considerable hands-on activities and allow students multiple ways to demonstrate their understanding may be more beneficial than classes taught in a more traditional lecture and note-taking format.

Scheduling should consider the student's energy level, sleep patterns, and the impact of medications taken. For students who struggle to make early morning classes, starting school at second period may be appropriate. Similarly, for students whose medication causes them to be particularly tired in the late afternoon, not scheduling courses during this time might be the best course of action. Some classes will be quite sedentary in nature, which could be beneficial for those students who need to remain calm following a tubal feeding. Other classes are more active, requiring students to move around a lot, which could best meet the needs

Table 7.1. Activity/IEP objective analysis for an eleventh grader

Student: Travis is 17 years old, curious, persistent, and active. He is deaf, has mental retardation, has very limited communication skills, and has difficulty with self-control.

Objectives	PE/weight training	Photography	Keyboarding	Chemistry	Art/drawing	Careers
Remains on task until completion	Works with partner Has pictorial routine of weights to do Checks off weights he does on laminated sheet	Stays with lab group or partner and does not wander off Finishes one small specific task per class	Stays at computer and finishes predetermined amount of work (data entry)	Stays with lab partners at table until assignment is completed or bell rings	Finishes one assignment before starting another Stays at work table throughout the period and does not roam	Stays with large group for discussions instead of running around room Looks at magazines with appropriate pictures
Expresses his needs without getting angry	Uses a card (attached with Velcro to a wrist sweatband) that says "Leave me alone", when Travis holds the card toward someone, that person leaves him alone	Gets someone's attention and signs help when he needs help Does not throw equipment	Signs break or uses break card to indicate need to stop working Does not throw keyboard	Raises hand instead of running up to the teacher when he wants to do the experiment or hand out papers	Signs help when frustrated, rather than tearing up paper	Requests attention by appropriately touching classmate or teacher or by raising his hand instead of biting his hand
Gets along with others	Works cooperatively with partner during weight training Together they decide who goes first and amount of weight	Shares equipment with classmate and decides with classmate what to photograph Responds to teachers' and classmates' greetings by looking and signing "Hi"	Responds to teachers' and classmates' greetings by looking and signing "Hi"	Follows gestural directions from chemistry teacher Shares materials with classmates	Sits close to other students at art table, not by himself Responds to their requests (via pointing and gestures) for materials he has	Shares materials (books, magazines) when doing a project such as a collage on possible careers Does not hit or bite others

(continued)

145

Table 7.1. (continued)

Student: Travis is 17 years old, curious, persistent, and active. He is deaf, has mental retardation, has very limited communication skills, and has difficulty with self-control.

Objectives	PE/weight training	Photography	Keyboarding	Chemistry	Art/drawing	Careers
Easily makes the transition from one task to the next	Uses pictorial/written schedule to determine when one activity is completed and what happens next; is given reminder of approaching transition 5 minutes before class ends; is learning to match clock time with time on schedule					
Initiates interactions with others	Approaches classmate and gives him or her a pictorial card that asks, "Want to work with me?" (part of his weight training routine)	Signs hello to teacher and to at least one classmate Asks that student's opinion of his (Travis's) photograph by pointing to it and using facial expressions	Turns in software program to teacher when leaving class and signs good-bye When appropriate, asks other students if he can see what they are doing; he extends a pictorial/written card for this ("What are you doing?")	Signs hello to chemistry teacher and signs help when he does not understand what to do	Uses pictorial card ("What are you doing?") or uses pointing and facial expressions to find out about others' work; points to own work to elicit comments about it	Uses pictorial card ("What are you doing?") or points and uses facial expressions to ask other students about their projects (life goals); pictures used to clarify understanding

of a very active student. For some students, following a schedule similar to that of close friends may be the best choice.

Find Supportive Teachers

Teachers who welcome students with diverse needs into their classes should be considered first (Fisher, Sax, & Pumpian, 1999). Facing negative attitudes from the beginning is exhausting to all concerned and can interfere with effective learning. Students without disabilities who follow the lead of the teacher are not going to be as welcoming or helpful in classrooms in which it is clear that the teacher would rather not have a certain student in class. Certainly, teachers need to be prepared to welcome students with severe disabilities into their classrooms (see Chapter 9). Some teachers, however, are more naturally inclined than others to regard inclusion in a positive light. These teachers make good use of the diversity of students to teach valuable lessons. They recognize that the presence of a classmate with severe disabilities presents unique problem-solving situations to students. They also use cooperative learning strategies and encourage students to work together. These teachers can ease the transition into general education classes by convincing their colleagues of the benefits of having a student with severe disabilities in their classes.

Determine Availability of Support

Determining when additional support is available may also affect a schedule. Some periods of the day may have more peer tutors than others. Some high schools employ part-time paraeducators who only work during the morning. Some classes are offered more than once a day, and choosing times when extra support is available (if needed) may be an important consideration. In some classes, the natural support of classmates and teachers may be sufficient. This type of support is depicted in Figure 7.1 as two classmates edit a promotional videotape on individuals with disabilities as part of a tenth-grade video production class. Volunteer programs may already be in place, serving as a valuable resource for additional support once volunteers have received training and are aware of the goals of the program.

Work to Overcome Challenges

The perfect schedule for a given high school student is probably just as difficult to achieve for a student with severe disabilities as without. For instance, the class that really intrigues the student may be at 7:30 in the morning, which may not be an ideal time for the student. Or, the student may want to take both chemistry and marching band, which are offered at the same time. The pros and cons of any schedule must be weighed and compromises made.

Some problems may initially seem overwhelming but in actuality are not that difficult to overcome. For instance, a class meets on the second floor of a nonaccessible building, which makes it impossible for a student using a wheelchair to attend. The easiest solution is to move this class to a first-floor location. Some schools, however, have opted to use an existing service elevator, put in an elevator, or use a stair climber designed for wheelchairs. A ramp may go into one

Figure 7.1.   A student in a tenth-grade video production class helps a classmate with a project. (Photograph by Margo Yunker.)

room of a two-classroom portable, which requires the student to go through the wrong room and into the desired room. This arrangement has the potential to be distracting, especially if the student is late for class. The obvious solution, of course, is to change rooms so that the desired location is directly attainable via the ramp.

Inaccessible restrooms can pose another problem, especially when several students require assistance of this kind. When students are attending their neighborhood high school, the probability of several students' using wheelchairs is small. Sometimes, however, students live in group homes that cater to the needs of individuals with a particular disability. Although this is not considered recommended practice, it can and does happen, and therefore, a larger number of students with the same or similar disabilities would attend the same high school. The real problem occurs when only one of the restrooms is accessible for students using wheelchairs, and all of these students are being assisted to use the restroom at the same time. Such a situation causes a drain on resources (e.g., insufficient number of paraeducators and teachers) and makes it difficult for these students to use the restroom and get to class in a timely fashion. Solutions may include staggering the time that students use the restroom, making other restrooms physically accessible, or using the restroom in the nurse's office.

Highly academic content can present a challenge if teachers are unfamiliar with ways to identify important learning objectives for students with severe and multiple disabilities from the core content. General educators may be concerned that the student will get nothing out of the class. How the teacher instructs the class, however, may be far more important than what is taught. Teachers who encourage students to demonstrate understanding and mastery in diverse ways according to different intelligences may be much more beneficial to a student than a class in which students must all perform in a similar manner. Therefore, avoiding academic classes is not recommended. Rather, identifying classes that allow for and encourage hands-on applied learning, whether academic or not, is the best strategy (Jorgensen, 1999).

For example, in a ninth-grade English class, students study Homer's *Odyssey* as part of a unit on Greek and Roman mythology. One assignment is to determine what constitutes heroic traits. Students research this topic from books and the Internet and have the option of writing a paper, writing a script for a play, drawing a mural, creating a fictitious interview with a hero from the past, or using a variety of other methods to demonstrate their understanding of the subject. Aidan, who does not read and has hearing and visual impairments, opts to create a collage of heroes from sports magazines (a high-interest area), stickers, and comic books (e.g., Superman, Batman, Spiderman). Aidan's primary objective is to use decision-making skills to create products as a leisure activity. He makes numerous choices with regard to color of background, pictures to use, layout of pictures and additional lines with markers he decides to add. He signs his name to his work using personalized labels and turns in his work with his classmates. The recognition that students can demonstrate knowledge in a variety of different formats makes it relatively easy to include a student like Aidan, who does not display highly academic skills.

EXAMPLES OF EFFECTIVE INCLUSIVE PRACTICES

Each situation is different. Successful placement in general education classes will depend on student needs, the make-up of the team, school schedule, and the attitudes of school personnel. Although no one recipe exists that will ensure success for all students, the following examples of different high school-age students in various general education classes may facilitate the inclusion of other high school students with similar abilities in other schools across the country. In addition to the examples that follow, the reader is referred to Jorgensen's (1998) *Restructuring High Schools for All Students: Taking Inclusion to the Next Level* and Fisher, Sax, and Pumpian's (1999) *Inclusive High Schools: Learning from Contemporary Classrooms*.

Tenth-Grade Biology Class

A tenth-grade science class is studying plant physiology. The students' primary objective is to identify plant parts and their function in photosynthesis and why that process is important. The teacher lectures for approximately 20 minutes to explain what is in the textbook and then assigns activities related to the lecture. Students may work independently or in small groups. For Lance, a determined and eager student who has severe sensory impairments and a significant intellectual impairment, the team decides that the importance of the topic for his everyday life focuses on the appreciation of plants, how they add to people's lives, and how to obtain and adequately care for them. Adaptations for Lance involve using several real plants, a watering can or something suitable, plant food, a water-measuring device to avoid overwatering, and advertisements from stores on plants and plant prices.

During the lecture portion of the class, Lance is assisted by a peer tutor (a work-study high school student) who teaches Lance how to discriminate between pictures of stores that do and do not sell plants and that money is required to obtain plants. The tutor uses pictures to explain the difference between large and small plants, healthy and unhealthy plants, as well as various types of plants to teach awareness of preferences. This instruction occurs quietly at Lance's assigned seat, using pictures to identify and categorize plants by similarity and a wallet with a variety of bills to practice the necessary money exchange.

During the remainder of the class, three classmates work with Lance to label parts of the plant (by matching a picture of the part of the plant with its name on a sticky label to the worksheet) while they discuss photosynthesis. Lance learns to check on and take care of the plants and seedlings in the classroom, including use of the necessary plant care equipment. As part of his community-based instruction, which occurs during another segment of his school day, Lance has gone to plant stores to find preferred plants and has purchased plants, seeds, and the necessary materials to maintain these plants. The community-based instruction supports what Lance is learning in science class. The skills he learns can continue at home with his parents, who have verified that having and caring for plants is a normal occurrence and pastime for the family. Furthermore, Lance can use these skills after graduation and after leaving home, when he lives on his own with a roommate or with more formal support.

Eleventh-Grade Home Economics Class

When the home economics class prepares meals, bakes, or cleans up, Vicki can participate with the rest of her class. Her classmates help her to do the physical aspects of tasks that she is unable to do herself, and they ask her directions for various steps that keep her actively involved and learning. For example, they might show her a measuring cup and measuring spoons, state that they need 1 cup of flour, and ask her which one they should use. When putting food items away following a cooking activity, Vicki's opinion is asked in the following way. A peer will stand next to the refrigerator, hold two items in front of Vicki (e.g., salt and milk), and ask her which one goes into the refrigerator. Vicki indicates her choice by looking, touching, or reaching toward the item. Her IEP goals and objectives of responding to peers and increasing her understanding of general knowledge are addressed continuously throughout these hands-on activities.

Not every class period in home economics, however, involves hands-on activities. Substantial time is spent in more sedentary activities, such as planning menus, discussing related topics, reading, taking notes during lectures, and taking examinations. During these times, Vicki requires more significant adaptations to be actively included. For example, Vicki, who does not speak and has very limited expressive communication skills, cannot adequately contribute to a group discussion on recommended dietary allowance requirements for various minerals and vitamins. During the discussion and lecture on this subject, Vicki works with a paraeducator or work-study student (peer tutor) to create a pictorial report of foods that are healthy and those that are not. She is shown two pictures, such as a candy bar and cereal, and is told that the cereal is good for her and makes a good breakfast. Similar types of pictures (taken from colored advertisements in newspapers and from actual food containers) are shown to her and sorted according to whether they are healthy or not. Healthy foods are placed on a piece of paper showing young athletes in action, whereas unhealthy foods (junk foods) are placed on a piece of paper showing an adolescent who is *very* overweight and looking unhappy.

Following this instruction, which occurs at Vicki's desk and is done using a soft voice, the pictures are mixed up and placed in one pile, and Vicki is presented with two pictures at a time to sort. If she is correct, she receives verbal praise and uses a glue stick to paste the picture to the appropriate piece of paper. If incorrect, she is given the necessary feedback, re-instructed, and offered two more choices. Vicki is learning basic knowledge about foods and health, recognizing pictured information and acting on it, and attending to the task in a quiet manner. Data are kept on the number of correct choices made per class period to monitor her progress. Tests for Vicki follow this same basic procedure, with pictures of two foods (one healthy and one not) shown to her. She uses a large marker to indicate which one is healthy. These are scored and recorded by the general educator who will use the scores to contribute to progress reports based on her IEP objectives.

Tenth-Grade Government Class

Raphael's tenth-grade government class is studying the three branches of the government by reading, listening to lectures, watching videotapes, role-playing, and researching various aspects. Raphael is deaf and has severe intellectual disabilities and mild cerebral palsy that makes the production of some signs difficult. Raphael does know a few signs that he uses expressively and understands more signs receptively. He primarily communicates via facial expressions, natural gestures, use of objects, and moving toward what he wants or is interested in. Although Raphael would have considerable difficulty learning the concepts in this class, he has a few friends in class who sign and who enjoy supporting him.

During lectures and when students are researching different topics on the Internet, library books, and other sources, Raphael works on different pictorial reports. He typically works with a computer and IntelliKeys that accommodate for his inability to just hit one key at a time. He designs borders and graphic designs using a paint program. He is learning to find the colors red, white, and blue and to sign those colors, as well. He is also learning the sign for *flag*. These signs are all within his physical ability, and to support his learning, members of his class have learned these signs as well. The class does a lot with voting for different aspects of lessons (e.g., deciding what activities to do first, what materials to use, or what activities to do in lieu of others). Raphael is learning about voting (although he typically raises his hand when his friends raise theirs) and about majority rule.

Raphael seems to enjoy watching videotapes, role-playing in skits, and going on fieldtrips to the state capitol, so for those activities few adaptations are needed. Classmates ensure that he stays with the group, and he is encouraged to remain as actively involved in each activity as possible. His primary goals during these activities are to follow directions, respond to peers' comments/questions, and use his expressive sign vocabulary. Because others in this class know some signs from taking American Sign Language (ASL) as a foreign language requirement, they are eager to interact with Raphael. As a result, every lesson offers some vocabulary that they can all learn in ASL.

Tenth-Grade Earth Science Class

For the study of erosion, a tenth-grade earth science teacher presents his lecture on the topic using transparencies and an overhead projector before having his class engage in the experiment to follow. Students are to attend to the presentation, take notes, and then work in small groups to perform the experiment. In this class, Reggie relies on visual representations of what to expect. Reggie has a severe bilateral hearing loss and a moderate level of intellectual impairment. He needs to be kept involved in lessons, or he becomes frustrated, leaves the activity, and may demonstrate aggressive behavior toward others.

Reggie uses a pictorial guide to follow for different class activities. Often the first step in earth science involves getting materials and setting them up for each group. A paraeducator assists him to "read" his guide and perform this set-up task. During the presentation, especially if there are no materials to prepare, Reggie maintains control of the file folder containing the transparencies the teacher uses. When the teacher signals him for a transparency, he puts the top one on the overhead projector. Often the transparencies are numbered, and Reggie is shown a numbered card and then finds the corresponding transparency. He is learning to identify and match numbers, so this adaptation supports such an objective. When possible, a picture or photograph of a trip taken by his family that is related to the lecture (e.g., a geographical location visited on a trip) is incorporated into the presentation. Then, Reggie uses a few signs and gestures (pointing to the picture and himself) to express his recognition of this picture.

Reggie follows the directions of his peers to perform the experiments (using gestures and modeling) and uses pictures (and photographs) to write his reports in this class. He writes his first name on these reports and chooses between three last names on labels to "write" his last name. For clean up activities, Reggie follows a similar pictorial guide that contains both graphic designs or photographs and one or two words (see Figure 7.2). In this way, he is learning to improve his reading skills and use them to follow written directions. He also is learning to sign either BREAK or HELP to his peers, the paraeducator, or teacher instead of becoming frustrated when he doesn't understand what to do or is overwhelmed by the task.

Ninth-Grade Health Class

Many different topics are covered in this ninth-grade health class. Students typically engage in reading, researching topics, writing brief reports, discussing in groups, watching videotapes, and occasionally debating the pros and cons of a given topic. The teacher also invites guest speakers (e.g., nutritionists, former drug addicts, medical personnel) to address different topics from different perspectives. She also takes the class on at least one field trip a semester that is related to a specific topic.

Many different adaptations are used to help Ruthie be an active learner in this class. Ruthie is nonverbal and deafblind; she has slight peripheral vision. She also uses a wheelchair as a result of cerebral palsy. Ruthie has a high need to maintain her health (a goal strongly stated by her grandmother) and to improve her social interactions with others her age. Others interact with her primarily through touch cues and objects that are placed under her hands.

CLEAN-UP

1. PICK UP TRASH

2. THROW TRASH AWAY

3. GET SPONGE

4. WIPE TABLE

5. WASH HANDS

Figure 7.2. Sample pictorial/written instructions for a student to read. The Picture Communication Symbols (PCS) are copyright © 1981–2001 and are used with permission.

For one unit, the class learns about the impact of drugs on one's health and social/emotional well-being. During this unit, Ruthie concentrates on learning how to organize and take her pills for seizure control. She takes a certain amount of phenobarbital and Tegretol on a daily basis. While the class can study about "not so good" and "good" drugs, including the ones that Ruthie takes, Ruthie learns a tactual system of organizing the drugs she must take.

Twelfth-Grade English Class

Darcy's twelfth-grade English class has a mix of sedentary activities (e.g., individual work on reading and writing) and more active aspects (e.g., games to learn facts). Darcy has a great smile, enjoys being with friends, and likes to be actively involved in classes. She uses a wheelchair and has very limited movement of her limbs. She does not have a formal communication system, but uses switch-activated VOCAs, facial expressions, and eye contact to convey messages.

Darcy sits in her wheelchair at a table with four other students. When students read from their literature book, Darcy listens to a greatly simplified version of the story on her cassette player using headphones. Her reading was prerecorded by the special educator, peer tutor, or sibling depending on their availability. Darcy uses a mercury switch attached to her headband to hear the recording. To check for understanding, the person supporting her (e.g., peer, special educator, paraeducator, SLP) asks very simple questions using two different graphics that are held up for her to look at or are put on her rotary scanner, which she also activates using the mercury head switch.

When class discussions occur, Darcy contributes information when directly asked by the teacher some preselected questions. She uses her dial scanner and pictures with attached comments to respond. Cues to help her may be color codes, matching numbers, or highlighted comments. Darcy is working on her receptive understanding, picture identification, following directions, and matching skills.

Darcy, like her classmates, enjoys the games played in this class. For instance, for a Jeopardy-style game of Medieval Europe, which sets the tone for literature being read from that time period, Darcy operated an Ablenet spinner to select questions to ask each team. Darcy uses a touch-sensitive momentary switch that she activates with her elbow because her arms are flexed up by her chest. The English teacher asks her to come up with a question via numbers on the Ablenet spinner that correspond to a question number that the teacher reads. One student picked from each team must place the colored flag of his or her team by Darcy's tray before the team can respond. Darcy keeps score by looking at the appropriate colored flag offered to her after each point earned. Darcy is not held responsible for the facts targeted by this activity; rather, she is learning to follow directions, consistently use her switch, and match by color to keep score.

Ninth-Grade Woodshop Class

Barry has a wonderful sense of curiosity. He uses his hands to accomplish many activities using small items and can get totally absorbed in activities of choice (e.g., wood burning, rolling stacks of coins in wrappers). He responds to five tactile signs and cues. Barry has no vision or hearing and usually conveys his intent through body movements, facial expressions, and manipulation of different objects.

Barry is a student in Mr. Jamison's ninth/tenth-grade woodshop class. He has a work partner who sits at his table. Barry helps Mr. Jamison with all of the demonstrations and explanations at the beginning of each class. He hands Mr. Jamison pieces of wood or equipment and turns equipment on and off as directed. Participation of this nature helps Barry stay more focused with the group and provides him more information and practice anticipating cues than if he were just sitting at his table. Mr. Jamison uses touch cues and objects to communicate with Barry, and a paraeducator or special educator is present to assist when Barry has difficulty.

Following the demonstration with Mr. Jamison, Barry works with his work partner (if a joint project), or he works with a paraeducator on independent projects. He enjoys this class and can perform most steps after tactually being shown what to do and examining a finished product. Barry does not participate in written examinations or lectures. Because he takes more time to finish projects than students without disabilities do, he uses times during examinations or writing assignments to continue working on projects. There is thus no need to rush Barry through projects, and he can see each project through to completion, working at his own pace. Photographs of finished projects are put in his portfolio for assessment.

Barry's goals are to follow tactile (touch and object cues) and occasionally signed instructions, handle materials appropriately, and remain on task for a specified time period without engaging in self-stimulatory behavior (e.g., head tapping), which interferes with his performance.

Tenth-Grade Drama Class

Ben, a student in a tenth-grade drama class, often follows verbal directions, takes good care of his own materials, and performs many tasks involving fine motor skills without assistance. Ben has been blind since birth and has a mild hearing loss. He also has significant cognitive impairments and can exhibit severe behavioral outbursts when frustrated (e.g., when not getting his way). Ben is ambulatory and uses the sighted guide technique as well as a cane (diagonal technique) for walking in familiar places. He has a few signs that he uses spontaneously (EAT, MORE, FINISHED), and he vocalizes many sounds.

Ben's drama class offers him the opportunity to work on skills such as following directions, handling materials appropriately, expressing frustration in an appropriate manner, and interacting with same-age peers. Ben seems to enjoy role playing, during which students can practice different skills (e.g., getting in character, projecting one's voice, changing voice style). When appropriate, Ben assumes roles of people who are not vocal or who have a few repetitive lines (such lines are prerecorded by a classmate on an Ablenet Step-by-Step Communicator[75], which Ben activates for the lines to be heard). Ben often plays the "straight man" in these skits. He also helps decide what props may be necessary and assists in obtaining or creating them. Ben is responsible for responding to classmates' or teacher's requests to get a certain prop for a scene as needed (e.g., chair, lamp, coffee cups).

To maximize Ben's opportunities to improve his skills, the support teacher, who works with the drama teacher, identifies the many situations that naturally exist as well as those that could be developed to enable Ben to receive sufficient skills practice. An activity analysis is completed for this class (as well as for all of Ben's classes), delineating how Ben's learning objectives are being addressed. This analysis clarifies expectations for everyone supporting Ben (drama teacher, classmates, special educator, SLP, and paraeducator).

Twelfth-Grade World History Class

Jemma's world history teacher tries to keep students actively involved in the learning process. He has students enact different historical events, compare and contrast current political events with past events, and choose favorite historical time periods/events to report on them using a manner of their choice. His emphasis on cooperative group instruction provides many opportunities for interacting and supports a learning environment best suited for Jemma's needs.

Jemma has a moderate sensorineural bilateral hearing loss and also has a difficult time understanding what she does hear. She uses pictorial information to help her understand others and has several different pictorial-based AAC devices that she uses in different situations (e.g., class, nutrition break, PE). She enjoys learning and playing on the computer given appropriate software programs (e.g., Teen Tunes Plus, Drawing Program).

In her world history class, Jemma works on social interaction with her teacher and classmates using her AAC devices. She also works on writing by sequencing pictures/photographs and printing her name with a dotted outline for some letters (which she adds to work that is turned in). With help from her grandmother and siblings, she cuts out of the newspaper or news magazine pictures of events that her teacher can use in class.

The class is working on making a time line of historical events for the classroom. Different groups of students work on different periods of time and make decisions as to what should be included. Jemma helps the group decide on what pictures to include when offered choices by the classmates in her group. To help her understand what the project represents, a paraeducator also works with her in developing her own "historical" time line of events in her life. Her grandmother has selected different photos of Jemma at different ages, and Jemma sequences these photos with the paraeducator's instructional support to represent a personal time line. Using numbers on yellow sticky notes and a number line as a guide, Jemma orders the photos and adds the appropriate sequence numbers. Given this example using her life, Jemma can more easily recognize that the class is working on a similar type of task.

Twelfth-Grade Life Enrichment Class

Sierra is a young woman of 18 who displays a love of music and a desire to be around her peers. Sierra can see very bright light or movement. She uses a wheelchair and can make a very slight movement of her head, which she uses to activate switches to control different appliances. She has considerable difficulty making basic needs known and has minimal responses under her control. As part of her school day, Sierra attends a life enrichment class (see Table 7.2 for a complete schedule of Sierra's school day).

Life enrichment is one part of a year-long sequence of courses in home economics (foods and clothing). Considerable discussion of life issues occurs as part of this class, and the teacher frequently changes scheduled activities to follow the needs of individual students in the class who want to discuss personal problems. The focus on discussion makes it difficult for Sierra to participate, yet her classmates want her to continue to be part of the group and want her to listen. For many of the class periods, students engage in various creative activities, such as designing collages that reflect their present life, future dreams, career goals, and so on. Students work alone or in groups and are encouraged to interact during these projects.

Sierra is assisted by a special educator or paraeducator who offers her choices of brightly colored pictures or other materials to include in her collages. Classmates, too, occasionally find things they think Sierra would like in her collages and present them as choices to her. Sierra is learning to make her selection by looking slightly in the direction of the desired choice. When her choice is unclear, her peers choose for her, show her their choice, and ask her to tell them if she disagrees. Adult assistance is provided until classmates finish their work and are free to work more with Sierra. When this happens, the adult fades out of the situation to help the teacher and other students as needed.

When students are working on projects, the teacher allows music to be played. If this is an option, Sierra controls the music via a momentary switch that

Table 7.2. Sample schedule of twelfth grader

Student: Sierra (age 18) comes from a supportive family and has several friends. She expresses herself by facial expressions and vocalizations. She loves to listen to others and to music. Sierra responds occasionally to very bright light and colors. She uses a wheelchair and activates switches with a slight movement of her head. She uses an object schedule throughout the day to learn the representational meaning of each item and to anticipate her day.

Period	Class	Adaptations/support	Goals
First period	Physical education (PE) (soccer)	Sierra is taken to PE by a paraeducator and is helped out of her wheelchair and onto mats. She is positioned prone on a slant board for medical reasons. She receives her physical therapy while she watches her classmates play soccer. Students not playing sit next to her and converse.	Social response to others
Second period	Life enrichment (class discusses issues relevant to their needs as young men and women)	Sierra's mother makes sure that she comes to class with photographs depicting trips taken and family members. These are used for discussions surrounding relationships, life goals, and so on. During class discussions (which often involve appearance), Sierra and her classmates experiment with putting on nail polish (Sierra both chooses color and indicates which hand by looking). She also responds to questions concerning how she wants her hair to look. The paraeducator works with all students.	Switch use Choice making Social interactions
Third period	Art (learning about different art forms)	Sierra operates the slide projector to show slides to the class. When requested to do so, she turns on a switch by using slight head movement. When producing art, Sierra uses her eyes to select color, texture, shape, tools, and so on, needed during the process. Paraeducator, art teacher, and classmates provide instruction.	Switch use Choice making Increased time on task
Fourth period	Computers	Sierra uses a gurney during this class (for a change in position). She is assisted by an inclusion support teacher who has her select her software programs and sets up the touch-sensitive switch by her head. She also listens to music or books on tape (her choice) using a Walkman.	Choice making Switch use
Fifth period	Lunch	Sierra is pushed in her wheelchair to the cafeteria by a classmate she selects by looking. She is fed through a gastrostomy tube that an adult sets up for her. She sits with her classmates from the life enrichment class. She lifts her head and turns toward the person who talks to her.	Choice making Social interaction
Sixth period	Choir	Sierra sits with classmates in choir after helping to pass out the books. She lifts her head to look at each student when they say "Thanks, Sierra." She tapes segments that the teacher wants recorded (using her head switch) and plays them back when directed. A classmate provides additional support for her to pass out the books (they are placed on her tray) and to record and play back a practice segment.	Social interactions Switch use Following directions
Seventh period	Computers	Sierra has two computer classes. She attends this one in her wheelchair. The paraeducator supports her and all other students in this class. This class is more interactive than the previous computer class, and Sierra is more alert. Students check each other's work and offer suggestions. Sierra operates her software programs with her head switch and responds to peers when they ask her to show them what she is doing (age-appropriate musical, visual programs such as Teen Tunes Plus).	Switch use Time on task

At the end of the day, classmates make sure Sierra has what she needs to take home. They help her get to the bus.

157

she activates with her head. Classmates help her decide on the desired station and set the allowed volume. Classmates also remind Sierra to continue the music if she does not keep the switch on. This creates a teasing situation, which Sierra seems to enjoy.

Sierra is working on responding to her peers by turning her head toward them, making choices, and controlling the environment via switch activation. She benefits from the social stimulation in this classroom because the effects of her medication make it very difficult to remain attentive and awake under less-stimulating circumstances.

Sierra uses the same techniques to show her family at home what she has been doing at school. Slides have been taken (either by teachers or by classmates) of Sierra's day. Explanations are sent home with the slides, and Sierra then has the opportunity to "discuss" her day using her head switch. Slides are updated periodically.

Block Scheduling

Block scheduling provides an alternative to the traditional scheduling, allowing teachers to explore a topic for a longer period of uninterrupted time. Schools using a block schedule often alternate days when certain classes meet for as much as 90 minutes instead of the traditional 50 minutes. Students with severe and multiple disabilities may benefit from the expanded time period in a preferred course and/or may be able to spend more time receiving instruction in block scheduling. Certainly, the longer time period allows teacher to make more effective use of co-operative learning opportunities (Jorgensen, Fisher, Sax, & Skoglund, 1998).

In addition to an extended learning period to explore a subject, block scheduling means fewer subjects per day that will need to be adapted for the student with severe and multiple disabilities. Also, when students are taking elective courses for a 90-minute block, general educators and special educators teaching core subjects can have access to a longer period of time for co-planning (Eshilian et al., 2000). By teaching fewer subjects per day, general educators have fewer students on a daily basis, and the planning can be less rushed. In general, block scheduling is perceived as a more effective schedule for all students when the focus is on collaborative teaching, active learning, high levels of student engagement, and interaction among students of different abilities (Jorgensen, 1998; Sage, 1997).

DETERMINING WHEN COMMUNITY-BASED INSTRUCTION IS APPROPRIATE

Secondary school students quickly approach the time when they will be graduating and involved in nonschool activities. To complement the student's interests and abilities and make this inevitable transition as smooth as possible, teachers and parents must plan ahead (Hughes & Carter, 2000; Rusch & Chadsey, 1998). Students at this age need experience in how to make use of public facilities, determine job preferences, obtain and keep jobs, gain access to community resources, and live safely and comfortably in a given neighborhood. The potential skills to be acquired before formal schooling ends are numerous and require considerable advance planning (Everson, 1995). The impact of community-based instruction on the student's ability to become a competent and actively involved community member should not be underestimated. Numerous benefits have been reported for secondary-age students who have received this type of instruction (Agran, Snow, & Swaner, 1999; Gent & Gurecka, 1998; McDonnell, Hardman, Hightower, Kiefer-O'Donnell, & Drew, 1993). Because the student with severe and multiple disabilities may have had limited experiences and generally requires longer learning periods before skill mastery, the educational team must ensure that sufficient time and opportunities are provided to enhance the learning of these critical skills.

The most efficient environment for learning community-based skills is the environment in which they are required and expected (Everson, 1995; McDonnell, 1997). Therefore, many students at this age may spend at least a portion of their day receiving direct instruction in the community. The amount of time spent in such instruction typically varies with the student, as determined by individual and family needs and beliefs. However, because in most states formal educational services end when the student reaches age 22, as the student approaches this age, more and more time may be spent appropriately in community environments (Certo, Pumpian, Fisher, Storey, & Smalley, 1997; Fisher & Sax, 1999). In addition, because most typical high school students have left school by age 17, students with special needs beyond this age are no longer with their peer group, and learning in the community is therefore perhaps more beneficial. Transition teams may thus wish to consider basing the student's entire educational program at a community college, university, vocational-technical school, or place of employment.

Community-Based Instruction as a Shared Experience

Criticism of community-based instruction revolves around issues of segregation and isolation for students with disabilities (Tashie, Jorgensen, Shapiro-Barnard, Martin, & Schuh, 1996). Off-campus teaching or instruction based in the community for students with severe and multiple disabilities has triggered some concerns regarding the resulting separation from typical peers (Tashie & Schuh, 1993). When the focus is on bringing students together to learn in general education classrooms, community-based instruction seems to be in conflict with this goal. This separation, however, does not need to occur, and the benefits of quality community-based instruction can be used to facilitate inclusive efforts, as well.

Community-based instruction should not interfere with the student's sense of belonging to a school or specific class. For instance, if a student is appropriately placed in an English class that meets daily, it would be inappropriate to remove the student from this class for periodic community-based instruction. Rules for attendance should apply to all students equally. Rather, community-based instruction could occur on a daily basis for one or two consecutive periods during a time that does not interfere with any previously assigned class that also meets educational needs. An alternative option may be to have a regularly scheduled, longer block period for instruction in the community (but not every day), and on those days when community instruction does not occur, the student could be assigned to study hall or work experience at the school.

An important consideration is that students with severe and multiple disabilities have similar schedules to those students without disabilities. Because students at the secondary level follow highly individualized schedules on the basis of both required and elective coursework, students with severe and multiple disabilities who take some classes on campus and some "classes" off campus will not draw undue attention. They will not be pulled from a particular class to receive special instruction. Furthermore, with the use of block scheduling, students can have the longer periods of time necessary for community-based learning, given the need for transportation to and from the site.

Off-campus instruction can mean recreation or work experience, service learning, and team research. All of these forms of community-based instruction can involve students with and without disabilities (Gent & Gurecka, 1998; Kluth, 2000; Krystal, 1999). Because general education also recognizes the value of students becoming involved in their community (Hamilton & Hamilton, 1997; Kesson & Oyler, 1999; Martin, 1995), considerable opportunity exists to bring students of very diverse abilities together for this purpose. Depending on the school program, students with and without disabilities can spend part of their school day at different worksites learning specific vocational skills. School–business partnerships allow students of different abilities to acquire practical vocational skills while they experience the work world. Such participation also allows for very real and practical career exploration. Rusch and Chadsey (1998) stated that successful student transitions depend on several factors including parent involvement, community-based instruction, and paid work experience during high school.

Although service learning can occur at any age, as part of the student's high school program, it can be particularly relevant with regard to future work possibilities. Service learning is designed to teach all students how they can contribute to their community and how to fulfill their civic responsibilities. In service learning, students choose a community service project that reflects personal interest as well as a community need (e.g., building homes for the homeless, visiting older adults in their homes, removing graffiti from a neighborhood.) Students of all ability levels can work to this end, and students without disabilities can see that their classmates with disabilities can be contributing members. In fact, Burns, Storey, and Certo (1999) studied the effect of service learning on the attitudes of typical high school students toward students with severe and multiple disabilities and found that their attitudes were much more positive when they shared service learning experiences with students with disabilities than when they had no contact with students with disabilities. Students with disabilities do not have to be seen in a helpee role.

Research teams as part of community-based instruction allow students to investigate issues in their community. Depending on interests, groups of students can work together in their investigation. Different members of a team may be assigned different areas to investigate, and students with very different ability levels can work together to reach the same end result. Many options exist using this model. Table 7.3 provides a sample schedule for a high school student as one example of integrating both school and community-based learning.

PLANNING COMMUNITY-BASED INSTRUCTION

As with all instructional planning, decisions related to where instruction will occur, how it will occur, and what skills will be taught are made by the educational team. Family members obviously play a critical role in planning community-

Table 7.3. A high school schedule demonstrating a blend of on- and off-campus instruction

Student: Carter is a 17-year-old senior in his final year at his high school. He enjoys swimming in the ocean, listening to rap music, and eating out. He also values his time alone and control of situations. He has Down syndrome with severe myopia that is not correctable. He has limited speech, and others essentially do not understand his speech. Carter also has severe mental health issues.

Time	Class	Adaptations/support
7:30–8:30 A.M.	Yearbook	Carter reads his pictorial/written daily schedule to help develop reading skills, recognize numbers, and organize his day. He participates in all activities in this class with the support of classmates (a paraeducator or special educator is in a classroom nearby and can provide assistance if needed). Carter makes decisions regarding projects using pictures and is learning to vote on various issues by raising his hand. When he is having a difficult morning, he is allowed to listen to music using headphones while he works. (He sees the school counselor once a week at this time.)
8:36–12:04	Community-based instruction (a combined two-block time period)	With support from a paraeducator or vocational specialist, Carter checks his daily schedule (reading) and crosses off his first period (writing). He then reads the pictorial reminder to gather certain belongings from his locker (opening the locker involves number recognition and memory skills). Carter is learning a simple bus route to a video store close to his home and high school, which involves reading and money skills. He works at the video store with the employees there, learning to check in; greet his supervisors, co-workers, and customers; open cartons of videotapes received; check returned videotapes to determine if they have been rewound and rewind them if they are not; stock shelves; empty the trash; and other related tasks. Carter is also learning to socially interact appropriately with co-workers during breaks and other appropriate times. He is also learning the bus route back to school.
12:04–12:45 P.M.	Lunch	Some days, classmates from his yearbook or marine biology classes meet Carter for lunch at a fast food place close to campus (on Carter's return from his job). On other days, Carter returns to school and joins classmates for lunch. He is learning to recognize a $5.00 bill from a $1.00 bill to pay for lunch, receive change and put it in his wallet, make choices for lunch in a timely fashion, and maintain a conversation with classmates using pictorial/written conversation books. He checks his schedule (reading and crossing off what he has already finished for the day) and goes to his locker to get materials for his next class. Other students support him for these skills.
12:45–2:19	Marine biology	With support from either the special educator or paraeducator, Carter is learning concepts of same and different using pictures of marine life and using color cues. With classmates he helps care for the class aquarium following pictorial/written directions to do so (reading and following a numerical sequence). He is learning to use a computer to access information off the web (e.g., selecting pictures related to the topic and printing them). He particularly enjoys going on field trips with this class (e.g., aquariums, beaches) and prepares for each trip by studying photographs and brochures (reading). He uses photographs taken on these trips as well as information collected during these trips to demonstrate what he has learned and share the information with his family. He checks his schedule (reading and crossing off the last period) and prepares for the next class.
2:25–3:25	Band	Carter is a member of the school band and enjoys playing drums. He is learning to attend to the director and to follow directions. He is learning to handle the drumsticks appropriately and to deal with frustrations in a positive way (he likes to play in his own way). He particularly enjoys practicing outside and is learning the routines while marching. A peer tutor provides support in this class and helps him read his schedule before this class and at the end of the day. He marks off all the classes he has done for the day and goes to his locker to collect what he needs to take home. The peer tutor (and sometimes other students as well) go with him to find his bus.

Note: The speech-language pathologist works with Carter directly during two lunch periods per week. She also provides consultation to other team members as they work with Carter on his communication skills using augmentative devices. The vision teacher works with Carter once per week at his place of employment to see if he needs any adaptations or accommodations visually and to help him make the best use of his vision.

based instruction because they are most knowledgeable about the community environments that are frequented (or need to be frequented) by the student (e.g., grocery store, convenience store, library, clothing store, fast-food and sit-down restaurants, movie theater, Laundromat). Although all teaching may not occur in these most commonly accessed environments, it may be preferable for initial instruction to occur in these places so that the student is given opportunities to practice skills after school and on weekends with family members.

Once the student is familiar with the physical layout of such commonly used environments and demonstrates appropriate skills there, teaching in similar environments to broaden skill acquisition and use will be necessary (Rosenthal-Malek & Bloom, 1998; Test & Spooner, 1996). For example, one student lives down the block from a convenience store frequently used by his younger brothers and parents. Although this student has limited vision, no speech, and mental retardation, his parents believe he could use this store on his own or with a friend, given the necessary adaptations (e.g., sufficient money in an adapted wallet that gives written instructions to the cashier). Community-based instruction, therefore, will occur at that convenience store for this particular student. When skills have been mastered (or nearly mastered), the student can receive training at other convenience stores in the community.

Community-based instruction is highly individualized and should not be confused with large-group awareness outings (e.g., a twelfth-grade government class visiting a political campaign headquarters). Of course, if a student with severe and multiple disabilities is a member of a class scheduled to go on a field trip or perform a service to the community, that student would accompany classmates. Due to the highly individualized nature of community-based instruction, the number of students with disabilities learning in a given environment would be small (one or two). In this way, individual needs for instruction can be met without drawing a lot of attention from the general public. Students without disabilities could provide additional support for instruction while receiving their own vocational work-study credit, credit for service learning or participating in research teams.

BLENDING GENERAL CLASS
PLACEMENT WITH COMMUNITY-BASED INSTRUCTION

Determining the most appropriate educational plan for a student is done on an individual basis and reflects a number of variables such as the student's age, present and future goals, abilities, needs, community, culture, and religion. As a result, no two students will have the same educational goals, daily schedule of activities, or amount of educational support. Some students will have minimal community-based instruction because their parents believe that such instruction is unnecessary and removes them from their peers (see Sierra's schedule in Table 7.2). Other students will have considerable instruction in the community because, to reach their goals, this kind of instruction is critical. It is therefore difficult even to suggest guidelines for teachers at the high school and college levels. The critical goal is to find a balance for each student between attending classes with peers who do not have disabilities and learning skills in the community (McDonnell, 1997). The following example of one high school student's schedule may help to clarify some of the decision-making processes that enter into a student's program.

Rick's Schedule

Rick is 16 years old and a junior in his local high school. He is interested in many things, likes to tease, is stubborn, and enjoys being with people. Rick uses a wheelchair and has a severe hearing loss even with bilateral hearing aids. He also has a visual field loss and is quite nearsighted. Rick uses his hands to grasp objects and then release them quickly. When interested in an object, he can maintain his grasp for a lengthy period. Rick is learning to make choices and to indicate his preferences using objects that represent items and activities. Rick uses an object schedule throughout the day to help with transitions and to help him identify representative items. Rick's daily schedule is as follows.

7:40–8:30 A.M. Band: Rick has an interest in music. In band he chooses among different rhythm instruments. He grasps the instrument and keeps time with the band as they play their songs. He can hear the rhythm and appears to enjoy this class.

8:35–9:25 A.M. Home economics: Rick's parents felt this would be a very practical class for him. Rick participates in all aspects of food preparation. He locates utensils and food items and helps prepare the work area. He mixes and stirs ingredients with assistance from others in his group and uses a switch at times to activate a blender or mixer when needed. He also helps with all cleanup activities. When the teacher is giving a lecture or when the class is involved with written tasks, Rick gathers the used, dirty linens and washes them in the washing machine, then puts them in the dryer. He also unloads the dishwasher and puts items away that are within his reach. He does this by visually matching the item to be put away with others already in their place. This class also participates in a local Meals on Wheels program with students helping to prepare food packages for senior citizens in the community. Rick volunteers on weekends with others in this class to make some of these deliveries.

9:35–10:25 A.M. Art: Rick enjoys art class because it is so active and involves many different textures and objects. Rick participates in all class activities: obtaining materials, working on projects, cleaning up, and putting materials away. He particularly likes sculpting with clay and wire but also likes painting and collage. When lectures occur or considerable verbal information is shared by the teacher, Rick helps set up the work area and begins his projects earlier than other class members.

10:30–11:20 A.M. Woodshop: Rick likes the loud sounds and vibrations from the tools used in woodshop class. He also likes working with different kinds of woods and stains, experiencing their feel and smell. Rick partially participates in all of the activities of this class, although, like art, his finished products may look uniquely his own. At the end of each class period, Rick uses an electric blower to remove wood chips and shavings from his hands and clothes. Rick uses a switch to activate the blower and really seems to enjoy the intensity of the forced air. His classmates ask him to use the blower on them, which gives him opportunities to socially interact.

11:30 A.M.–12:10 P.M. Lunch: Rick eats in the cafeteria with at least one classmate from his morning classes. He is working on making choices as he goes through the lunch line, keeping his food on the tray, eating with a spoon without excessive spillage, responding to peers, and cleaning up when finished. On Tuesdays and Thursdays, he occasionally goes out into the community earlier and has lunch at a fast-food restaurant. He is sometimes accompanied by one or two of his classmates who want to go.

12:15–1:05 P.M.   School job: Rick has several jobs on the school campus. On Mondays, he works in the library, putting books that are lying on tables and shelves in a large bucket to be reshelved. He also waters the plants for the librarian and helps to open new shipments of books as they arrive. On Wednesdays, he works in the administrative office, helping with mailings, putting messages in staff boxes, and making copies. On Fridays, he volunteers in the school's recycling program by helping to sort items collected and crushing cans and plastic bottles. On Tuesdays and Thursdays, he goes into the community for the last two periods of the day, exploring—or actually training—at places of employment. For example, he works at a pet store bagging animal feed, checking water in the pet cages, and stocking shelves with pet food. (Rick has at least four job internships a year, in order to provide him with the experiences he needs to determine his strengths and preferences.)

1:10–2:00 P.M   Study hall (Monday, Wednesday, and Friday): When Rick finishes with his jobs around school, he ends his day in study hall. He goes over his schedule of the day (object representation) in preparation for telling his parents when he arrives home. He has a choice of listening to music using headphones or creating object and part-of-object books to serve as conversation tools during lunch or other classes. Sometimes other students work with him if appropriate. They show him how to operate the cassette recorder, adjust volume, and choose desired audiotapes and help him compile his conversation books by adding appropriate phrases. On Wednesdays and Fridays, Rick leaves school early to receive physical therapy at home. (Therapy is also embedded into many activities throughout each day.)

Care has been taken in developing Rick's schedule to build on his strengths and preferences (e.g., his social nature, his ability to see and grasp objects) so that he can use these skills in a variety of ways to achieve purposeful outcomes. He is supported by different team members throughout the day as determined by his needs. Each year, Rick and his educational team will need to choose specific courses and evaluate alternative options to allow him to continue to develop useful skills. The teachers of these courses, as well as course format and structure, will determine the appropriateness of fit to Rick's needs. In addition, the amount of time Rick spends learning in the community (e.g., at various places of employment, public facilities, community college) will depend on a number of factors, including Rick's health, his changing preferences, his increased abilities, and his personal goals. For Rick, therefore, as for high school students with disabilities in general, coordinating learning time at school with time away from school in the community does not follow a predetermined plan. Rather, it is highly individualized and dynamic as the student's skills and goals change.

TRANSITION TO POSTSECONDARY SCHOOLS AND ADULT LIFE

By age 14, students with special needs are required by law (IDEA Amendments of 1997, PL 105-17) to have a formal transition plan as part of their IEP. The importance of such a plan cannot be overemphasized for a student with severe and multiple disabilities. These graduates may well require ongoing support in most areas of adult life (work, home, recreation, and community involvement) (Everson, 1995). They will require time to adjust to new expectations beyond school, and they need opportunities to make decisions about their adult life so as to maintain as much control as possible over the quality of their lifestyle.

As stated previously, during high school each student with severe and multiple impairments needs to have exposure to different job or volunteer options in order to make an informed choice about future work goals. Each student also needs to experience as many leisure and recreational pursuits as possible to determine the ones that he or she most enjoys. Students with limited or no reading skills cannot easily explore career and recreational options unless they have the opportunity to actually experience them. The transition plan for each high school student with severe disabilities, especially when those disabilities involve sensory impairments, must allow for hands-on experiences to which the student can respond.

Transition plans build on skills acquired during the school years. Therefore, the importance of an appropriate school program that continues to plan ahead for its students is obvious. The inclusion of students with severe and multiple disabilities in typical activities with others who do not have disabilities, as described in this chapter, should not end with graduation, but needs to be continued in the years following. The interactive skills learned by both students with and without severe disabilities throughout their elementary and secondary years should continue to support the inclusion of adults in typical homes, places of employment, higher education, recreational pursuits, and community activities in general. The presence of individuals with severe and multiple disabilities will not come as a surprise to adults without disabilities who have experienced inclusive education. In fact, one of the goals of inclusive educational practices is to remove any consideration of separating individuals by ability/disability as adults and to view their full participation in all adult activities as appropriate, expected, and desired.

Following a 4-year high school education, students can opt for more education at an institute of higher education (2-year or 4-year colleges and universities), obtain employment, engage in volunteer work, or select a combination of these options. Opportunities may be great or more limited depending on what the community has to offer. What is important is that these opportunities and options should be similar for students with and without disabilities. For example, further education at institutes of higher education should not be automatically rejected as too difficult for students with severe and multiple disabilities. Considerable benefits have been noted for students with and without severe disabilities in university programs (Hall, Kleinert, & Kearns, 2000; McDonald, MacPherson-Court, Frank, Uditsky, & Symons, 1997).

While still supported by the school district as part of their IEP/ITP, students ages 18–22 may be physically based at a university, college, community center, apartment, or business. Teachers and paraeducators would provide instructional support at these locations, not the high school. The accommodations that were made to include students with severe and multiple disabilities in their high school general education program should be continued after graduation as needed. Certainly adaptive materials and equipment will need to be available for those with physical, sensory, communicative, and intellectual disabilities.

Young adults with severe and multiple disabilities, like other graduates, should have the opportunity to move into typical places to live, work, and recreate as determined by individual preferences and not by the availability of existing programs. To this end, the creativity, problem-solving skills, and commitment of individual team members will continually be challenged to ensure successful transitions for students with severe and multiple impairments.

REFERENCES

Agran, M., Snow, K., & Swaner, J. (1999). A survey of secondary level teachers' opinions on community-based instruction and inclusive education. *Journal of The Association for Persons with Severe Handicaps, 24,* 58–62.

Burns, M., Storey, K., & Certo, N.J. (1999). Effect of service learning on attitudes towards students with severe disabilities. *Education and Training in Mental Retardation and Developmental Disabilities, 34,* 58–65.

Certo, N., Pumpian, I., Fisher, D., Storey, K., & Smalley, K. (1997). Focusing on the point of transition. *Education and Treatment of Children, 20,* 68–84.

Demchak, M.A., & Greenfield, R.G. (2000). A transition portfolio for Jeff, a student with multiple disabilities. *Teaching Exceptional Children, 32*(6), 44–49.

Eshilian, L., Falvey, M.A., Bove, C., Hibbard, M.J., Laiblin, J., Miller, C., & Rosenberg, R.L. (2000). Restructuring to create a high school community of learners. In R.A. Villa & J.S. Thousand (Eds.), *Restructuring for caring and effective education: Piecing the puzzle together* (2nd ed., pp. 402–427). Baltimore: Paul H. Brookes Publishing Co.

Everson, J.M. (Ed.). (1995). *Supporting young adults who are deaf-blind in their communities: A transition planning guide for service providers, families, and friends.* Baltimore: Paul H. Brookes Publishing Co.

Fisher, D., & Sax, C. (1999). Noticing differences between secondary and postsecondary education: Extending Agran, Snow, & Swaner's discussion. *Journal of The Association for Persons with Severe Handicaps, 24,* 303–305.

Fisher, D., Sax, C., & Pumpian, I. (1999). *Inclusive high schools: Learning from contemporary classrooms.* Baltimore: Paul H. Brookes Publishing Co.

Gent, P., & Gurecka, L. (1998). Service learning: A creative strategy for inclusive classrooms. *Journal of The Association for Persons with Severe Handicaps, 23,* 261–271.

Hall, M., Kleinert, H.L., & Kearns, J.F. (2000). Going to college! Postsecondary programs for students with moderate and severe disabilities. *Teaching Exceptional Children, 32*(3), 58–65.

Hamilton, S., & Hamilton, M. (1997). When is learning work-based? *Phi Delta Kappan, 78,* 677–681.

Hughes, C., & Carter, E.W. (2000). *The transition handbook: Strategies high school teachers use that work!* Baltimore: Paul H. Brookes Publishing Co.

Individuals with Disabilities Education Act Amendments of 1997, PL 105-17, 20 U.S.C §§ 1400 *et seq.*

Jorgensen, C.M. (Ed.). (1998). *Restructuring high schools for all students: Taking inclusion to the next level.* Baltimore: Paul H. Brookes Publishing Co.

Jorgensen, C.M. (1999). A community of learners born of trust, respect, and courage: The foundation of inclusion and school reform at Jefferson High School. In D. Fisher, C. Sax, & I. Pumpian (Eds.), *Inclusive high schools: Learning from contemporary classrooms* (pp. 103–130). Baltimore: Paul H. Brookes Publishing Co.

Jorgensen, C.M., Fisher, D., Sax, C., & Skoglund, K.L. (1998). Innovative scheduling, new roles for teachers and heterogeneous groupings: The organizational factors related to student success in inclusive, restructuring schools. In C.M. Jorgensen (Ed.), *Restructuring high schools for all students: Taking inclusion to the next level* (pp. 49–70). Baltimore: Paul H. Brookes Publishing Co.

Kesson, K., & Oyler, C. (1999). Integrated curriculum and service learning: Linking school-based knowledge and social action. *English Education, 31,* 135–149.

Kluth, P. (2000). Community-referenced learning and the inclusive classroom. *Remedial and Special Education, 21,* 19–26.

Krystal, S. (1999). The nurturing potential of service learning. *Educational Leadership, 56,* 58–61.

Martin, J. (1995). A philosophy of education for the year 2000. *Phi Delta Kappan, 76,* 355–359.

McDonald, L., MacPherson-Court, L., Frank, S., Uditsky, B., & Symons, F. (1997). An inclusive university program for students with moderate to severe developmental disabilities: Student, parent and faculty perspectives. *Developmental Disabilities Bulletin, 25*(1), 43–46.

McDonnell, J. (1997, February). Isn't it about achieving a balance? *TASH Newsletter, 23*(2), 23–24, 29.

McDonnell, J., Hardman, M.L., Hightower, J., Kiefer-O'Donnell, R., & Drew, C. (1993). Impact of community-based instruction in the development of adaptive behavior of secondary-level students with mental retardation. *American Journal on Mental Retardation, 97,* 575–584.

O'Brien, J., & O'Brien, C.L. (1998). *A little book about person centered planning.* Toronto: Inclusion Press.

Rosenthal-Malek, A., & Bloom, A. (1998). Beyond acquisition: Teaching generalization for students with developmental disabilities. In A. Hilton & R. Ringlaben (Eds.), *Best and promising practices in developmental disabilities* (pp. 139–155). Austin, TX: PRO-ED.

Rusch, F.R., & Chadsey, J.G. (Eds.). (1998). *Beyond high school: Transition from school to work.* Belmont, CA: Wadsworth.

Sage, D. (1997). *Inclusion in secondary schools: Bold initiatives challenging change.* Port Chester, NY: National Professional Resources.

Tashie, C., Jorgensen, C., Shapiro-Barnard, S., Martin, J., & Schuh, M. (1996, September). High school inclusion: Strategies and barriers. *TASH Newsletter, 22*(9), 19–22.

Tashie, C., & Schuh, M. (1993). Why not community-based instruction? High school students with disabilities belong with their peers. *Equity and Excellence, 1,* 15–17.

Test, D.W., & Spooner, F. (1996). *Community-based instructional support.* Washington, DC: American Association on Mental Retardation.

Chapter 8

The Important Role of
Peers in the Inclusion Process

June E. Downing and Joanne Eichinger

Many schools and school districts, especially those in remote rural areas, may never have access to an adequate number of qualified and experienced teachers and related services personnel to support an inclusive educational process. When students have multiple impairments that include a severe sensory loss, obtaining knowledgeable educators for such schools is particularly difficult (Erin, 1986; Giangreco, Edelman, MacFarland, & Luiselli, 1997; Izen & Brown, 1991). As a result, school districts must look for other avenues of support to ensure the successful inclusion of these students. One resource for schools that is free and in abundant supply is their students. Capitalizing on the valuable resource that students without disabilities (or with less severe disabilities) represent is critical to the inclusion process (Ryndak, 1995; Villa & Thousand, 1992).

The use of peers to assist in including all students, regardless of the severity of their disability, has been well documented (Staub & Hunt, 1993; Staub, Schwartz, Gallucci, & Peck, 1994; Vacc & Cannon, 1991). Students have been used in the capacity of peer tutors, cross-age tutors, data collectors, and peer buddies or peer helpers. They have aided directly or indirectly in the instruction of gross and fine motor skills, communication skills, social skills, academic skills, and community living skills. Their impact has been impressive. The benefits that these peers have received are also innumerable (Fisher, Sax, & Jorgensen, 1998; Giangreco, Edelman, Cloninger, & Dennis, 1993; Peck, Donaldson, & Pezzoli, 1990).

Including peers as active members in the education of their classmates is critical to the full-time placement of students with severe and multiple disabilities in typical classrooms. Yet, it is not meant to be a one-sided benefit for students with disabilities. Learning and achievement are the goals of quality education for all students. Careful attention must be taken to ensure that learning together does not detract from any student's education and that it contributes to all. For example, a study by Hunt, Staub, Alwell, and Goetz (1994) on the achievement of second-grade students learning mathematics in cooperative learning groups verified that all students did master learning objectives; the presence of a student with severe multiple disabilities as a member of the group did not interfere with other students' learning of mathematics. A study by McDonnell, Thorson, McQuivey, and

Kiefer-O'Donnell (1997) reported similar findings regarding engaged time of students without disabilities when students with severe disabilities shared the same learning environment.

SUPPORTING PEER INVOLVEMENT

In general, students of any age appear willing and able to offer assistance when needed. In fact, peers have been so enthusiastic and eager to assist, especially in the younger grades, that another problem arises—that of modifying their enthusiasm so it is does not interfere with any student's learning. Not all students, however, will feel comfortable interacting with a classmate who has obvious physical, sensory, and intellectual differences (although this may change with time). No student should ever be forced to help, and peer assistance should never be used as punishment. There are plenty of students who are interested in becoming involved with such a classmate, and therefore, not all students in a given class or school need to do so. There is no reason to expect that all students will want to be involved. In fact, it would be unusual in any school situation for all students to enjoy being with every other student. Students naturally choose their friends and study partners. This should be no different for the student with significant impairments. If interactions do not occur naturally, some suggestions for the more formal recruitment of peers are found in Table 8.1.

Salisbury, Gallucci, Palombaro, and Peck (1995) conducted a qualitative study to determine strategies used by general educators to promote social interactions among students with and without severe disabilities in general classrooms. The five major approaches identified were: 1) active facilitation of social interactions, 2) empowering students, 3) building a sense of classroom community, 4) modeling acceptance, and 5) developing school organizational supports. For additional information, Haring, Haring, Breen, Romer, and White (1995) have described specific strategies for the selection and recruitment of peers in inclusive environments.

Elementary School Students

At the elementary school level, students usually express a desire to assist and work with a student with severe and multiple impairments, just as they would any classmate, and little formal recruitment is needed (Jorgensen, 1994; Staub et al., 1994). Students at this age are naturally curious about differences and are interested in discovering why such differences exist. Students can be encouraged to work together (e.g., in pairs, in small groups, in cooperative learning groups), and the teacher can ensure that all students have an equal opportunity to get to know one another. The students who desire to work together and those who have the skills to do so become readily apparent. As much as possible, the student with severe and multiple disabilities should be allowed to choose a work partner (especially if other students are allowed to do so). The student with disabilities can make this choice by looking at, reaching toward, or touching the desired partner or by using individual class photographs. The same students, however, should not serve as partners all the time. Students need to keep up with their own work and should not be relied on to help another student for all assignments and activities. Some teachers rotate students so that everyone eventually works with

Table 8.1.   Suggestions for supporting peers to assist students with disabilities

Informally ask students if they would like to interact with a given student, and provide opportunities to do so.

Ask the teacher who might benefit academically, socially, and emotionally from working with a student with severe and multiple impairments.

Ask the school counselor, especially at the secondary level, to identify students who may benefit from such interactions.

Help students with severe and intellectual impairments join extracurricular activities and clubs.

Ask the student council or other school leaders if they are interested in getting to know or supporting some students.

Develop a credit course for peer tutoring.

Establish a peer buddy club.

everyone else. Other teachers allow peer tutoring or helping only by those students who are performing well with their work. Being in a helping role thus becomes a privilege, not a duty.

In a qualitative study examining the way in which five elementary teachers used peer intervention to promote the inclusion of students with moderate or severe disabilities, Janney and Snell (1996) conducted interviews with teachers who implemented partial integration, inclusion (but not at the student's neighborhood school), and inclusion at the student's home school. They determined that the teachers attempted to promote inclusion by using peer assistance and peer social interactions. They also noted that teachers perceived the students with disabilities as instrumental to the inclusion process. One difference they noted between the home school inclusion and the other two environments was that students with disabilities were expected to follow the same rules as the rest of the students in the home school situation, whereas there was a departure from this in some instances in the other two environments.

Middle and High School Students

Pressure to be like everyone else, to be part of the "in" crowd, and to appear to defy adult authority may present some initial challenges when encouraging middle and high school students to become involved with a classmate who appears to be quite different. Despite this potential hindrance, finding interested students to become involved in another student's life has not been overly difficult (Hughes et al., 1999; Kennedy, Shukla, & Fryxell, 1997; Peck et al., 1990; York, Vandercook, MacDonald, Heise-Neff, & Caughey, 1992). The greater difficulty, perhaps, is that of encouraging the paid adult support to fade out and provide opportunities for students to interact (Ferguson, Jeanchild, & Meyer, 1992; Giangreco, Edelman, Luiselli, & MacFarland, 1997). Students are less likely to involve themselves in another student's life if it necessitates tolerating the presence of an adult. Students at this age typically view an adult's presence as decidedly unnecessary. Once students understand that their involvement is desired and they are provided with some initial suggestions for becoming acquainted (if necessary), adults probably should maintain as low a profile as possible.

Students at this age can work together as lab partners in a science class, participate in the same study group for English or history, or accompany the student with disabilities from one class to the next. Depending on school district policy, classmates can help students with severe physical disabilities as well as their positioning equipment (e.g., standers, gurneys) move to various classes. In addition to the social benefits for both students, such peer assistance can greatly relieve pressure on paid personnel to be in several places at the same time.

HELPING STUDENTS UNDERSTAND SEVERE AND MULTIPLE DISABILITIES

Although students with severe and multiple disabilities share many similarities with other children their age in terms of interests and desires, the lack of typical communication skills and the need for certain adaptations may pose initial barriers to the development of friendships. Students may need to understand about their classmate's specific strengths and needs in order to feel more comfortable in their interactions (Bowden & Thorburn, 1993; Helmstetter, Peck, & Giangreco, 1994; York & Tundidor, 1995).

Information can be provided informally or formally, depending on the student's age and the given situation. At the preschool and elementary levels, all students at a given school may want and need the information. This information can focus on the fact that the entire class is learning together, even though each individual has slightly different ways to learn that work best for that person. The idea is to share information while building respect and appreciation of differences. A question box can be used by the teacher on a weekly basis. Students can ask specific questions anonymously (if they like), and the responses can be discussed as a class. For instance, a student may want to know why his classmate never looks directly at him. This child's greater use of peripheral vision needs to be explained so that the lack of eye contact is not misunderstood.

During such information-sharing sessions, the student with severe disabilities may or may not be present. Family members, with assistance from their child's teachers, will determine what would be most appropriate. Hunt, Alwell, Farron-Davis, and Goetz (1996) described an intervention designed to facilitate social inclusion of three elementary-level students with multiple disabilities, including sensory impairments. One of the components of the intervention involves providing ongoing information relative to how the students learn and what adaptive equipment they used. This information was provided at naturally occurring times within the context of social interactions.

At the secondary level, schoolwide training may be neither feasible nor desirable. Informing just those students who have classes with someone having these multiple disabilities may be the most direct and appropriate course of action. These students, in turn, can educate other students who are interested and want more information. In addition, naturally infusing disability-related information into certain appropriate classes, such as civics or government, English, biology, and drama, may be the most effective and least conspicuous way of bringing attention to issues of disability. Instead of special assemblies or even special lessons, information about disabilities is a natural part of the curriculum and can be studied along with other aspects of the typical curriculum (Hamre-Nietupski et al., 1989). Table 8.2 presents some suggestions for sharing information with students.

Students at any age will need to know how to effectively communicate and what to expect regarding visual, hearing, and physical capabilities. The emphasis

Table 8.2.   Sharing information about a student's special condition with classmates

A parent or sibling can present information to a class about a student using home videos, slides, photograph albums, and items collected from the student's life.

Teachers (general and special educators) can hold a formal discussion about a student's abilities and disabilities. The student with disabilities may or may not be present, depending on student and family preference.

Teachers can have the class read books about individuals who have similar disabilities to those of a classmate and then discuss them.

Teachers can wait for questions to emerge and address them informally as they occur.

Information can be infused into a curriculum topic (e.g., civil rights, journalism, discrimination, diversity of the human species).

A student's friends can disseminate information informally to other students in other classes and around the school.

Students can be assigned a project to research different types of abilities.

on information sharing focuses on the abilities of individuals and provides clear strategies for effective interactions. Students are shown the similarities between themselves, with differences explored matter-of-factly and in a manner that does not diminish the student. The appreciation of diversity should be stressed, with all students recognizing the strengths that a diverse population brings.

TEACHING INTERACTION SKILLS

Perhaps one of the most important requirements for initiating and maintaining friendships is effective interaction skills. When children do not use speech to communicate their thoughts and desires, interactions can become difficult and may be avoided. Students without disabilities will need to learn the modes of communication used by a classmate so that they will feel more comfortable initiating interactions and remaining in these interactions for longer periods of time.

Students who share a class with and have an interest in getting to know a student who has severe and multiple disabilities need to learn how to express their thoughts and how to understand the student's expressive communications. Students may need to learn how to use their classmate's AAC system (of pictorial or object symbols), how to visually or tactually sign, or how to make use of objects and touch cues (Downing, 1999). If their classmate is slow to respond, peers will need to receive training to wait for this student so as to avoid dominating the interaction (Buzolich & Lunger, 1995). Learning such interaction skills is not necessarily difficult and provides the student with severe and multiple disabilities many different role models and communicative partners throughout the day.

Students without disabilities may need instruction on how to avoid treating their classmate with multiple disabilities in a juvenile manner, especially if that student is very small in stature. Students without disabilities may interact with any student having a significant intellectual impairment in a manner considerably younger than that used with a student of the same age with no disabilities (Janney & Snell, 1996). Girls, in particular, tend to adopt "mothering" and disciplining roles that may hinder the development of true friendships (Evans, Salisbury, Palombaro, Berryman, & Hollowood, 1992; Kishi & Meyer, 1994). Role-playing different scenarios using students without disabilities in the role of a student with a severe disability—taking care not to demean that student—and then exaggerating the interactions allows the class to see ways to improve the situation. It is critical for the classroom teacher, all support personnel, administrators, and any adult who interacts with the student having a severe and multiple impairment to do so in a way that provides a positive model for students without disabilities. When adults model inappropriate behavior, such as using language that is immature, raising their tone of voice when speaking, holding the student's hand when walking (for many upper elementary and older students), and giving students juvenile things to play with and do, they set the stage for the same unequal interactions to occur among students.

Teaching Accommodations for Physical Disabilities

Some students have physical disabilities in addition to their sensory and intellectual impairments. These students use certain devices to accommodate these limitations. Although classmates may not need in-depth information on etiology (if students ask, they should receive information at a level they can understand), they do need to know what the student can do, what the student is expected to do independently, and where assistance may be appreciated. Students need to learn how to assist their classmate when necessary (e.g., safely push someone in a wheelchair, guide someone using a walker). They need to know to present items or choices within the student's range of motion. Some students will feel comfortable stabilizing a classmate's arm to allow maximal use of the other arm when performing certain tasks.

Understanding physical limitations can serve as a catalyst for classmates to devise creative adaptations to allow a student greater ability to participate. For example, students in a woodshop class made a slant board with small shelves to hold object choices for a classmate, whereas other students made a rotary board that allowed a classmate a variety of pictorial choices. In a sewing class, students made an adapted shopping bag to fit alongside a classmate's wheelchair to accommodate her limited range of motion for taking items off store shelves and carrying them to the counter.

Teaching Adaptations Unique to Sensory Loss

A severe visual or hearing loss (or combination of the two) can alter interactions and require certain adjustments in how peers interact. If a student has usable hearing but limited or no vision, then classmates need to be aware of the importance of using their voices to help the student anticipate their actions. They should also remember to identify themselves when approaching the student with disabilities (e.g., "Hey, Jane, it's me, Cindi. Want to go to lunch with me?"). Such use of verbal cuing may also reduce the startle reflex of a student with limited vision and severe physical disabilities. Students need to be given feedback on using certain verbal expressions that are visual in nature and therefore not very helpful (e.g., "Put it there," "Go over there," "It's by the brown one"). Verbal instructions and comments should be clear and relate to the student's abilities.

When giving the student something, a classmate needs to learn to put it into the student's hands or on a table in front of the student and let him or her know where it is, rather than silently holding it in front of the student. Classmates need to understand that it is appropriate to gently touch the student to provide needed information that will increase participation. For example, when a science model is placed before each cooperative learning group, one member of that group should guide the student's hand to the model so that this student will not miss vital information available to the rest of the group visually. When moving with the student with limited or no vision around the classroom or from class to class, it may be appropriate for classmates to offer to be a sighted guide. Serving as a sighted guide does not require much training and helps to develop responsibility on the part of the student.

For the student with limited or no hearing, classmates will need to obtain either visual or tactile attention before trying to exchange information. Yelling at a student across a room or playing field should be discouraged, and alternative visual ways of attracting attention substituted. Using gestures, body language, and other visual cues (objects or pictures) needs to be emphasized over an abundance of verbal output.

Understanding Unexpected and Undesired Behavior

Students with severe and multiple disabilities may have learned to engage in certain behaviors that seem unusual and perhaps somewhat frightening. They may sometimes spin in circles with their head back, looking at lights in the ceiling, or rock their head back and forth repeatedly while making a unique sound. Such behaviors initially may be difficult to understand and can have a negative impact on interactions (Ogletree, Wetherby, & Westling, 1992). Students without disabilities can be taught the rationale for these behaviors (e.g., to stimulate or calm oneself) and can see the relationship between these behaviors and the behaviors they themselves commonly engage in for the same purposes (e.g., swinging legs, clicking pens, twirling hair, chewing gum). Students without disabilities can also be asked why such behaviors are different across different people.

Recognizing similarities in the reasons that people engage in certain behaviors can greatly reduce the fears and uncertainties that may threaten the development of positive relationships. Once the reasons for the behaviors are better understood by class members, then students without disabilities can brainstorm ways of helping a particular student (with or without a disability) substitute an unacceptable behavior for a more socially acceptable one. It is also important for students to know how to respond to unacceptable behavior, particularly when the behavior is aggressive and hurtful. A common reaction to aggression against oneself is to strike back, either physically or verbally. Students must be allowed to reason through the consequences of such reactions to determine for themselves the overall impact. With some guidance from adults, if necessary, students of any age often volunteer that reacting to aggression with aggression will only aggravate the situation. Other means need to be employed. Frequently, aggressive behavior from a student with a significant intellectual impairment is tolerated by classmates, who probably do not understand why it occurred, realize that it would be inappropriate to retaliate, and end up trying to avoid the individual. This situation can lead to isolation for the student as classmates avoid interactions. Such isolation is exacerbated by support personnel who may maintain an overly high profile in their efforts to ensure that aggressive behavior is controlled.

Students without disabilities must be helped to understand the reasons behind more aggressive behavior, especially when it is usually not meant to hurt another. Students of any age are quick to see the frustration that a classmate may feel when the ability to effectively communicate is limited. They can relate the behavior to similar behaviors they express when extremely frustrated. Although understanding is critical to avoid the isolation that could result, students also need to know specific things they should and can do when the student engages in the aggressive behavior. Often, students can arrive at specific strategies designed to reduce their avoidance of the individual and simultaneously assist the student to gain greater self-control.

Knowing exactly what to do will help to alleviate the uncertainty and fear surrounding the situation. For example, the class has decided that, when Danny (age 10) becomes angry and tries to grab someone's hand and bite it, they will tell him "No" quite firmly and then move away from him. When he appears to be calmer, they will return to where they were (next to him). In addition, they will try to be sensitive to what makes Danny angry and try to help him avoid those situations by offering other choices or giving him more assistance.

ROLES FOR STUDENTS WITHOUT DISABILITIES

Students without disabilities offer a valuable form of support to their classmates with severe and multiple disabilities. Whether in the role of formal peer tutor or as a friend, students without disabilities offer assistance when needed and provide opportunities for social closeness and potential friendships.

Peer Tutoring

The use of trained peer tutors to support students with severe and multiple disabilities in general education classrooms has been implemented in several school districts (Villa & Thousand, 1996). Peer tutors typically receive credit for fulfilling the role of a same-age teaching assistant. They are not in a given class to learn the subject matter but rather to deliver support as needed to a specific student. They may help a student check his or her schedule, aid the student in getting to the right class, ensure that the student works on specific IEP objectives, adapt materials, encourage the student's interaction with classmates, and collect data on the student's progress. Consequently, peer tutors can represent a major form of support to students. Although peer tutors can be an invaluable aid to students with disabilities, especially in schools where staffing is limited, heavy reliance on peer-tutoring programs should be avoided. A peer tutor is not a trained teacher, and overreliance on peer tutors may hinder the development of more natural supports, such as the general educator and classmates (Martin, Jorgensen, & Klein, 1998).

In addition, developing friendships with students without disabilities may be hindered if the student with disabilities is always placed in a subordinate role of being helped by a peer tutor (Staub, 1998). Van der Klift and Kunc (1994) cautioned against the practice of placing the student with disabilities at the receiving end of the relationship. This helper–helpee relationship is clearly evident in peer tutoring programs; however, peer tutors can be instrumental in facilitating peer interaction and helping students with severe and multiple disabilities belong to various social groups. Peer tutors can definitely be friends, as illustrated by a middle school student and her peer tutor in Figure 8.1.

Figure 8.1.   A peer tutor in seventh grade provides educational support as well as companionship. (Photograph by Margo Yunker.)

Friends and Natural Supports

The most important role for a peer without disabilities is that of a true friend to a student with severe and multiple disabilities. This is an important role for any student. Although classmates can serve in the official role of peer tutor, being a friend provides invaluable support in numerous ways throughout each school day. (The two fifth graders in Figure 8.2 are very good friends who provide each other mutual support.) A student without disabilities, for example, can play an active role in encouraging a friend with severe and multiple disabilities to engage in social interactions and to clarify communicative attempts. As a friend, the student without disabilities is more likely to expect his or her classmate to make his or her needs or desires known and is more apt to give that student enough time when trying to communicate. A friend will also serve as an interpreter to allow interactions to occur with another student who may be less familiar with a unique communicative style. Classmates who are friends also provide valuable information to teachers concerning the types of messages they feel need to be included on augmentative communication systems. Research has proven that being in classes together promotes stronger friendships and support networks for students with and without severe disabilities (Kennedy et al., 1997).

Furthermore, students without disabilities can provide natural support for a classmate who has difficulty engaging in expected and desired behavior. Friends can be understanding of their classmate's unique way of expressing him- or her-

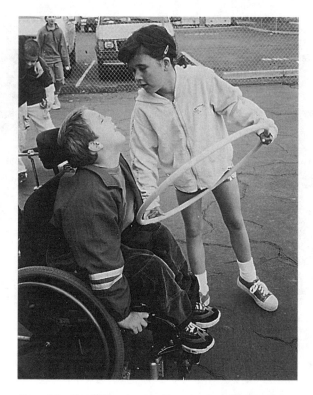

Figure 8.2. Two fifth graders provide each other with mutual support and friendship. (Photograph by Lavada Minor.)

self and provide feedback to the student concerning that behavior. They can also explain the occurrence of undesired behavior to another student who may be annoyed or put off by the behavior. For example, Ian, a second grader, frequently flaps his hands in front of his face and makes repetitious vocal sounds. His friend, Troy, asks him if he's bored and then provides him with something he likes to manipulate and explore. Jeremy, an eighth grader, occasionally grabs books or magazines and crinkles them up in his hands and bites them. His friend, Eric, tells him to cut it out, directs him to put the materials down on the table, and gets him to do something else with different material. Besides specific incidences such as those just mentioned, the daily presence of so many students without disabilities in the course of any school day provides the student with severe and multiple disabilities with numerous appropriate role models. Of course, the teacher needs to ensure that the student notices these role models (e.g., "Where is everyone going?" "Is anyone else screaming?").

When students without disabilities consider themselves friends of students with disabilities, there is a natural inclination to include the students with disabilities in class and school activities. Depending on the students' disabilities, being included in all activities could require a number of adaptations. Classmates can be encouraged to consider different ways to include their friends. For instance, students without disabilities can remind the teacher of the need for a wheelchair-accessible bus and place of destination for field trips. They may determine the need to present material in a different manner (e.g., using objects versus just talking). They can develop ways of working together, making joint

Table 8.3. Types of peer support

Direct student's attention to the teacher or activity.

Assist student to take out and prepare his or her materials.

Assist student with mobility (e.g., sighted guide, pushing wheelchair).

Assist student with moving and setting up equipment and materials.

Learn and use the student's mode(s) of communication.

Plan to be with the student for lunch, recess, and assemblies. Serve as an appropriate role model.

Provide corrective feedback when inappropriate behavior occurs.

Provide information about what a particular student needs to say via an augmentative or alternative communication device.

Design and make adaptive equipment or materials as part of a class (e.g., woodshop) or at home.

Brainstorm ways to include a classmate in a given activity.

Be part of a telephone tree to call student at home.

presentations, and turning in final projects. To encourage such involvement (which can be highly beneficial), teachers need to listen to students and incorporate their ideas when appropriate. Students can make adaptations for a friend (e.g., a book holder in woodshop, photographs for an AAC device in photography class), or they can decide on the level of participation to be expected of their friend. This involvement develops creative thinking skills, problem-solving skills, and respect for everyone's right to be included.

Finally, students without disabilities can help ensure that their classmate moves with the class and gets to the next activity in a timely fashion. Students can push their classmate who uses a wheelchair, provide sighted guidance, or encourage a student who is using a walker to keep up. Sometimes students require that positioning equipment move with them in the classroom and from one class to the next. Classmates can be particularly helpful in this regard, taking responsibility for moving wedges, standers, corner chairs, and so forth, so that their friend can have access to necessary equipment when and where needed. Students at the secondary level can be asked to help move equipment that is large and bulky to transport. Table 8.3 lists a number of potential types of peer supports.

STRUCTURING THE DEVELOPMENT OF INTERACTIONS

Sometimes interactions do not occur naturally, for whatever reason. When this happens, teachers may need to implement structured groups. Approaches such as MAPS (originally known as the McGill Action Planning System; Forest & Pearpoint, 1992; Vandercook, York, & Forest, 1989), Circle of Friends (Forest & Lusthaus, 1989), and creative problem solving (Giangreco, Cloninger, Dennis, & Edelman, 2000) have been used to support interactions among students of vastly different abilities. Also, these may be incorporated in more global interventions designed to promote social interactions and friendship. For example, Hunt et al. (1996) included a support circle, a recess club, and a sign club in their validated intervention model. MAPS was described in Chapter 3. Circle of Friends and creative problem solving are described next.

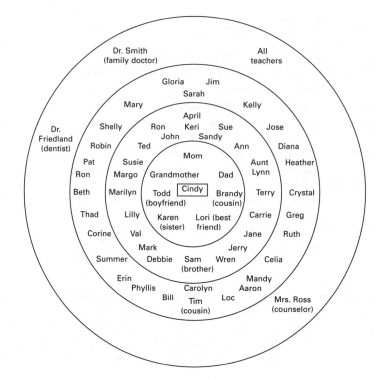

Figure 8.3.   A typical seventh-grader's Circle of Friends.

Circle of Friends

Circle of Friends is a method for developing relationships among students with-out disabilities and a student included in a general education environment. In this process, an adult asks the students without disabilities to fill in four concentric cir-cles representing their current relationships. The first and innermost circle in-cludes the names of people closest to them; the second, people they like and see frequently, but not with the same intimacy as those in the first circle; the third, people they know and occasionally do things with; and the fourth, people who are paid to be in their life (e.g., doctors, teachers). See Falvey, Forest, Pearpoint, and Rosenberg (1994) for more detailed information on this process.

Figure 8.3 provides an example of a typical child's Circle of Friends. After all circles are completed, the facilitator shares a circle of a student who has disabili-ties and highlights the fact that this student's circle contains mostly paid people. Figure 8.4 shows an example of a Circle of Friends for a boy who is deafblind. The facilitator generates responses from the students about how this must feel and asks students to think of ways they might become part of the student's circle. Table 8.4 provides one example of how some high school students became more involved in their classmate's life.

The resulting plan of action may take the form of a social club built around common interests. Originally organized and facilitated by adults (e.g., special ed-ucator, school counselor, parent), the intent of a true circle of friends is to exist without adult intervention. That is, initially students may be encouraged to meet and engage in entertaining activities such as making popcorn and watching videotapes or painting murals (with an adult setting the meeting date and ensur-

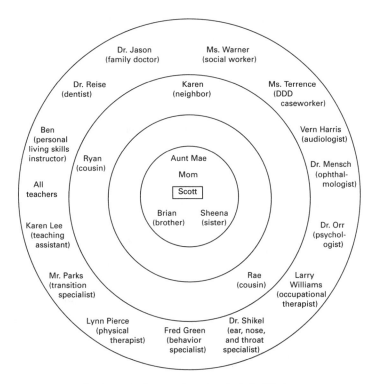

Figure 8.4.   Circle of Friends of a seventh-grader who is deafblind.

ing that necessary materials and refreshments are obtained). Once the group starts meeting on a regular basis, the adults should be able to fade from the group, with the students assuming the responsibility to continue to meet.

Creative Problem Solving

Another suggested approach for including students with severe disabilities in general education environments is the use of the creative problem-solving method developed by Osborn (1953) and Parnes (1981). This method has been employed extensively for various applications. It has also been used to help students without disabilities generate ideas for actively engaging a particular student with severe disabilities in general education classroom activities (Giangreco et al., 2000).

In this six-step process, participants first describe the problem facing them. For example, in one high school class the problem faced was that Pedro, a student with severe and multiple disabilities, was sitting in class making noises and being disruptive. Next, participants compile facts about the problem. In this case, some facts included Pedro's lack of interest in the topic, his inability to do the math involved, and his isolation from others in the class. This step is followed by restating the problem so that ideas can be generated. For example, it might be stated, "In what ways can Pedro be involved in our unit on consumerism?" The fourth step is to brainstorm ideas, deferring judgment. This is followed by evaluating each idea using set criteria to determine solutions. The final step involves refining targeted solutions and developing and implementing an action plan.

Applying this process in a classroom can provide an opportunity for students at any age level to practice and hone problem-solving skills in a real-life situation.

Table 8.4.   Some results of a high school student's Circle of Friends

Student	Sierra is a twelfth grader who has developed a number of good friends. Sierra is blind and can move her head only about ½ inch to either side. She does not speak and has a difficult time making her wants and needs known.
Facilitator	A student teacher from the local university initiated the idea of a Circle of Friends in Sierra's life enrichment class. She explained that the hoped-for outcome would be lasting and close friendships in and out of school. She helped the class compare opportunities that most of the students have to develop friendships to Sierra's opportunities and abilities (e.g., sharing classes for several years, hanging out, talking on the telephone). The student teacher then let the students suggest ways to enhance Sierra's opportunities to make friends.
Ideas	Sierra's class developed a system of sign-up sheets whereby students signed up to eat lunch with Sierra, to meet and walk to and from classes with her, or to telephone her after school and on weekends. They put these sheets in a folder and passed it around during class. The girls also started a gossip notebook (no adults allowed, except for Sierra's mother who responded for her). The girls learned a lot about Sierra and began to feel comfortable talking to her about many things. One of the boys recommended that a cassette tape be started the same way as the notebook. This worked well and gave Sierra the opportunity to share her responses with the class independently (via a head switch). The students were pleased with their ideas and at how well they appeared to work.
Results	After 3 weeks, students stopped signing up and would just come up to Sierra and say, "See you for lunch," and "See you after art." They were approaching, speaking, and treating Sierra on the same level as they treated all their other friends. The facilitator had a hard time keeping up with all of Sierra's dates.

Students are also more likely to use the process in other situations requiring problem-solving abilities. Because students are actively engaged in curricular modification and adaptations, the process also aligns closely with a child-centered approach as opposed to a model in which the teacher dominates as an authority figure.

VALUE OF FRIENDSHIPS

One of the most highly rated outcomes of the educational process for any student and certainly for the student with severe and multiple disabilities is that he or she has friends (Bishop & Jubala, 1994; Hunt et al., 1996; Turnbull & Turnbull, 1999). Certainly, the value of friendships cannot be underestimated for anyone. The impact on the student's performance at home and school is obvious. Although friendships cannot be specifically taught, they can and should be encouraged by adult team members who recognize the positive impact of friendships on the academic, behavioral, social, communicative, and motor skills of most students.

Certain research has focused on friendship development in inclusive environments. Hendrickson, Shokoohi-Yekta, Hamre-Nietupski, and Gable (1996) conducted a study involving 1,137 sixth through twelfth graders in three states, who attended schools with students with severe disabilities. Survey results indicated that students thought that friendships with students with severe disabilities were possible (38.2% noted that they had such a friendship), that students with severe disabilities benefit from these friendships, and that students without disabilities should attempt to be friends with students with severe disabilities. As would be expected, when asked, "In what educational settings are these friend-ships likely to develop?" the most frequent answer was general education class for the entire day. The top three ratings for who should be responsible for facili-tating friendships were: students themselves, special educators, and youth clubs and organizations. The top five strategies that students felt teachers and schools should use to promote friendships were 1) use teaching strategies that involve students working together, 2) provide information on disabilities to students, par-ents and teachers, 3) provide social activities for all students, 4) teach students without disabilities to be tutors, and 5) use Circle of Friends. Furthermore, the majority of the respondents indicated that they might not know what to do or say to a peer with a severe disability, heightening the importance of some adult sup-port intervention.

One model with documented effectiveness for developing friendships be-tween students with severe and multiple disabilities and students without dis-abilities was developed by Hunt et al. (1996). This multifaceted intervention con-sisted of 1) providing ongoing information about the communication system, adaptive equipment, and educational activities during social interactions between students with severe and multiple disabilities and their peers without disabilities; 2) identifying and using media (e.g., computers, communication devices) that would facilitate social interactions; and 3) facilitating interactions by staff via a buddy system, interactive activities, and prompting and interpreting communica-tive exchanges when needed.

The researchers examined the effectiveness of the intervention for three stu-dents with severe and multiple disabilities and found that the intervention in-creased reciprocal interactions with peers and student-initiated interactions, and decreased assistance interactions with paraprofessionals. A second facet of the study involved socially validating the outcomes via teacher and student inter-views. All nine of the elementary and general education students identified them-selves as friends of the students with disabilities. Two themes emerged regarding the motives of their friendship: playing and helping.

ENHANCING THE ROLE AND IMAGE OF STUDENTS WITH SEVERE AND MULTIPLE DISABILITIES

When students with severe disabilities have obvious educational needs, there may be a tendency to perennially cast them in the role of recipient of help from classmates. One aspect of facilitating interactions calls for teachers to stress simi-larities and strengths between students. Although students with severe and mul-tiple disabilities may need assistance at times to perform as desired, there are also times when these students can help others. Students can hold doors open for oth-ers, pick up dropped items and return them to their owners, pass out homework and other materials, collect homework and turn it in, hold the flag for the Pledge of Allegiance, sharpen pencils, and obtain necessary materials for a group. With support from home, students can bring in requested items for school or class proj-ects, such as used clothing for the clothing drive, food for a community food bank, and items to be recycled. In cooperative learning groups, students with se-vere and multiple disabilities can perform the important role of timekeeper with the aid of a kitchen timer or, if need be, a vibrating timer.

Teachers need to be aware of the many opportunities that occur daily that allow a student with severe and multiple disabilities to serve in a helping role. Expecting the student to assist others and assume valued roles in the classroom (e.g., hall leader) helps classmates to perceive this student on a more equal basis. In a study by Williams and Downing (1998), middle school students reported that teachers played an important role in helping their classmates with severe and multiple disabilities attain true membership in their classes. Teachers were believed to promote a sense of belonging and equality when they used different strategies to increase the participation of *all* students.

AFTER-SCHOOL HOURS

A major goal of promoting interactions among students of different abilities during school hours is for these interactions to occur after school, as well. As stated, students who have difficulty communicating their thoughts and desires and who have other impairments that make interactions more difficult do not usually have an easy time developing friendships (Ferguson, 1994; Haring et al., 1995). By creating daily, ongoing opportunities for these students to interact and become familiar with a group of students who can be responsive communicative partners, the chance to develop friendships is enhanced (Schnorr, 1997; Staub, Peck, Gallucci, & Schwartz, 2000). Parents have reported that friendships do carry over to after-school times when students are taught together in inclusive classrooms (Bennett, DeLuca, & Bruns, 1997; Ryndak, Downing, Jacqueline, & Morrison, 1995).

To facilitate the development of friendships and to provide structured leisure activities for after-school hours, enrolling students with severe and multiple disabilities in typical community activities is one option. Depending on the student's age and interests, the possibility of Boy Scouts or Girl Scouts (and their younger counterparts, Cub Scouts and Brownies, respectively) should be explored. Scout troops offer structured opportunities for students to work together on various projects (many of which do not require substantial adaptation). The most critical consideration is to find a troop leader who is open to new ideas, flexible, eager to learn, and able to recognize the benefit of including all students. Having a student join a scout troop with familiar students from school should also be a consideration.

In addition, many cities feature parks and recreation department programs covering a range of leisure and recreation areas. Although these classes may be offered during the school year, they are more typically available during summer months. Classes can include martial arts, crafts, exercise, dance, swimming, basketball, drama, music lessons, jewelry, photography, yoga, ASL, and other special interest activities. During the summer months, extended school-year programs for a student with disabilities may occur in the community, with the student involved in appropriate activities with peers without disabilities (Alper, Parker, Schloss, & Wisniewski, 1993). As part of the student's extended school-year plan, the school district can offer much-needed support to ensure active participation and continued growth. Instead of assembling children with similar disabilities at a special site that is unfamiliar to all involved, a district can provide the necessary support on an individual basis to allow students to participate in the local community in summer activities that promote progress according to the IEP.

YMCAs and YWCAs also provide various course offerings for children and youth. These activities do not have to be geared for individuals with special needs, so long as such students have the necessary support from home, the department of developmental disabilities, volunteers, or trained employees at the facility. The objective is to provide organized and structured activities that facilitate interactions among students and enable friendships to develop. Without such structured opportunities that complement efforts at school, meeting new people and making friends will remain difficult.

Extracurricular activities such as 4-H, pep clubs, and an array of sporting activities and clubs can offer the social structure needed to develop or maintain relationships with other students. Falvey, Coots, and Terry-Gage (1992) provided lists of typical extracurricular activities for preschool, elementary, and secondary students. The interests of individual students with severe and multiple disabilities will determine which extracurricular activities are most suitable and beneficial.

SUMMARY

This chapter has highlighted the crucial role that peers play in the education of students with severe and multiple impairments. Given the opportunity, students of all abilities can and do learn from one another. Bringing students together to learn is an important role that adults in schools can assume, while also providing opportunities for friendships to develop. Although friendships cannot be dictated, they can be encouraged. Social and communication skills can and should be taught so that interactions among students of different abilities can be rewarding and isolation does not occur. As one parent lamented, "They—students with disabilities—know how to interact with their teachers, and they know how to respond to their aides, but they don't know how to respond to each other" (Hanley-Maxwell, Whitney-Thomas, & Pogoloff, 1995, p. 10).

The importance of friendships in everyone's life is indisputable. Allowing (and encouraging) students to learn and play together is one way to assist students with severe and multiple impairments to achieve valued friendships.

REFERENCES

Alper, S., Parker, K., Schloss, P., & Wisniewski, L. (1993). Extended school year programs: A community-driven curriculum model. *Mental Retardation, 31,* 163–170.

Bennett, T., DeLuca, D., & Bruns, D. (1997). Putting inclusion into practice: Perceptions of teachers. *Exceptional Children, 64*(1), 115–131.

Bishop, K., & Jubala, K. (1994). By June, given shared experiences, integrated classes, and equal opportunities, Jaime will have a friend. *Teaching Exceptional Children, 21*(1), 36–40.

Bowden, J., & Thorburn, J. (1993). Including a student with multiple disabilities and visual impairments in her neighborhood school. *Journal of Visual Impairments and Blindness, 87*(7), 268–272.

Buzolich, M.J., & Lunger, J. (1995). Empowering system users in peer training. *Augmentative and Alternative Communication, 11,* 37–45.

Downing, J.E. (1999). *Teaching communication skills to students with severe disabilities.* Baltimore: Paul H. Brookes Publishing Co.

Erin, J. (1986). Teachers of the visually handicapped: How can they best serve children with severe and profound handicaps? *Education of the Visually Handicapped, 18*(7), 15–25.

Evans, I.M., Salisbury, C.L., Palombaro, M.M., Berryman, J., & Hollowood, T.M. (1992). Peer interactions and social acceptance of elementary-age children with severe disabilities in an inclusive school. *Journal of The Association for Persons with Severe Handicaps, 17,* 205–212.

Falvey, M., Coots, J., & Terry-Gage, S. (1992). Extracurricular activities. In S. Stainback & W. Stainback (Eds.), *Curriculum considerations in inclusive classrooms: Facilitating learning for all students* (pp. 229–237). Baltimore: Paul H. Brookes Publishing Co.

Falvey, M.A., Forest, M., Pearpoint, J., & Rosenberg, R.L. (1994). Building connections. In J.S. Thousand, R.A. Villa, & A.I. Nevin (Eds.), *Creativity and collaborative learning: A practical guide to empowering students and teachers* (pp. 347–368). Baltimore: Paul H. Brookes Publishing Co.

Ferguson, D.L. (1994). Is communication really the point? Some thoughts on interventions and membership. *Mental Retardation, 32*(1), 7–18.

Ferguson, D.L., Jeanchild, L., & Meyer, G. (1992). *When inclusion isolates: Dimensions in the creation of "bubble kids."* Eugene: University of Oregon, Specialized Training Program.

Fisher, D., Sax, C., & Jorgensen, C.M. (1998). Philosophical foundations of inclusive, restructuring schools. In C.M. Jorgensen (Ed.), *Restructuring high schools for all students: Taking inclusion to the next level* (pp. 29–47). Baltimore: Paul H. Brookes Publishing Co.

Forest, M., & Lusthaus, E. (1989). Promoting educational equality for all students: Circles and maps. In S. Stainback, W. Stainback, & M. Forest (Eds.), *Educating all students in the mainstream of regular education* (pp. 43–57). Baltimore: Paul H. Brookes Publishing Co.

Forest, M., & Pearpoint, J.C. (1992). Putting all kids on the map. *Educational Leadership, 50*(2), 26–31.

Giangreco, M.F., Cloninger, C.J., Dennis, R.E., & Edelman, S.W. (2000). Problem-solving methods to facilitate inclusive education. In R.A. Villa & J.S. Thousand (Eds.), *Restructuring for caring and effective education: Piecing the puzzle together* (2nd ed., pp. 293–327). Baltimore: Paul H. Brookes Publishing Co.

Giangreco, M., Edelman, S., Cloninger, C., & Dennis, R. (1993). My child has a classmate with severe disabilities: What parents of nondisabled children think about full inclusion. *Developmental Disabilities Bulletin, 21*(1), 77–91.

Giangreco, M.F., Edelman, S.W., Luiselli, T.E., & MacFarland, S.Z. (1997). Helping or hovering? Effects of instructional assistant proximity on students with disabilities. *Exceptional Children, 64*, 7–18.

Giangreco, M.F., Edelman, S.W., MacFarland, S., & Luiselli, T.E. (1997). Attitude about educational and related service provisions for students with deaf blindness and multiple disabilities. *Exceptional Children, 63*, 329–342.

Hamre-Nietupski, S., Ayres, B., Nietupski, J., Savage, M., Mitchell, B., & Bramman, H. (1989). Enhancing integration of students with severe disabilities through curricular infusion: A general/special educator partnership. *Education and Training in Mental Retardation, 24*, 78–88.

Hanley-Maxwell, C., Whitney-Thomas, J., & Pogoloff, S.M. (1995). The second shock: A qualitative study of parents' perspectives and needs during their child's transition from school to adult life. *Journal of The Association for Persons with Severe Handicaps, 20*, 3–15.

Haring, T., Haring, N.G., Breen, C., Romer, L.T., & White, J. (1995). Social relationships among students with deaf-blindness and their peers in inclusive settings. In N.G. Haring & L.T. Romer (Eds.), *Welcoming students who are deaf-blind into typical classrooms: Facilitating school participation, learning, and friendships* (pp. 231–247). Baltimore: Paul H. Brookes Publishing Co.

Helmstetter, E., Peck, C.A., & Giangreco, M.F. (1994). Outcomes of interactions with peers with moderate or severe disabilities: A statewide survey of high school students. *Journal of The Association for Persons with Severe Handicaps, 19*, 263–276.

Hendrickson, J.M., Shokoohi-Yekta, M., Hamre-Nietupski, S., & Gable, R. (1996). Middle and high school students' perceptions on being friends with peers with severe disabilities. *Exceptional Children, 63*, 19–28.

Hughes, C., Guth, C., Hall, S., Presley, J., Dye, M., & Byers, C. (1999). They are my best friends: Peer buddies promote inclusion in high school. *Teaching Exceptional Children, 31*(5), 32–37.

Hunt, P., Alwell, M., Farron-Davis, F., & Goetz, L. (1996). Creating socially supportive environments for fully included students who experience multiple disabilities. *Journal of The Association for Persons with Severe Handicaps, 21*, 53–71.

Hunt, P., Staub, D., Alwell, M., & Goetz, L. (1994). Achievement by all students within the context of cooperative learning groups. *Journal of The Association for Persons with Severe Handicaps, 19*, 290–301.

Izen, C.L., & Brown, F. (1991). Education and treatment needs of students with profound, multiply handicapping, and medically fragile conditions: A survey of teachers' perceptions. *Journal of The Association for Persons with Severe Handicaps, 16,* 94–103.

Janney, R., & Snell, M. (1996). How teachers use peer interactions to include students with moderate and severe disabilities in general education classes. *Journal of The Association for Persons with Severe Handicaps, 21,* 72–80.

Jorgensen, C.M. (1994). Developing individualized inclusive educational programs. In S.N. Calculator & C.M. Jorgensen (Eds.), *Including students with severe disabilities in schools* (pp. 27–74). San Diego: Singular Publishing Group.

Kennedy, C.H., Shukla, S., & Fryxell, D. (1997). Comparing the effects of educational placement on the social relationships of intermediate school students with severe disabilities. *Exceptional Children, 64,* 31–48.

Kishi, G.S., & Meyer, L.H. (1994). What children report and remember: A six-year follow-up of the effects of social contact between peers with and without severe disabilities. *Journal of The Association for Persons with Severe Handicaps, 19,* 277–289.

Martin, J., Jorgensen, C.M., & Klein, J. (1998). The promise of friendship for students with disabilities. In C.M. Jorgensen (Ed.), *Restructuring high school for all students: Taking inclusion to the next level* (pp. 145–181). Baltimore: Paul H. Brookes Publishing Co.

McDonnell, J., Thorson, N., McQuivey, C., & Kiefer-O'Donnell, R. (1997). Academic engaged time of students with low-incidence disabilities in general education classes. *Mental Retardation, 35*(1), 18–26.

Ogletree, B.T., Wetherby, A.M., & Westling, D.L. (1992). Profile of the prelinguistic intentional communicative behaviors of children with profound mental retardation. *American Journal on Mental Retardation, 97,* 186–198.

Osborn, A. (1953). *Applied imagination: Principles and procedures of creative thinking.* New York: Charles Scribner's Sons Reference.

Parnes, S.J. (1981). *The magic of your mind.* Buffalo, NY: Creative Education Foundation in association with Bearly Ltd.

Peck, C.A., Donaldson, J., & Pezzoli, M. (1990). Some benefits nonhandicapped adolescents perceive for themselves from their social relationships with peers who have severe handicaps. *Journal of The Association for Persons with Severe Handicaps, 15,* 241–249.

Ryndak, D.L. (1995). Natural support networks: Collaborating with family and friends for meaningful education programs in inclusive settings. In D.L. Ryndak & S. Alper (Eds.), *Curriculum content for students with moderate and severe disabilities in inclusive settings* (pp. 61–76). Needham Heights, MA: Allyn & Bacon.

Ryndak, D.L., Downing, J.E., Jacqueline, L.R., & Morrison, A.P. (1995). Parents' perceptions after inclusion of their child with moderate or severe disabilities in general education settings. *Journal of The Association for Persons with Severe Handicaps, 20,* 147–157.

Salisbury, C., Gallucci, C., Palombaro, M.M., & Peck, C.A. (1995). Strategies that promote social relations among elementary students with and without severe disabilities in inclusive schools. *Exceptional Children, 62,* 125–137.

Schnorr, R.F. (1997). From enrollment to membership: "Belonging" in middle and high school classes. *Journal of The Association for Persons with Severe Handicaps, 22,* 1–15.

Staub, D. (1998). *Delicate threads: Friendships between children with and without special needs in inclusive settings.* Bethesda, MD: Woodbine House.

Staub, D., & Hunt, P. (1993). The effects of social interaction training on high school peer tutors of schoolmates with severe disabilities. *Exceptional Children, 60,* 41–57.

Staub, D., Peck, C.A., Gallucci, C., & Schwartz, I. (2000). Peer relationships. In M. Snell & F. Brown (Eds.), *Instruction of students with severe disabilities* (pp. 381–408). Upper Saddle River, NJ: Merrill.

Staub, D., Schwartz, I.S., Gallucci, C., & Peck, C.A. (1994). Four portraits of friendship at an inclusive school. *Journal of The Association for Persons with Severe Handicaps, 19,* 314–325.

Turnbull, A., & Turnbull, R. (1999). Comprehensive lifestyle support for adults with challenging behavior: From rhetoric to reality. *Education and Training in Mental Retardation and Developmental Disabilities, 34,* 373–394.

Vacc, N.N., & Cannon, S.J. (1991). Cross-age tutoring in mathematics: Sixth graders helping students who are moderately handicapped. *Education and Training in Mental Retardation, 26*(1), 89–97.

Vandercook, T., York, J., & Forest, M. (1989). The McGill Action Planning System (MAPS): A strategy for building the vision. *Journal of The Association for Persons with Severe Handicaps, 14,* 205–215.

Van der Klift, E., & Kunc, N. (1994). Beyond benevolence: Friendship and the politics of help. In J.S. Thousand, R. Villa, & A. Nevin (Eds.), *Creativity and collaborative learning: A practical guide to empowering students and teachers* (pp. 391–401). Baltimore: Paul H. Brookes Publishing Co.

Villa, R.A., & Thousand, J.S. (1992). Student collaboration: An essential for curriculum delivery in the 21st century. In S. Stainback & W. Stainback (Eds.), *Curriculum considerations in inclusive classrooms: Facilitating learning for all students* (pp. 117–142). Baltimore: Paul H. Brookes Publishing Co.

Villa, R.A., & Thousand, J.S. (1996). Student collaboration: An essential for curriculum delivery in the 21st century. In S. Stainback & W. Stainback (Eds.), *Inclusion: A guide for educators* (pp. 171–191). Baltimore: Paul H. Brookes Publishing Co.

Williams, L.J., & Downing, J.E. (1998). Membership and belonging in inclusive classrooms: What do middle school students have to say? *Journal of The Association for Persons with Severe Handicaps, 23,* 98–110.

York, J., & Tundidor, M. (1995). Issues raised in the name of inclusion: Perspectives of educators, parents, and students. *Journal of The Association for Persons with Severe Handicaps, 20,* 31–44.

York, J., Vandercook, T., MacDonald, C., Heise-Neff, C., & Caughey, E. (1992). Feedback about integrating middle school students with severe disabilities in general education classes. *Exceptional Children, 58,* 244–257.

Chapter 9

Working Cooperatively

The Role of Team Members

June E. Downing

Teamwork plays a critical role in a successful inclusion experience. Instead of viewing the situation from the perspective of "my" class and "your" class, and "my" students and "your" students, all teachers share the responsibility for each classroom and for the learning of all students. Bringing students together requires bringing adults together. In addition, the value of individual team members is not determined by labels (titles or degrees), but simply by the shared desire to contribute to a student's educational program. Establishing equal parity across all team members is an essential component of true collaboration (Idol, 1997; Rainforth, York, & Macdonald, 1992; Walter-Thomas, Korinek, & McLaughlin, 1999). All participants need an equal voice in the decision-making process and time to openly discuss concerns and make suggestions for increased participation of all students.

Resistance to including students may come from a fear of not knowing what to do to make the process successful (Coots, Bishop, & Grenot-Scheyer, 1998; Downing, Eichinger, & Williams, 1997; Evans, Bird, Ford, Green, & Bischoff, 1992). Considerable resistance can be avoided when all players feel comfortable with program goals and performance expectations. Sharing information and working as a collaborative team from the time of the program's inception can serve to alleviate concerns and resistance.

WHO IS ON THE EDUCATIONAL TEAM?

In general, anyone who has something to contribute and who wants to be on a student's educational team can be a team member. In the past, the make-up of the team may have been determined by matching the student's disabilities to the professional who had training or expertise in the disability (Rainforth & York-Barr, 1997). Yet, training and certification in a given disability area may or may not provide the professional with the motivation or knowledge to contribute to a student's educational program. In other words, being a licensed SLP does not mean that that person should be solely responsible for addressing the child's communication difficulties. Such an expectation places considerable stress on a given professional that is both unwarranted and unproductive. A student's communicative needs, like other skill areas, are complex and require the ongoing commitment of several people interested in and knowledgeable about those needs.

Depending on training and past experiences, the SLP may not have all the necessary information or skills to assist a particular student (at least initially). The most effective support for a given student will probably be a combined effort from a number of people, both professionally trained and not professionally trained, who share a common goal for the student's success. The blending of all team members' skills and knowledge leads to a more holistic program for the student.

WHO PROVIDES SUPPORT?

Determining who provides the necessary support for a given student at any given time is a dynamic and ongoing decision. The dynamic nature of this decision rests on the fact that students do acquire skills, learn to recognize and meet expectations, and need more or less support depending on the activity as well as their changing ability to handle the activity. Obviously, students have both "good" and "bad" days depending on a number of physical and emotional factors (e.g., sickness, lack of sleep, hunger). For these reasons, support must be considered in a flexible rather than fixed manner. Those providing support must be alert to when assistance is needed and when it is not. The goal is to fade external support for the individual and rely on natural supports that exist in various situations (e.g., friends, co-workers, supervisors). For many students with severe and multiple disabilities, however, additional support will be necessary at times. Making sure the right amount and kind of support is available is as important as ensuring that too much support is avoided.

NATURAL SUPPORTS

The first choice for sources of support are the individuals who are typically available in general education classrooms—the teacher and classmates. These supports are the most natural and readily available sources of assistance, as depicted in Figure 9.1, a student with disabilities and her classmate. Classroom teachers need to perceive the student with severe and multiple disabilities as a full-time class member, not a visitor or guest (Martin, Jorgensen, & Klein, 1998; Williams & Downing, 1998). This perception alone can provide considerable support to the student's sense of belonging. Other forms of support by the teacher and classmates can and should be easily provided. Many activities, for example, require no more support than a peer to offer to be a sighted guide or to tactually remind the student to take out needed classroom materials. At times, the teacher can intervene to repeat directions, tactually cue a student to go to the appropriate lab group, ask a student to be quiet, or help a student use the desired playground equipment. Salisbury, Gallucci, Palombaro, and Peck (1995) interviewed 10 elementary general educators and found that these teachers felt they could do several simple things to enhance the membership of students with severe and multiple disabilities in their classrooms. Teachers mentioned such strategies as encouraging students to work together, promoting a caring and sharing environment, and modeling acceptance of the student by talking to the student, walking with the student, and encouraging the student to become involved in activities.

Figure 9.1.   A student in a seventh-grade art class provides some natural support to a classmate with severe and multiple disabilities. (Photograph by Margo Yunker.)

Other sources of natural supports include other classroom teachers, students in other classes, the school principal, parent volunteers, bus drivers, cafeteria workers, librarians, and any staff members who are at the student's school and interact with this student. These people need to feel comfortable interacting and supporting the student when needed and should not rely on someone else to provide all the support. For instance, if a student accidentally knocks over some books in the library, the librarian should feel comfortable asking the student to pick up the books via verbal directions, gestures, physical prompts, or modeling. This is much more natural than looking to a special educator or paraeducator to intervene. Likewise, the cafeteria worker and a peer can help a student locate and present his lunch ticket without seeking out someone who is specifically trained to work with students with disabilities. Natural support relies on individuals in the natural environment knowing not only that they can assist when it is logical to do so, but that they *should* assist. In sum, everyone assumes some of the responsibility for everyone else. This policy affords the student greater contact with different people and provides more learning opportunities across different activities, environments, and individuals.

The school principal, as school leader, can facilitate the development of natural supports by setting a tone of shared accountability for all students. The principal can recognize and commend the efforts of teachers and staff when they assume responsibility for students who have unique needs. By interacting with each student equally, the principal also can model for faculty, staff, parents, and

students the importance and positive aspects of such interactions. Helping everyone to see the value of looking out for one another can provide considerable support throughout the day.

Nevertheless, there will be times when natural supports are insufficient to
produce the desired results. A careful analysis of each activity with ongoing feedback from the classroom teacher can help determine when a student may need
extra support.

ADDITIONAL SUPPORTS

When natural supports cannot adequately meet a student's needs, the necessary
support can be found elsewhere. Paid and unpaid adults as well as students other
than classmates can provide varying levels of support. The different sources of potential support are described in the following pages.

Special Educator and Paraeducator Support

Perhaps the most consistent and expected source of additional support (when
natural supports are insufficient) is the special educator or paraeducator who is
designated to ensure appropriate programming for a given student. These individuals are typically trained to meet the unique educational needs of students
with severe and multiple disabilities. Their support will be directed toward assessing the compatibility of fit between individual goals and the curriculum and
adapting instruction and materials accordingly to best meet learning needs within
the typical activities of the class. As emphasized in previous chapters, care must
be taken not to provide excessive support or attention so that the student is isolated from classmates, the classroom teacher, or the activity. The special educator
or paraeducator should be perceived as additional support for the teacher and
class, providing one-to-one assistance only when absolutely needed (Giangreco,
Broer, & Edelman, 1999). To reflect this type of role change, special educators
may go by the title of support teacher or inclusion support teacher. Avoiding the
term *specialist,* as in *inclusion specialist,* is recommended so as to create greater parity across teachers on the team (Goessling, 1998).

The manner in which support is provided also must be given careful thought,
so that high expectations for performance are maintained. A study by York and
Tundidor (1995) revealed that secondary-age students felt that paraeducators "ba-
bied" students with disabilities and that these students were not expected to adhere to the same classroom rules. Support does not mean having low expectations
or doing assignments for the student. Ideally, the right amount of support allows
the student to make maximal learning gains while participating in typical and valued activities. To ensure that students receive the most appropriate kind of support, paraeducators need training and guidance from professional staff. Several
studies have reported the valuable support paraeducators provide to the inclusive
classroom and thus, the critical need for these individuals to receive quality training (Downing, Ryndak, & Clark, 2000; French, 1998; French & Chopra, 1999).

Special educators and paraeducators usually support several students across
different classes and grades. They, therefore, move in and out of classrooms, providing support as needed. Their schedules fluctuate according to the changing

skill levels and needs of the students they support. They must learn the delicate balance of providing whatever support is needed, but no more.

Related Services Support

Professionals trained to address specific areas of need are a valuable resource for additional support in inclusive classrooms. These professionals could be vision teachers, hearing specialists, SLPs or communication specialists, interpreters, occupational therapists, physical therapists, orientation and mobility instructors, adaptive physical education specialists, and behavior specialists. Although these individuals (owing to large caseloads) may serve primarily in a collaborative and consultative manner (Rainforth & York-Barr, 1997), the direct time they spend with students in classrooms can provide needed support at critical times of the day.

Given some flexibility in their work schedules, related services providers may be able to support students at different times and in varying activities to gain a clearer, more comprehensive picture of a student's program. For instance, the vision teacher may be able to work with a student in his or her class for 30 minutes on a Monday morning 1 week and then 2 weeks later see the same student on a Thursday afternoon. In this way, the support professional can help identify strengths and needs and monitor intervention plans that directly relate to what the teacher is targeting.

Related services providers do not take the student out of class to work on unrelated subject matter, but support what the teacher is trying to accomplish within the classroom. They also provide the teacher with specific information regarding the student's unique needs. According to a study by Giangreco, Edelman, and Nelson (1998), specialists who knew what to do were highly regarded by teachers. In addition, if the special educator knows when specialists will be available to support a given student, he or she can rearrange the schedule of additional direct services providers to support other students, collect data, monitor other programs, adapt materials, or plan with another team member (e.g., paraeducator, general educator).

Professionals who represent different disciplines (e.g., visual impairments, hearing impairments, communication disorders, motor impairments) need to have access to the student's overall educational program in order to know how best to contribute to the program. By observing the student in as many different situations and activities as possible, these professionals can obtain a better understanding of the student's needs and of how they can best help the student. Improving skills in isolation that relate to a given specialty area is not the goal. For instance, the goal of "seeing better" is too vague and difficult to measure. Rather, the goal should be to support the student in achieving IEP objectives that are meaningful and activity based and that address desired areas for improvement. For example, one student's objective is to independently move through the lunch line and make food choices. Currently, the student stops, holds up the line, flicks his hand in front of his face, and does not look at the food choices. Observing this activity, the vision teacher can confer with the rest of the team to implement a program that teaches the student to look for the cafeteria workers as natural cues for the appropriate behavior, scan the food options, and respond appropriately when asked to make choices. The student will learn to use his vision during this activity to be more successful and will have opportunities to practice this same visual skill in other activities (e.g., choosing art materials, choosing a library book, choosing a partner for physical education).

Volunteer Support

Developing a volunteer program for a given school can help alleviate some of the need for additional support that certain students have. Volunteers can either provide support to a student with severe disabilities or can provide instructional support to other students so that the classroom teacher can spend more time with students who have special needs. Volunteers can also help make and adapt materials as needed.

Volunteers can be older adults; retired individuals; parents or other family members; university or college students in education, psychology, social work, or a related field; or members of various organizations (e.g., Knights of Columbus, Big Brothers/Big Sisters, sororities/fraternities). Volunteers (like everyone else) require training to understand the classroom teacher's expectations and to feel comfortable with the level of support they themselves can provide. They need to know how best to interact with and teach a student. They also need to have a definite schedule and to realize that they are needed and appreciated.

Peer Tutors

The benefits of students supporting students are detailed in Chapter 8; however, it is important to mention that adults on the educational team need to keep in mind the valuable resource peer tutoring is when planning ways to support students who need extra help. In the Coots et al. study (1998), peers were reported by teachers to be providing a great deal of support to their classmate having significant disabilities. Students who are older, are in different grades or classes, or attend different schools can serve as peer tutors at various times in a student's day. Creative scheduling is needed so that peer tutors do not miss out on other learning opportunities critical for their own success. Many students, however, finish their work early and need a constructive outlet for their free time and energy. Being a peer tutor (or being given the title of teaching assistant) provides these students the chance to help another student learn. Students can practice skills already acquired, learn creative ways of communicating and teaching, express their creativity by making and adapting materials, and develop strong feelings of self-esteem (Longwell & Kleinert, 1998; McDonnell, 1998). These benefits apply to gifted and talented students as well as those who are at risk for academic failure.

Middle and junior high school students may be able to acquire credit for serving as teaching assistants while also developing valuable skills that could lead to a related career choice. Secondary-age students can leave their school campus when classes are finished or between classes to assist younger students with severe disabilities at elementary schools. Many schools use peer tutoring to supplement instructional support by paid professionals (Longwell & Kleinert, 1998; Staub, Spaulding, Peck, Gallucci, & Schwartz, 1996). These tutors must be trained to communicate effectively with all students, to systematically and positively shape desired behavior versus doing for the student, and to accurately and objectively collect data to help measure progress. Training takes time, but the long-term benefits to the teacher and students in the class are obvious.

BRINGING THE TEAM TOGETHER

With respect to the professionals involved, the concept of including all students with diverse learning needs, especially those with severe and complex needs, may not initially be conducive to creating the desired partnership between general and special education. Instead, already overwhelmed teachers with large classes and limited, if any, experience working with such students may express resentment and an unwillingness to participate (Downing et al., 1997). In addition, the new role for special educators and other specialists (vision teacher, hearing specialist, SLP) of blending with general education and supporting the classroom teacher may create turf problems and an unwillingness to relinquish control. The benefits for everyone involved must be clearly articulated (Hamre-Nietupski et al., 1999; Idol, 1993), and the overall educational goals for individual students must guide the process (Giangreco et al., 1998; Rainforth & York-Barr, 1997). Professionals will need to relax their unilateral hold on their areas of expertise and work together to develop a unified program for a student within natural settings. Such a change may be more difficult for special educators to accept as these professionals lose their separate classrooms and locus of control and "move in" with another teacher who is already established in a given room. In addition, specialists accustomed to removing the child from a given classroom and going to a special place to work will need to adapt to the demands of the classroom, adjusting their intervention techniques accordingly. These specialists also lose control of how they provide services and instead must consider the dynamics of the typical learning environment (e.g., teacher style, activity in progress, physical layout of classroom, acceptable noise level).

The lack of time experienced by most educational team members is a potential barrier to collaborative teaming (Bardak, 1995; Friend, 2000; Hamre-Nietupski et al., 1999; Walter-Thomas et al., 1999). Yet, team members must have the time to meet and develop the skills needed to successfully support students in inclusive settings. Once team members feel comfortable working cooperatively together, less meeting time may be needed. Strategies for sharing information with team members in quick and efficient ways are suggested in the following sections.

SHARING INFORMATION TO FACILITATE COLLABORATION

One critical component in facilitating cooperative collaboration among educational team members is the ongoing sharing of information about the student and the overall program. Several research studies have shown that attitudes toward inclusion are more favorable given the appropriate support, training and experience (Gallagher et al., 2000; Janney, Snell, Beers, & Raynes, 1995). All team members need to be kept informed of program goals and expectations for the student so that they can all see how each person can contribute to the success of the program. Classroom teachers may be reluctant to include a student with severe and multiple disabilities if they do not understand how they can contribute to the student's learning. After interviewing general and special educators who were teaching students with severe disabilities, Wood (1998) found that general educators craved information concerning their role. In general, teachers want to feel that they can have a positive impact on a student's education (Coots et al., 1998). Once the student's goals, as well as ways that the classroom teacher can help the student meet these needs, have been clearly stated, the initial reluctance will ease. Therefore, it is recommended that the team (or at least the general educator and special educator) complete an activity analysis form (described in Chapter 3) to clarify exactly how each goal and objective will be addressed by subject matter or activity. A student profile that concisely provides pertinent information on the student's skills, likes, and means of communication can be a particularly effective way of helping the general educator understand a student's needs. Figure 9.2 provides a sample student profile form used for this purpose.

Demystifying Students with Severe and Multiple Disabilities

Students with severe and multiple disabilities have obvious impairments, and special labels tend to accompany them. This combination can be overwhelming to a teacher with no prior experience interacting with anyone with such seemingly complex challenges. Special educators who use medical and technical jargon with teachers in discussing students with such disabilities do little to relieve fears. Stressing the student's strengths and the similarities among all children will do much to demystify the disability and enhance the possibility of inclusion. Teachers desire and need appropriate information in order to support the child and help him or her feel welcome in the classroom (Coots et al., 1998; Janney et al., 1995; Wood, 1998).

Explaining How to Interact

As discussed in previous chapters, the individual characteristics of a given student need to be explained so that everyone will feel as comfortable as possible interacting with this student. The student with severe and multiple disabilities often communicates in unique ways. Everyone involved with such a student needs to know how the student receives information (e.g., speech, sign, pictures, touch cues) and how the student shares information with others (e.g., gestures, pointing, using objects, facial expressions). The entire school community needs to be aware of the importance of interactions, even when they are brief or when the expected or desired response does not occur. Students with severe and multiple disabilities need many opportunities to interact with others to practice their social-communicative skills. They also need to know that all members of the school community are potential communicative partners, not just those trained in special education.

Perhaps the most beneficial aspect of sharing information involves reassuring teachers, administrators, and all other school staff that interactions are encouraged, desirable, and not to be feared. When a student appears to differ markedly from others in communication and social skills, a hesitancy to even try to interact may result from a fear of doing something "wrong." Alleviating these fears and stressing to individuals that the worst mistake is to ignore and avoid this student might help to increase the frequency of interactions for the student. The adults in the school also need information about communicating with students

Student Information Form (Confidential)

Student _____ Grade _____ School Year _____

Current Teachers _____ Last Year's Teachers _____

Special Education & **Related Services** ____ Academics (list): ____ Speech: ____ Occupational Therapy: ____ Physical Therapy: ____ Aide Support: ____ Sp. Ed. Instruction: ____ Sp. Ed. Consultation: ____ Other:	**Likes** **Dislikes**
Medical/health	**See guidance counselor/** **principal for other relevant** **confidential information?** ____ yes ____ no **Behavior Plan?** ____ yes (attach) ____ no
What works/learns best when **What does not work/** **does not learn when**	**Other important information/** **areas of concern**

Figure 9.2.   Sample student profile for sharing information with team members. (From Janney, R., & Snell, M.E. [2000]. *Modifying schoolwork: teacher's guides to inclusive practices* [p. 76]. Baltimore: Paul H. Brookes Publishing Co.; reprinted by permission)

with disabilities—not only regarding how to interact but also what to do when a student's response is lacking, not understood, or unwelcome. People will react differently according to their unique personalities, confidence, and skills working with different students, as well as the time they have to deal with a given situation. Knowing that there is not just one right way to respond to the student, but that there is a range of "best" options, may help reduce the reluctance to become involved.

Explaining How to Respond to Unconventional Behavior

Many students with severe disabilities may convey their intent or desires through behaviors that are destructive, disruptive, or harmful to themselves or others (Durand & Kishi, 1987; Sigafoos, 2000). The reasons behind these behaviors need to be carefully explained to all potential communicative partners so that the behaviors can appear less strange or abnormal. When not understood for their communicative potential, behaviors that are socially unconventional or unacceptable can create a barrier to enhancing interactions, thus highlighting the differences between people rather than bringing them together. For example, adults, as well as student peers, need to know that when a student engages in behaviors such as pulling out his or her hair, destroying papers, scratching others, screaming, or hitting his or her head, the student may be expressing excessive frustration over having to do a given task or not understanding what is expected. Awareness of the student's frustration can make it easier to understand and accept the student. The importance of assisting the individual to communicate desires and feelings in alternative ways also becomes a clearer goal. Sharing this information with teachers, paraeducators, support staff, and principals is critical to building an understanding network of support for the student.

Sensory impairments also can have an impact on the type of self-stimulatory or self-amusing behaviors that an individual can express. All of us engage in such behavior for a number of reasons (e.g., to relieve boredom, to reduce stress). Self-stimulatory behaviors of people who can see clearly, hear well, and move their bodies fluently look different from the behaviors of people with disabilities who cannot see, hear, or move well. For example, instead of doodling, twirling hair, fidgeting in a chair, or clicking pens, children with severe and multiple disabilities may make vocalizations that they can feel in their throat, may flick their fingers in front of their face, or may pat their chin repeatedly. Without adequate vision or hearing, these children may not have received the feedback to know that these behaviors are not typically done or acceptable and may not have been able to model more socially acceptable behaviors.

In the same way, the more customary behaviors of typical students are understood and accepted, the more unique behaviors of students with severe and multiple disabilities need understanding and acceptance. Explanations of stereotypical or self-stimulatory behavior in individuals with sensory impairments, especially with severe and multiple impairments, have been provided by several researchers (Durand & Carr, 1987; Leonhardt, 1990; Mar & Cohen, 1998). Knowing why students engage in certain unique types of self-stimulatory behaviors reduces the perception of strangeness that can develop and allows for greater understanding and acceptance. Team members can recognize the need to intervene to find out what the student is trying to convey. Sharing this type of information also stresses the similarities among all individuals, rather than concentrating on the differences.

Strategies for Information Sharing

Critical information about how a student communicates and otherwise behaves can be shared in a number of ways. Formal presentations to the entire staff can be given. Information can also be shared in smaller staff meetings (e.g., cafeteria workers, playground monitors, teachers of a certain grade level). Because information shared must be ongoing as the student and situations change, much of the information will probably be exchanged informally when teachers have a few minutes together in class, in the staff lounge, over lunch, walking down a hall together, while watching children on the playground, and through written correspondence in the form of notes and messages. Teachers in a study by Snell and Janney (2000) reported that discussing students' problems took place "on the fly" and involved brief, hurried interactions that occurred where and when they could. Despite the rushed nature of such interactions, care must be taken to convey information positively, in a way that shows respect for the student and does not impinge on confidentiality of records. Derogatory language can be harmful and isolating, and it is never appropriate to refer to any child by an undesirable label (e.g., "runner," "biter," "screamer"). Students need to be referred to by their names and the grade they attend.

The type of information shared and the way it is presented varies depending on the situation. For instance, some classroom teachers like to share information briefly with a paraeducator while students are in the midst of changing activities. Other teachers prefer to use this limited time for preparation or checking students' work. Team members need to inform each other regarding how and when they prefer to receive information, and there needs to be a clear procedure for requesting information. Again, demonstrating respect for the student and each team member is critical. For instance, when trying to conduct class, few classroom teachers appreciate two or three adults' exchanging information at the back of the room. The temptation to engage in this behavior may be great, especially if one of the adults is a related services provider (e.g., occupational therapist, vision teacher) who has limited time at any one school. In addition, it is sometimes easier to exchange information when the student is involved in an activity and the need for modifications is apparent to everyone. The author recommends that teachers videotape classroom activities and use videotaped segments of the student to discuss problem areas and share ideas with team members, especially parents and related services providers who may not be on campus often. Videotapes can be used before or after school or during planned staff meetings to serve as a focal point for brainstorming ideas and discussions. Videotapes also can be taken home with specific questions attached for a particular service provider or the parent. These questions can be responded to via telephone, e-mail, or written messages if face-to-face meetings cannot occur in a timely fashion. Whatever the option, an alternative must be found to the group huddle of adults in a given classroom. When adults are in the classroom, they are there to support each other as well as the learning of all students.

Initially, greater time may be needed to adequately explain a student's behaviors and how the adult should strive to interact. As adults become more comfortable with the student, less assistance in this area will be needed and requests for information will become more sporadic and on an as-needed basis. For example, one second-grade teacher requested weekly meetings for at least 1 hour with the special educator and paraeducator when she first included a child with severe and multiple disabilities in her room. After 1 month, she reported feeling much more comfortable with this child and decided that the meetings were no longer necessary. The need to meet to exchange information and problem-solve will depend on a range of variables including student performance, transition issues, familiarity, changing needs, and changes in the team. Retaining some degree of flexibility with regard to the number and scheduling of meetings is a necessity.

One way to share information with team members regarding preferred ways to help the student acquire skills is a simply written lesson plan. Although the overall lesson for the class will be co-planned with the general educator, the specific strategies and adaptations used to shape the desired responses for the student with severe and multiple disabilities will ultimately be the support teacher's responsibility. To communicate effective strategies to all team members, these plans need to be brief and clearly stated. The sequence of prompts to be used by adults working with the student should be clearly delineated so they are easy to read and understand. Some examples can be found in Chapter 11.

WORKING COOPERATIVELY AND COLLABORATIVELY

A considerable body of literature exists on parents and professionals working as collaborative teams (e.g., Corrigan & Bishop, 1997; Thousand & Villa, 2000; Turnbull & Turnbull, 1997). Although information abounds on the characteristics of truly cooperative and collaborative teams, achieving the ideals of such a team is difficult. Furthermore, the more individuals on a given team, the more difficult true collaboration may be (Friend, 2000; Lake & Billingsley, 2000). Students with complex educational needs such as those with severe and multiple disabilities typically have many professionals serving on their teams. To further complicate matters, considerable turnover of team members can occur, disrupting the team's functioning (Giangreco, Edelman, Nelson, Young, & Kiefer-O'Donnell, 1999). Many of these professionals (e.g., occupational therapists, physical therapists, hearing specialists, orientation and mobility instructors) have large caseloads and may be assigned multiple schools and even school districts. As a result, their time to work as part of a cohesive team is extremely limited. These professionals also may not have received training in collaborative teaming and may feel more comfortable working independently. In their survey of special educators, occupational therapists, and physical therapists, Utley and Rapport (2000) discovered that these professionals were only willing to share between 55% and 56% of their expertise. Even though participants in this survey had been teaming for as long as 13 years, they still struggled with issues of trust necessary for a true role release.

Bringing different professionals and parents together is necessary to integrate their skills and knowledge to help the student achieve valued outcomes. Without a truly collaborative approach, the intervention for students can become fragmented and overly specialized, with related outcomes for students even conflicting. Keeping valued outcomes determined by the entire team (especially family members) firmly in mind will help to focus the team on the child as part of a classroom, school, family, and community, and not on isolated deficit areas.

Table 9.1.   IEP objectives showing shared team input

Student #1:	Sharon—first grade
Objective:	During mathematics class, Sharon will indicate which is the greater of two amounts by reaching toward the appropriate pile of items with 80% accuracy for 10 trials.
Team Input:	
Parent	Recognizes importance of keeping Sharon with class for all subjects; encourages interest in basic academics
First-Grade Teacher	Determines math curriculum and activities and helps establish criteria
Special Educator	Recommends physical adaptations and limited options
Speech-Language Pathologist	Suggests method of clarifying the request to Sharon and helps determine how she will respond
Vision Teacher	Works with Sharon on looking and shifting gaze from one choice to the next; suggests ways to create greater contrast
Student #2:	Tara—fifth grade
Objective:	While reading with a peer and using page fluffers on each page, Tara will turn the page within 3 seconds of the peer finishing reading a given page for 70% of each book for 10 different books.
Team Input:	
Parent	Recognizes importance of sharing with a peer, showing respect for property; would like her to do the same skill at home
Fifth-Grade Teacher	Stresses importance of reading and criteria for mastery
Special Educator	Targets responding to classmate, staying on task
Occupational Therapist	Determines method of turning pages, adaptations
Speech-Language Pathologist	Encourages positive interactions with peers
Student #3:	Simon—tenth grade
Objective:	While positioned in a standing table, Simon will make at least four choices of materials to use in art class by pointing within 5 seconds of a request for 10 consecutive classes.
Team Input:	
Parent	Suggests the need for clear communication and self-determination
Art Teacher	Suggests art materials as a choice and presents project
Special Educator	Determines number of choices and criteria for mastery
Physical Therapist	Determines best position
Vision Teacher	Identifies looking as a way to make choices; determines best visual field to present choices
Occupational Therapist	Suggests a modified point as a way to indicate choice; suggests modified holders/brushes
Speech-Language Pathologist	Suggests listening to a peer, responding to a peer; helps determine criteria for mastery

Table 9.1 provides examples of how various team members collaborate to write the IEP objectives. Each student should have one unified IEP based on achieving important activities, not multiple IEPs written by individuals acting on their own.

Building Shared Responsibility for Students

As stated at the outset of this chapter, recognizing that all adults can help all students at a given school learn helps to diminish the separation that occurs when teachers refer to "your" and "my" students. Providing classroom teachers with specific information regarding interactions with certain students also helps to clarify roles and responsibilities. These strategies should be easy to perform and

Table 9.2. Ways the classroom teacher can demonstrate responsibility for students with disabilities

Model appropriate behavior toward student with disabilities:
- Avoid language that is too juvenile.
- Ignore (if possible) some of the student's inappropriate behavior.

Avoid seating student on the periphery of the class.

Expect the child with disabilities to participate:
- Call on the student to respond.

Recognize the need to stand near the student when giving instructions.

Have student help with demonstrations to maintain interest.

Ask student to collect and hand out papers/materials.

Assign the student to cooperative learning groups/lab groups.

Encourage students to help each other.

Praise appropriate behavior/work.

Discipline when needed—make expectations clear.

Assist with lifts/transfers when needed.

Determine some adaptations for lessons.

Work directly with student on specific skills while other adult (paraeducator, therapist) works with rest of the class.

Avoid assigning special education support solely to the student with special needs.

Talk directly to the student, not through the support person.

Actively participate in staffings and IEP meetings.

Establish regular lines of communication with parents.

to blend into the teacher's natural teaching style (Salisbury et al., 1995). The teacher should be able to recognize that assuming some responsibility for a student will not add to an already challenging role. For example, classroom teachers need to feel comfortable calling on students who are learning to raise their hands, even if the students do not respond when called on. In addition, if the students are working with peer buddies, the teacher can call on both children for a response to a particular question. This teacher behavior is natural and expected and conveys the message of acceptance and high expectations for behavior to other students. See Table 9.2 for more specific suggestions for teachers.

Working in partnership with the classroom teacher, the special educator or paraeducator can facilitate interactions among students with and without disabilities and their teacher. The adult who is trained to work with children with severe challenges can cue the student to respond to a communicative request or statement. Such an adult can ensure that the student has necessary adaptations and materials and then fade back to work with other students. This allows the classroom teacher to work with the student having severe and multiple disabilities as well as with others in the same group. The direct involvement of the classroom teacher in the instruction of the student with severe and multiple disabilities not only supports teacher ownership, but also may have a positive impact on student learning (Giangreco et al., 1998). Table 9.3 lists responsibilities often assumed by the special educator. Whereas the special educator and classroom teacher should work together as equal teachers, some special educators report feeling like aides when they teach in typical classrooms. Such feelings should be openly explored and addressed. Each adult needs to be valued and respected for the unique skills and abilities he or she brings to the shared learning environment. The same is true for each student.

Table 9.3.   Role of the special educator in the inclusive classroom

Work with general educators and other team members to support all students in class
Adapt materials and curriculum as needed
Modify instruction to student's learning styles
Model appropriate ways to interact
Facilitate peer supports and friendships
Coordinate supports (e.g., paraeducators, related services personnel, volunteers, peer tutors)
Share ideas for teaching various subject areas
Co-teach, instruct small groups, or occasionally teach whole class
Obtain specific information from various specialists and share with classroom teacher
Collect data on student performance

Professionals providing related services such as speech-language pathology, physical therapy, hearing and vision instruction, and adaptations for these sensory losses provide some direct assessment and instruction in the general education classroom and other environments such as libraries, computer labs, cafeterias, and so forth. They also instruct other team members in providing these services, so there is no disruption of a student's program. These professionals infuse their expertise into the student's typical day to facilitate the student's attainment of desired objectives (Anderson, Hawkins, Hamilton, & Hampton, 1999; Ryndak, 1995; Snell & Janney, 2000; York, Giangreco, Vandercook, & Macdonald, 1992). In this way, classroom teachers can see how specialists help them work toward common goals (e.g., how positioning, adaptive switches, and AAC devices improve the student's performance in an activity); classroom teachers can thus feel comfortable interacting with the student with disabilities when the specialists are not in the room.

In a study by Giangreco, Dennis, Cloninger, Edelman, and Schattman (1993), classroom teachers expressed the desire for specialists to work with them and to respect the dynamics of the classroom. They did not perceive separate goals and objectives that were taught in separate environments to be particularly helpful. Echoing these findings, Goessling (1998) found that general educators did not appreciate the overspecialization of services that can occur when team members work from their disciplines and not from a holistic perception of the student.

Scheduling Support for Students

Making sure that all students have the support they need to be successful learners may be one of the most challenging tasks a teacher faces. When a teacher's caseload of students with severe disabilities is not congregated in one room but in different classrooms throughout the school based on chronological age, the teacher must rely on others to implement programs effectively. While the special educator may hold considerable responsibility for ensuring the implementation of appropriate educational programs for each student, he or she obviously will not be physically with each student throughout each day. As a result, special education teachers must work closely with all team members to ensure that curricular adaptations are made and implemented appropriately, that goals and objectives are addressed within general education classrooms, and that strategies to teach students skills are employed consistently across team members.

The special educator, in conjunction with general educators, will determine who will support each student as needed. To alleviate excessive coming and going of various team members, individual team members may teach in a specified classroom for a 2- to 3-hour block of time. Coordinating team movement in different classes will depend to a large degree on individual teacher schedules and student needs. For instance, Ms. Myers starts her second-grade class with a language arts block of 2 hours that incorporates several listening, reading, writing, and spelling activities. During this period, she prefers to have one other adult from the team in her room to support her efforts. When her class goes outside for recess and returns to do an art project based on the morning's activities, she does not feel the need for extra support. Therefore, either the special educator or one of the paraeducators scheduled to be in Ms. Myers's room in the morning goes to another classroom at this time. Someone comes back to this class when Ms. Myers has science following the art activity.

Instead of team members removing students from typical classrooms, services are provided to students within different classrooms according to their learning objectives (Fisher, Sax, & Grove, 2000). For instance, the occupational therapist may see Courtney, a high school student, during her art class, lunch, and keyboarding. The SLP works with her during her leadership class and during the nutrition break. When related services providers are not available to provide support, the special educator, paraeducator, peer tutor, or volunteer may step in as needed. Sample schedules in Figures 9.3 and 9.4 provide examples of how team members make the transition from room to room to support students.

INTEGRATING THE ADULTS

Keeping children learning together is problematic if the adults involved in teaching are kept separate from one another. The separation of special education from general education can lead to a separate culture—to a separate world with little connectedness (Goessling, 1998). Separate rooms result not only in physical isolation but also in a cultural isolation that makes it very difficult to see a student's total program. Adults must feel comfortable sharing the educational environment (e.g., classrooms, playground, gym) instead of "protecting" their specialized space. Physically sharing the same work environments facilitates information exchange and awareness of each other's interests and skills. Special educators and related services personnel will become much more knowledgeable about typical educational curricula, which will help them be more efficient team players and more mindful of necessary adaptations. By the same token, classroom teachers will become more aware of the different ways children learn and of how various adaptations help students to compensate for missing skills. Kronberg, Jackson, Sheets, and Rogers-Connolly (1995) offered several suggestions for teachers and administrators to integrate themselves into the learning process for all students, including role release, learning strategies to teach diverse learners, and brainstorming ideas to solve problem areas. By working together, all teachers can appreciate the skills and knowledge that comprise teaching a diverse group of learners. As a result, everyone's skill level should improve.

A major advantage of integrating adults in the process of providing truly inclusive and supportive education is that all students benefit from an increased number of teachers in the classroom. Any student can seek assistance from any adult, thus the time students spend waiting for the teacher's attention is reduced.

Time	Special education teacher	Paraeducator 1	Paraeducator 2	Speech-language pathologist	Physical therapist	Occupational therapist	Vision teacher	Behavior specialist
7:30-8:00	Quick meeting and prep with some teachers							
8:00-8:30	Third grade (James & Travis)	First grade (Annie & Mike)	Fourth grade (Hannah & Eduardo)	(Mike) Tuesday, Thursday			Second grade (Jeremy) Tuesday	
8:30-9:00				(Annie) Tuesday, Thursday		(Hannah) Monday, Wednesday		
9:00-9:30	Fifth grade (Carrie)		Third grade (James & Travis)	(Travis) Tuesday, Thursday				
9:30-10:00	Second grade (Jeremy)	(9:30-9:45 break) Third grade (James & Travis)	(9:45-10:00 break)	(Carrie) Tuesday, Thursday		(Mike) Monday, Wednesday		
10:00-10:30			Fourth grade (Hannah & Eduardo)		(Annie) Monday, Wednesday			Third grade (Travis) Friday
10:30-11:00	Fourth grade (Hannah & Eduardo)	Fifth grade (Carrie)	Third grade (James & Travis)		Mike Monday, Wednesday	(Jeremy) Monday		
11:00-11:30								
11:30-12:00		Lunch						
12:00-12:30	Lunch	First grade (Annie & Mike)						
12:30-1:00	First grade (Annie & Mike)	Third grade (James & Travis)	Lunch					
1:00-1:30			Second grade (Jeremy)					
1:30-2:00	Fifth grade (Carrie)							
2:00-2:30	Meeting to debrief for the day and prepare for the next day			Twice a month all team members attend this meeting.				
2:30	Plan and meet with teachers	Leave	Leave					

Figure 9.3.   Sample schedule for team members at an elementary school (eight students). Schedule may remain the same for a 2- to 3-week period before being changed. This will depend on student progress, general education activities, and other factors. Related services providers see students two or three times weekly. Not all services are shown.

Periods	Special education teacher	Paraeducator 1	Paraeducator 2	Adaptive physical educator	Speech-language pathologist	Occupational therapist	Physical therapist	Peer tutors	Vocational specialist
1	Ninth grade (Chloe & Jarod) *English*	Twelfth grade (David & Randy) *consumer ed*	Eleventh grade (Kelly) *journalism*	Tenth grade (Loren & Mia)				(Brett) *general choir*	
2	Tenth grade (Loren & Mia) *algebra*	Twelfth grade (David & Randy) *swimming*	Ninth grade (Chloe & Jarod) *keyboarding*	Eleventh grade (Kelly) *PE*			(David) *swimming*	(Brett) *art*	
Nutrition	(Brett & Mia)	(Jarod & Loren)	Break					(David & Randy)	(Kelly)
3	Tenth grade (Loren & Mia) *Spanish*	Ninth grade (Chloe & Jarod) *algebra*	Eleventh grade (Brett) *English*		Tenth grade (Loren & Mia) *Spanish*	(David) *photography*		(Randy) *sign language*	(Kelly)
4	Eleventh grade (Kelly) *English*	Eleventh grade (Loren & Mia) *health*	Tenth grade (Chloe & Jarod) *science*		(David & Randy) *drama*			(Brett) *weightlifting*	
Lunch	(Randy)	(Brett & Kelly)	(Loren)						
5	Eleventh grade (Brett & Kelly) *algebra*	Ninth grade (Chloe & Jarod) *weights*	Twelfth grade (David & Randy) *art*	(Chloe & Jarod)		(Loren) *art*		(David & Randy) *art*	(Mia)
6	Twelfth grade (David & Randy) *geometry*	Ninth grade (Chloe & Jarod) *chorus*	Eleventh grade (Brett & Kelly) *keyboarding*		(Loren) *study hall*				(Mia)

Figure 9.4. Sample high school support schedule by team member (eight students). This schedule will remain as is for 1 month. Paraeducator 1 has a 15-minute break during swimming and lunch for 30 minutes of fifth period. Paraeducator 2 has a 15-minute break during nutrition and a 30-minute lunch break during fifth period. Special educator takes 30 minutes for lunch during third or fourth period (relieved by SLP or peer tutor). Related services providers see students 2–3 times weekly. Paraeducators and special educator meet briefly before first period and after sixth.

206

In addition, all students can benefit from the ideas generated from more than one person. In general, it should be apparent that teams of people problem solve more effectively than one individual (Skrtic, Sailor, & Gee, 1996). For example, a special educator may have wonderful ideas for teaching some science units and can share these ideas with the classroom teacher and help present them to the entire class. At the same time, classroom teachers have devised clever adaptations to allow for increased learning and involvement in their classrooms of students with severe and multiple impairments. For example, one first-grade teacher brought in some apples and a mechanical apple corer and had her student with visual, intellectual, and mild physical disabilities be the first one to demonstrate the use of the peeler. This activity helped to clarify the lessons on machines and the benefits of machinery for all of her students. The roles that define individual team members should not interfere with creatively constructing the best instruction for all students.

SUMMARY

Bringing adults together to share teaching responsibilities for all students in schools may be more difficult than bringing children together to learn. The benefits are obvious in terms of more instruction for students, greater learning by adults, and a greater abundance of resources for problem solving and task achievement; however, the type of cooperation and collaboration required of adults in inclusive educational programs will be new to the majority of adults and therefore initially uncomfortable. Working together as a team necessitates an initial desire and commitment on the part of everyone, specific skills to make it happen, and time to provide opportunities for practice. As with any new system, working through problem areas will take time and effort. Supporting the adults in the educational system is a critical component of inclusive education (Fisher et al., 2000; Kronberg et al., 1995). Personnel preparation programs for all professionals involved on the team could support the development of collaborative teams in schools by initiating training programs that are collaborative across disciplines. School principals working toward shared responsibility of all students by all faculty and staff can support this development by providing team members both with sufficient time to meet and with external resources for direction and guidance if needed.

Again, achieving the desired results takes time. Teams are also constantly changing, which affects the team's performance. Meanwhile, students have a right to an appropriate education in the least restrictive environment. They also have a right to feel that they belong. These rights must be kept in mind as a constant guide while adults struggle to achieve their sense of belonging.

REFERENCES

Anderson, N.B., Hawkins, J., Hamilton, R., & Hampton, J.D. (1999). Effects of transdisciplinary teaming for students with motor disabilities. *Education and Training in Mental Retardation and Developmental Disabilities, 34*, 330–341.

Bardak, J. (1995). Collaboration in schools: Meeting the needs of all students. *Developmental Disabilities Bulletin, 23*(1), 120–138.

Coots, J.J., Bishop, K.D., & Grenot-Scheyer, M. (1998). Supporting elementary age students with significant disabilities in general education classrooms: Personnel perspectives on inclusion. *Education and Training in Mental Retardation and Developmental Disabilities, 33,* 317–330.

Corrigan, D., & Bishop, K.K. (1997). Creating family-centered integrated service systems and interprofessional educational programs to implement them. *Social Work in Education, 19,* 149–163.

Downing, J., Eichinger, J., & Williams, L. (1997). Inclusive education for students with severe disabilities: Comparative views of principals and educators at different levels of implementation. *Remedial and Special Education, 18,* 133–142.

Downing, J.E., Ryndak, D.L., & Clark, D. (2000). Paraeducators in inclusive classrooms: Their own perceptions. *Remedial and Special Education, 21,* 171–181.

Durand, V.M., & Carr, E.G. (1987). Social influences on "self-stimulatory" behavior: Analysis and treatment application. *Journal of Applied Behavior Analysis, 20,* 119–132.

Durand, V.M., & Kishi, G. (1987). Reducing severe behavior problems among persons with dual sensory impairments: An evaluation of a technical assistance model. *Journal of The Association for Persons with Severe Handicaps, 12*(1), 2–10.

Evans, J., Bird, K., Ford, L., Green, J., & Bischoff, R. (1992). Strategies for overcoming resistances to the integration of students with special needs into neighborhood schools: A case study. *Case in Point: The Journal of the Council of Administrators of Special Education, VII*(1), 1–16.

Fisher, D., Sax, C., & Grove, K.A. (2000). The resilience of changes promoting inclusiveness in an urban elementary school. *The Elementary School Journal, 100,* 215–227.

French, N. (1998). Working together: Resource teachers and paraeducators. *Remedial and Special Education, 19,* 359–369.

French, N.K., & Chopra, R.V. (1999). Parent perspectives on the roles of paraprofessionals. *Journal of The Association for Persons with Severe Handicaps, 24,* 259–272.

Friend, M. (2000). Myths and misunderstandings about professional collaboration. *Remedial and Special Education, 21,* 130–132.

Gallagher, P.A., Floyd, J.H., Stafford, A.M., Taber, T.A., Brozovic, S.A., & Alberto, P.A. (2000). Inclusion of students with moderate or severe disabilities in educational and community settings: Perspectives from parents and siblings. *Education and Training in Mental Retardation and Developmental Disabilities, 35,* 135–147.

Giangreco, M.F., Broer, S.M., & Edelman, S.W. (1999). The tip of the iceberg: Determining whether paraprofessional support is needed for students with disabilities in educational settings. *Journal of The Association for Persons with Severe Handicaps, 24,* 281–291.

Giangreco, M.F., Dennis, R., Cloninger, C., Edelman, S., & Schattman, R. (1993). I've counted Jon: Transformational experiences of teachers educating students with disabilities. *Exceptional Children, 59,* 359–371.

Giangreco, M.F., Edelman, S.W., & Nelson, C. (1998). Impact of planning for support services on students who are deaf-blind. *Journal of Visual Impairment and Blindness, 92,* 18–29.

Giangreco, M.F., Edelman, S.W., Nelson, C., Young, M.R., & Kiefer-O'Donnell, R. (1999). Changes in educational team memberships for students who are deaf-blind in general education classes. *Journal of Visual Impairment and Blindness, 93,* 166–173.

Goessling, D.P. (1998). Inclusion and the challenge of assimilation for teachers of students with severe disabilities. *Journal of The Association for Persons with Severe Handicaps, 23,* 238–251.

Hamre-Nietupski, S., Dvorsky, S., McKee, A., Nietupski, J., Cook, J., & Costanza, C. (1999). Going home: General and special education teachers' perspectives as students with moderate/severe disabilities return to rural neighborhood schools. *Education and Training in Mental Retardation and Developmental Disabilities, 34,* 235–259.

Idol, L. (1993). *Special educator's consultation handbook* (2nd ed.). Austin, TX: PRO-ED.

Idol, L. (1997). *Creating collaborative and inclusive schools.* Austin, TX: Eiter Press.

Janney, R.E., Snell, M.E., Beers, M.K., & Raynes, M. (1995). Integrating students with moderate and severe disabilities into general education classes. *Exceptional Children, 2,* 425–439.

Kronberg, R., Jackson, L., Sheets, G., & Rogers-Connolly, T. (1995). A toolbox for supporting integrated education. *Teaching Exceptional Children, 27*(4), 54–58.

Lake, J.F., & Billingsley, B.S. (2000). An analysis of factors that contribute to parent-school conflict in special education. *Remedial and Special Education, 21,* 240–251.

Leonhardt, M. (1990). Stereotypes: A preliminary report on mannerisms and blindness. *Journal of Visual Impairment and Blindness, 84,* 216–218.

Longwell, A.W., & Kleinert, H.L. (1998). The unexpected benefits of high school peer tutoring. *Teaching Exceptional Children, 30*(4), 60–65.

Mar, H.H., & Cohen, E.J. (1998). Educating students with visual impairments who exhibit emotional and behavior problems. In S.Z. Sacks & R.K. Silberman (Eds.), *Educating students who have visual impairments with other disabilities* (pp. 263–302). Baltimore: Paul H. Brookes Publishing Co.

Martin, J., Jorgensen, C.M., & Klein, J. (1998). The promise of friendships for students with disabilities. In C.M. Jorgensen (Ed.), *Restructuring high schools for all students: Taking inclusion to the next level* (pp. 145–181). Baltimore: Paul H. Brookes Publishing Co.

McDonnell, J. (1998). Instruction for students with severe disabilities in general education settings. *Education and Training in Mental Retardation and Developmental Disabilities, 33,* 199–215.

Rainforth, B., & York-Barr J. (1997). *Collaborative teams for students with severe disabilities: Integrating therapy and educational services* (2nd ed.). Baltimore: Paul H. Brookes Publishing Co.

Rainforth, B., York, J., & Macdonald, C. (1992). *Collaborative teams for students with severe disabilities: Integrating therapy and educational services.* Baltimore: Paul H. Brookes Publishing Co.

Ryndak, D.L. (1995). Education teams and collaborative teamwork in inclusive settings. In D.L. Ryndak & S. Alper (Eds.), *Curriculum content for students with moderate and severe disabilities in inclusive settings* (pp. 77–96). Needham Heights, MA: Allyn & Bacon.

Salisbury, C.L., Gallucci, C., Palombaro, M.M., & Peck, C.A. (1995). Strategies that promote social relations among elementary students with and without disabilities in inclusive schools. *Exceptional Children, 62,* 125–138.

Sigafoos, J. (2000). Communication development and aberrant behavior in children with developmental disabilities. *Education and Training in Mental Retardation and Developmental Disabilities, 35,* 168–176.

Skrtic, T.M., Sailor, W., & Gee, K. (1996). Voice, collaboration, and inclusion: Democratic themes in educational and social reform initiatives. *Remedial and Special Education, 17,* 142–157.

Snell, M.E., & Janney, R.E. (2000). Teachers' problem-solving about children with moderate and severe disabilities in elementary classrooms. *Exceptional Children, 66,* 472–490.

Staub, D., Spaulding, M., Peck, C.A., Gallucci, C., & Schwartz, I.S. (1996). Using nondisabled peers to support the inclusion of students with disabilities at the junior high school level. *Journal of The Association for Persons with Severe Handicaps, 21,* 194–205.

Thousand, J.S., & Villa, R.A. (2000). Collaborative teaming: A powerful tool in school restructuring. In R.A. Villa & J.S. Thousand (Eds.), *Restructuring for caring and effective education: Piecing the puzzle together* (2nd ed., pp. 254–291). Baltimore: Paul H. Brookes Publishing Co.

Turnbull, A.P., & Turnbull, H.R. (1997). *Families, professionals, and exceptionality: A special partnership* (3rd ed.). Upper Saddle River, NJ: Prentice-Hall.

Utley, B.L., & Rapport, M.J.K. (2000). Exploring role release in the multidisciplinary team. *Physical Disabilities: Education and Related Services, XVIII,* 89–118.

Walter-Thomas, C., Korinek, L., & McLaughlin, V.L. (1999). Collaboration to support students' success. *Focus on Exceptional Children, 32*(3), 1–18.

Williams, L.J., & Downing, J.E. (1998). Membership and belonging in inclusive classrooms: What do middle school students have to say? *Journal of The Association for Persons with Severe Handicaps, 23,* 98–110.

Wood, M. (1998). Whose job is it anyway? Educational roles in inclusion. *Exceptional Children, 64,* 181–195.

York, J., Giangreco, M.F., Vandercook, T., & Macdonald, C. (1992). Integrating support personnel in the inclusive classroom. In S. Stainback & W. Stainback (Eds.), *Curriculum considerations in inclusive classrooms: Facilitating learning for all students* (pp. 101–116). Baltimore: Paul H. Brookes Publishing Co.

York, J., & Tundidor, M. (1995). Issues raised in the name of inclusion: Perspectives of educators, parents, and students. *Journal of The Association for Persons with Severe Handicaps, 20,* 31–44.

Chapter 10

Are They Making Progress?

Assessing the Skills of Students with Severe and Multiple Disabilities in General Education Classrooms

June Downing

The preceding chapters of this text have highlighted the many ways that students with very challenging disabilities can be educated in general education classrooms—the key word being *educated*. Being physically present in classrooms with students without disabilities is not the goal, rather it is the premise. The foundation of this book is that special and separate places do not have to be created in order for students with severe and multiple disabilities to learn. In fact, these students have a legal right to be educated in the least restrictive environment (IDEA Amendments of 1997); however, this education should be appropriate, which means that students are learning critical skills to meet their individual needs. Teachers have the responsibility of making sure this happens. In fact, accountability with regard to effective instruction is a requirement of IDEA 1997 (Kleinert, Haigh, Kearns, & Kennedy, 2000). This chapter addresses the need to document student learning.

IMPORTANCE OF ASSESSING STUDENT PROGRESS

Accountability is a critical educational issue. A major concern regarding inclusion for students with severe disabilities is that they will merely be placed in general education classrooms for social reasons and will not be expected to acquire meaningful skills (Billingsley & Albertson, 1999; Chelsey & Calaluce, 1997). This concern is valid and should be addressed seriously by all educators. The least restrictive environment clause of IDEA requires that students learn in their educational placement, not just have access to students without disabilities. Therefore, if general education classrooms are to be least restrictive for a particular student, educators need to ensure that the student can meet learning goals and objectives.

The IEP determines a student's placement, and documenting progress on IEP goals and objectives represents a meaningful way to measure student learning (Hock, 2000). The contents of the IEP, therefore, become critical not only for determining the student's program but also for accountability. In addition, progress toward meeting IEP goals and objectives provides feedback to the educational team with regard to the effectiveness of the intervention. Therefore, documenting student progress helps to guide team members to implement appropriate programs (Fisher & Kennedy, 2001).

ASKING THE RIGHT QUESTIONS

Measuring meaningful change in a student's behavior means targeting the most important aspects of a student's program. In other words, educators need to make sure they are asking the right questions about what the student is to learn, which in turn will be reflected in a high-quality IEP. IEPs that address minimal skills in isolation may be very easily measured; however, if they fail to give a comprehensive and realistic picture of the student's ability, then the measurement may be meaningless. For instance, it may be relatively easy to measure whether a student can cut on a line for 3 inches; however, considering the student and desired outcomes (i.e., to develop relationships with other students, express needs effectively, entertain himself for at least 15 minutes), progress on such a skill is of dubious merit. Educators must be careful not to become too involved in the attainment of specific skills without keeping in mind the bigger picture or desired outcome for the student. Translating information obtained from interviewing family members or from doing a person-centered assessment such as MAPS (Falvey, Forest, Pearpoint, & Rosenberg, 1997) into a meaningful IEP is of particular importance if educators are going to make any socially valid claims regarding student progress.

In the following example, a MAP reveals that Maria's team is concerned about her lack of friends. This concern was mentioned by Maria's family, teachers, and a second-grade classmate. Past assessment information revealed that Maria did not have strong social interaction skills that were conducive to forming relationships. One of the dreams for Maria was to improve her relationships with classmates and ultimately to have friends. As a result of the MAPS process, one of Maria's goals was the following: *Maria will engage in 5-minute social conversations with a peer buddy in three of five attempts daily for 3 consecutive weeks.*

Objectives supporting this goal of engaging in social conversation targeted the skills of initiating a conversation, responding to comments (maintaining the conversation), and ending the conversation in an acceptable manner (e.g., not just walking away). For example, one objective stated the following: *Maria will initiate one response during lunch and recess by pointing to pictorial symbols in her conversation book for 3 consecutive weeks.*

Other results from Maria's MAPS process revealed that members of her team felt that one of Maria's strengths was her interest in pictures and photographs. They also expressed concern that she did not have a lot of interests. In particular, she didn't enjoy any sedentary activities and tended to wander around the classroom. Therefore, when the team wrote goals for her IEP they addressed this finding from her MAP. For example, one objective stated, *Maria will remain seated at her desk and engaged in a task for at least 15 minutes daily for 9 of 10 consecutive days.* Different skills to meet this goal were addressed in IEP objectives. Some of these skills were choosing a photograph album to look at, orienting it to the right position, looking at the pictures and turning the pages. One objective was written in the following way: *During language arts and when offered her choice of three different photograph albums, Maria will choose one album and with the help of a peer or teacher to turn the pages, she will look at the pictures on at least five pages four times per week for 2 weeks.*

Although this objective specifies language arts, these same skills are targeted across several different classes (e.g., science, social studies) and at Maria's home, allowing for plenty of practice. These objectives reflect what is considered important for Maria and differ considerably from previous objectives that addressed Maria's ability to put three-piece puzzles together, throw away trash, and balance on one foot for a specified amount of time. Although Maria did not perform these skills, they also were not considered very critical for improving her quality of life.

Listening to individuals who know the student and care about his or her future is a good way to develop an IEP that will really help the student acquire meaningful life skills. A recommended practice reported by experts of inclusive education was that assessment information be authentic, reflect student performance in meaningful activities across environments, and address social validation concerns (Jackson, Ryndak, & Billingsley, 2000).

MEASURING STUDENT PROGRESS

Accurately and objectively documenting a student's progress sometimes does not receive the attention it deserves. Team members may resort to guessing or estimating progress. In a study of instructional practices in general education classes, Agran and Alper (2000) found that 46% of the respondents stated that subjective judgements were used rather than frequency data (6%) to measure IEP objectives. Furthermore, these researchers found that few teachers ever task-analyzed activities or set schedules for data collection. These results raised concerns that students with severe disabilities may not be receiving the systematic instruction they need.

Sometimes methods of collecting objective data are so complex that teachers, paraeducators, and other team members (e.g., related services providers) cannot easily determine how to collect data. In addition, time to collect data may be minimal depending on the student's support needs and the situation. As a result, data collection procedures must be very clear, simple, convenient, and planned. To determine efficient means to measure a student's progress on IEP goals and objectives, it is recommended that IEP goals and objectives be clearly written and easily measured. Of course, they should also be written to reflect what is meaningful for a given student. Criterion measures should be carefully considered so that they truly address the desired outcome (see Chapter 3). When IEP objectives are vaguely written, collecting data is much more difficult. Clearly written objectives should specify exactly what is being measured, under what conditions, and the level of mastery expected of the student. The following examples highlight the difference between objectives that are vague and those that are more specifically written and clearly measurable.

Example 1

Original IEP objective: *Abby will improve communication skills 80% of the time.*
Revised IEP objective: *When a classmate or teacher asks her a question, Abby will look at him or her and then point to the appropriate person, object, or picture on her communication device within 3 seconds for 8 of 10 consecutive questions.*

In the original objective, what the word "improve" refers to is not clear. The communication skills being addressed are also unclear. As a result, each team member working with Abby can decide what is meant by a "communication skill" and how improvement will be measured. Consistency across team members in gathering relevant data may be lost without greater specificity in this objective. The criterion of "80% of the time" is equally confusing because it's not clear what time period is being considered. It is doubtful that all opportunities for communication for an entire school year can be observed by teaching staff.

With the revised objective, the situation is stated ("when a classmate or teacher asks her a question"), and it is clear that the communication skill addressed is that of responding to a question. The objective also states how Abby will communicate (by looking and pointing) and how often she must perform the skill to reach criterion. Given Abby's skill level, the team decided that if Abby independently performed the skill as stated in the objective for 8 of 10 consecutive questions asked of her, mastery would be sufficiently indicated. (Of course, it is critical for all team members to know Abby's present level of performance so that an appropriate IEP objective can be written that will indicate real growth).

The data collection sheet in Figure 10.1 was developed to capture the necessary information to measure progress on this objective. The information gathered on this data sheet goes beyond the IEP objective in that it also allows for information on the exact question responded to, the person asking the question, what activity is taking place, and what the student uses in her response. Although this information is not needed to indicate Abby's mastery of the objective, such information can be very informative regarding intervention and generalization of skills. The data may indicate that over time Abby has clear preferences with regard to conversation partners and activities. Other IEP objectives that target additional communication skills for Abby may also be necessary to measure real progress in this area.

Example 2

Original IEP Objective: *Tom uses his schedule with 100% accuracy.*
Revised IEP Objective: *When presented with his schedule and asked by his peer tutor what is next, Tom will find the object or part of object representing the current class and then will find the next object that represents the next class and hand it to the peer tutor at least four times per day for 2 weeks.*

The original objective is unclear about how or when Tom is to use his schedule and whether he should be asked to do so or should simply do it on his own. In addition, the definition of 100% accuracy is not clear. The revised IEP objective addresses these problems. The specifics of the situation (a peer tutor will prompt Tom) and what Tom is to do with the schedule are clarified. In addition, 100% accuracy has been replaced with a performance criterion that is straightforward and easily measured. Figure 10.2 shows the data form created to document progress made on this objective.

Example 3

Original IEP Objective: *Savannah will demonstrate understanding of the concept greater than.*

Revised IEP Objective: *During math and using an adapted number line, Savannah will point to or put her hand on the larger of two written numbers (from 1 to 20) when asked to find the one that is more four out of five times per day for 5 days.*

In the original objective, how Savannah will demonstrate her understanding of "greater than" is not clear, nor is it clear what criterion will be used to indicate mastery of this concept. This objective is not measurable as stated.

The revised objective specifies where and how the objective will be met. The adaptation needed is stated as a condition, and how Savannah will demonstrate her achievement is apparent. The criterion is clear and measurable, as well. Fig-

---

Student: *Abby*

Objective: *When a classmate or teacher asks her a question, Abby will look at him/her and then point to the appropriate person, object, or picture on her communication device within 3 seconds for 8 or 10 consecutive questions.*

Date: *1/30*

Questions asked/where	Looks at person?	Pointed to?	Person who asked?	Prompting strategies
1. What do you want to drink? (at lunch)	Yes (No)	(Chocolate milk) White milk Other	*Tim* (peer)	* Wait time = 3 seconds between all prompts * Repeat question * Point to options * Tap elbow
2. What do you want to do? (at recess)	(Yes) No	–	*Mrs. T* (aide)	
3. Do you want to play on the swings or with the girls? (at recess)	Yes (No)	–	*Mrs. T* (aide)	
4. Where do you want to sit? (at music)	(Yes) No	*Points at Tim (peer)*	*Mrs. T* (aide)	

Directions:

Write the question asked in the first column.

Circle Y=yes or N=no if the student looks at the speaker.

Write down options (if not on the sheet) and circle or mark what the student pointed to (third column).

Figure 10.1.   Sample data sheet for a student's communicative responses.

Student:	Tom				

Objective: When presented with his schedule and asked by his peer tutor what is next, Tom will first find the object or part of object representing the current class and then will find the next object that represents the next class and hand it to the peer tutor at least 4 times a day for 2 weeks.

Date Skill sequence	3/19/01 1st to 2nd period	3/19/01 2nd to 3rd period	3/19/01 3rd period to nutrition	3/19/01 Nutrition to 4th period	Strategies to teach/adapt *** Wait time = 5 seconds before all prompts**
Visually and tactually looks for object on schedule	P	+			* Place schedule near hands * Tap schedule

Finds object
representing
present activity
	–	–			* Praise if
					  correct
					* Give corrective
					  feedback if
					  wrong

Finds next
object in
schedule
	–	–			* Tap around
					  object
					* Ask what's next
					* Move object
					  into hand

Takes off schedule and hands to peer	P	+			* Hold hand out to receive object * Praise

Figure 10.2.   Sample data sheet to document schedule use (Key: + = independent performance; P = prompted behavior; – = did not perform behavior).

ure 10.3 is a sample data sheet that could be used to collect data for this objective. This data sheet also goes beyond the required information for meeting IEP objectives and provides critical information pertaining to the numbers used, the order in which they were presented, and the prompts used. Such information helps the team determine more accurately what Savannah has mastered and what the reasonable next steps should be.

Student: _Savannah_   Date: _2/16/01_

Objective: _During math and using an adapted number line, Savannah will point to or put her hand on the larger of two written numbers (from 1-20) when asked to find the one that is more 4 out of 5 times a day for 5 days._

Problems		Chose larger number		Level of prompt used **(4 second delay between prompts)**
2	10	(Y)	N	__ Ask which number is more and say number as you point to it __ Add manipulatives __ Model __ Tap near larger number
11	4	Y	(N)	__ Say number as you point to it __ Add manipulatives __ Model __ Tap near larger number
7	1	(Y)	N	__ Say number as you point to it __ Add manipulatives __ Model __ Tap near larger number
3	15	(Y)	N	__ Say number as you point to it __ Add manipulatives __ Model __ Tap near larger number
7	14	Y	(N)	__ Say number as you point to it __ Add manipulatives __ Model __ Tap near larger number
3	15	(Y)	N	__ Say number as you point to it __ Add manipulatives __ Model __ Tap near larger number

Directions:
In the first column, write the numbers and the order presented to the student.
Circle Y = yes or N = no for student performance (second column).
Check all prompts used (third column).

Figure 10.3.   Data sheet for determining the larger of two numbers.

Example 4

Original IEP Objective: *Eric will independently initiate interactions with his peers once a day.*
Revised IEP Objective: *While on the playground, Eric will independently approach a peer and by pointing to a picture on a waist clip, ask him or her to play with him in a chosen activity at least one time for outdoor play sessions for 4 consecutive weeks.*

In the original objective, how Eric will initiate interactions is not described, and therefore, it is questionable what an initiation will look like. Furthermore, when the desired behavior will occur or where is not explicit. Although the criterion in the original objective states once a day, the question remains as to how many days must this behavior occur before the student can be credited with this skill.

In the revised objective, much greater specificity has been added to address these concerns. How Eric will initiate an interaction specifies the use of an AAC device. The criterion is much more detailed and consequently, measurable. It is unambiguous when Eric will be given credit for mastering this objective. Information to be collected for this objective can be found in Figure 10.4. This data sheet captures not only the data required by the objective but also additional information concerning the peer who was approached, the activity chosen, and the prompts required for Eric to perform the skill.

DECIDING WHAT TYPE OF DATA TO COLLECT

To show that students are acquiring skills as desired, it is important to collect the right kind of data. A tendency to use accuracy as the sole criterion on IEP objectives may obfuscate the need to collect other kinds of data leading to a more accurate or measurable criterion. For example, an IEP objective that states that a student must stay with his group during a center time with 80% accuracy presents a problem in terms of accountability. In this situation, accuracy does not address what the student is to accomplish. A more appropriate criterion to capture what skills the student has acquired would be the length of time he is to stay with the group (duration) and the number of times he is to do this (frequency). To clarify the desired outcome further, describing his behavior while he is staying with the group (e.g., facing the teacher, being quiet, and not hitting) would be advisable. A more accurately and clearly stated IEP objective might read: *During center time, Cliff will stay with his group for at least 10 minutes, face the teacher, listen to directions, and respond to at least one modified question without hitting his peers or screaming once a day for 2 consecutive weeks.* With these conditions and criteria a part of the IEP objective, the team knows what data need to be collected and for how long. Oftentimes, the desired objective will require more than one criterion (as in the previous example) to demonstrate student acquisition of the desired skill(s). The team must decide what makes the most sense and what will most accurately reflect student achievement.

Frequency Data

Collecting some kind of frequency data is demanded by most, if not all, objectives. Using frequency of behavior as a criterion, the team needs to consider how often they must see the target behavior(s) in order to affirm that the student has mastered the skill or at least met the desired objective. For example, a team may de-

Student: _Eric_

Activity: _Outdoor playtime_

Objective: _While on the playground, Eric will independently approach a peer, and by pointing to a picture on a waist clip, ask him/her to play with him with a chosen activity at least one time per outdoor play session for 4 consecutive weeks._

Playground	Date:	Date:	Date:	Date:
Peer chosen	2/21/01			
Activity chosen	Slide ___ Swing ✓ Climber ___ Ball ___ Clip clops ___ Parachute ___	Slide ___ Swing ___ Climber ___ Ball ___ Clip clops ___ Parachute ___	Slide ___ Swing ___ Climber ___ Ball ___ Clip clops ___ Parachute ___	Slide ___ Swing ___ Climber ___ Ball ___ Clip clops ___ Parachute ___
Prompt required to get peer's attention. (Check the last prompt needed.)	1. No prompt ___ 2. Initial encouragement ___ 3. Question only (who?) ___ 4. Question and point ___ 5. "Let's go ask" ___ 6. Visual (tap at peer) ✓ 7. Verbal instruct to tap ___ 8. Hand over hand tap ___	1. No prompt ___ 2. Initial encouragement ___ 3. Question only (who?) ___ 4. Question and point ___ 5. "Let's go ask" ___ 6. Visual (tap at peer) ___ 7. Verbal instruct to tap ___ 8. Hand over hand tap ___	1. No prompt ___ 2. Initial encouragement ___ 3. Question only (who?) ___ 4. Question and point ___ 5. "Let's go ask" ___ 6. Visual (tap at peer) ___ 7. Verbal instruct to tap ___ 8. Hand over hand tap ___	1. No prompt ___ 2. Initial encouragement ___ 3. Question only (who?) ___ 4. Question and point ___ 5. "Let's go ask" ___ 6. Visual (tap at peer) ___ 7. Verbal instruct to tap ___ 8. Hand over hand tap ___
Name of peer chosen	Stephen			
Prompt required to communicate to peer what he wants to play. (Check the last prompt needed.)	No prompt ___ Visual cue ___ Tap elbow ___ Push elbow ✓ Model "I want to" and guide hands ___ Display choices ___	No prompt ___ Visual cue ___ Tap elbow ___ Push elbow ___ Model "I want to" and guide hands ___ Display choices ___	No prompt ___ Visual cue ___ Tap elbow ___ Push elbow ___ Model "I want to" and guide hands ___ Display choices ___	No prompt ___ Visual cue ___ Tap elbow ___ Push elbow ___ Model "I want to" and guide hands ___ Display choices ___

Figure 10.4.   Sample data sheet for documenting initiations with a peer.

219

cide that if a student comes back to class following recess once a day without any prompting for 9 of 10 consecutive recess periods then he or she understands what to do in this situation and has mastered the desired skill. Of course, the team may want this student to perform this skill at every opportunity throughout the school year; however, they set the mastery criterion at 9 of 10 consecutive times, making the decision that this frequency indicates mastery.

Duration Data

At times, a criterion other than frequency is important for a given situation or activity. Collecting duration data may be very important if the person is to engage in a behavior for a given period of time (e.g., play appropriately with peers, stay on task, stay with the group). Typically, duration of time would be combined with frequency in setting the criterion, as in the previous example of Cliff. The team needs to ask itself how long the student needs to engage in the behavior and how many times the behavior must be observed before the team can feel comfortable claiming mastery for the student.

Latency Data

The latency between when a direction or other stimulus is given and the response expected of the student may be critical information to include when setting the criterion. For example, if a student responds to a greeting or a question but not until 5 minutes or more have passed, then the interaction will break down. Typically, teachers want students to respond almost immediately to directions, greetings, or questions. If the student has difficulty responding in a timely fashion, then adding a specific time limit to the desired behavior may be very appropriate. An example of an IEP objective using latency as part of the criterion is as follows. *When asked a question, Ysella will respond by looking, using a picture or object within 4 seconds of the question asked for 12 of 15 consecutive questions.* As in previous examples, multiple criteria may be needed per objective (in this case, latency and frequency) in order to create a measurable objective. The determination of how long to set the latency criterion will depend on the student's ability to respond and the demands of the situation. Table 10.1 describes different types of data that may be appropriate for the team to consider when assessing student progress.

STRATEGIES TO COLLECT STUDENT PERFORMANCE DATA

Several strategies exist to collect meaningful data needed to assess student progress. How data are collected will depend on team members, their preferences, and their availability. Data can be collected via direct observation as the student performs the behavior, periodic samples of the student's work, and videotaped observations of the student's performance over time. More qualitative types of data can be collected periodically by interviewing individuals who interact with the student (e.g., family members, general educators, bus drivers) to determine whether they have noted changes in performance. However data are obtained, it should be ongoing and occur on a regular basis. These types of data collection strategies are presented in greater detail in the following pages.

Table 10.1.   Types of behavior to target for IEP criterion

Frequency of behavior—number of times a specific behavior occurs (e.g., the number of times a student chooses her name stamp to sign her name to her papers).

Duration of behavior—length of time that a specific behavior lasts (e.g., a student's time on task); unit of measure could be seconds, minutes, or hours depending on the behavior.

Latency of behavior—duration of time between the stimulus given and the desired behavior (e.g., time between when the teacher asks students to line up and when the student performs this behavior).

Direct Observation

Perhaps the most obvious way to collect assessment data is to directly observe the targeted behaviors as they occur. The closer the assessment is to what is being assessed, the more valid the procedure (Schloss & Smith, 1999); however, this method of data collection may be difficult if the team member who is to collect the data is also expected to support the student in acquiring the behavior. One way to make data collection convenient is to make it a part of the lesson plan or a part of formal directions to follow. Combining the procedure for instruction with the form to collect student progress can serve as a reminder to those responsible for this important aspect of teaching. Figures 10.1–10.5 are examples of data sheets that also contain a prompting strategy for the adult to follow. Using a clipboard with an attached pen or pencil and making sure it is readily available also eases the process of documenting student behavior. Of course, including the importance of data collection in the training of all adults or peer tutors is critical. Collecting data needs to become a part of the instructional routine so that it is not perceived as an additional burden.

The form used for data collection will vary depending on the IEP objective and the targeted skills within that objective. Forms may need to be devised to collect information on the frequency of behaviors (e.g., the number of times a student greets a peer), their duration (e.g., the length of time maintained during a conversation), and/or the latency between a stimulus and the desired response (e.g., the time that is allowed between when a peer greets a student and when the student responds). Some IEP objectives may involve several steps of an activity that the student is to master, whereas other objectives may target only one small skill. For example, in the activity of conversing with a peer, the sequence of steps or skills depicted in Figure 10.5 is needed. Data would need to be collected on all steps or skill sequences to determine which skills are being performed consistently and which skills are causing the student more difficulty. The criterion in the IEP objective will determine when the student has mastered the objective. For example, if the criterion for mastery in the present example is set at a minimum of three responses per conversation for at least six consecutive conversations, the data sheet should be able to reflect this. All steps of this interaction must have at least three positive (indicating independent) signs in each box for at least six different conversations. The more information that is preprinted on the data collection forms, the less writing will be needed by data collectors; however, enough space should be provided to write in additional comments as necessary.

If the objective is for the student to use sign to communicate during appropriate times of the day, the data sheet would probably look different. It would be

Student: _Michele_

Objective: _Michele will take at least 3 turns during a social conversation with a peer by_
pointing to appropriate pictures in her conversation book for 8 of 10 consecutive
conversations.

Activity: _Nutrition_

Conversations

	1	2	3	4	5
Looks at peer	+ (P) – Prompt: _a_ Peer: _Leah_	+ P – Prompt: Peer:	+ P – Prompt: Peer:	+ P – Prompt: Peer:	+ P – Prompt: Peer:
Responds to peer's initiation by looking at conversation book	+ (P) – Prompt: _b_	+ P – Prompt:	+ P – Prompt:	+ P – Prompt:	+ P – Prompt:
Points to appropriate picture	+ (P) – Prompt: _d_ Picture: _family_	+ P – Prompt: Picture:	+ P – Prompt: Picture:	+ P – Prompt: Picture:	+ P – Prompt: Picture:
Looks at peer	+ P (–) Prompt: _a_	+ P – Prompt:	+ P – Prompt:	+ P – Prompt:	+ P – Prompt:
Responds to peer's comments	+ P (–) Prompt: _d_ Picture:	+ P – Prompt: Picture:	+ P – Prompt: Picture:	+ P – Prompt: Picture:	+ P – Prompt: Picture:

Directions:
First row: Circle the level of response (=, P, –), write in the highest level of prompt used,
   and write in the peer's name.
Second row: Circle the level of response and write in the highest level of prompt used.
Third row: Circle the level of response, write in the highest level of prompt used, and write
   in the picture the student used.
Prompting strategy (wait 3 seconds before each prompt):
a) Point to the person; b) touch the book; c) start to scan pictures in the book with finger;
d) tap near the appropriate picture.

Figure 10.5.   Data sheet showing a task analysis of skills needed (Key: + = independent performance; P = prompted performance; – = did not perform skill).

Student: _Clarisse_		Date: _3/26/01_	

Objective: _At appropriate times during the school day, Clarisse will independently use at least 3 different signs twice a week for a 2-week period._

Signs used	Level of independence	When used	With whom
Eat	+	_30 minutes before lunch_	_Terri (aide)_
Help me	_I_	_Putting things away_	_Terri (aide)_
Play?	_I_	_Looking at recess picture in schedule_	_Annie (peer)_
Yes	_C_	_At lunch, asked if she wanted something_	_Terri (aide)_
Yes	+	_(same)_	_Terri (aide)_

Directions:
Write in the words signed by the student (first column).
Use the key to add the level of performance (second column).
Briefly state when the sign was used (third column).
State the recipient of the signed expression (fourth column).

Figure 10.6.   Data sheet for documenting use of sign (Key: + = independent performance; I = imitation; C = cued with touch).

important to document what signs are being used, when, and with whom. Figure 10.6 depicts a format for documenting progress of such skills.

To clarify mastery, the objective would have to state how many signs needed to be used, how often, and at what level of independence. For example, it could be worded, _At appropriate times during the school day, Clarisse will independently use at least three different signs twice a day for a 2-week period._ Although the social component (to whom) is not addressed in the objective, it could provide important information with regard to Clarisse's social network. If the paraeducator is the primary person to whom Clarisse signs, it could mean that she does not have opportunities to interact with other students, that other students do not know how to interact with her, or that she has only learned to sign to an adult. Such information, although not directly applicable to the IEP objective, does provide meaningful information that could lead to a needed change in the educational program and/or teaching strategy.

Table 10.2.   Things to consider when designing data forms

Does the form collect all the data needed to measure the IEP objective?

Can it collect additional information that may aid further instruction?

Is it in its simplest form (easy to read, minimal writing required)?

Is the key clear and easy to use?

Is there sufficient space to add information as needed?

Are individual team members encouraged to modify the form as needed?

Table 10.2 provides some things to consider when developing data forms. As with any skill that a teacher employs, practice performing it is critical. After making an initial draft of a data form, using it to collect data will determine its appropriateness for the task. Revisions of forms should be expected. Feedback from other members of the team who make use of the form will help to identify its usefulness and probable need for modification.

Videotaped Observations

For maintaining an accurate picture of a student's progress, videotaping holds considerable merit (Burford, 1996; Siegel-Causey & Allinder, 1998). Lessons targeting similar skills can be videotaped at different intervals creating a readily available comparison of change over time. The videotaped format is easily accessible to all team members and can demonstrate a change in behavior that may be much easier to discern than similar data in another format. Everyone can easily see the progress made. Furthermore, videotaped information provides a more qualitative approach to assessment that allows for a holistic and comprehensive picture of a student's performance (Schwartz & Olswang, 1996).

Videotaped observations do not need to be long, just brief excerpts of activities deemed to be representative of a student's performance in different and critical activities at a specific point in time. Videotaping the student in similar activities across different grades can clearly document progress. For example, videotaped segments for one elementary-age student may include listening to a story read by the teacher (large group), using a schedule to transition from one activity to another, using manipulatives and a calculator for individual seat work in math, doing a hands-on science experiment for small-group work, and completing a reading or writing exercise with a peer buddy. Videotaped assessment of this nature provides information regarding how a student performs in different learning arrangements (e.g., large group, individual seat work, small group, in pairs) as well as information on skills of following directions, reading, writing, social interactions, math and tool use. Depending on this student's IEP, videotaped segments also might include having access to a computer via a switch, purchasing lunch, eating lunch, and socially interacting during recess.

If a team member or volunteer is not available to videotape target activities, a tripod can be used to allow videotaping of large segments of the day. This videotaped information then can be edited to show the most important information in a more time efficient format. One copy of the videotape can stay in the student's portfolio gathering cumulative data while another copy can remain with the student's family as a means of gaining a clearer idea of what happens in school. As the student transitions from grade to grade and school to school, future team members can get a relatively quick idea of the abilities of the student they will be receiving.

Student Work

Products completed by the student also provide a means of assessing progress. Added to more traditional types of assessment data, samples of student work provide another dimension to the assessment process (Schwartz & Olswang, 1996). Such products could include a student's signature, a sequence of pictures to write a sentence, an art creation, a vocabulary worksheet showing how a student has drawn lines from the word to its picture, a tactile science project, and a book cowritten with a peer using photographs and computer graphics. All work should be clearly dated and contain a brief description of how the student completed the project and how much was done independently.

Collecting similar samples of the student's work can make comparison across time easier. For example, a 5-year-old child may initially sign her name by identifying it from two others on sticky labels (hers is bold and highlighted), peeling it off, and placing it on her work. In third grade, this same student can write the first letter in her name, and by fifth grade, she can print her full name, although some letters are not as legible as others. The progress toward reaching the goal of signing her name is obvious.

ORGANIZING THE INFORMATION

To get a holistic understanding of a student's increased abilities, no one data source will suffice. Multiple forms of data can be combined to demonstrate not only that the student has made progress, but also *how* the student has progressed and what the progress entails. Data on IEP objectives from MAPS, videotaped observations, and student projects need to be organized in a manner that is easily accessible and makes discerning the student's progress easy. An individual student portfolio offers an effective means of maintaining information on a student over a given period of time.

Portfolio Assessment

An alternative to standardized assessment procedures involves the development of individualized portfolios that reflect student work and progress made (Kleinert, Kearns, & Kennedy, 1997; Siegel-Causey & Allinder, 1998; Wesson & King, 1996). The naturally individualized nature of portfolios precludes the necessity of all students demonstrating progress in the same manner. Students do not have to conform to a set process but can demonstrate their skills, strengths, and interests in a variety of ways that tell a lot about them. Furthermore, portfolio assessments apply equally well to all students. For instance, a student who is gifted musically may include a musical piece she created, whereas another student may have a videotaped segment of a choral performance in which she took part. Likewise,

Table 10.3.   Selected sections for a student's portfolio

Student profile
MAPS (Making Action Plans)
Videotapes of performance (academic subjects, nonacademic subjects, work)
Samples of work (pictorial essays, tactual representations, signatures, tape recording of
    student reading/talking)
Narrative progress reports
Performance data
Photographs of student performing tasks and/or photographs of completed projects
Lists of preferred activities/items/people
Samples of augmentative and alternative communication device overlays

one student may have a copy of a research paper on a topic of interest, and another student may have a pictorial collage to represent what he has learned on a topic. Portfolio assessment involves both quantitative and qualitative data and can clearly demonstrate how every student has access to the general education curriculum, regardless of ability level (Kleinert & Kearns, 1999).

Portfolios on students will be dynamic, changing with the student as the student progresses through school and acquires different skills. Students should have ready access to their portfolios so they can check on past work, compare to current work, make decisions to replace some work with others, and add new categories as the need arises (Swicegood, 1994). Even though students with severe and multiple disabilities may not understand the rationale for or use of the portfolio, simple choices can still be offered. Portfolio selections should be dated so that the progression of skill acquisition can be easily noted. In addition, a brief explanation of how the student completed the work (e.g., what choices were given, what prompts were used) should be attached to included work to clarify the learning process. This practice helps to organize the material and provides valuable information for present and future educational teams. Review of a student's portfolio can help the team focus on a student's strengths and better plan future IEP goals and objectives (Carpenter, Ray, & Bloom, 1995). Table 10.3 provides some suggestions for information to include in a student's portfolio.

Collaborative Progress Report

"A well-planned and executed assessment that results in each team member having a well-balanced understanding of a student's performance is one of the most important contributions to generating critical objectives, effective instruction, and meaningful outcomes" (Gilles & Clark, 2001, p. 80). Reporting on student progress is not delegated to one individual (usually the special educator) but rather is shared by those working directly with the student. For students with severe and multiple disabilities, this policy could mean that a large number of people will contribute to the assessment reporting process. Not all members of a team, however, will necessarily collect information on every objective. The type of information needed and when and where a student engages in the targeted skills will determine what team members will be able to collect the desired data.

Although the special educator on the team may have considerable responsibility for assessing student progress, the classroom teacher shares the responsibility for reporting student progress. Some team members have been disappointed with the lack of communication from the general educator regarding their child's performance (Downing, Ryndak, & Clark, 2000). Because the classroom teacher has access to the IEP and has participated in its development, the objectives that require documentation of progress should be known. Furthermore, the teacher should spend sufficient time with the student to know where progress is being made. As Giangreco, Edelman, and Nelson (1998) found, a positive relationship exists between student progress and teacher involvement. The classroom teacher's perspectives are important and need to be part of any assessment process.

Besides teacher input (whether special or general education), the paraeducator can provide valuable information concerning student progress. Because these individuals often work directly with a student, they are in an excellent position to collect data. They can be the first members on a team to notice progress or to recognize that an intervention is not working. Soliciting their input (both formal and anecdotal) adds to a high-quality and accurate report.

Other members of the team (e.g., SLP, hearing specialist, occupational therapist) may be specifically targeting certain skills. Although individual team members will assess different aspects of a student's program, in compiling their information and presenting it as a collaborative effort, a more comprehensive look at a student's program can be achieved (Gilles & Clark, 2001). Depending on when related services providers work with the student, they may be in the best position to collect specific data for the rest of the team. These team members can also draw attention to progress made in specific areas (e.g., greater use of a pincer grasp, evidence of more efficient visual tracking) that may have gone unnoticed by others on the team.

Parents and other family members may be instrumental in verifying if the student is engaging in any target behavior at home. Although the IEP usually addresses skills that the student is to learn at school, the carryover of these skills from school to home is the desired social outcome. For instance, teachers and paraeducators may note that a student is increasing the frequency of his choice-making behavior and is making these choices in less time (decreasing the latency between being asked and choosing). When the student's father verifies that he is noticing a similar change in behavior at home, the generalization of these critical skills can be confirmed.

SHARING INFORMATION WITH PARENTS

Parents want to be notified of their child's progress. They want to know that their child is learning, and they want to know how they can support their child's learning. Having access to information on their child at regular intervals helps to enhance communication and parent involvement (Hughes & Carter, 2000; Sommerstein & Smith, 2001). In addition, IDEA requires that parents be informed of their child's performance at least as frequently as parents of children without disabilities.

One way to enhance communication with parents regarding the progress of their child is through the use of portfolios (Alberto, Mechling, Taber, & Thompson, 1995; Ezell, Klein, & Ezell-Powell, 1999; Salend, 1998; Siegel-Causey & Allinder, 1998). Compared with a score on a standardized test or a statement that an IEP objective was met, a student's portfolio provides parents and family members with more concrete information regarding their child's progress. This portfolio allows parents to see how their child has mastered IEP objectives. The focus of this form of assessment is on what the student can do, not on his or her deficits (Ezell et al., 1999). There are no negative comparisons made to students without disabilities, yet parents can easily see where their child needs help.

Videotaped samples of work, which are part of the student's portfolio, provide another very concrete way of quickly sharing information about a student's performance in school. This form of assessment can be particularly critical for parents who are unable to visit the classroom on a regular basis. In a study by Guidry, Van den Pol, Keeley, and Neilsen (1996), parents of young children with disabilities reported that they liked the videotaped records of their child and felt the tapes provided valuable information that they could not get otherwise. Such records of student performance may be particularly important for working parents who cannot easily visit their child's classroom. Similarly, Alberto et al. (1995) reported that parents found videotaped information of their child's program very accessible and very convenient to review repeatedly. Videotaped information served as a pictorial report card to show parents the progress their child had made as well as the instructional techniques used.

Regardless of how information is shared with family members, it should be done in a manner that is clear, easy to understand, and respectful of familial and cultural values. Student progress should pertain to outcomes desired by the family and emphasize skills the student has attained. If students have not made the anticipated progress, family members, as part of the team, can help determine alternate strategies to use. The focus should remain on ways to help the student learn as well as plans to modify the intervention, rather than more negative labels attributed to a student.

USING DATA CONSTRUCTIVELY

Ongoing assessments can help team members determine student progress and answer questions regarding desired outcomes. In this manner, the team can adjust its teaching strategies as needed (McGregor & Vogelsberg, 1998; Schwartz & Olswang, 1996). Data collected on student performance needs to be reviewed frequently to ensure that the student is becoming more proficient. Quickly checking the data as it is collected and comparing it to previously collected data (on the same form) may be the easiest approach for objective and quantitative type of data. If the student has reached the expected criterion for performance, lessons should be adapted to expect more from the student, allowing the student to acquire greater competence. If anticipated progress isn't made, teachers should ask, "Why not?" and determine how to change the intervention so that the student can be more successful. The team needs to raise issues and brainstorm alternative strategies.

Lack of success may be due to a number of factors including lack of motivation, irrelevance of task, distractions, difficulty of task, and ineffectiveness of the intervention. Depending on the reason for the lack of progress, the program will need to be adapted or changed altogether. Activities that hold no meaning for the student need to be replaced with those that do (e.g., throwing a ball in PE did not meet any of Shana's needs, whereas parachute play was more meaningful). Tasks that are too difficult need to be made easier to perform with the use of various assistive technology devices. Tasks that are important but hold little interest for the student may need to be accompanied by a rather powerful reinforcer for the student (e.g., putting away materials and cleaning up after a task hold little enjoyment, but Roger does them because he'll get time on the computer if he does).

Additional analysis of tasks may help identify where the student is having the greatest difficulty. Types of tasks that are particularly problematic may require more intensive instruction, greater adaptation, or may need to be eliminated if possible. For example, when analyzing data on a student's progress toward matching numbers from an enlarged math worksheet to a large calculator, it became evident that mistakes were made for numbers in the middle columns (2, 5, 8) more often than other numbers. By recording what number was selected by the student and what number should have been selected, the teachers were able to see that the student selected the number next to the correct number, which may indicate a difficulty controlling the physical movement of the adapted pointer. This information can then lead to needed change in the instructional program.

SUMMARY

This chapter has targeted the critical importance of measuring student progress and program effectiveness when students with severe and multiple disabilities receive their education in general education classrooms. By law, students with disabilities have the right to an appropriate education. Appropriateness is determined if the student is making progress toward meaningful goals and objectives.

An inclusive education does not just refer to an acceptance of diversity. Learning must occur. Documenting student progress is necessary in order to document the effectiveness of the program and to ensure high standards. Although parents may be pleased that their child is a regular member of the general education classroom, this fact does not mean that they have forfeited their right to have their child acquire valuable skills. Assessment data shows progress made by the teaching staff as well as the progress made by the student. This process keeps everyone on the right track.

REFERENCES

Agran, M., & Alper, S. (2000). Curriculum and instruction in general education: Implications for service delivery and teacher preparation. *Journal of The Association for Persons with Severe Handicaps, 25,* 167–174.

Alberto, P.A., Mechling, L., Taber, T.A., & Thompson, J. (1995). Using videotapes to communicate with parents of students with severe disabilities. *Teaching Exceptional Children, 27*(3), 18–21.

Billingsley, F.F., & Albertson, L.R. (1999). Finding a future for functional skills. *Journal of The Association for Persons with Severe Handicaps, 24,* 298–302.

Burford, B. (1996). A way of assisting careers of children with profound learning disabilities to share what they know about communication. *Network, 5*(1), 31–37.

Carpenter, C.D., Ray, M.S., & Bloom, L.A. (1995). Portfolio assessment: Opportunities and challenges. *Intervention in School and Clinic, 31,* 34–41.

Chelsey, G.M., & Calaluce, P.D. (1997). The deception of inclusion. *Mental Retardation, 35,* 488–490.

Downing, J.E., Ryndak, D.L., & Clark, D. (2000). Paraeducators in inclusive education: Their own perspectives. *Remedial and Special Education, 21,* 171–181.

Ezell, D., Klein, C.E., & Ezell-Powell, S. (1999). Empowering students with mental retardation through portfolio assessment: A tool for fostering self-determination skills. *Education and Training in Mental Retardation and Developmental Disabilities, 34,* 453–463.

Falvey, M., Forest, M., Pearpoint, J., & Rosenberg, R. (1997). *All my life's a circle. Using the tools: Circles, MAPS, and PATHS.* Toronto: Inclusion Press.

Fisher, D., & Kennedy, C.H. (2001). Linking assessment to accountability and instruction. In C.H. Kennedy & D. Fisher, *Inclusive middle schools* (pp. 73–88). Baltimore: Paul H. Brookes Publishing Co.

Giangreco, M.F., Edelman, S.W., & Nelson, C. (1998). Impact of planning for support services on students who are deaf-blind. *Journal of Vision Impairment and Blindness, 92*(1), 18–29.

Gilles, D., & Clark, D. (2001). Collaborative teaming in the assessment process. In S. Alper, D.L. Ryndak, & C.N. Schloss (Eds.), *Alternate assessment of students with disabilities in inclusive settings* (pp. 75–87). Needham Heights, MA: Allyn & Bacon.

Guidry, J., Van den Pol, R., Keeley, E., & Neilsen, S. (1996). Augmenting traditional assessment and information: The videoshare model. *Topics in Early Childhood Special Education, 16,* 51–65.

Hock, M.L. (2000). Standards, assessments, and individualized educational programs: Planning for success in the general education curriculum. In R.A. Villa & J.S. Thousand (Eds.), *Restructuring for caring and effective education: Piecing the puzzle together* (2nd ed., pp. 208–241). Baltimore: Paul H. Brookes Publishing Co.

Hughes, C., & Carter, E.W. (2000). *The transition handbook: Strategies high school teachers use that work!* Baltimore: Paul H. Brookes Publishing Co.

Individuals with Disabilities Education Act (IDEA) Amendments of 1997, PL 105-17, 20 U.S.C. §§ 1400 *et seq.*

Jackson, L., Ryndak, D.L., & Billingsley, F. (2000). Useful practices in inclusive education: A preliminary view of what experts in moderate to severe disabilities are saying. *Journal of The Association for Persons with Severe Handicaps, 25,* 129–141.

Kleinert, H.L., Haigh, J., Kearns, J.F., & Kennedy, S. (2000). Alternate assessments: Lessons learned and roads to be taken. *Exceptional Children, 67,* 51–66.

Kleinert, H.L., & Kearns, J.F. (1999). A validation study of the performance indicators and learner outcomes of Kentucky's alternate assessment for students with significant disabilities. *Journal of The Association for Persons with Severe Handicaps, 24,* 100–110.

Kleinert, H., Kearns, J., & Kennedy, S. (1997). Accountability for all students: Kentucky's alternate portfolio assessment for students with moderate and severe cognitive disabilities. *Journal of The Association for Persons with Severe Handicaps, 22,* 88–101.

McGregor, G., & Vogelsberg, R.T. (1998). *Inclusive schooling practices: Pedagogical and research foundations.* Baltimore: Paul H. Brookes Publishing Co.

Salend, S.J. (1998). Using portfolios to assess student performance. *Teaching Exceptional Children, 31*(2), 36–43.

Schloss, P.J., & Smith, M.A. (1999). *Conducting research.* New York: Merrill.

Schwartz, I.S., & Olswang, L.B. (1996). Evaluating child behavior change in natural settings: Exploring alternative strategies for data collection. *Topics in Early Childhood Special Education, 16,* 82–101.

Siegel-Causey, E., & Allinder, R.M. (1998). Using alternative assessment for students with severe disabilities: Alignment with best practices. *Education and Training in Mental Retardation and Developmental Disabilities, 33,* 168–178.

Sommerstein, L., & Smith, J. (2001). Summarizing and communicating assessment information: Empowering students and families. In S. Alper, D.L. Ryndak, & C.N. Schloss (Eds.), *Alternate assessment of students with disabilities in inclusive settings* (pp. 183–198). Needham Heights, MA: Allyn & Bacon.

Swicegood, P. (1994). Portfolio-based assessment practices. *Intervention in School and Clinic, 30*(1), 6–15.

Wesson, C.L., & King, R.P. (1996). Portfolio assessment and special education students. *Teaching Exceptional Children, 28*(2), 44–49.

Chapter 11

Common Concerns
and Some Responses

June E. Downing

This chapter uses a question-and-answer format to address specific concerns or issues that may remain for readers. The response accompanying each question encompasses one of many possible ideas to consider and should not be perceived as the only possible or even the best response. Each situation is different, and ideas must be considered and applied in context to have optimal value. Suggestions provided here have been employed successfully with specific children in distinct situations. It is hoped that some of these strategies, in whole or in part, will prove helpful.

Question 1. How do I deal with a student who is disruptive in class (e.g., screams, hits, runs around, throws items)?

When students display disruptive behavior of this nature, they probably are trying to express thoughts and feelings that they cannot otherwise communicate effectively. For instance, they may be having a difficult time attending to a task, receiving the necessary information, or feeling competent to perform what is being asked. They may need more help, a different task, or another way to understand what is expected and why. They may feel sick or may be expressing frustration over an earlier interaction with someone that did not go well. Medications also may compound the problem, making some students more irritable, more easily frustrated, more tired, or less able to pay attention.

Whatever the reason, it is critical not to blame the child or use the undesired behavior as a reason to permanently remove the child from the typical learning environment. Instead, a thorough functional analysis of the behavior (Donnellan, Mirenda, Mesaros, & Fassbender, 1984; O'Neill et al., 1997) is needed to determine strategies to help the student gain greater self-control and also reduce the need for this inappropriate mode of communication. Changing the situation (e.g., whole task, aspect of the task, method of instruction, physical position in the room), while also providing the student with alternative communicative modes to express needs, feelings, and so forth, has been documented as a successful practice (Carr & Durand, 1985; Carr et al., 1994; Durand, 1993; Mirenda,

1997; Reeve & Carr, 2000; Scotti & Meyer, 1999). Offering the student choices (e.g., preferred versus nonpreferred task, where to sit, what materials to use) can have a definitive and positive effect on undesired behavior (Foster-Johnson, Ferro, & Dunlap, 1994). The idea behind offering students choices is to allow the student as much control as possible. Assisting the student to be as successful as possible at a given task can be another effective strategy to reduce the occurrence of negative behavior. Students who feel incompetent and unable to participate adequately will tend to engage in negative types of behavior to escape the task because it is aversive to them (Cipani, 1995).

When the student is out of control and potentially disruptive to the teacher and other classmates, helping the student to leave the classroom and to go into the hall, outside the building, into a teacher's office, or to the principal's office for a few minutes to regain control and interrupt the inappropriate behavior may be the best course of action. This does not mean permanent removal based on negative behavior, however. By not going to a special self-contained classroom, it remains clear to everyone that returning to the typical classroom as soon as possible is the immediate goal. Returning the student to the classroom after a disruption also does not reinforce the student who might engage in the disruptive behavior specifically to escape a given situation and go to a less-demanding environment. Instead, the student should be taken to an obviously temporary environment, shown how to request the need for a change in activity (or whatever the student intended to communicate), and then returned to the classroom to continue the task with more help or to engage in an alternative activity. In this way, it is made clear to the student that he or she belongs in the classroom, that disruptive behavior does not eliminate all expectations for performance, and that there are other appropriate ways to express frustration, boredom, or anger in a given situation.

For the student who is frequently disruptive in an effort to communicate, having quick and easy access to an AAC device may be most helpful. For instance, a student may wear a wrist sweatband with a pictorial symbol of an angry face with the message, "I need a break now," on it. When he or she touches this symbol or hands it to someone, the task ends for the moment, and he or she gets to step away from it. Individuals supporting this student should respond quickly and positively to the appropriate behavior (e.g., touching the AAC device) so that the student will not have to make his or her requests in a less desirable and more disruptive manner.

Question 2. How do I ensure appropriate language development and social interactions with classmates when the student is deaf?

This book has focused on the needs of individuals who have cognitive impairments and may be deaf, but the strategies listed can also benefit students without cognitive impairments and those for whom both cultural and language issues are critical (Kluwin, Gonsher, Silver, & Samuels, 1996; Kluwin, Moores, & Gausted, 1992; Luchner, 1991). Generally speaking, students who are deaf or have a significant hearing impairment as well as a cognitive impairment may use minimal signs to communicate (either receptively or expressively) and are not fluent users of ASL. They do not require teachers and classmates who are fluent in this manual language. Furthermore, they typically are not a part of and do not experience

Deaf culture. They, however, definitely need the opportunity to interact with class-mates and to learn as many communication skills as possible.

Teaching the general educator and all students some sign awareness as an ongoing language lesson and using the signed alphabet while practicing spelling in the younger grades will provide everyone with some of the skills needed to facilitate social interactions. Young children and their general education teachers often express great enthusiasm in learning some vocabulary from ASL, and teachers can see the benefit for all students of learning a second or third language. Zeece and Wolda (1995) reported on the benefits of signing for young children with a variety of disabilities in typical environments. The kinesthetic properties of using one's hands to communicate may contribute to the learning process (Luchner, 1991). Therefore, learning to sign may facilitate language learning for a wide array of children. Heller, Manning, Pavur, and Wagner (1998) felt that preschoolers who learned English Sign Language enhanced their language development, even though only two children had hearing impairments. At the secondary level, a formal sign language class or club can be developed (possibly with assistance from people in the Deaf community). Students of widely different abilities can be members of this club, with the student who has severe and multiple disabilities providing some of the instruction.

In addition to some sign awareness and instruction, students without disabilities, teachers, and other members of the school community need to exploit the many ways the student with disabilities interacts with others. As described in Chapter 8, communication partners will use facial expressions, natural gestures, body language, objects, pictures, photographs, and any number of other behaviors that allow the student with deafness and other impairments to communicate most effectively. In fact, multimodal approaches to communication are recommended (Beukelman & Mirenda, 1998; Downing, 1993, 1999; Reichle, Feeley, & Johnston, 1993). The intent is to provide a rich social environment in which all students can receive the stimulation they need.

Question 3.   How do I motivate a student to learn?

Some students appear to lack interest in many common activities and refuse to participate. Trying to provide an effective reinforcer for such a student to encourage participation may be difficult because the student shows little response to any potential reinforcer. Assessing the personal preferences and choices of students with severe and multiple disabilities, therefore, becomes a critical objective for teachers (Hughes, Pitkin, & Lorden, 1998; Lohrmann-O'Rourke, Browder, & Brown, 2000). A thorough interview with parents and other family members needs to be conducted to determine interests of the student that may possibly be used as reinforcers for less-desired activities. Some unique motivators may be discovered that can aid learning. For example, one 11-year-old would apparently work quite hard if he could play with a pine cone on occasion. Once teachers discovered this information from his parents, they used it not only as a reinforcer but also let him collect pine cones, sort them by size, use them in mathematics as manipulatives, and tear them apart to make artistic designs. These designs then became illustrations for poems and stories co-written with a classmate.

In addition to familial input, providing the student with diverse opportunities to explore new activities and items of potential interest is vital. Owing to sensory, cognitive, or physical limitations, students may not have been exposed to a sufficient array of options to develop interests and skills. Caregivers and teachers alike may have prejudged the value of certain activities, and the student may have been denied access or exposure to these as a result. Furthermore, simple exposure to activities or items may not be sufficient to foster interest. Repeated opportunities may be needed (as with all of us) before a true interest develops. The novelty of an activity or environment may be too confusing or stimulating to be perceived initially as a positive experience. For example, the author has known several students who initially appeared to hate swimming. They kicked, screamed, cried, and struggled to get out of the water. Repeated attempts to encourage the enjoyment of swimming and water play, however, resulted in increasingly more positive behaviors until the students perceived the activity as the fun event it was intended to be. A decision on the part of a caregiver that swimming was not a good activity for the students, based on their initial reactions, could have been very limiting for the students.

Part of a community-based program may be to increase exposure, develop interests, and nurture these interests. For example, some students show a special interest in birds and guinea pigs after being taken on repeated trips to a pet store. Others show interest in clocks, arcade games, and other novelty items (e.g., magnetic doodles; hard, rubberized knickknacks; strobe lights; onyx pieces) following excursions into the community with peers who do not have disabilities. To help cultivate a student's interest in activities—especially an older student who may have become comfortable with limited options and expectations for performance— educational staff will need to work closely with parents and significant others to experiment with all available options in the community.

In addition to expanding awareness of what is possible by increasing experiences and opportunities to learn, providing students with various choices throughout each activity of the day can have a major impact on increasing a student's motivation to perform as expected. Making choices of preferred activities, parts of activities, materials to use, partners to work with, and so forth not only aids in the development of decision making but also gives the individual a sense of control, which can in turn enhance positive self-esteem. Choice making has been linked to decreasing problem behaviors and increasing desirable behaviors (Johnson, Ferro, & Dunlap, 1994; Moes, 1998), to motivating the passive learner (Downing, 1999; Hughes et al., 1998), and to gaining control over the environment (Gothelf, Crimmins, Mercer, & Finocchiaro, 1994).

Question 4.   I do not have a one-to-one staffing ratio. How can I provide adequate support for all of the students in typical classes?

Most programs do not have the funding to provide one-to-one teacher–student staffing ratios, nor would that be advisable in all situations. Students with severe and multiple impairments often need considerable support for a variety of reasons; however, automatically assigning a paraeducator to a child based on his or her need for special education or particular disability is not an effective practice (Giangreco, Broer, & Edelman, 1999). An adult's being present with a student 100% of the time may seriously interfere with that student's ability to interact with others, make friends, and feel a true part of the class. It may also signal to other students in the class that they have little if any responsibility for getting to

know the student with a disability. Although paraeducators are extremely valuable in inclusive classrooms, they should not be solely responsible for assisting the
student with disabilities (Giangreco et al., 1999). Therefore, it is a good idea
early on to encourage assistance when needed from classmates so as to fade specialized adult support.

However, since there is a recognized need to adapt materials, use alternative
instructional techniques, help the student remain on task, and so forth, added
human resources may be necessary. Heterogeneously assigning students to the
special educator can help alleviate the need to provide extensive supports (physical and instructional) to all students at the same time. If a teacher's caseload involves a number of students with different abilities, there is a much greater
chance of providing extensive support to a few students as needed. In other
words, one teacher's caseload for inclusion might consist of 10 students, one of
whom has severe and multiple impairments and requires considerable assistance
throughout the day; the other 9 students have moderate to severe disabilities but
demonstrate varying levels of independence. Although all of these students need
support at various times throughout the day, their needs are not constant, and a
variety of supports can be used effectively.

If this heterogeneous arrangement is not in evidence, teachers may need to
solicit aid from a number of different resources, as described in Chapter 9. Non-
paid and nonprofessional support may come from classmates, older students from
either the same school or another school, volunteers, parents, and practicum students from university programs. Scheduling support for all students needs to be
creative and flexible and reflect individual needs as they vary throughout the
school day. For example, a special educator may have a caseload of 10 students,
but not all 10 students will experience the same needs for support at the same
time. All of the students may be in different classes depending on their chronological ages and their IEP objectives. That is, at any one time during the day, students could be in mathematics, language arts, science, PE, music, or study hall
or at recess or lunch. Obviously, supporting students with challenging learning
needs will vary depending on the subject being studied and the activities expected
of the student. If all students were in different classrooms and all were engaged
in mathematics at the same time, the problems for adequate support would be
obvious.

One of the primary responsibilities of the special education support teacher
is to develop (and keep modifying) a schedule of support for himself or herself,
paraeducators, related services providers, volunteers, and others. This will require
changing support assignments as needed and continually working to create the
best match possible between students' needs for assistance and the expertise of
available human support. The sample elementary and high school staff schedules
in Chapter 9 provide examples of how such scheduling might look.

Question 5. How do I find time to meet and plan collaboratively with all team members?

This question arises frequently and is perhaps the most challenging aspect of inclusive education for everyone involved in this type of service delivery. In general, educators often feel overwhelmed with work and very short on time (Snell
& Janney, 2000). In addition, every educational team supporting a given student

operates differently depending on a number of personal and work-related variables. As such, there are no clear guidelines to follow other than the recognized importance of meeting on a regular basis (Rainforth & York-Barr, 1997; Thousand & Villa, 2000; Wolery, Werts, Caldwell, & Snyder, 1995).

Because time is a critical factor for most educators and related services personnel, meetings should always be held on time and be brief, to the point, and constructive so that participants can leave feeling that the meeting was worthwhile. Guidelines exist for holding time-efficient meetings (see Villa & Thousand, 1993). It is also critical to consider who must actually meet and how often. Obviously, those working directly with the student on a daily basis will need to meet so that daily programming can continue as smoothly as possible. Therefore, the teachers involved (classroom teacher and special educator) and the paraeducators supporting these teachers need to find time to exchange information and to resolve issues on a fairly regular basis. Short meetings can be held during planning periods, lunch, recess, before or after school, and, in some districts, on early release days. Whenever they can, teachers must find a few minutes to confer on a student (Graham, 1998).

It is important to note that in the initial stages of including all students, meetings may be longer or more frequent as the team first learns to work together. As the team becomes comfortable working in this manner, the length and number of meetings should be reduced. Whatever is not resolved during these face-to-face meetings may be tabled until the next meeting or may require one of the participants to obtain necessary information to share with the other members. Information can be shared through notes, articles put in mailboxes, e-mail messaging, telephone calls in the evening, or brief exchanges when passing in the hall. Every effort should be made to exchange information as quickly as possible and in the most convenient fashion (which is seldom another meeting).

Question 6. How can I ensure consistency in programming with so many staff members?

Consistency in programming is difficult whenever more than one person is responsible for implementation. When support staff are working in different classrooms throughout the day, however, consistency in programming becomes an even greater challenge. As discussed in Question 5, arranging time to meet with critical support personnel is essential to effective inclusive programming; however, meetings alone will not ensure consistency in what and, especially, how a particular student is instructed. Considerable diversity in activities can exist in any classroom, and, as support staff (teachers, paraeducators, vision teachers, occupational therapists, physical therapists, volunteers, etc.) shift from room to room to meet individual instruction needs, consistency in implementation of IEPs easily could be jeopardized. A system is needed that quickly and clearly describes what the student is to be learning, how instructional support to reach the objective is to be implemented, and how it all fits into the general education curriculum.

Simply and clearly written lesson or participation plans that remain in the typical classroom with the student should serve as written reminders to all staff of the preferred way to support the student. This lesson plan should have the IEP goals or objectives clearly stated on it, so that incidental learning opportunities that address these objectives will not be lost. Data sheets per objective attached to lesson plans also serve as a reminder to collect data of emerging skills. The sample lesson plans provided in Figures 11.1–11.4 may serve as guidelines. Once individual team members become comfortable with the ways the student learns and participates in various activities, these individuals should be able to identify similar learning opportunities across many other activities. Therefore, initial training of team members may require considerable time, but subsequent training should be less demanding.

Question 7. How do I help the student communicate more effectively within typical classrooms?

Communication is a critical skill for all students and especially for students with severe and multiple disabilities. These students typically do not have effective means of making their needs known, of responding to direct questions, or of expressing their thoughts and feelings about a topic or situation (Reichle et al., 1993; Sigafoos, 2000). This limitation affects their ability to be actively involved in most learning situations and to make friends. Every effort, therefore, must be made to ensure that the student has access to and knows how to use as many different communication modes as possible for any given situation (Downing, 1999). This will take considerable teamwork and creative thinking on the part of team members; it is not the sole responsibility of the SLP or any other specially trained person. This effort will also be ongoing and dynamic as the skills of the student evolve and as team members change.

The first step in helping a student to communicate more effectively in any environment is to analyze what is needed or expected communicatively (both receptively and expressively) in that environment. Observing how a teacher interacts with his or her students at a given grade level and how students interact with the teacher and each other will help to establish a communicative base (see Chapter 3 for a description of this assessment process). Students may be expected to listen to the teacher for certain time periods, to raise their hands to gain the teacher's attention, to ask questions and respond to peers' questions when working in small groups, or to carry on an informal conversation during recess and lunch. Due to the limitations often imposed by severe and multiple disabilities, students may not be able to engage in these types of communicative interactions without considerable adaptations. It is important to know, however, what the typical expectations are for communicative behavior in a given classroom and during a specific activity to determine how the student with this severe disability can participate and what adaptations will be required.

AAC devices can greatly supplement a given student's present communicative behaviors (e.g., natural gestures, pointing, vocalizations). These devices can be small and flexible to accommodate different needs as activities change. One device will probably not suffice. Some devices will be specific to a given situation, such as pictorial symbols affixed to a wristband that a student uses at recess to make requests for snacks and to play with certain items (see Downing, 1999). Other devices will be used for other needs. Hunt, Alwell, and Goetz (1991) developed conversation books for students with multiple and sensory disabilities to use during different classroom and nonclassroom settings. Although these books did not meet all communication needs, they served a distinct purpose—to enhance social interactions. Students will need a means of making the same basic

Student Participation Plan

Student: Carly   **Age:** 6   **Grade:** First

Outcome for student: To express herself during school activities

Class activity: Sharing

Objective: Carly will make comments in class when asked by peer or teacher by using a switch-activated message in 70% of all opportunities for five class periods.

What students in class are expected to do: Students sit in circle, listen to each other, ask questions after raising their hands. A few students present something they have brought to share—they show it and describe it.

How Carly participates to achieve desired outcome: Carly sits on floor in adapted chair and looks at classmate presenting. She activates a prerecorded message of "You did a good job" by raising her right arm. When she presents, she holds what she brought with an adapted mitt and raises her hand for peers to see. She activates a prerecorded message about her item by pressing a switch.

Who provides support and how: Teacher calls on Carly when appropriate. She helps Carly respond to questions. She cues peers to ask yes/no questions. Peers ask questions, pass items for Carly to see. Paraeducator sets up switch devices, supports Carly at shoulder and elbow so she can activate switched. She puts the mitt on Carly and massages her arms/hands to relax them.

Sample #1 Data Sheet

Directions followed	Dates						Prompting strategies
1. Looks at student talking majority of the time	I III						• Point to student talking
2. Comments on peer's presentation by activating prerecorded message	I III						• Wait 5 seconds • Model head up • Tap elbow up
3. Responds to yes/no questions	II						• Wait 5 seconds • Ask again • Model head shake or nod • Ask peer to help

Figure 11.1. Sample #1: Student participation plan and data sheet for a sharing activity. Dates to be inserted above each column. Boxes below dates are for recording the number of appropriate responses over the number of opportunities given.

Student Participation Plan

Student: Doug   **Age:** 11   **Grade:** Fifth

Outcome for student: To gain greater control over social and physical environments

Class activity: Social studies—making maps

Objective: Doug will make at least three choices during four activities a day by vocalizing, looking, or reaching toward items within 5 seconds of being asked for a 2-week period.

What students in class are expected to do: Listen to teacher, watch demonstration, get materials, divide into groups, divide up responsibilities, choose colors for different regions, label regions, sign their names.

How Doug participates to achieve desired outcome: Doug looks at colors, extends arm to choose color, grasps adapted roll-on applicator filled with paint, places on paper, indicates by vocalizing when finished with color, uses signature stamp with adapted handle to sign name.

Who provides support and how: Teacher assigns Doug to a group, monitors group progress, comments on Doug's work. Classmates push Doug in wheelchair to group and to get materials. They ask him questions and provide model. Paraeducator supports him physically at shoulders to allow greatest movement. She massages his arms and hands in preparation (while teacher gives instruction).

Sample #2 Data Sheet

Skills	Trial 1 Chose to stop/ continue	Trial 2 Chose color, materials	Trial 3 Chose peer to work with	Trial 4 Chose where to sit	Prompting strategies
Chose by vocalizing	P				• Respond quickly to any behavior • Wait 5 seconds • Move one choice at a time and ask him to choose
Chose by reaching		+	—		• Wait 3 seconds
Chose by looking			—	—	• Point to/tap each item while label-ing it; repeat question • Wait 3 seconds • Ask a peer to model making a choice

Figure 11.2.   Sample #2: Student participation plan and data sheet for a social studies activity. (Key: + = independent within 5 seconds of direction, P = performed skill with prompts, – = did not perform skill)

Student Participation Plan

Student: Mark   **Age:** 13   **Grade:** Seventh

Outcome for student: To follow directions in order to be successful in activities

Class activity: Science—studying the impact of combining different chemicals

Objective: Mark will follow 50% of all directions given during 10 class periods (responding within 5 seconds of being told).

What students in class are expected to do: Students listen to teacher, watch demonstration, divide up into groups of four, get materials, perform experiments, write observations, sign their names, turn work in to teacher.

How Mark participates to achieve desired outcome: Mark assists teacher with demonstration by handing chemicals the teacher points to. Mark goes with peers to get materials. He follows directions of peers and handles items appropriately. He agrees or disagrees with written observations. He signs his name to paper with label and turns it in to teacher.

Who provides support and how: Teacher asks Mark to be a partner with him. Teacher monitors all groups, redirects Mark, and gives feedback. Peers provide guidance by modeling and cuing. Special educator cues appropriate behavior, prevents disruptive behavior, blocks Mark's movement to other groups. She cues peers to interact.

Sample #3 Data Sheet

Directions followed	Dates						Prompting strategies
Raised hand when named called	+	—					• Model hand up and tap under elbow • Fade prompts
Approached teacher when requested	—	P					• Wait 5 seconds • Point to teacher • Wait 2 seconds • Repeat request and point to teacher
Got materials	—	P					• Wait 5 seconds • Point to others getting materials and ask what he needs to do • Wait 2 seconds • Tap at elbow and guide to materials
Went to assigned table	+	P					• Wait 5 seconds • Point to table • Ask where he needs to go • Wait 2 seconds • Ask peer to assist him

Figure 11.3. Sample #3: Student participation plan and data sheet for a science activity. Dates to be inserted above each column. (Key: + = independent within 5 seconds of direction, P = performed skill with prompts, – = did not perform skill)

Student Participation Plan

Student: Sierra   **Age:** 18   **Grade:** Twelfth

Outcome for student: To enhance her interactions with others

Class activity: Life Enrichment—discuss life goals, problems; do projects around these issues; give class presentations

Objective: Sierra will lift her head and turn toward someone talking to her for the majority of all interactions for six class periods.

What students in class are expected to do: Listen to teacher, get materials, join in discussion, interact with each other, work independently and with partners.

How Sierra participates to achieve desired outcome: Sierra lifts head up and turns toward peers talking to her. She uses a head switch to turn on a radio or cassette if allowed. She chooses materials to be part of projects by looking. She listens to her classmates.

Who provides support and how: Teacher greets Sierra, makes sure she has materials and is included in all projects. She responds to Sierra if she vocalizes. Classmates help with all projects, sit close to Sierra, and talk to her. They offer her choices. Special educator sets up switch, provides therapy, and prompts her behavior.

Sample #4 Data Sheet

Skills	Dates						Prompting strategies
Head up	III						• Wait 3 seconds • Touch under chin • Ask speaker to say Sierra's name & touch her arm
	III						
Turns toward speaker	I						• Wait 3 seconds • Press against opposite side of cheek
	III						

Figure 11.4.   Sample #4: Student participation plan and data sheet for a life enrichment activity. Dates to be inserted above each column. Boxes below dates are for recording the number of appropriate responses over the number of opportunities provided.

requests as other students (e.g., to use the restroom, to get a drink of water). They will also need a means of sharing what they have learned with their class, as other students do. To meet their other needs to develop friendships, students unable to use speech will need ways to socialize before, during, and after class activities. The creative use of pictures, photographs, or parts of objects that change as topics change, in combination with facial expressions, body language, natural gestures, and manual signs (if known), needs to be explored with each student. Leaving a student in any environment with extremely limited means of communication may well lead to disruptive and negative behavior (Sigafoos, 2000). Considerable information has been written about the development and use of AAC devices for a variety of individuals. Appendixes B (Resources on Augmentative and Alternative Communication) and C (Augmentative and Alternative Communication System Hardware Manufacturers) at the end of this book list resources that deal with this subject.

Question 8. How can I be sure that the student with disabilities is learning what he or she needs to learn?

This question is often asked by general educators who are concerned that placement of a student with such obvious disabilities in their classroom will not benefit that student. They may see the social benefits for the student, but cannot see other reasons for including that student. Obviously, the question is of consequence to all educators, parents, and administrators who are interested in the education of all students. The best response to this question is to readdress the issue of assessment. Assessment procedures that start with the child and the family and are based on the identification of valued life outcomes (Giangreco, Cloninger, & Iverson, 1998) help ensure that the student is indeed in the appropriate learning environment and receiving the appropriate instruction. It should be clear that the skills being targeted across the different activities that occur in different classrooms lead to desired outcomes for the student. If these skills cannot be identified in a given activity or class, then changes need to be made.

Meaningful participation for each student is the desired goal, with the student being given opportunities to control social and physical events to the maximum extent possible (Brown & Lehr, 1993). To reach this goal, the team should consider whether the activity can be presented in another way (e.g., pictorial information added to verbal, information presented in shorter blocks of time). Perhaps the student's position needs to be changed or membership in a particular learning group changed. Expectations of students' performance (how they work together) may need to be adapted. For example, if a valued outcome for a student is to develop social relationships, social interaction skills need to be targeted across activities. Independent seat work by students does not support the teaching of such skills; however, allowing students to work together to share materials, make joint decisions, and otherwise cooperate on a project or assignment would provide the opportunity to learn valued skills. Giving students adaptive equipment (e.g., switch devices, rotary scanner with pictorial options, VOCA devices) provides an alternative way to participate. Sax (2001) provided several practical examples of the use of assistive technology to support students in inclusive classrooms.

At the secondary level, it may be possible to change classes altogether if a particular class is taught in a manner that is not conducive to meeting the learning needs of a given student; however, even in classes that complement a student's learning needs, every effort must be made to ensure that each activity has a sufficient number of opportunities for students to practice critical skills. If these do not naturally occur, it may be possible to alter the situation sufficiently to create the desired opportunity. For instance, a student could be asked to pass out home-work assignments or other materials to increase the number of opportunities a student has to appropriately handle materials, gain a classmate's attention, hand materials to a classmate, and respond to any socially interactive behaviors (e.g., "hi," "thanks") that might occur. Although materials might normally be laid out on a table or teacher's desk for students to pick up independently, this modifi-cation accomplishes the same objective. Furthermore, it greatly facilitates the op-portunity for one student to learn skills that may lead toward the development of friendships and the ability to obtain and handle a job. Other examples to enhance the learning opportunities of secondary-age students can be found in Chapter 6.

Question 9. What do I do when I've planned for one activity and the classroom teacher suddenly changes the lesson?

Unfortunately, the best planning in the world suffers when teachers suddenly make changes without notifying the student's support team. Although the gen-eral education teacher may have a great new lesson in mind, successfully includ-ing the student with severe and multiple disabilities (or any severe disability) will take quick and creative thinking. Such spur of the moment adaptations occur in all inclusive classrooms. If a change in plans means movement from the class-room, a note should be left for any related services personnel (e.g., vision teacher, hearing specialist, occupational therapist) who may be planning to provide sup-port services at that time. Flexibility on the part of all support staff is critical. With but a small delay, the person providing needed related services will likely be able to find the class in time to provide services in the changed environment.

Keeping in mind the student's learning goals and objectives will provide guidance when unexpected changes in lesson plans occur. If these goals and ob-jectives identify truly meaningful skills for the student to learn, addressing these same skills across different activities and settings should not be overly problem-atic. Knowing how the student acquires information most efficiently also helps teachers to quickly adapt to an unexpected activity.

Many teachers following an inclusive model maintain a collection of easily accessible materials (e.g., "bag of tricks") that allows quick (although not perfect) adaptations to most lessons. These materials might include index cards, felt-tip pens, glue sticks, magazine pictures, self-stick notes, thick paper or file folder sheets to hold textures and parts of objects, and adhesive to hold the objects to the paper. Larger items that can be practical across different activities are cassette recorders with blank tapes and the necessary switch adaptation for control by the student. Cassette recorders or other simple devices that allow a vocal output for a student and on which small messages can be easily recorded serve a number of purposes. For example, a sudden change in plans found a second-grade classroom in Arizona outside collecting items related to a unit on ecology (e.g., eroded rocks, rain-produced gullies). For Danielle, a popular student who had very limited movement, used a wheelchair, and had severe photosensitivity (sensitivity to light), exploring the desert was not practical. Instead, she remained in her wheel-chair in the shade of the school building and collected the items gathered by her classmates on her wheelchair tray. To involve Danielle in this activity, one of the girls in her class was asked to quickly record the message, "Thanks for bringing me this. Can you get more?" and Danielle was given access to her switch, which activated the recorded message. When her classmates brought her various items, they showed her what they had found and waited for the paraeducator to prompt her to state the prerecorded message. This quick adaptation to an unplanned, yet worthwhile, activity allowed Danielle greater participation with her classmates and also provided opportunities for her to control devices via switch use and respond to her peers. Both of these skills were targeted on her IEP.

Question 10.   How can a student with significant medical needs be taught in a typical class?

Students with significant medical needs will have medical personnel as members of their educational team. These professionals will play a significant role in how much time a student can safely spend at school. This decision obviously will be individually determined and will depend on a number of factors, including the student's health and the activity level and expectations of the classroom. Everyone on the team must be well informed so that one factor does not completely override others that are equally important. For example, there may be a misconception about what happens in a self-contained classroom as compared with a typical classroom (especially for medical personnel). Special education classrooms were never meant to be hospital rooms. They were designed to be places where the unique educational needs of the student could be met. If education is the primary purpose of schools, then environments geared toward teaching and learning should be considered when determining how much time a student attends school. Therefore, a special education room should not be considered a better environment for a student with severe medical needs because it is quiet and relaxing and the student will be able to sleep. This would represent a major misconception about special education in general.

In this situation, the importance of forming a true partnership among all team members (educational, therapeutic, and medical) is obvious. A study by Izen and Brown (1991) found that teachers felt unprepared to deal with students who have profound and multiple disabilities as well as significant medical needs. In other studies, early childhood special educators also indicated their lack of training regarding complex medical needs of students (Louman, 1997). If students with these challenging disabilities are to be successful in inclusive classrooms, the fear that can develop from educators feeling uncomfortable with these students must be addressed. Information must be shared so that all of the student's ongoing needs can be addressed and emergencies met efficiently.

Several authors have addressed the needs of students with serious medical conditions within typical classrooms (Lehr, 1996; Lynch, Lewis, & Murphy, 1992; Prendergast, 1995). These authors have stressed the need for shared information, teaming, emergency planning, and individualization to provide the appropriate education in typical classrooms. As with any student, the individual needs of the student with serious medical conditions must be met or the educational services cannot be considered appropriate. Furthermore, services must be provided in a way that respects the student's dignity and need for privacy, if desired. A student's medical needs (e.g., gastrostomy feedings, catheterization, suctioning), however, should not dictate placement in a special education environment (Jones, Clatterbuck, Marquis, Turnbull, & Moberly, 1996; Porter, Haynie, Bierle, Caldwell, & Palfrey, 1997). For example, students can and do receive gastrostomy feedings in the cafeteria, where they eat alongside their classmates. For those students who may be learning to ingest some food orally, watching their peers eat can be motivating. What determines where students receive support and educational services are the desired outcomes established for them by those people who know them best and care about their well-being. Therefore, if we want a student to be included in family outings to noisy restaurants, attend birthday parties, and, in general, have friends, then eating in a noisy cafeteria with classmates may be the best place to learn to deal with this type of noisy, yet very social, environment.

Students can and do receive some treatments (e.g., medication, suctioning) in general education classrooms. Obviously, consideration must be given to the potential for distracting other students and the teacher and to respecting the student's need for privacy. When the student must leave the classroom to receive medical treatments, the nurse's office is a logical option. For example, one second grader left his class every afternoon to go to the nurse's office to receive 10 minutes of respiratory therapy. Given that other students with no disabilities receive their medical assistance from the school nurse, it makes sense that students with disabilities also go to the nurse for this purpose. Catheterization can occur in either the boys' or girls' restrooms, although certain physical adaptations may be needed to accommodate students. One junior high school put in a fold-down single wall "bed" with a curtain running alongside it for privacy. The fold-down bed also hid shelves for diapers, clean clothes, and cleaning items. This system worked well for students needing to be changed or catheterized. When the bed was up against the wall, it was not noticeable and did not take up additional space.

These examples are provided to help individual teams for students with severe medical needs in addition to other multiple disabilities consider different options before immediately assuming that a student is too medically fragile to benefit from a typical educational environment. While their medical needs cannot be denied, they also have a need to be members of classrooms like other children (Ferguson, Willis, & Meyer, 1996). Parents interviewed in a study by Lynch et al. (1992) expressed a desire for normalization and enhanced quality of life for their children with chronic illnesses. As with any individual with a special need, we must guard against the tendency to allow one characteristic (usually a limitation) to determine where and how we interact. Creative and collaborative teamwork with clear attention to desired outcomes for children should be the basis for all decisions.

Question 11.   The family of one of my students just seems to want him to be comfortable. They want him to be included, but they don't want me placing any demands on him. I know I could teach this student a lot, even though he does have severe and multiple disabilities. What can be done?

When expectations for student performance differ substantially among individual team members, it is difficult to implement an effective program. Students do behave differently at school and home, which is to be expected. Students may really resist demands placed on them at home, and family members, seeing this resistance, may not want school staff to experience this. They also may fear repercussions to their child if he or she doesn't do as instructed (Lambie, 2000). Parents also may just want their child to be happy and accepted and fear that this won't happen if expectations are present and the child refuses to meet them. Parents may be very concerned about their child's disrupting the learning of other children (Bennett, Lee, Lueke, 1998; York & Tundidor, 1995). This concern can lead them to suggest that their child not be challenged to learn new things. Cultural differences may play a major role in the expectations parents hold for their child (Harry, Kalyanpur, & Day, 1999; Harry, Rueda, & Kalyanpur, 1999). Such cultural differences must be respected even if they interfere with what other team members feel is of crucial importance. In other words, family members may have very good reasons for resisting the wishes or demands of teachers.

Sharing information in a nonthreatening way about what is possible may help family members make more of an informed decision. Several high-quality professional videotapes on inclusive practices are available to share with families so that they can see what an inclusive education could mean for their child. A list of several excellent videos for this purpose can be found in Appendix D. These videotapes also can be used for faculty in-services to explain the purpose for inclusive education and the benefits for all involved. Another way to use videotaped information to share information with families is to videotape their children performing various activities (Alberto, Mechling, Taber, & Thompson, 1995). Family members who see their child actively engaged and learning may be more apt to consider it a real possibility. From the author's personal experiences, some families have been very positively surprised by what they saw on videotape. When family members can see how activities have been adapted and what is expected of the student, increasing expectations may be seriously considered.

Sharing information with families about what is possible for their children is of critical importance and distinctly different from judging families on their cultural and religious values. Families of children with disabilities may be more open and trustful of other families in similar situations. Therefore, pairing families to share information regarding expectations for the student and future goals may be a preferred approach. Such an approach may be particularly effective if both families share the same culture or religion.

Regular correspondence with family members is particularly important to establish and maintain trust regarding student performance. Family members want to know what is happening at school, especially if they are unable to visit on a regular basis (Bennett et al., 1998; Soodak & Erwin, 2000). Although they need to know when there are problems so they can help brainstorm solutions, they also want and need to know of successes that the child is experiencing. Short telephone calls home to relay positive information about what the student is achieving may help families raise expectations. An easy way to share information with families is to attach short messages on yellow sticky notes to the student's daily schedule following each activity or period. Then, as the family reviews the student's day at home with the student, members can quickly read what the student experienced and accomplished for the day.

Finally, if families continue to insist that expectations remain minimal for the student so that he or she will not be disruptive in class, respecting this preference is critical. Students with and without disabilities learn differently depending on many factors, one of which is certainly family expectations. Students with severe disabilities are no different in this regard than any of their classmates. Teachers must strive to help students be successful and reach desired goals, recognizing that there will always be limitations to what they can accomplish.

REFERENCES

Alberto, P.Q., Mechling, L., Taber, T.A., & Thompson, J. (1995). Using videotape to communicate with parents of students with severe disabilities. *Teaching Exceptional Children, 27*(3), 18–21.

Bennett, T., Lee, H., & Lueke, B. (1998). Expectations and concerns: What mothers and fathers say about inclusion. *Education and Training in Mental Retardation and Developmental Disabilities, 33,* 108–122.

Beukelman, D.R., & Mirenda, P. (1998). *Augmentative and alternative communication: Management of severe communication disorders in children and adults* (2nd ed.). Baltimore: Paul H. Brookes Publishing Co.

Brown, F., & Lehr, D. (1993). Making activities meaningful for students with severe multiple disabilities. *Teaching Exceptional Children, 25*(4), 12–17.

Carr, E.G., & Durand, V.M. (1985). Reducing behavior problems through functional communication training. *Journal of Applied Behavior Analysis, 18,* 111–126.

Carr, E.G., Levin, L., McConnachie, G., Carlson, J.I., Kemp, D.C., & Smith, C.E. (1994). *Communication-based intervention for problem behavior: A user's guide for producing positive change.* Baltimore: Paul H. Brookes Publishing Co.

Cipani, E.C. (1995). Be aware of negative reinforcement. *Teaching Exceptional Children, 27*(4), 36–40.

Donnellan, A.M., Mirenda, P.L., Mesaros, R.A., & Fassbender, L.L. (1984). Analyzing the communicative functions of aberrant behavior. *Journal of The Association for Persons with Severe Handicaps, 9,* 201–212.

Downing, J. (1993). Communication intervention for individuals with dual sensory and intellectual impairments. *Clinics in Communication Disorders, 3*(2), 31–42.

Downing, J.E. (1999). *Teaching communication skills to students with severe disabilities.* Baltimore: Paul H. Brookes Publishing Co.

Durand, V.M. (1993). Functional communication training using assistive devices: Effects on challenging behavior and affect. *Augmentative and Alternative Communication, 9,* 168–176.

Ferguson, D.L., Willis, C., & Meyer, G. (1996). Widening the stream: Ways to think about including "exceptions" in schools. In D.H. Lehr & F. Brown (Eds.), *People with disabilities who challenge the system* (pp. 99–126). Baltimore: Paul H. Brookes Publishing Co.

Foster-Johnson, L., Ferro, J., & Dunlap, G. (1994). Preferred curricular activities and reduced problem behaviors in students with intellectual disabilities. *Journal of Applied Behavior Analysis, 27,* 493–504.

Giangreco, M.F., Broer, S.M., & Edelman, S.W. (1999). The tip of the iceberg: Determining whether paraprofessional support is needed for students with disabilities in general education settings. *Journal of The Association for Persons with Severe Handicaps, 24,* 281–291.

Giangreco, M.F., Cloninger, C.J., & Iverson, V.S. (1998). *Choosing outcomes and accommodations for children (COACH): A guide to educational planning for students with disabilities* (2nd ed.). Baltimore: Paul H. Brookes Publishing Co.

Gothelf, C.R., Crimmins, D.B., Mercer, C.A., & Finocchiaro, P.A. (1994). Teaching choice-making skills to students who are deaf-blind. *Teaching Exceptional Children, 26*(4), 13–15.

Graham, A.T. (1998). Finding time to teach. *Teaching Exceptional Children, 30*(4), 46–49.

Harry, B., Kalyanpur, M., & Day, M. (1999). *Building cultural reciprocity with families: Case studies in special education.* Baltimore: Paul H. Brookes Publishing Co.

Harry, B., Rueda, R., & Kalyanpur, M. (1999). Cultural reciprocity in sociocultural perspective: Adapting the normalization principle for family collaboration. *Exceptional Children, 66,* 123–136.

Heller, I., Manning, D., Pavur, D., & Wagner, K. (1998). Let's all sign! Enhancing language development in an inclusive preschool. *Teaching Exceptional Children, 30*(3), 50–53.

Hughes, C., Pitkin, S.E., & Lorden, S.W. (1998). Assessing preferences and choices of persons with severe and profound mental retardation. *Education and Training in Mental Retardation and Developmental Disabilities, 33,* 299–316.

Hunt, P., Alwell, M., & Goetz, L. (1991). Interacting with peers through conversation turn-taking with a communication book adaptation. *Augmentative and Alternative Communication, 7,* 117–126.

Izen, C.L., & Brown, F. (1991). Education and treatment needs of students with profound, multiply handicapping, and medically fragile conditions: A survey of teachers' perceptions. *Journal of The Association for Persons with Severe Handicaps, 16,* 94–103.

Johnson, L., Ferro, J., & Dunlap, G. (1994). Preferred curricular activities and reduced problem behavior in students with intellectual disabilities. *Journal of Applied Behavior Analysis, 27,* 493–504.

Jones, D.E., Clatterbuck, C.C., Marquis, J., Turnbull, H.R., III, & Moberly, R.L. (1996). Educational placements for children who are ventilator assisted. *Exceptional Children, 63,* 47–58.

Kluwin, T.N., Gonsher, W., Silver, K., & Samuels, J. (1996). The E.T. class: Education together. *Teaching Exceptional Children, 29*(1), 11–15.

Kluwin, T.N., Moores, D.F., & Gausted, M.C. (1992). *Toward effective public school programs for deaf students: Context, process, and outcomes.* New York: Teachers College Press.

Lambie, R. (2000). Working with families of at-risk and special needs students: A system change model. *Focus on Exceptional Children, 32*(6), 1–22.

Lehr, D.H. (1996). The challenge of educating students with special health care needs. In D.H. Lehr & F. Brown (Eds.), *People with disabilities who challenge the system* (pp. 59–78). Baltimore: Paul H. Brookes Publishing Co.

Lohrmann-O'Rourke, O., Browder, D.M., & Brown, F. (2000). Guidelines for conducting socially valid systematic preference assessments. *Journal of The Association for Persons with Severe Handicaps, 25,* 42–53.

Louman, D.K. (1997). Planning for students with complex health care needs. *Physical Disabilities: Education and Related Services, VXI*(1), 7–22.

Luchner, J. (1991). Mainstreaming hearing-impaired students: Perceptions of regular educators. *Language, Speech, and Hearing Services in the Schools, 22,* 302–307.

Lynch, E.W., Lewis, R.B., & Murphy, D.S. (1992). Educational services for children with chronic illnesses: Perspectives of educators and families. *Exceptional Children, 59,* 210–220.

Mirenda, P. (1997). Supporting individuals with challenging behavior through functional communication training and AAC: Research review. *Augmentative and Alternative Communication, 13,* 207–225.

Moes, D.R. (1998). Integrating choice-making opportunities within teacher-assigned academic tasks to facilitate the performance of children with autism. *Journal of The Association for Persons with Severe Handicaps, 23,* 319–328.

O'Neill, R.E., Horner, R.H., Albin, R.W., Sprague, J.R., Storey, K., & Newton, J.S. (1997). *Functional assessment and program development: A practical handbook* (2nd ed.). Pacific Grove, CA: Brooks/Cole Publishing Co.

Porter, S., Haynie, M., Bierle, T., Caldwell, T.H., & Palfrey, J.S. (1997). *Children and youth assisted by medical technology in education settings* (2nd ed.). Baltimore: Paul H. Brookes Publishing Co.

Prendergast, D.E. (1995). Preparing for children who are medically fragile. *Teaching Exceptional Children, 27*(2), 37–41.

Rainforth, B., & York-Barr, J. (1997). *Collaborative teams for students with severe disabilities: Integrating therapy and educational services* (2nd ed.). Baltimore: Paul H. Brookes Publishing Co.

Reeve, C.E., & Carr, E.G. (2000). Preventing severe behavior problems in children with developmental disabilities. *Journal of Positive Behavior Intervention, 2,* 144–160.

Reichle, J., Feeley, K., & Johnston, S. (1993). Communication intervention for persons with severe and profound disabilities. *Clinics in Communication Disorders, 3*(2), 7–30.

Sax, C. (2001). Using technology to support belonging and achievement. In C.H. Kennedy & D. Fisher (Eds.), *Inclusive middle schools* (pp. 89–104). Baltimore: Paul H. Brookes Publishing Co.

Scotti, J.R., & Meyer, L.H. (1999). *Behavioral intervention: Principles, models, and practices.* Baltimore: Paul H. Brookes Publishing Co.

Sigafoos, J. (2000). Communication development and aberrant behavior in children with developmental disabilities. *Education and Training in Mental Retardation and Developmental Disabilities, 35,* 168–176.

Snell, M.E., & Janney, R.E. (2000). Teachers' problem-solving about children with moderate and severe disabilities in elementary classrooms. *Exceptional Children, 66,* 472–490.

Soodak, L.C., & Erwin, E.J. (2000). Valued member or tolerated participant: Parents' experiences in inclusive early childhood settings. *Journal of The Association for Persons with Severe Handicaps, 25,* 29–41.

Thousand, J.S., & Villa, R.A. (2000). Collaborative teaming: A powerful tool in school restructuring. In R. Villa & J. Thousand (Eds.), *Restructuring for caring and effective education: Piecing the puzzle together* (2nd ed., pp. 254–291). Baltimore: Paul H. Brookes Publishing Co.

Villa, R.A., & Thousand, J.S. (1993). Redefining the role of the special educator and other support personnel. In J.W. Putnam (Ed.), *Cooperative learning and strategies for inclusion: Celebrating diversity in the classroom* (pp. 57–91). Baltimore: Paul H. Brookes Publishing Co.

Wolery, M., Werts, M.G., Caldwell, N.K., & Snyder, E.D. (1995). Experienced teachers' perceptions of resources and supports for inclusion. *Education and Training in Mental Retardation and Developmental Disabilities, 30*(1), 15–26.

York, J., & Tundidor, M. (1995). Issues raised in the name of inclusion: Perspectives of educators, parents, and students. *Journal of The Association for Persons with Severe Handicaps, 20,* 31–44.

Zeece, R.D., & Wolda, M.R. (1995). Let me see what you say: Let me see what you feel! *Teaching Exceptional Children, 27*(2), 4–9.

Appendix A

Systematic Teaching Resources

Belfiore, P.J., & Toro-Zambrana, W. (1994). *Innovations: Recognizing choices in community settings by people with significant disabilities.* Washington, DC: American Association on Mental Retardation.

Biederman, G.B., Fairhall, J.L., Raven, K.A., & Davey, V.A. (1998). Verbal prompting, hand-over-hand instruction, and passive observation teaching children with developmental disabilities. *Exceptional Children, 64,* 503–562.

Billingsley, F.F., Liberty, K.A., & White, O.R. (1994). The technology of instruction. In E.C. Cipani & F. Spooner (Eds.), *Curricular and instructional approaches for persons with severe disabilities* (pp. 81–116). Needham Heights, MA: Allyn & Bacon.

Farlow, L.J., & Snell, M.E. (1994). *Innovations: Making the most of student performance data.* Washington, DC: American Association on Mental Retardation.

Fetco, K.S., Schuster, J.W., Harley, D.A., & Collins, B.C. (1999). Using simultaneous prompting to teach a chained vocational task to young adults with severe intellectual disabilities. *Education and Training in Mental Retardation and Developmental Disabilities, 34,* 318–329.

Schepis, M.M., Ownbey, J.B., Parsons, M.B., & Reid, D.H. (2000). Training support staff for teaching young children with disabilities in an inclusive preschool setting. *Journal of Positive Behavior Interventions, 2,* 170–178.

Schuster, J.W., Morse, T.E., Ault, M.J., Doyle, P.M., Crawford, M.R., & Wolery, M. (1998). Constant time delay with chained tasks: A review of the literature. *Education and Treatment of Children, 21,* 74–106.

Snell, M.E., & Brown, F.E. (2000). *Instruction of students with severe disabilities* (5th ed.). Upper Saddle River, NJ: Prentice-Hall.

Sternberg, L. (1994). *Individuals with profound disabilities: Instructional and assistive strategies.* Austin, TX: PRO-ED.

Westling, D.L., & Fox, L. (2000). *Teaching students with severe disabilities.* (2nd ed.). Upper Saddle River, NJ: Prentice-Hall.

Wolery, M., Ault, M.J., & Doyle, P.M. (1992). *Teaching students with moderate to severe disabilities.* New York: Longman.

Appendix B

Resources on Augmentative and Alternative Communication

ARTICLES

Brady, N.C. (2000). Improved comprehension of object names following voice output communication aid use: Two case studies. *Augmentative and Alternative Communication, 16,* 197–204.

Calculator, S.N. (1999). AAC outcomes for children and youth with severe disabilities: When seeing is believing. *Augmentative and Alternative Communication, 15,* 4–12.

Durand, V.M. (1993). Functional communication training using assistive devices: Effects on challenging behavior and affect. *Augmentative and Alternative Communication, 9,* 168–176.

Iacono, T., Mirenda, P., & Beukelman, D.R. (1993). Comparison of unimodal and multimodal AAC techniques for children with intellectual disabilities. *Augmentative and Alternative Communication, 9,* 83–94.

McGregor, G., Young, J., Gerak, J., Thomas, B., & Vogelsberg, R.T. (1992). Increasing functional use of a nonassistive communication device by a student with severe disabilities. *Augmentative and Alternative Communication, 8,* 243–250.

Rowland, C., & Schweigert, P. (2000). Tangible symbols, tangible outcomes. *Augmentative and Alternative Communication, 16,* 61–78.

Schepis, M.M., & Reid, D.H. (1995). Effects of a voice output communication aid on interactions between support personnel and an individual with multiple disabilities. *Journal of Applied Behavior Analysis, 28,* 73–77.

Schweigert, P., & Rowland, C. (1992). Early communication and microtechnology: Instructional sequence and case studies of children with severe multiple disabilities. *Augmentative and Alternative Communication, 8,* 273–286.

BOOKS

Beukelman, D.R., & Mirenda, P. (1998). *Augmentative and alternative communication: Management of severe communication disorders in children and adults* (2nd ed.). Baltimore: Paul H. Brookes Publishing Co.

Downing, J.E. (1999). *Teaching communication skills to students with severe and multiple disabilities.* Baltimore: Paul H. Brookes Publishing Co.

Glennen, S.L., & DeCoste, D.C. (1997). *Handbook of augmentative and alternative communication.* San Diego: Singular Publishing Group.

Johnson, J.M., Baumgart, D., Helmstetter, E., & Curry, C.A. (1996). *Augmenting basic communication in natural contexts.* Baltimore: Paul H. Brookes Publishing Co.

Light, J.C., & Binger, C. (1998). *Building communicative competence with individuals who use augmentative and alternative communication.* Baltimore: Paul H. Brookes Publishing Co.

McCormick, L., Loeb, D.F., & Schiefelbusch, R.L. (1997). *Supporting children with communication difficulties in inclusive settings: School-based language intervention.* Needham Heights, MA: Allyn & Bacon.

Reichle, J., York, J., & Sigafoos, J. (1991). *Implementing augmentative and alternative communication: Strategies for learners with severe disabilities.* Baltimore: Paul H. Brookes Publishing Co.

Romski, M.A., & Sevcik, R.A. (1996). *Breaking the speech barrier: Language development through augmented means.* Baltimore: Paul H. Brookes Publishing Co.

Van Tatenhove, G.M. (1993). *What is augmentative and alternative communication (AAC)?* Wooster, OH: Prentke Romich Co.

VIDEOTAPES

Augmentative and alternative communication. (1994). Van Nuys, CA: Child Development Media. (Available from Child Development Media, Inc.; 5632 Van Nuys Boulevard, #286, Van Nuys, CA 91401; 818-989-7221)

Augmentative communication: Communication alternatives for people with disabilities. (1999). (Available from Program Development Associates, 5620 Business Avenue, Suite B, Cicero, NY 13039; 800-543-2119)

Communication: Forms and function. (1990). Sacramento: California Department of Education. (Available from California Deaf-Blind Services, 650 Howe Avenue, Suite 300, Sacramento, CA 95825; 916-641-5855)

Tangible symbol systems: Symbolic communication for individuals with multisensory impairments. (1990). Tucson, AZ: Communication Skill Builders. (Available from Communication Skill Builders, 555 Academic Court, San Antonio, TX 78204; 800-232-1223)

Appendix C

Augmentative and Alternative Communication System Hardware Manufacturers

Ablenet
1081 Tenth Avenue, SE
Minneapolis, MN 55414
(800) 322-0956

Apple Computer, Inc.
Office of Special Education
20525 Mariani Avenue
Cupertino, CA 95014
(408) 996-1010

Assistive Technology, Inc.
7 Wells Avenue
Newton, MA 02459
(800) 793-9227

Attainment Company
Post Office Box 930160
Verona, WI 53593
(800) 327-4269

Linda Burkhart
Professional in communication and
    assistive technology
8503 Rhode Island Avenue
College Park, MD 20740
(301) 345-9152

Canon USA, Inc.
One Canon Plaza
Lake Success, NY 11042
(516) 488-6700

Consultants for Communication Technology
508 Bellevue Terrace
Pittsburgh, PA 15202
(412) 352-5678

Creative Communicating
Post Office Box 3358
Park City, UT 84060
(801) 645-7737

Crestwood Company
6625 N. Sidney Place
Milwaukee, WI 53209
(414) 352-5678

Daedalus Technologies, Inc.
2491 Vauxhall Place
Richmond, BC V6V1Z5
CANADA
(800) 561-5570

Don Johnston, Inc.
26799 W. Commerce Drive
Volo, IL 60073
(800) 999-4660

Dragon Systems, Inc.
320 Nevada Street
Newton, MA 02460
(617) 965-5200

Dunamis, Inc.
3545 Cruse Road, #312
Lawrenceville, GA 30044
(800) 828-2443

DynaVox, Inc.
2100 Wharton Street
Pittsburgh, PA 15203
(800) 344-1778

Edmark Corporation
Post Office Box 97021
Redmond, WA 98073
(800) 691-2986

Epson America, Inc.
2780 Lomita Boulevard
Torrance, CA 90505
(800) 873-7766

Flaghouse, Inc.
604 Flaghouse Drive
Hasbrouck Heights, NJ 07604
(800) 793-7900

Franklin Learning Resources
1 Franklin Plaza
Burlington, NJ 08016
(800) 525-9673

IBM
National Support for Persons with
  Disabilities
1000 NW 51st Street
Internal Zip 5432
Boca Raton, FL 33432
(800) 426-4832; (800) 426-4833 (TDD)

Innocomp
26210 Emery Road, #302
Warrensville Heights, OH 44128
(800) 382-8622

Innoventions
5921 S. Middlefield Road, #102
Littleton, CO 80123
(800) 382-8622

Intellitools, Inc.
55 Leveroni Court, Suite 9
Novato, CA 94949
(800) 899-6687

Kurzweil Applied Intelligence, Inc.
411 Waverly Oaks Road
Waltham, MA 02154
(800) 894-5374

Laureate Learning Systems, Inc.
110 E. Spring Street
Winooksi, VT 05404
(800) 562-6801

Luminaud, Inc.
8688 Tyler Boulevard
Mentor, OH 44060
(440) 255-9082

Mayer-Johnson Company
Post Office Box 1579
Solano Beach, CA 92075
(619) 550-0084

Nanopac
4832 S. Sheridan Road, Suite 302
Tulsa, OK 74145
(918) 665-0329

Phonic Ear, Inc.
3880 Cypress Drive
Petaluma, CA 94954
(800) 227-0735

Prentke Romich Co.
1022 Heyl Road
Wooster, OH 44691
(800) 262-1984

Sentient Systems Technology
2100 Wharton Street
Pittsburgh, PA 15203
(800) 344-1778

Switchworks
Post Office Box 64764
Baton Rouge, LA 70896
(225) 925-8926

TASH International, Inc.
Unit 1-91
Station Street
Ajax, Ontario L1S 3H2
CANADA
(800) 463-5685

Therapeutic Toys, Inc.
Post Office Box 418
Moodus, CT 06469
(800) 638-0676

Toshiba America Information Systems
9740 Irvine Boulevard
Irvine, CA 92713-9724
(800) 999-4273

Toys for Special Children/Enabling Devices
385 Warburton Avenue
Hastings-on-Hudson, NY 10706
(914) 478-0960

Trace Research and Development Center
University of Wisconsin–Madison
S-151 Waisman Center
1500 Highland Avenue
Madison, WI 53705
(608) 263-5776

Words +, Inc.
1220 W. Avenue J
Lancaster, CA 93534
(800) 869-8521

Zygo Industries, Inc.
Post Office Box 1008
Portland, OR 97207
(800) 234-6006

Appendix D

Videotapes on Inclusion

Choices. (1995). Evanston, IL: Comforty Media Concepts. (Available from www.comforty.com)

Collaborating for change: Including all of our students. (1997). Baltimore: Paul H. Brookes Publishing Co. (Available from www.brookespublishing.com)

Disability awareness in an inclusive setting. (1994). Hampton, NH: AGH Associates, Inc. (Available from www.schoolhousedoor.com)

Effective education: Adapting to include all students. (1996). South Dakota Department of Education and Cultural Affairs, The Utah Projects for Children with Dual Sensory Impairments, and the Blumberg Center, Indiana State University. (Available from [800] 438–9832)

Essential characteristics of inclusive schools: Education in the real world. (2000). South Dakota Department of Education and Cultural Affairs and the Blumberg Center for Interdisciplinary Studies in Special Education, Indiana State University. (Available from [800] 438-9832)

Families, friends, futures. (1995). Evanston, IL: Comforty Media Concepts. (Available from www.comforty.com)

Heather's story: Program highlights. (1995). Evanston, IL: Comforty Media Concepts. (Available from www.comforty.com)

High school inclusion: Equity and excellence in an inclusive community of learners. (1999). Baltimore: Paul H. Brookes Publishing Co. (Available from www.brookespublishing.com)

Instructional strategies for all students. (1997). Baltimore: Paul H. Brookes Publishing Co. (Available from www.brookespublishing.com)

Plain talk: Teacher to teacher. (1993). Hampton, NH: AGH Associates, Inc. (Available from www.schoolhousedoor.com)

Regular lives. (1987). State of the Art, Inc. (Available from www.PDAccoc.com)

Standards and inclusion: Can we have both? (1998). Baltimore: Paul H. Brookes Publishing Co. (Available from www.brookespublishing.com)

Step by step: Heather's story. (1995). Evanston, IL: Comforty Media Concepts. (Available from www.comforty.com)

Index

Page numbers followed by "*f*" indicate figures; those followed by "*t*" indicate tables.

259